American Gangsters, Then and Now

American Gangsters, Then and Now

An Encyclopedia

Nate Hendley

A B C CLIO

Santa Barbara, California • Denver, Colorado • Oxford, England

Cataloging-in-Publication data is on file with the Library of Congress

ISBN 978-0-313-35451-9: hard cover
ISBN 978-0-313-35452-6: eBook

14 13 12 11 10   1 2 3 4 5

This book is also available on the World Wide Web as an eBook.
Visit www.abc-clio.com for details.

ABC-CLIO, LLC

130 Cremona Drive, P.O. Box 1911
Santa Barbara, California 93116-1911

This book is printed on acid-free paper ∞
Manufactured in the United States of America

This book is dedicated to
Victor Riesel, Robert St. John,
and
Michel Auger.

Contents

List of Entries

Guide to Related Topics

Preface

This book defines a gangster as someone who controls or participates in a criminal organization that uses violence and illicit means to amass money and power. By this definition, Al Capone, John Gotti, and Jesse James (leader of the notorious bank-robbing James-Younger Gang) are all gangsters. The Dead Rabbits, the Bloods and the Crips, and Murder, Inc., are all gangster organizations.

For reasons of space, this book will not look at criminals who fall outside of the "gangster" definition, such as serial killers, mass murderers, presidential assassins, white collar criminals, violent cult leaders, etc. This encyclopedia does not include terrorists either (who might belong to groups that commit criminal acts, but are generally more interested in advancing a social/political/religious agenda than getting rich).

The entries in this encyclopedia are designed to offer a broad sweep of history and demonstrate that the gangster is not a new phenomenon. "The Wild West" era (roughly 1850–1890) was selected as the start-point simply because it is so rich with gunfighter/outlaw lore. Also, readers are more familiar with Wild West figures than criminals from earlier times in American history.

Though the James-Younger gang, the Daltons, and Billy the Kid are all examined in detail, criminal developments in "the Wild East" are not ignored either. The late Victorian-era saw the emergence of urban crime bosses such as "Monk" Eastman and Paul Kelly, who mixed feral criminal cunning with an astute grasp of corrupt municipal politics. Both are featured within.

The Prohibition era (1920–1933) was an obvious choice for inclusion, both for the famous mobsters it spawned (Al Capone, Dutch Schultz, the Purple Gang, etc.) and its impact on organized crime. Thanks to Prohibition, local crime bosses began operating on a national, even international, scale. Prohibition offered a template for contemporary criminals—the bootlegger has an obvious counterpart in today's drug trafficker. The illicit drug trade, like Prohibition, is covered in detail.

This book examines crimes that were once widespread but have largely disappeared, such as the "numbers" racket and "Black Hand" intimidation. The involvement of organized crimes in all forms of gambling (and the establishment of Las Vegas as a major tourist draw) is also documented. Not surprisingly, murder, assault, extortion, and prostitution figure prominently in several entries throughout the book.

The history of the American Mafia, from its first faint stirrings in late-19th Century New Orleans to the rise and fall of John Gotti and his successors, is outlined in detail. I have endeavored to show that organized crime is not the sole preserve of any one particular ethnic group. Whereas Italian-American gangsters dominate the Mafia entries, other pieces examine Jewish, Irish, and African-American mobsters, such as (respectively) Meyer Lansky, Dion O'Banion, and Leroy "Nicky" Barnes.

In a similar manner, I have tried to cover a wide base of organized crime gangs, from the Bloods and Crips to outlaw bikers and Mara Salvatrucha (better known as MS-13). Gang origins are analyzed as are dramatic changes of heart, as in the case of former gangster turned peace activist Stanley "Tookie" Williams.

Gangster myths, such as the widespread belief that underworld financier Arnold Rothstein "fixed" the 1919 World Series, are deconstructed and sifted through for elements of truth. Gangster weapons through the ages (from clubs, slingshots, and "luparas" to machine-pistols and Thompson sub-machine guns) are given an in-depth look as well.

A few prominent voices from the side of law and order are also included, most notably FBI agent Joseph Pistone (who successfully posed as a Mafia associate for several years). Entries on the ill-fated Apalachin conference and turncoat Joseph Valachi's testimony underscore how FBI director J. Edgar Hoover came to grudgingly acknowledge the existence of the Mafia. Original surveillance and case files, as well as office memos detailing the FBI's inconsistent pursuit of organized crime figures feature prominently in this history. The impact of the RICO (Racketeer Influenced and Corrupt Organizations) Act and electronic surveillance in the federal government's war on crime also receive attention.

Although foreign developments—from Benito Mussolini's crackdown on the Mafia to the vicious biker war in Quebec—are examined, the encyclopedia's focus is on American crime. It's worth noting that most of the gangsters cited in this book—with the exception of early Mafia leaders and their associates—were born and bred in the United States. Arguably, these men couldn't have risen to prominence in any other country and this book explains why.

Introduction

A gangster is simply a criminal who commits felonies for power and profit in the company of a gang. Al Capone, Dutch Schultz, and John Gotti were gangsters, but so were Stanley "Tookie" Williams, Jesse James, and Ralph "Sonny" Barger.

Some gangsters, like Edward "Monk" Eastman, legendary head of a 1,200-strong band of street warriors in turn-of-the-20th-century New York City, took a personal hand in murder, muggings, and robbery. Other gangsters prefer to keep their distance and merely reap the benefits of criminal activity. Arnold Rothstein, financier of the underworld, is the perfect example of a "gentleman" gangster who never sullied his hands no matter how dirty his peers got.

Gangsters earn their keep by running "rackets"—illegal schemes that generate income. Common rackets include murder for hire, counterfeiting, gambling, prostitution, drug trafficking, theft, kidnapping, arson, extortion, embezzlement, labor racketeering, and, more recently, computer and credit card theft. Some rackets come and go: from 1920 to 1933, the most lucrative racket in America was bootlegging. After liquor was legalized, gangsters moved on to other fields. Other rackets morph into legal diversions. The numbers racket, for example, now has to compete with legal lotteries and "scratch and win" cards available at corner convenience stores.

Gangsters are frequently compared to legitimate businessmen. Meyer Lansky, for example, was nicknamed "The Chairman of the Board." The comparison doesn't work, however. Unlike real business people, gangsters operate in an environment of total secrecy and violence, implied and explicit. Gangsters do not hold public meetings or try to buy out a competitor's stock. Dissatisfied customers will not be sent to the complaints desk, but ignored or even threatened.

Utter contempt for their own customers is a unique characteristic of the gangster. Gangsters operate in a completely unregulated market in which they are not subject to any kind of standards, codes, or even considerations of basic ethics. During the 1920s, the terrible Genna brothers of Chicago made bootleg liquor from industrial alcohol that they knew could blind or kill anyone who drank it. On the black market, the reigning principle is caveat emptor: buyer beware.

That said, most gangsters have to forge some kind of alliance, or at least an accommodation, with the "upper world." This means paying off judges, politicians, police officers, journalists, and anyone else in a position to affect the gangster's bottom-line. This element of corruption is perhaps the worst aspect of organized crime. Gangsters are not merely the mirror-image of mainstream businesspeople. They are a completely different breed of entrepreneur with a worldview most people would find appalling.

During his six-year stint undercover in a Mafia family, FBI agent Joseph Pistone made two interesting observations about gangsters. According to Pistone, all Mafiosi fully expect to either be arrested at some point and incarcerated or murdered by a rival gang. Not fearing sudden death or jail gives the mobster a huge edge over normal people, who are rightly terrified of either prospect.

Ironically, the handful of gangsters who have made it to middle or old age often come to regret their chosen occupation. At the end of his life, Lansky (who was hailed as the financial genius of the underworld) sadly mused that he probably could have earned more if he'd gone legit. Gangsters cannot own anything or invest their profits, for fear the government will seize their assets as proceeds of crime. Gangsters also have to spend a huge amount of money on "overhead" (bribes, lawyer's fees, bail money, etc.). Still, it's unlikely that Lansky would have changed anything if he actually was given the chance to live things over once again. The mindset of the gangster tends to be fixed; as Pistone observed, Mafiosi regard themselves as canny businessmen, not criminals. To the gangster, vice is not something to be ashamed or fearful of, but merely an avenue for earning wealth.

"The basic creed of the gangster and for that matter of any other type of criminal, is that whatever a man has is his only so long as he can keep it, and that the one who takes it away from him has not done anything wrong, but merely demonstrated his smartness," wrote Herbert Asbury in his 1927 book, *The Gangs of New York*. Asbury made these comments almost a century ago, but they remain prescient. The gangster is not about to disappear from modern society. Being a gangster today still holds the same appeal as it did a century ago in the slums of New York: the promise of easy money, power, sex, peer respect, action, and the inherent thrill of operating outside the law.

A

APALACHIN CONFERENCE

The botched Mafia conference in Apalachin, New York, was a major embarrassment to the underworld and a turning point in the FBI's approach to organized crime. The conference was held in mid-November 1957 on the bucolic estate of Joseph Barbara, president of the Canada Dry Bottling Company and long-time Mafia associate. It is believed the meeting was called at the behest of crime boss Vito Genovese. There were several items on the agenda. Genovese wanted to justify the recent murder of mob boss Albert Anastasia and the near-assassination of Frank Costello. Genovese was also eager to put himself forward as "boss of bosses" in New York City.

Another topic of discussion was the Mafia's role in drug trafficking. Mafiosi leaders were squeamish about illegal drugs, partly out of "moral" concerns but mostly because trafficking penalties were so severe. Mob bosses worried that their underlings, if arrested on drug charges, would crack under the threat of spending decades in jail and break the

Sgt. Edgar D. Croswell, the first witness in the federal conspiracy trial of 21 men who attended the Apalachin gangland conference in 1957. Croswell identified a photo of the site of the meeting, the home of the late Joseph Barbara, Sr. [AP photo/Jack Harris]

Mafia's much-vaunted code of silence (omerta).

It was a full agenda, but the 60–100 mobsters who descended on Barbara's estate never had a chance to discuss any

1

of it. On November 13, 1957, a state trooper named Edgar Croswell became intrigued by the number of big, black limousines driving through the countryside. With another trooper in tow, he drove out to Barbara's place, where he spotted even more limousines and cars. Sergeant Croswell figured something was up. His suspicions were confirmed when a local merchant mentioned that Barbara had placed an enormous food order with him for steak, veal cutlets, and cold cuts.

Croswell sought help from the local unit of the federal Alcohol and Tobacco Tax Division (a forerunner of the Bureau of Alcohol, Tobacco, Firearms and Explosives). Sergeant Croswell and another trooper, backed by two agents from the Alcohol and Tobacco Tax Division, drove out to Barbara's house on November 14, 1957. The officers spotted about 30 vehicles parked at the residence. Prominent crime bosses present included Joseph Bonanno, Joseph Profaci, Paul Castellano, Santo Trafficante, Sam Giancana, and many others. The gangsters, who were getting ready to enjoy a nice barbeque, panicked at the sight of the police. Some mobsters took to the woods and tried to run through brush while clad in dress shoes and expensive overcoats.

Croswell called for reinforcements, and police quickly established roadblocks. Authorities detained about 46 men who tried to get past the roadblocks in vehicles. They caught another dozen or so who were running around the forest. Police were astonished at the amount of cash each mobster had on hand. Some of them carried thousands of dollars in bills. They were also amazed to discover the mobsters had come from across the United States. Clearly, this was not just a local gathering

of small-time criminals. For their part, the men detained by police claimed to be visiting Barbara because he had a heart condition and was sick.

The gangsters were smart enough not to carry concealed weapons (which would have left them open to criminal charges), so the police let them go. It was obvious that the mob bosses were plotting criminal activities at Barbara's house, but police couldn't prove it.

Some of the attendees were indicted by a federal grand jury for conspiracy to commit perjury, charges they beat. Still, the botched conference was extremely embarrassing for the Mafia. For a start, it punctured the aura of secrecy that made the Mafia such a potent force (the names of all those detained were published in newspapers). Also, the image of mob bosses taking to the forest to flee a handful of cops was humiliating. As quoted in *The Valachi Papers*, Mafia soldier turned informer Joseph Valachi sneered at this blatant display of cowardice:

> I'll tell you the reaction of all us soldiers when we heard about the raid. If soldiers got arrested in a meet like that, you can imagine what the bosses would have done. There they are, running through the woods like rabbits, throwing away money so they won't get caught with a lot of cash and some of them are throwing away guns. So who are they kidding when they say we got to respect them?

There is some suggestion that the police were tipped off about the conference by an insider who wanted the event to flop. It was noted, for example, that Jewish financial mastermind Meyer Lansky had been invited to the meeting but didn't show up. Mafia gossip suggested that opponents of Genovese were scheming to knock the rising mobster off his pedestal.

The botched conference did ruin Genovese's career trajectory. Within a few months of Apalachin, Genovese and some of his gang members were arrested on drug charges. In 1959 the mob boss was sentenced to fifteen years in jail. He died in prison in 1969.

Apalachin also had a dramatic impact at the FBI. For decades, FBI director J. Edgar Hoover had denied the existence of a national, organized crime body along the lines of the Mafia. After Apalachin, it became much harder for Hoover to say the Mafia didn't exist. To save face, Hoover fixed on the term "La Cosa Nostra," claiming it was a brand-new organization. According to Hoover, authorities everywhere had missed out on the birth of this new criminal body.

Post-Apalachin, Hoover had his aides put together a special report on the Mafia. The study, completed in July 1958, was top secret at the time. The authors of the

DEFINING ORGANIZED CRIME

It's important to distinguish between "organized crime" and "ordinary crime." "Ordinary crime" refers to offenses committed by individuals. Organized crime, on the other hand, reflects a collective effort. The FBI defines organized crime as "any group having some manner of a formalized structure and whose primary objective is to obtain money through illegal activities. Such groups maintain their position through the use of actual or threatened violence, corrupt public officials, graft or extortion and generally have a significant impact on the people in their locales, region, or the country as a whole." According to the Omnibus Crime Control and Safe Streets Act of 1968, "Organized crime means the unlawful activities of the members of a highly organized, disciplined association engaged in supplying illegal goods and services, including but not limited to, gambling, prostitution, loan sharking, narcotics, labor racketeering and other unlawful activities of members of such organizations." A burglar operating alone is not engaged in "organized crime" any more than a serial killer who murders people out of personal grievances. Unless the burglar or killer is part of a larger group, their crimes are viewed as solo efforts in the eyes of the law.

This might be cold comfort for crime victims, but it does make an enormous difference in terms of prosecution. Ordinary criminals can be convicted only when they break the law. Merely belonging to an organized underworld group, however, can be a crime under federal law. In spite of such draconian punishment, there's no shortage of people clamoring to join organized crime groups in the United States. The main appeal is power and money: global organized crime revenues have been estimated at between $750 billion and $1 trillion a year, and are probably higher.

Sources: Federal Bureau of Investigation–Organized Crime (http://www.fbi.gov/hq/cid/orgcrime/ocshome.htm); Klaus von Lampe, Organized Crime Research (http://www.organized-crime.de/); Selwyn Raab, *Five Families: The Rise, Decline and Resurgence of America's Most Powerful Mafia Empires*, 2005; David Southwell, *The History of Organized Crime: The True Story and Secrets of Global Gangland*, 2006.

study (which was officially called the "Mafia Monograph") were blunt in their assessments:

The roundup of 61 Sicilian-Italian hoodlums at Apalachin, New York on November 14, 1957, once again focused the public spotlight on the Mafia in the United States. For years, there have been speculations as to the existence or nonexistence of such an organization in this country. Available evidence shows that beyond the shadow of a doubt, the Mafia does exist today in the United States, as well as in Sicily and Italy, as a vicious, evil and tyrannical form of organized criminality. The Mafia represents one of the most ruthless, pernicious, and enduring forms of criminality ever to exist in the United States.

See also: Castellano, Paul; Mafia; Valachi, Joseph

Further Reading

Federal Bureau of Investigation, *Mafia Monograph*, 1958. http://foia.fbi.gov/foiaindex/mafiamon.htm.

Peter Maas, *The Valachi Papers*, 1968.

Thomas Reppetto, *American Mafia: A History of Its Rise To Power*, 2004.

Thomas Reppetto, *Bringing Down the Mob: The War Against the American Mafia*, 2006.

B

BARGER, RALPH "SONNY" (1938–)

Ralph "Sonny" Barger did not found the Hells Angels—the largest and most notorious outlaw motorcycle gang in the world—but he is their most famous member. For several decades, Barger has served as the Angels' de facto national media spokesman. Now a senior citizen, Barger freely admits to beating, whipping, and shooting people, and selling hard drugs as part of the gang. At the same time, he strives to depict his chosen band of outlaws as exemplars of freedom and rebellion against a conformist society.

Born in 1938, Barger grew up in Oakland, California, the son of an alcoholic father and runaway mother. Openly combative, Barger gravitated towards trouble at an early age: "What I really liked to do at school was fight," he wrote in his autobiography. "I fought at least once a week in junior high school. For me, fighting was always a contest. There was always somebody to test, and a fight was a fight."

He barely bothered with school, despite an interest in reading (mostly western titles by Zane Grey or Louis L'Amour). In the mid-1950s, Barger formed a youth gang called the Earth Angels (after the song of the same title) that mostly just hung out on the sidewalks, trying to look tough. Barger began using drugs, smoking marijuana (a very rare commodity at that time) as a young teenager.

Wanting some direction in life, Barger forged a birth certificate and enrolled in the U.S. Army at age sixteen. He was sworn into the service on July 14, 1955. He found military life physically exhausting, but appreciated the sense of group discipline and esprit de corps. After he had been serving for fourteen months, army brass discovered Barger's true age, and he was drummed out of the service.

Back in Oakland, Barger hung around with fellow street toughs and rode motorcycles. At eighteen, he bought his first real motorcycle—a Harley Davidson, of course. In April 1957 Barger and some friends founded

Hells Angels leader Ralph "Sonny" Barger and his wife Sharon, after his release on $100,000 bond in 1980. He spent more than a year in jail on Federal racketeering conspiracy charges. [AP Photo/Robert Houston]

the Oakland chapter of the Hells Angels Motorcycle Club (HAMC). The Hells Angels had existed in some form or another for about a decade in various California cities. That same month he was arrested for the first time. Booked for drunk driving, Barger was briefly incarcerated, an experience that didn't seem to faze him. In 1958 Barger became president of the Oakland club. Barger wasn't particularly big (he stood 5'9" tall) but he was confident and charismatic, two qualities that endeared him to biker prospects (i.e.,

people looking to join the Angels or other motorcycle clubs).

Barger's inspiration was to combine the outlaw spirit of jail with the discipline and camaraderie of the army: "To become a real man, you need to join the army first, and then do time in jail. Serving time in the barracks and the slammer teaches you discipline and survival. Jail teaches you to be on time: when those doors open and close each day, you'd better be set. After doing the army and jail, you're ready for anything," Barger later wrote.

Under Barger, the Angels established a clubhouse where they could hang out. Some members worked (typically in garages, gas stations, and factories) while others remained unemployed. A collectivist ethos prevailed, with members sharing motorcycle parts and pooling their money to buy groceries for communal meals. A distinctive "winged death's head" emblem was created for the Angels, which "full-patch" members wore on the back of their leather or denim jackets.

In addition to riding and racing high-powered motorcycles (primarily Harley-Davidsons), the fledgling Angels had a proclivity towards violence. The HAMC fought police, other biker gangs, and even wayward chapters of their own organization. The early 1960s, for example, saw the Oakland Angels at war with the San Francisco branch. "We battled long and hard and it wasn't pretty," noted Barger. "If you ever ended up on the ground, forget about it, you got the boot. Your face got smashed in. We did the same to them."

Wanton violence was accompanied by a deliberately foul public image. Angels were rude, dirty, and loud, decorating their bikes and clothes with Nazi regalia, including swastikas and iron crosses. Barger claims to have started the fascist fashion trend after a member gave him a vintage Nazi-era belt buckle bearing an engraved swastika. Barger insists, however, that the Angels only wore this gear for shock value and didn't adhere to Nazi principles.

As vile as the Angels were, Barger stood out by dint of personality and ability. In an early book about the gang, *Hell's Angels*, famed "gonzo" journalist Hunter Thompson wrote:

In any gathering of Hell's Angels, from five to a possible hundred and fifty, there is no doubt who is running the show: Ralph "Sonny" Barger, the Maximum Leader, a six foot [sic], 170-pound warehouseman from East Oakland, the coolest head in the lot, and a tough, quick-thinking dealer when any action starts. By turns he is a fanatic, a philosopher, a brawler, a shrewd compromiser and a final arbitrator.

Thompson, who was badly beaten by an Angel during his time observing the gang, had no illusions about the HAMC. Far from glamorizing the gang (as other journalists have done over the years), he made it clear that most Angels and their peers were ill-educated thugs with a propensity for violence.

While essentially an apolitical gang, the Angels have on occasion displayed a warped sense of patriotism. Barger and his comrades were outraged, for example, by peace marchers during the Vietnam War era. The HAMC didn't appreciate what they perceived to be the demonstrators' upper-class airs and jaundiced attitude towards army veterans. Like Barger, many of the Angels were military veterans with a chauvinistic love of country. Barger decided to launch a counter-demonstration to show where he stood. On October 16, 1965, Barger and a handful of Angels violently disrupted an anti-Vietnam War march in Oakland, California. While taking pains not to hit women or children, Barger and his compatriots began brawling with the peace marchers. Barger attempted to reach a platform at the front of the march, where rally leader and future counter-culture sage Jerry Rubin was giving a speech. Barger was stopped by a knot of police officers, who beat him with truncheons.

The run-in at the rally was the last time the Angels clashed with peace marchers. On every subsequent march in Oakland, Barger was served with a restraining order prior to any demonstrations. Barger sent a telegram to the White House offering the services of the HAMC as "a crack team of trained guerrillas" to battle the Vietcong. President Lyndon Johnson did not take Barger up on this offer. Emissaries from the peace movement, meanwhile, met with the HAMC and more or less smoothed over their considerable differences.

In spite of their actions, the Angels were embraced by the burgeoning hippie counter-culture of the late 1960s. Because they had long hair and enjoyed drugs, motorcycles, rock 'n' roll, and shocking "the establishment," the bikers were accepted by hippies as rowdy brothers-in-arms. This association would have disastrous consequences at the notorious Altamont, California music festival in late December 1969. Altamont was a huge, hastily organized outdoor rock festival headlined by the Rolling Stones, hot off a major U.S. tour. The Angels were hired as "security" and were paid for their efforts with $500 worth of beer. Thanks to the combination of booze, power, and an overflow crowd estimated at half-a-million, the Angels went berserk. Bikers with sawed off pool cues mercilessly tore into the crowd, beating people at will. The mayhem extended to the stage; during an opening set by the Jefferson Airplane, an HAMC member knocked lead singer Marty Balin unconscious after he tried to intervene in a fight. The concert reached its apocalyptic peak during the Stones' notorious performance.

In his autobiography, Barger doesn't downplay the violence at Altamont. He causally alludes to beating "some of the a**holes vandalizing our bikes" at Altamont. He also claims to have forced Stones guitarist Keith Richards (who threatened to quit the show because of the Angels' brutality) to keep performing at gunpoint. During the Stones' set, a black teenager named Meredith Hunter was stabbed to death by the Angels, an event captured on film. Barger insists that Hunter drew a gun and even shot one of the Angels on security detail. The injury was minor, apparently, and the victim not eager to report to a hospital where his identity might be revealed to police.

Altamont is one in a series of violent episodes Barger touches on in his autobiography. At one point, he details the fate of a pair of criminals who foolishly tried to pass themselves off as HAMC members: "Once the cops left, I went out and rounded up both guys. We roughed them up pretty damned bad. We stuck their hands in vices and beat them senseless with bullwhips and mallets." When Barger's prized, customized motorcycle (called "Sweet Cocaine") was stolen by a low-level biker club called the Unknowns, retribution was swift and terrible. The Angels kidnapped the Unknowns and brought them to Barger's house. There, they inflicted terrible torture on the hapless wannabe bikers, bullwhipping the lot, beating them with dog collars, and breaking their fingers with ball-peen hammers. As if that wasn't enough, the Angels also seized the gang's motorcycles and forcibly disbanded their club.

Evidently no one involved in the incident pressed charges, which is why Barger can get away with talking about it in his book.

Thanks to sensational media coverage and Barger's stalwart leadership, the Angels expanded rapidly in the 1960s and 1970s. Chapters popped up across the country and even in Europe and Asia. Oakland became the unofficial flagship chapter for Angels worldwide. Even as the HAMC thrived, Barger's personal life remained chaotic. His first wife, Elsie, died from a self-induced abortion in the late 1960s. He married his second wife, Sharon Grunhlke, in December 1973 while serving time in jail. A third wife would follow later on.

While vague on specifics, Barger admits to sinking deeper into the criminal underworld as the HAMC gained strength and notoriety. "The seventies were a gangster era for us," writes Barger, in his autobiography. He was put on trial for some of his activities, including a case involving a triple homicide. He was tried and found not guilty of this offense in the early 1970s, but was eventually incarcerated for other drug charges, gun charges, and false imprisonment. He landed at Folsom Prison in California (the same penitentiary Johnny Cash famously performed at). In the mid-1970s Barger was also charged with income tax evasion and more gun charges.

Following some tricky legal maneuvers, Barger was released from Folsom in November 1977. In October 1979 Barger along with other Angels and associates went on trial again, charged with violations of the RICO (Racketeer Influenced and Corrupt Organizations) statute. The federal government accused the Angels of being a criminal organization, deeply involved in trafficking drugs, particularly methamphetamine, and murdering people for sport and profit. Authorities painted the HAMC as a massive underworld enterprise that ruled through sheer brute force. When it came time to testify, Barger insisted that the Angels were not a criminal band, but a benign social club. While sticking to this position today, Barger does concede that individual Angels, himself included, have been known to break the law on occasion. On July 2, 1980, the RICO trial of Barger and other Hells Angels ended in a hung jury. A mistrial was declared.

Barger didn't have long to celebrate. In 1983 he underwent extensive surgery for throat cancer caused by a heavy smoking habit. Four years later, he was imprisoned again in Arizona on conspiracy charges connected with a plot to blow up a clubhouse belonging to the Outlaws, bitter biker rivals of the Angels. Barger served his time and was released in 1992. Six years later, Barger transferred his Angels membership from Oakland to Arizona, where he currently resides. Barger is now an author, having published his autobiography in 2000. The book features Barger's criminal rap sheet, which includes twenty-one separate arrests. Barger has since penned a series of other tomes with titles such as *Freedom: Credos from the Road* and *Ridin' High and Livin' Free*. His career switch from Hells Angels spokesman to bestselling author has not gone unnoticed by law enforcement.

"The legendary leader of HAMC, Sonny Barger, travels across the United States promoting his autobiography at various events and presents an image of HAMC as a group of average working men who are simply motorcycle enthusiasts who like to have a good time," reads a profile on outlaw motorcycle gangs written by the U.S. Department of Justice. The same agency estimates that the bike club Barger helped popularize now numbers between 2,000–2,500 members in over two hundred and thirty chapters worldwide. Far from being law abiding motorcycle enthusiasts, the Department of Justice accuses the HAMC of being heavily involved in drug trafficking, assault, murder, extortion, money laundering, and motorcycle theft.

See also: Hells Angels; Outlaw Motorcycle Gangs

Further Reading

Ralph "Sonny" Barger (with Keith and Kent Zimmerman), *Hell's Angel: The Life and Times of Sonny Barger and the Hell's Angels Motorcycle Club*, 2001.

Sonny Barger–An American Legend. http:// sonnybarger.com/index3.html.

Federal Bureau of Investigation report on— Hells Angels. http://foia.fbi.gov/foiaindex/ hellsang.htm.

Hells Angels Motorcycle Club. http://www .hells-angels.com.

William Marsden and Julian Sher, *Angels of Death: Inside the Bikers' Global Crime Empire*, 2006.

National Drug Intelligence Center, Drugs and Crime—Outlaw Motorcycle Gang Profile: Hells Angels Motorcycle Club. October 2002.

Hunter Thompson, *Hell's Angels: The Strange and Terrible Saga of the Outlaw Motorcycle Gangs*, 1966.

U.S. Department of Justice—Motorcycle Gangs. http://www.usdoj.gov/criminal/ gangunit/gangs/motorcycle.html.

BARNES, LEROY "NICKY" (1933–)

Leroy "Nicky" Barnes remains a figure of controversy. Viewed as a hero to some African-Americans, a "rat" and a gangster to others, he earned millions peddling dope to black communities. Barnes was a gangster who rose to the pinnacle of success only to break the code of the jailhouse and inform on his business associates. Once prominent enough to raise the wrath of a President, Barnes' status in the underworld is still open to debate. Some accounts depict Barnes as a "Black Godfather" who answered to no one and was treated as an equal by white mobsters. Another take suggests he was merely a figurehead, a tool of the Italian Mafia who wanted an African-American to serve as point man for their drug operations in Harlem.

Born in 1933 into a poor Harlem family, Barnes might have remained an obscure street criminal were it not for a fortuitous encounter with a high-ranking Mafiosi. Jailed on drug charges in 1965 in New York's Green Haven penitentiary, Barnes made the acquaintance of fellow prisoner "Crazy Joe" Gallo. Gallo was an eccentric underworld chieftain who had a reputation for being mentally unstable (a reputation that might have been merely an act to unnerve opponents). Unusual for a Mafia leader, Gallo didn't look down on blacks and saw them as potential business partners and customers for the drugs he sold. Gallo served as something of a mentor to Barnes, instructing the young man on the finer points of running a large-scale drug operation. He taught the fledgling gangster the benefit of organization and structure, which was to insulate the boss

Leroy "Nicky" Barnes, seated at right, testifies clad in a black hood and under heavy security during a hearing before the Presidents Commission on Organized Crime, 1985. [AP Photo/Jim Witmer/ Miami News]

from the actions of his underlings. When Gallo was released from jail, he instructed his lawyer to look into Barnes' case. The lawyer got Barnes' conviction overturned on a technicality, and the mentor and student went into business together. Gallo served as a wholesaler, providing huge amounts of drugs (primarily heroin) to Barnes, who retailed the dope on the streets of New York. Barnes was expected to provide Gallo with a cut of the profits and occasionally some "muscle," black street thugs, for unspecified purposes. Barnes had nothing to do with actually smuggling the drugs into the United States; that remained the Mafia's responsibility. Barnes also had no say on internal Mafia policy.

Crazy Joe Gallo was assassinated on April 7, 1972, but Barnes' Mafia drug links remained intact. Barnes did more than just buy drugs from the mob. He modeled his criminal organization after traditional Mafia "families." To this end, Barnes made sure there were several layers of authority between himself and the street thugs who did his bidding. Just as police find it difficult to pin specific

Mafia crimes on the family boss, Barnes seemed immune from punishment. While arrested many times, Barnes always seemed to beat the rap, earning the nickname "Mr. Untouchable."

Organization was Barnes' forte. In 1973 he brought together a handful of Harlem's biggest drugs dealers to set up a city-wide syndicate called "the Council." Barnes himself was on the Council, which sought to regulate illicit drug operations and settle disputes between black mobsters. The Council was very similar to "the Commission," the regulatory body created by Charles "Lucky" Luciano back in the 1930s. The difference was in scale; while the Commission was concerned with Mafia activity throughout the United States, the Council's purview was generally limited to New York City. By the mid-1970s, Barnes had become one of the biggest drug dealers in America, with the earnings to match. For 1975 Barnes reported an income of $288,750 to the IRS. Of this total, he itemized $1,750 as "wages" and the rest as "miscellaneous income." "By 1976, Barnes had at least seven major lieutenants working for him, each of whom controlled a dozen mid-level distributors who in turn supplied up to 40 street level retailers each," states a backgrounder from the Drug Enforcement Administration (DEA). "His syndicate made enormous profits by cutting and packaging low-quality heroin. Barnes controlled heroin sales and manufacture throughout New York State and extended his business into Canada and Pennsylvania."

In the fall of 1976, Barnes held a memorable birthday party for himself. As slack-jawed police looked on, over two hundred black gangsters parked their Rolls Royces and Cadillacs and flocked to a private rooftop club on top of a New York skyscraper. Such flamboyant antics helped endear Barnes to the very same communities he was flooding with drugs. He was a folk hero to many blacks, an African-American who worked with the Italian Mafia on his own terms and became enormously wealthy in the process. Barnes strutted around town with an air of bravado and a sense of invincibility. He also enjoyed toying with authorities. He was fond of taking police "tails" on wild goose chases. He would drive aimlessly around New York City, making constant stops, for no other purpose than irritating police observers who had to follow behind him in a car.

In June 1977 Barnes was the subject of a cover story in the *New York Times* magazine. The cover featured a photograph of a haughty Barnes plus the title "Mr. Untouchable." Barnes posed specifically for the shot, as per the *New York Times'* request. *The Times* achieved this goal by telling Barnes they would run an unflattering mug shot of him on the magazine cover unless he would allow himself to be formally photographed. Ever image conscious, Barnes agreed. According to the article, Barnes owned three hundred custom-tailored suits, sixty pairs of custom-made shoes, twenty-seven full-length leather coats, two Citroën-Maseratis, four Mercedes, and five homes. The cars couldn't be seized because Barnes registered them with phony leasing companies. Federal authorities would eventually get wise to this scheme and seize his wheels.

The fall out from the magazine article was intense. The story infuriated President Jimmy Carter who ordered the Justice Department to come down hard on Barnes. This was done, and in late 1977 Barnes and several of his associates found themselves in federal court, charged with various drug crimes. Following nine weeks of testimony, Barnes and ten associates were found guilty. On January 19, 1978, the Federal District Court in Manhattan served sentence on Barnes. Mr. Untouchable received life in prison.

Barnes was not happy behind bars. He felt he was being disrespected by Council members who remained on the outside and believed his lawyers were cheating him. He was angered to hear that one of his lieutenants was bedding a favorite mistress. Convinced his colleagues were running down the empire he built up, Barnes decided to start talking. As *TIME* magazine memorably put it, "Mr. Untouchable Turned into Mr. Tell All." Throughout the early 1980s, Barnes operated as an undercover informer, luring associates into making compromising statements in prison visits. Then, starting in 1984, Barnes served as a prosecution witness in a series of trials. He helped convict 14 defendants, most of them fellow African-American business associates. Barnes isn't remorseful about turning into a "rat": "When I realized they left me on the battlefield to die . . . I said, 'I'll pull [them] in, let them see what it's like.' . . . I don't regret it," he was quoted as saying in an October 2007, article in *New York* magazine. In the same story, Barnes spoke dismissively about the underworld code against "snitching": "I can't see how a guy can be considered strong if he lets a bunch of a**holes walk all over him and he

doesn't respond, just because of some code that a bunch of idiots have cooked up."

Authorities certainly appreciated Barnes' change of heart. In the 1980s then U.S. Attorney Rudolph Giuliani petitioned to get a presidential pardon for Barnes in return for the assistance he had provided. At the time, Giuliani was unsuccessful and a pardon was not forthcoming. In February 1992, authorities tried again. Otto G. Obermaier, United States Attorney in Manhattan, filed papers with a federal judge requesting a lighter sentence for Barnes in return for services rendered. Barnes was not released, however, until August 1998. With an alleged $1 million price tag on his head courtesy of his underworld colleagues, Barnes was put into the Witness Protection Program. It is not clear where he lived or what he did for a living, although apparently at one point he was employed by a chain of automated car wash centers.

In 2007, Barnes released his autobiography. Called *Mr. Untouchable*, this memoir was written with the help of Tom Folsom, a documentary filmmaker. Of course, the book put the best possible spin on Barnes's actions. One topic it didn't touch on were unresolved killings Barnes was aware of (a smart move, given that Barnes could still be charged if he said too much). That same year, a documentary film based on the book was released. Barnes was also depicted in the 2007 feature film *American Gangster*. His character was played by Oscar-winning actor Cuba Gooding Jr. While pleased to be on the silver screen, Barnes was reputedly annoyed that the movie primarily focused on drug dealer Frank Lucas, an old rival.

In late 2007, Barnes was able to swallow any professional jealousy he might have felt for Lucas and agreed to chat with the man for an article in *New York* magazine. This tête-à-tête was the first time the two men had spoken together in decades. The dialogue revealed a great deal of mutual respect between the two drug lords. That said, Barnes was critical of his former role as a drug dealer and slammed Hollywood for glamorizing criminals. "No one should be elevated because of what they did in the drug business. The way we operated— there was a lot of violence, like 10 to 12 homicides, to keep the whole operation running. You can't glorify that. It's not something Frank or I would tell any of our children to get into," stated Barnes. "Heroin has wreaked a lot of havoc and a lot of pain in the black community. I shouldn't have done it. . . . [but] I wanted to make money and that's what I did," he added. Barnes also used the occasion to note that, "Giuliani would make a good president because he's a principled guy."

The *New York Times* magazine tracked down Barnes for a follow-up story in late 2007. According to *the Times*, Barnes (who is now in his mid-70s) lives in a white neighborhood in an undisclosed locale, and holds down a legitimate job. He has two children (who were put into foster care when their father went to federal prison in the late 1970s) and several grandchildren. None of the fortune he earned as a mob boss remains. The former crime boss told the *New York Times*:

Nicky Barnes is not around anymore. Nicky Barnes' lifestyle and his value system is extinct. I left Nicky Barnes behind. I live within my paycheck. I want to get up every day and get in the car and go to work and be a respected member of my community. And I am respected. I know I am. I'm not looking in the rear view mirror to see if anyone is tailing me anymore. I don't turn on the blender when I'm at home so I can talk [without being overheard on a covert listening device]. That is not part of my life. Sure, I'd love to have more money but I am not willing to do anything but go to my job to get it

See also: Drug Trade; Johnson, Ellsworth "Bumpy"

Further Reading

"Bad, Bad Leroy Barnes," *TIME*, December 12, 1977.

Mark Jacobson, "Lords of Dopetown," *New York*, October 25, 2007.

Sam Roberts, "Crime's 'Mr. Untouchable' Emerges From Shadows," *New York Times*, March 4, 2007.

Ronald Sullivan, "U.S. Attorney Seeks Release of Informer," *New York Times*, February 22, 1992.

"Telling Tales," *TIME*, January 30, 1984.

U.S. Drug Enforcement Administration history, 1975–1980. "The Arrest of Nicky Barnes."

BILLY THE KID

See: Bonney; William

BLACK HAND

The Black Hand racket was a simple scam that was extremely common in Italian-American communities from the late 19th century to the early 20th century. In this racket an anonymous note would arrive at the home of an Italian immigrant threatening all manner of torture and violence unless a large fee was paid. The extortionist sending the letter would typically "sign" it by dipping their hand in black ink and pressing their palm against the paper. This would leave the impression of a black hand, which is how the scam got its name. The racket was prevalent in any city with a large Italian population. Many new Italian immigrants were poorly educated, deeply superstitious, and had an inbred mistrust of police, who tended to be very corrupt in their homeland. Italians were unlikely to report Black Hand intimidation to authorities. These factors allowed the racket to flourish.

Italian-Americans ascribed all manner of quasi-mystical powers to the Black Hand "organization" which was viewed as all-knowing and all-powerful. In reality there was no Black Hand organization beyond a few solo operators who counted on their countrymen's ignorance to propagate the scam. It wasn't only poor immigrants who were victimized either. The famous singer Enrico Caruso was once the target of Black Hand intimidation. Unlike most victims, Caruso reported the intimidation to police, who set a trap and arrested his would-be extortionists. Strangely enough, some Black Handers also tried the scam on fellow criminals. Big Jim Colosimo, crime boss of Chicago in the early 20th century, was on the receiving end of countless Black Hand threats. Annoyed, Colosimo brought his wife's nephew, Johnny Torrio from New York City, to deal with the problem. Torrio's solution was to organize hit squads to murder the Black Handers who were bothering his uncle. With the problem resolved, Torrio elected to stay in Chicago and introduce

an up-and-coming gangster named Al Capone to the city.

Some brave Italians fought back against the Black Handers. In one famous case in 1909, New Orleans mobster Paul Di Cristina was rebuffed by a grocer named Pietro Pepitone, who refused to pay Black Hand tribute. Di Cristina decided a personal visit was in order. When he arrived at Pepitone's store, the plucky grocer pulled out a shotgun and blasted the gangster at point-blank range. Pepitone was sentenced to twenty years in jail for his act of defiance, but only served six.

Several dedicated policemen also fought against the Black Hand scam. One of the most notable was Italian-born police lieutenant Joseph Petrosino. Petrosino headed up a squad in New York City that dealt specifically with crime in the Italian immigrant community. Fearless, Petrosino made virtually hundreds of Black Hand related arrests in spite of death threats from mobsters. He also didn't hesitate to apply a little rough street justice, beating up Black Handers in public to lower their status in the eyes of their victims. In early 1909 Petrosino made a brave but foolhardy solo mission to Sicily to get more information about criminals who had left the island to plague New York. Petrosino was set up and murdered in Palermo on March 12, 1909. His body was brought back home and Italian immigrants mourned the loss of a very courageous officer. An estimated 250,000 people viewed his coffin as it passed by on the street. Petrosino was the only New York City police officer killed while on assignment in a foreign country.

The Black Hand scam eventually petered out around the early 1920s due to a combination of factors. For one, the

Italian community had become more acclimatized to their new surroundings and less likely to fall for blatantly obvious extortion scams. Also, the federal government began cracking down on Black Hand extortionists, charging them with using the mail to defraud. What really killed the Black Hand racket, however, was Prohibition. Italian gangsters realized there was more money to be had selling illegal alcohol than extorting cash from their countrymen. Although the Black Hand racket disappeared, extortion hasn't. Threatening merchants or local business people with murder and dismemberment (or threatening the same to their families) remains a tried and true gangster racket. The only difference is, today extortionists generally don't send their victims notes containing inky palm prints and dire warnings of violence.

See also: Mafia; Saietta, Ignazio "Lupo the Wolf"

Further Reading

Pierre de Champlain, *Mobsters: Gangsters and Men of Honour*, 2004.

Officer Down Memorial Page—Joseph Petrosino. http://www.odmp.org/officer/10600 -lieutenant-giuseppe-(joseph)-petrosino.

Thomas Reppetto, *American Mafia: A History of Its Rise to Power*, 2004.

David Southwell, *The History of Organized Crime: The True Story and Secrets of Global Gangland*, 2006.

BLOODS

The Bloods were formed from the merger of various Los Angeles street gangs such as the L.A. Brims, Denver Lanes, the Inglewood Family, the Swans, and the Pueblo Bishops, who opposed the rise of the Crips megagang in the 1970s. The Bloods were also strengthened by the presence of the Piru Street Boys, who were once allied to the Crips. It is suggested that the name "Bloods" came from the word black soldiers used in Vietnam to identify themselves. "Blood" simply meant African-American.

Aside from the intense animosity between the two gangs, there is little that separates the Bloods from the Crips. Both are largely made up of disenchanted, young African-American men who don't hesitate to use violence and intimidation to support their criminal lifestyles. Like the Crips, members of the Bloods got heavily involved in the crack cocaine trade during the 1980s. Both groups also drastically boosted their firepower during this period, using drug profits to purchase expensive, military-grade automatic weapons. Battles between Bloods and Crips were often waged over drug turf. Crips and Bloods both use elaborate hand signals to indicate their gang and set affiliations. Sets are smaller subdivisions within a larger gang. Members of different sets might find each other at war, even though both groups are technically part of the same gang. Code words are common as well; "C.K." is Bloods code for "Crip Killer." Crips themselves are called "crabs" in the Bloods vernacular. Crips, in turn, deride Bloods as "snoops" or "slobs." Bloods try to avoid using the letter "C" when identifying their gang set (as in "Kompton" not "Compton"). They also use the color red to identify themselves. This is to contrast the gang from the Crips, who use blue as an identifier. This color war traces its origins to correctional facilities run by the California Youth Authority. The latter would hand

Members of the Bloods gang in red headbands, far right and second from left, Los Angeles, 1993.
[AP Photo/Nick Ut]

out blue handkerchiefs to their youthful charges. The Crips took up the blue hankies as a gang emblem, so the Bloods naturally started using the color red to distinguish themselves from other gangs.

The U.S. Department of Justice estimates there are 5,000–20,000 members of the Bloods, in over 120 cities. "The main source of income for the Bloods is derived from the street-level distribution of cocaine and marijuana," reads a U.S. Department of Justice report. "Bloods members are also involved in the transportation and distribution of methamphetamine, heroin and to a lesser extent PCP (phencyclidine). The Bloods are also involved in other criminal activity, such as assault, auto theft, burglary, carjacking, drive-by shooting, extortion, homicide, identification fraud and robbery."

See also: Crips; Mara Salvatrucha (MS-13); Shakur, Sanyika; Williams, Stanley "Tookie"

Further Reading

Leon Bing, *Do Or Die*, 1991.

Detective Wayne Caffey, Los Angeles County Sheriff's Office, "Crips and Bloods," 2006. http://www.eremedy.org/doc/crips_bloods .pdf.

Sanyika Shakur (aka Monster Kody Scott), *Monster: The Autobiography of an L.A. Gang Member*, 1993.

U.S. Department of Justice—Street Gangs (http://www.usdoj.gov/criminal/gangunit/ gangs/street.html)

BONNEY, WILLIAM "BILLY THE KID" (1859 OR 1860–1881)

Unlike most outlaws of the Old West, Billy the Kid never robbed banks or held up trains. He wasn't motivated by

William H. Bonney, aka "Billy the Kid," western outlaw (1859–1881). [Circer, Hayward, ed., Dictionary of American Portraits, *1967]*

money, but by a twisted sense of justice. High-spirited and boyish in appearance and attitude, the Kid was also a cold-blooded killer.

Billy was born in New York City; as to when, the record is unclear. The year is usually given as 1859 or 1860. Even his real name is open to dispute. Different sources give his first name as either William or Henry, and his family name as Bonney or McCarty. Billy's parents, William and Catherine Bonney, were both Irish Catholics. They had another son named Joseph (some accounts say Edward) a couple years after Billy was born. In 1862 the young family moved to Kansas where William Bonney promptly died. His widow moved her two boys to Colorado, but didn't stay there long. A census from June 18, 1868, placed the widow (identified as "Catherine McCarty") and sons William and Joseph in Indiana. While in Indiana, Catherine met a man named William Antrim, whom she married on March 1, 1873. Shortly after the wedding, the Antrim family moved to Silver City, New Mexico. Catherine opened a boarding house to supplement the family income. William Antrim tried his hand at panning for silver. When Catherine died of tuberculosis in September 1874, her two boys were shuttled around various foster homes. William Antrim drifted to Clifton, Arizona, abandoning his stepsons.

Left to his own devices, young Billy found work in Silver City as a dishwasher. He also started hanging out with some tough local kids. One of them stole some laundry and gave it to Billy to hide. Billy was caught and arrested for the first time on September 23, 1875. He was locked up, but escaped. Billy tramped his way to Clifton, Arizona and located his stepfather. Antrim wanted nothing to do with the boy, however, so Billy became a drifter. During 1875 to 1876 Billy wandered the countryside, going from ranch to ranch looking for work. He was employed, alternately, as a ranch hand and gambler. His fellow ranch hands taught him how to shoot, use a knife, and lasso and rustle cattle—skills he would later put to good use. Billy also befriended a horse thief named John Mackie. Under Mackie's guidance, Billy was soon rustling horses as well—a very serious crime in the Old West. In March 1877 Billy and Mackie were caught and placed in prison in Fort Grant, Arizona. Once again, Billy escaped.

In the summer of 1877 Billy committed his first murder. The victim was a blacksmith and bully in Fort Grant named Frank Cahill. According to the most reliable accounts, Billy and Cahill got into an argument at a saloon. Cahill rushed his much smaller opponent, slamming him onto the ground. Cahill proceeded to slap Billy's face with his work-hardened palms. Billy managed to get a hand free and grabbed a revolver—either his own or Cahill's. The gun went off and Cahill was shot in the stomach. As Cahill writhed on the ground, Billy jumped up and ran. Cahill died and Billy became a murderer and outlaw. Calling himself "William Bonney," Billy fled Arizona and went back to New Mexico.

By this point, Billy had reached his full adult height. He was 5'8" tall and weighed about 140 pounds. His eyes were gray, and his hair was light brown and worn fairly long, as per outlaw style. "In appearance, Billy was one of the mildest persons imaginable," stated a *New York Times* article written after Billy's death. "His soft blue eye (sic) was so attractive that those who saw him for the first time looked upon him as a victim of his circumstance. In spite of his innocent appearance, however, Billy the Kid was really one of the most dangerous characters which this country has ever produced." Indeed, Billy was developing a reputation as a crack shot. He practiced shooting all the time. He also worked on his quick draw skills—seeing how fast he could remove his pistol from his holster. *The Saga of Billy the Kid*, one of the best known biographies of the rangy teenager, described the outlaw as jovial, friendly, witty, and generally upbeat. The same book also speculated that he was largely devoid of empathy or any deep-seated feelings. There was " . . . a hiatus in his character—a sub-zero vacuum devoid of all human emotions. He was upon occasion the personification of merciless, remorseless deadlines . . . he had no remorse. No memories haunted him," stated the book.

In September 1877 Billy joined forces with outlaw Jesse Evans, who led a group of thugs called "the Boys." Billy also picked up his nickname during this period. One of the members of Evans' gang started referring to Billy as "the Kid," a reflection of his youth, and the tag stuck. Billy and the Boys rode into Lincoln County, New Mexico in the fall of 1877. At the time, New Mexico was only a territory, not a state. Statehood wouldn't arrive until well into the 20th century. In the late 1870s New Mexico Territory was populated with restive Mexicans, Indians, and a handful of determined settlers. One such settler, an Englishman named John Tunstall, had dreams of getting into the cattle business. After arriving in Lincoln County, Tunstall befriended John Chisum, another settler who owned 10,000 head of cattle. Tunstall purchased a ranch and opened a store. He aligned himself with a third settler, a deeply religious lawyer named Alexander McSween.

Wittingly or not, Tunstall helped spark a conflict dubbed the Lincoln County War. This war pitched Tunstall, Chisum, and other ranchers against a fellow store owner named James Dolan and his allies. Prior to Tunstall's arrival, Dolan had run the only general store for miles around. His shop sold food, animal feed, clothes, saddles, and farm and ranch equipment. Dolan also sold beef to Indian reservations and the U.S. Army. He had a monopoly on trade in the area and wanted to keep it that way. Dolan ran his business with a fellow merchant named A.G. Murphy (identified as Lawrence Murphy by some sources), who controlled grazing and water rights for the surrounding ranches. This gave Murphy an enormous amount of power over local ranchers. Murphy was also politically connected and could count on New Mexico Territory Governor Samuel Beach Axtell as an ally. Dolan and Murphy did their best to drive Tunstall out of business. Tunstall fought back, unsuccessfully, with legal actions. Realizing he was getting nowhere, Tunstall changed tack. He hired a band of gunmen/ranch hands, whose ranks included Billy the Kid. Billy worked for Tunstall as a cattle guard, field hand, and gunman. Billy took a liking to the determined Englishman, who respected Billy in return. While Tunstall was only in his early 20s, there is evidence that Billy regarded him as a father figure.

On February 18, 1878, Billy was herding horses with Tunstall and another man named Dick Brewer. Billy and Brewer became separated from their employer, who was ambushed by a posse led by Dolan. As Billy and Brewer watched helplessly in the distance, Tunstall was gunned down. His death galvanized his ranch hands. A faction led by Brewer dubbed themselves "The Regulators" and sought justice. Billy was part of this group. A day after their boss was assassinated, the Regulators tried to serve arrest warrants on his killers. The group was disarmed instead, and taken prisoner by Sheriff William Brady, who sided with the Dolan/Murphy gang. At the end of the month, having missed Tunstall's funeral, Billy and his companions were released from jail.

The Regulators gave up their legal fight. On March 6, 1878, the group arrested Bill Morton and Frank Baker, two members of the Dolan/Murphy gang. The Regulators decided not to hand their prisoners over but to kill them. One account says Morton and Baker were murdered in cold blood. Another suggests they were cut down by

Billy while trying to escape on horseback. On April 1 a group of Regulators, including Billy, ambushed Sheriff Brady and his deputies. Brady and a deputy were killed. Four days later, the Regulators murdered "Buckshot Bill" Roberts, a local man viewed as an ally of the Dolan/Murphy faction. Before Roberts died, he killed Dick Brewer with a well-aimed shot from his rifle. Two weeks after Roberts' death, Billy and two Regulators were indicted for murdering Sheriff Brady.

On July 15, 1878, new Lincoln County Sheriff George Peppin, who was allied with the Dolan/Murphy gang, led a forty-man posse to the home of the lawyer McSween. About fifteen Regulators—including Billy—were staying at the home, using it as an informal barracks. The sheriff's posse opened fire on the residence in the middle of the night. Their volleys smashed windows, blasted holes in the walls, and shattered the house structure. Aroused from their sleep, the Regulators traded shots with the posse. The latter could have stormed the house, but were content to simply lay siege. Five days into the siege, the posse set the house on fire. By nightfall, it was burning bright. Inside, there was panic, except for Billy, who stayed cool. Assuming leadership, Billy arrayed the men into two groups. The first group, led by Billy, raced out of the house one way, while the second group ran in the opposite direction. Shots rang out. Three Regulators and one posse member were killed, but Billy and most of his comrades got away. McSween, who stayed inside his blazing home, praying out loud, was shot dead by the posse.

During the summer of 1878, Billy stole cattle and gambled, unaware that powerful interests wanted to squash him and his friends. In Washington D.C. President Rutherford Hayes was determined to put an end to the Lincoln County War. President Hayes eased corrupt Governor Axtell out of office and replaced him with Lew Wallace, a tough-minded leader who had served as a Union officer in the Civil War. Once in office, Governor Wallace issued an amnesty proclamation that would allow most of the participants in the Lincoln County War to escape prosecution as long as they weren't under indictment. Billy was selling stolen horses in Texas when he heard the news. He returned to Lincoln County at the end of 1878.

In February 1879 a drifter named Pat Garrett sauntered into Fort Sumner, New Mexico. Garrett was very tall (6'4") and gaunt. Born in 1850 in Alabama, Garrett had headed west after the Civil War. He took employment as a ranch hand and professional buffalo hunter. In Fort Sumner he began working for a rancher named Pete Maxwell. The same month that Garrett showed up in Fort Sumner, Billy secured a shaky truce between the Regulators and the Dolan/Murphy gang. The rough peace accord was broken almost immediately, however, after some of Dolan's men murdered Huston Chapman, a lawyer who was helping McSween's widow.

On March 13, 1879, Billy penned a letter to Governor Wallace offering to surrender and testify against Chapman's killers. In exchange, he wanted a pardon. A meeting was arranged between the governor and the outlaw. On March 17, 1879, Billy showed up at the governor's mansion, rifle and revolver in hand. The governor was shocked to discover that the notorious outlaw was a youthful, innocent looking boy. A deal was struck. Billy would submit to a false arrest and testify in court. He would receive a pardon for his actions. Billy was supposed to stay in jail until the various trials concluded. The plan went into effect on March 21, 1879. Billy was arrested and brought to Lincoln County. The next month he testified against the men who murdered Chapman. He also testified at other trials. After three months in prison, Billy realized he'd been tricked. The governor had no intention of pardoning him. Not only that, he would be put on trial for killing Sheriff Brady and other men. Billy escaped from jail, stole a horse, and rode off. An outlaw once more, Billy reverted to form and began rustling cattle again.

On January 10, 1880, in Fort Sumner, a drunk named Joe Grant foolishly challenged the Kid in a saloon. Billy asked if he could inspect Grant's sidearm. Grant handed the weapon over. Like most men of the era, Grant only loaded five rounds in his six-shooter. He kept the hammer resting on an empty chamber, so the gun wouldn't go off accidentally if jostled. Billy pretended to inspect the weapon. He spun the cylinder and made sure the hammer would fall on an empty chamber. Then he handed the weapon back. Triumphant, Grant gripped his gun and aimed it at the outlaw. Grant pulled the trigger and looked mystified when the hammer clicked on an empty chamber. Billy smiled and drew his own weapon, and killed the dumbfounded drunk.

By the fall of 1880, Billy was wearying of the outlaw lifestyle. He penned another note stating his willingness to fix things with Governor Wallace. Nothing ever came of this second request. While hanging around Fort Sumner, he became acquainted with Pat Garrett. Some accounts say Billy attended Garrett's

wedding. On November 2, 1880, however, Garrett was elected Sheriff of Lincoln County. Billy's former acquaintance was now his sworn enemy. Later that same month, a posse led by Deputy Sheriff James Carlysle tracked Billy and his gang to a ranch. During the ensuing chaos, Carlysle was accidentally killed by his own men. The Kid escaped with his associates, but was blamed for the deputy's death.

By mid-December 1880, Billy had a $500 bounty on his head for his capture. Later that same month, a member of Billy's gang was killed in an ambush orchestrated by Garrett. The rest of the gang got away, and hid out in an abandoned stone house. Garrett's posse caught up with the gang and opened fire. Another member of Billy's crew was killed. A shot from Sheriff Garrett's gun killed a horse belonging to Billy's gang. The animal sprawled in such a way as to block the only door to the stone house. A stand off ensued. After a couple days, Billy and gang—cold, and low on bullets and supplies—surrendered.

During the Christmas season, Billy was transported in shackles first to Las Vegas, and then to a small, obscure desert town. He was placed on board a train and taken to Santa Fe, New Mexico Territory. While in jail, Billy composed yet another note for Governor Wallace, pleading for his intervention. No reply was forthcoming. Billy and his companions tried to dig their way to freedom, only to be caught. Billy was placed in a dark, solitary confinement cell and chained to the floor. He continued writing fruitless letters to the governor. In March 1881 Billy was put on trial in La Mesilla, New Mexico Territory for the murder of Buckshot Bill Roberts (other sources say the trial was for killing an

Indian agent). After a few days, the Roberts case was dismissed on a technicality. Billy was promptly put on trial for murdering Sheriff Brady. Found guilty, he was scheduled to be hanged on May 13, 1881, in Lincoln County.

The Kid was transported to Lincoln and placed in a cell at the local courthouse. He was guarded by two deputies: James Bell and Bob Olinger. Bell was a decent man who treated Billy respectfully. Olinger was a bully who tormented the Kid about his impending hanging. During the afternoon of April 28, 1881, Billy escaped from jail for the last time. While playing cards with Bell—the only guard on duty—Billy pretended to drop a card on the floor. Deputy Bell reached to pick it up and Billy seized his gun. The dazed deputy tried to run, so Billy shot him dead. He worked his small wrists out of the handcuffs that bound him, and then stole a shotgun from the courthouse armory. Billy leaned out of the second floor window of the courthouse and waited. Eventually, Deputy Olinger came into view, tromping towards the courthouse. Billy called to him. The startled deputy looked up and the Kid blasted him to pieces. Billy forced an old cook, who made meals for prisoners in the courthouse cells to split his leg irons with an axe. He used twine to bind the broken ends of the leg irons, which were still attached to his feet. Billy stole a horse and disappeared. He made his first stop at a blacksmith shop, where he got the remainder of his leg irons removed. A free man, Billy rode off to Fort Sumner, New Mexico.

Garrett had heard rumors of Billy's arrival and was on alert. On the evening of July 14, 1881, the sheriff and two deputies rode out to the home of Pete Maxwell, Garrett's former employer.

Garrett wanted to ask him if he had seen the Kid. Garrett ordered his two deputies to wait on the porch while he went inside. The sheriff entered the darkened home and made his way to Maxwell's room. He woke up the man was trying to explain his mission when he heard a familiar voice. It belonged to Billy the Kid. He was hiding out in a nearby house and had sauntered over, to see if he could buy some beef from Maxwell. The Kid had a butcher knife and a pistol on him but wasn't wearing boots. Billy spotted the deputies on the porch but didn't stop. Billy cat-footed into Maxwell's bedroom and asked in a whisper who the strangers on the porch were. Billy caught the silhouette of Garrett's tall frame, crouched by the bed. According to *The Saga of Billy the Kid*, he called out, "Who is it?" in Spanish. By way of reply, Sheriff Garrett fired two shots at the Kid. One round pierced his heart and killed him instantly. The second shot went wild. Billy was buried in the Fort Sumner graveyard, next to two of his buddies, Tom O'Folliard and Charlie Bowdre.

The Kid's murder was headline news: "the fact that he is at last out of the way will be received with a sense of relief . . . his killing is regarded (in the west) as one of the most fortunate events which has occurred for years," reported the *New York Times* on July 31, 1881.

The actual tally of Billy's victims isn't known, although he probably killed under a dozen people. Tales that he murdered twenty-one men (supposedly one for each year of his life) abound but are not historically accurate. On July 15 a coroner's jury decided that Billy's death was justifiable homicide. Garrett would face no charges for the execution style murder of the Kid.

With the help of some ghost writers, Garrett published a quickie book in early 1882 entitled, *The Authentic Life of Billy the Kid*. While a huge hit at the time, the book was largely a work of fiction, replete with myths, legends, untruths, and falsehoods. Billy had only been dead for a few months, and his life was already being mythologized, ironically, by the man who killed him.

See also: James, Jesse

Further Reading

Marcelle Brothers, About Billy the Kid. http://www.aboutbillythekid.com.

"Billy the Kid's Life and Death," *New York Times*, July 31, 1881.

"Billy the Kid's Slayer Thanked," *New York Times*, July 20, 1881.

Walter Noble Burns, *The Saga Of Billy the Kid, 1953*.

Officer Down Memorial Page (Deputy Sheriff James W. Bell). http://www.odmp.org/officer/1713-deputy-sheriff-james-w.-bell.

Officer Down Memorial Page (Sheriff William Brady). http://www.odmp.org/officer/2168-sheriff-william-brady.

Officer Down Memorial Page (Deputy Sheriff James Carlysle). http://www.odmp.org/officer/2797- deputy-sheriff-james-carlysle.

Officer Down Memorial Page (Deputy Sheriff George Hindman). http://www.odmp.org/officer/6526-deputy-sheriff-george-hindman.

Officer Down Memorial Page (Deputy Marshal Robert Olinger. http://www.odmp.org/officer/10157-deputy-marshal-robert-olinger.

C

CAPONE, AL (1899–1947)

During the Prohibition era, Al Capone was the most powerful criminal in America. He ordered violent assassinations, including a mass murder in a cold, Chicago garage. He personally beat three associates to death with a baseball bat, aroused the wrath of a president, and most likely had syphilis, which affected his judgment. In the end he was brought down by accountants, not policemen.

Al Capone's background gave no hint of the monster he would eventually become. His parents, Gabriele Capone and Teresina (called Teresa) hailed from Naples. Although his family was working class, they were not poverty-stricken. Gabriele was a barber by trade, and literate. He had dreams of opening a barbershop in America and brought his family to the United States in 1894. They were part of a massive wave of immigrants fleeing poverty in southern Italy and Sicily for opportunities abroad. Mostly poor, Mediterranean, and Catholic, these immigrants inspired fear and loathing upon their arrival in America. They were

Al Capone at a football game in Chicago, 1931. [AP Photo/File]

called "wops" and "dagos" and were viewed as shifty, criminal, and cunning by the Protestant majority.

By this point, the Capone family consisted of two children, a toddler named Vincenzo, and an infant called Raffaele. Teresa was pregnant with a third child when they made the journey to America. The Capones moved into a cold-water tenement flat near the Brooklyn Navy Yard in New York City. There was no indoor toilet and the district was a slum, not made any more charming by the proximity to the naval yard. Off-duty sailors prowled the area, looking for alcohol, women, and opportunities to gamble. Because he was literate, Gabriele Capone got a job in a grocery store that serviced the Italian community. This was quite a step up from the basic pick and shovel drudge work most males from Italy were forced to accept in the new world. Teresa also worked, taking in sewing piecework.

In 1895 Salvatore, the family's third child, was born. Four years later, on January 17, 1899, a fourth male child arrived, whom his parents called Alphonse. The child had literally been bred and born in America. Alphonse Capone was a product of the United States, not a foreign shore. While they suffered from the anti-Italian prejudices of the day, the Capones were not a maladjusted bunch. The family was quite close. Gabriele wasn't violent or a heavy drinker. He was a hardworking, conventional man. Teresa was equally practical, sober, and family-oriented. The Capones were not criminal, psychotic, or any much different than thousands of other struggling Italian-American families in New York City.

The family adapted relatively quickly to life in America. Outside the home, the Capone boys anglicized their names. Vincenzo became James, Raffaele became Ralph, Salvatore became Frank, and Alphonse was simply called Al. Shortly after Al was born, Gabriele opened a barber shop at 69 Park Avenue in Brooklyn. The Capone family moved into an apartment above the barber shop. The community was not entirely Italian. There were Germans, Swedes, and even Chinese immigrants living in the neighborhood.

The Capones lived near St. Michael's Church, which was the parish for the area. Alphonse was baptized there. The neighborhood was noisy, crowded, and active, but not exceptionally poor. Kids played in the street, and stickball—an inner city version of baseball—was a popular pastime. Food carts were abundant, as were horse-drawn wagons. Trains raced by on the nearby "El" (elevated railroad).

In 1904, at the age of five, Al was sent to school. Mandatory public education was still something of a novelty at the time. Italian students were looked down upon by education officials. They were seen as unteachable and ignorant. Al, however, did all right in school and generally had a B average. He kept plugging along until grade six. At age 14, Al got into an argument with a teacher. She hit him so he hit her back. Al was expelled and that was the end of his academic career.

Around the same time, the Capone family moved once more to 21 Garfield Place. One of the most prominent citizens in the area was a rising mobster named Johnny Torrio. Torrio's headquarters were located a few blocks from the Capone residence. Unlike many mob bosses who were violent and impulsive, Torrio favored structure, organization, and diplomacy. He was slight and small, and survived by his wits, not his brawn. In public Torrio behaved like a gentleman, albeit one who worked as a pimp and racketeer. Young Al greatly admired Torrio, who was one of the most visibly successful men in the neighborhood. Capone became one of several youths who ran errands for Torrio in exchange for pocket money. Capone observed Torrio carefully. He noted that Torrio kept his home-life rigidly separate from his "work." Torrio wasn't around for long, however; in 1909 he headed to Chicago at the behest of another rising gangster named "Big Jim" Colosimo.

When Capone was growing up in New York, immigrant kids typically banded together and formed ethnic gangs. These gangs—Italian, Jewish and Irish predominantly—fought each other and stole from merchants and push-carts. Capone belonged to such a youth gang, which offered an outlet for his adolescent energies. Being in a street gang also offered the opportunity to drink alcohol and smoke cigarettes. In spite of his gang membership, Al was still regarded as a relatively average kid. Even as he ran with gangs, he was steadily employed. Among other jobs, he toiled briefly in a munitions factory. All told, Capone spent about six years after leaving school in a series of menial gigs. By this point, Gabriele was prospering. He owned his own barbershop and had become an American citizen. As his career horizons expanded, so did his family. Teresa continued to produce kids—a slew of boys, and then finally two girls. Although close to his family, Al was more interested in emulating the adult criminals in the neighborhood than following in his father's earnest footsteps.

In 1917 Capone was hired to work as a bartender in a Coney Island dive bar called the Harvard Inn. The Inn was owned by a gangster named Frankie Yale (real name, Francesco Ioele) who hailed from Calabria, Italy. Unlike Torrio, Yale was openly violent and believed in using brute force to get his way. Yale respected Torrio's opinion however; it was Torrio's recommendation that got Capone the job at the Harvard Inn. In addition to bartending, Capone was expected to work as a waiter and, if necessary, a bouncer. Young Capone became a popular figure

with Yale and the customers at the Inn. He served something of a mentorship there, learning how to run rackets and behave like a crime boss. Yale specialized in extortion and loan-sharking. He also collected "tribute" from local pimps and bookies, and ran a "protection" racket. Yale's men would threaten to beat local merchants unless they handed over some of their profits to the mobster.

One dispute, however, would literally mark him for life. Capone was serving an attractive young woman and a man. Entranced by the lady's beauty, Capone bluntly informed her that she had a very attractive derriere. The remark was apparently intended as a compliment, but the young beauty's escort took it as an insult to her honor. The escort happened to be the girl's brother. His name was Frank Gallucio and he felt bound to defend his sister's good name. Infuriated by Capone's crack, Gallucio leapt to his feet and punched the fresh interloper. A fight ensued. Gallucio suddenly produced a knife and slashed the young bartender on the face three times. Then he grabbed his sister and ran out of the place. Capone ended up with a four-inch slash mark on his left cheek, a two-inch gash on the left side of his jaw, and a third wound behind his left ear. From that point on, whenever he posed for a photograph, he tried to present his right, unscarred side. A "sit-down" with Yale, Gallucio, and Capone was arranged. Local sentiment favored Gallucio. Capone was made to apologize for insulting his sister. He was also instructed not to seek out vengeance against the man who permanently scarred him, and he didn't.

Around 1918 Capone met his future wife, Mae Coughlin. She was blonde, pretty, and two years Capone's senior.

Her family was Irish and middle-class, and none too thrilled by the relationship. Capone and Coughlin began having sex and she became pregnant, which further estranged her from her family. On December 4, 1918, Coughlin gave birth to a boy. The parents named the child Albert Francis Capone, but generally called him Sonny. Johnny Torrio served as godfather. A couple weeks after the birth, Coughlin and Capone were married at Brooklyn's St. Mary Star of the Sea Church. Unknown to his parents, their boy was born with a severe impairment in the form of congenital syphilis. Capone had been infected prior to his marriage (but apparently didn't alert Coughlin to the fact). Capone's syphilis soon went into remission and he didn't seek treatment. With a wife and child to support, however, he briefly became respectable. He moved to Baltimore and worked as a bookkeeper for a construction firm. Capone did well in this position. He had a good head for numbers and was a reliable employee.

On November 14, 1920, Gabriele Capone died of heart disease at age 55. Following his father's death, Capone renewed his friendship with Johnny Torrio. By this point, Torrio was well ensconced in the Chicago criminal underworld. Torrio urged Capone to give up bookkeeping and move to Chicago to work with him. Were his father still alive, Capone might have turned Torrio down. As it was, Capone welcome Torrio's offer and in early 1921, moved to the Windy City. In doing so he abandoned any attempt at legitimate work. Located in the Midwest next to Lake Michigan, Chicago had a tradition of violence, raw capitalism, and political corruption. Pigs, sheep and cows raised in the Midwest were shipped to Chicago to be killed in the city's many abattoirs. The slaughterhouse was an apt symbol for what the city would become. The biggest Chicago gangster of the early 20th century was Torrio's boss, Big Jim Colosimo. With his wife and business partner, a madam named Victoria Moresco, Colosimo had a lock on the local prostitution trade. They owned a string of brothels that produced huge profits. Colosimo flaunted his wealth, wearing flashy clothes complete with diamond cufflinks and diamond-studded belt buckles. Torrio did not share his boss' flashy exuberance. He was a serious-minded businessman who didn't smoke, drink, curse, or cheat on his wife, Anna. Torrio ran the day-to-day operations in Colosimo's brothels in an efficient, sober manner.

Colosimo could have ruled Chicago for decades, but for the fact that he fell in love with a young singer named Dale Winter. He began accompanying Winter about town and eventually divorced his wife to marry her. This was considered a shocking breech of gangster etiquette. Mobsters had no problem with adultery, but considered it bad manners to humiliate their wives. Deeply in love, Colosimo stopped attending to business. Despite Torrio's pleas, Colosimo refused to make more than a token investment in bootlegging, an up-and-coming racket at the time, as Prohibition had just become national law. He was content being a newlywed pimp. Torrio felt Colosimo was holding his organization back. He worried other mob bosses might overtake Colosimo. With this in mind, Big Jim was shot dead in his nightclub on May 11, 1920. His assassin was Frankie Yale, Capone's old acquaintance from New York. Yale was arrested for shooting Colosimo, but avoided prosecution when the only witness to the assassination, a waiter, refused to testify. Yale intended to take over Colosimo's criminal empire, which included thousands of brothels, gambling joints, and a few speakeasies. Torrio moved faster, however, and seized the reins of the organization.

All of this happened prior to Capone's arrival; he had nothing to do with Colosimo's assasination. When Capone showed up in Chicago, he was assigned to manage a handful of brothels. While he felt the work was beneath him, Capone proved to be a good manager. He impressed Torrio with his ability to handle finances, keep the brothels stocked with supplies, and lure in new customers. Capone was still a diamond in the raw, however. He was crude and drunk much of the time during his early days in Chicago. Nonetheless, he got along well with Torrio and was soon moved up the criminal ladder. Capone became manager of a Torrio establishment called the Four Deuces. Located at 2222 South Wabash, the Four Deuces served as a combination speakeasy, brothel, gaming house, and headquarters of the expansive Torrio crime empire. Once again, Capone showed a flair for management. With Torrio's approval Capone began bringing family members into the Chicago underworld. Ralph Capone arrived first, and was put to work by Torrio.

Capone soon met another mentor named Jack Guzik. Guzik was an Orthodox Jew, who operated a family-run prostitution ring. Capone had no problem doing business with a Jew. He was never the type of mobster who only associated "with his own kind." Short, quiet, and dumpy, Guzik liked Capone and became something of a big brother to the rising young gangster. Capone

soon found himself a nearly equal partner to Torrio. With money coming in steadily, Capone bought a two-story, red brick house at 7244 Prairie Avenue for his family. The home was relatively modest, but had plenty of rooms—fifteen in total. Capone installed Mae and Sonny there, as well as his mother and other family members. To his neighbors Capone claimed to be a second-hand furniture dealer. He even had business cards made up to this effect. He was friendly, neighborly, and didn't strut around like a gangster.

Torrio and Capone faced some stiff competition in Chicago. One of their main rivals was a mentally-addled Irish gangster named Dion "Deanie" O'Banion. When he wasn't taking care of bootlegging operations, O'Banion spent time arranging flowers in a florist shop he owned. His gang was notoriously eccentric. After one of their members died when he was thrown from a horse, O'Banion's troops tracked the horse down and killed it. O'Banion was friendly, charming, ruthless, and impulsive. The horrible Genna brothers were another major power. This Sicilian born clan of bootleggers were allies of Torrio. The six fierce Genna brothers were earning a fortune making low-grade liquor.

Other up-and-coming gangs included a pack led by the O'Donnell brothers on the West Side. This crew included William "Klondike" O'Donnell, Myles O'Donnell, and Bernard O'Donnell. They were a fearsome bunch, but nowhere near as big as the Torrio, O'Banion and Genna gangs. Torrio managed to establish a shaky truce with O'Banion and the Gennas. Torrio argued that there was more than enough cash to go around and there was no need for rival gangsters to be at each other's throats. Each gang would stick to their own territory and not intrude on anyone else's turf.

The Chicago underworld benefited from the fact that the city government was in the hands of an extremely corrupt, buffoonish mayor named "Big Bill" Thompson. Thompson opposed Prohibition and did little to halt the spread of organized crime. He made florid, bizarre speeches in which he mused on conspiracy theories involving English royalty (a topic that went over extremely well with anti-British Polish and German voters). Unfortunately for the gangs, Thompson decided not to run for another term in 1923. He was replaced by a wannabe reformer named William Dever. Torrio and Capone, who by this point was Torrio's main lieutenant and a powerful mobster in his own right, saw the writing on the wall. They decided to move many of their operations outside of the city. They were particularly attracted to the suburb of Cicero. An all-white enclave, Cicero was heavily populated by central Europeans who thought Prohibition was ridiculous and didn't seem to mind the presence of bootleggers and gangsters. The Torrio/Capone organization purchased a property called the Hawthorne Inn and set about taking over Cicero. They came to completely dominate the municipal government, one of the few times in American history when an entire town was run by mobsters.

Torrio decided to take his aged mother home to Italy for a visit. He left Capone in charge of things during his absence. Capone encouraged his older brother Frank to move to Cicero and act as front man for the Capone/Torrio gang in dealings with government officials. Dark-haired and handsome, Frank

looked respectable, unlike his dumpy, scarred younger brother. Capone put his brother Ralph in charge of a low-end brothel called the Stockade, which serviced the working-class men of Cicero. Capone, meanwhile, put much of his energy into gambling. He bought a piece of a Cicero gambling joint called The Ship, and also took over the Hawthorne Race Track in the same town.

Most Cicero residents went along with the gangster conquest. One brave newspaper editor with the *Cicero Tribune* refused to buckle, however. His name was Robert St. John and he wrote biting exposes about Torrio and Capone's business interests in Cicero. Capone worried about St. John's impact on a local municipal election he was trying to rig. Held April 1, 1924, the election proved to be a brutal affair. Capone's men kidnapped election workers and threatened men at the polls. The violence grew so out-of-hand that police from Chicago were dispatched to re-establish law and order. A posse of seventy-nine officials, some in uniform and many in plain clothes, raced to Cicero in a caravan of unmarked cars. Frank Capone happened to be walking about on the street when the heavily armed flotilla arrived in town. There is some confusion about what happened next. Police claim that Frank pulled a gun on them, which was entirely possible given that most of the cops weren't in uniform and might have been mistaken for members of another gang. The peace officers opened fire with their own weapons, and Frank Capone was cut down. Understandably upset, Al rose to new levels of violence. He had more officials kidnapped and ballot boxes stolen. The rising gangster remained sullen and bitter throughout Frank's funeral, which took place a few days after his murder. He had good reason to sulk. The funeral was watched over by some of the same police officers who had killed his older brother.

Shortly after Frank's death, Capone got into a dispute with Joseph Klenha, (the puppet mayor he'd helped elect) on the steps of city hall. To underscore who was really in charge, Capone knocked the mayor off his feet and kicked him as he lay prostrate on the ground. St. John continued to add to Capone's woes. The intrepid editor disguised himself as a workingman and went to a country brothel run by Capone and Torrio. Once inside, he managed to interview a pair of prostitutes. St. John learned that many of the working girls had been lured to the city from farms and small towns by fast-talking con men promising legitimate work. Once in Chicago, the girls were brutalized and forced to turn tricks. They usually only lasted a few years on the job before becoming too damaged from disease, drink, and drugs to be of any value to the Capone/Torrio organization. At that point, the girls would be cut loose and forced to fend for themselves.

When Capone read all this in print, he was beside himself with rage. What really stoked his ire was the fact St. John appeared immune to bribery. The plucky newspaper editor turned down offers of money from Capone in return for more complimentary coverage. Capone's rage reached new heights when a local group of vigilantes, aroused by St. John's reporting, burned the brothel the editor had visited to the ground. Capone's men ambushed St. John and severely beat him on the streets of Cicero. The reporter still refused to give in. Capone contacted the owners of the paper and forced them

to sell-out to him. This made Capone St. John's boss. It was a fate the editor couldn't stomach, so he left Cicero for a job in Vermont.

Capone handled another crisis with even less finesse. On May 8, 1924, a low-level thug named Joe Howard got into a screaming match with Jack Guzik on a Chicago sidewalk. Even when Howard called him anti-Semitic names, Guzik failed to respond physically. He raced off and informed Capone of the incident. Enraged, Capone armed himself with a pistol and set out to find Howard in Chicago. Capone caught up with the thug in a bar on Wabash Avenue. He confronted Howard and ordered him to apologize to Guzik. Howard refused to do this. He laughed at Capone and called him a "dago pimp." Capone took out his pistol and shot Howard dead at point-blank range. Capone biographers disagree on whether this was the first murder he committed or not. Some accounts say Capone killed a man years before in New York City. Regardless, murdering Howard was a foolish move. Although he escaped prosecution, the barroom bloodbath drew the ire of the assistant state attorney, William McSwiggin. Nicknamed the "hanging prosecutor," McSwiggin had a reputation for being tough on crime. He was outraged when the bar patrons who witnessed Howard's death refused to testify. Capone was now firmly in McSwiggin's sights.

In the spring of 1924 Johnny Torrio finally returned to his fiefdom from Italy. He was immediately confronted with a major problem. The Gennas and O'Banion were at each other's throats. O'Banion was furious with the Gennas for flooding his turf with cheap, rot-gut liquor.

Just when it looked like war was going to break out, O'Banion suddenly announced he was retiring. The Gennas were making his life miserable, said the wily Irishman. To prove his sincerity, O'Banion said he was willing to sell his share in the Sieben Brewery (a facility co-owned by Torrio, O'Banion, and Capone) for $500,000.

Torrio agreed to this deal and on the night of May 19, met the erratic gang leader at the Sieben Brewery. All at once, the place was raided by police, led by federal investigators. Torrio, O'Banion, and their respective gang members were hauled off to a federal holding tank.

It slowly dawned on Torrio that he had been set up. O'Banion knew the police were going to make a raid and set up his supposed ally for arrest. O'Banion had a clean record, which meant he would most likely get a fine as a result of the raid. Torrio, however, already had one Prohibition charge on his record, which meant he faced serious jail-time.

O'Banion found it marvelously amusing that a wily crime boss such as Torrio could be so easily tricked.

As the cliché goes, Torrio had the last laugh. In November 1924 O'Banion was gunned down in his florist shop as he arranged flowers for a funeral. O'Banion had a splendidly gaudy funeral featuring twenty-six cars carrying flowers, three bands, and a police escort. An estimated 10,000 people joined the funeral cortege to see off the dead gangster. Torrio and Capone feigned grief, but were delighted that one of their biggest rivals was gone. Now they could move in on O'Banion's turf. What Torrio and Capone didn't appreciate was that they had made a determined enemy out of Earl Wajciechowski, also known as "Hymie" Weiss, who was a close friend of

O'Banion. Another O'Banion associate waiting in the wings was George Moran. George was better known as "Bugs" Moran, "bugs" being slang at the time for crazy.

Over the next two years, former O'Banion associates would try to kill Capone at least a dozen times. Capone, by this point, kept two bodyguards around him whenever he ventured from home, and only traveled by car, which was flanked by more bodyguards. His chauffeur was armed, and to make his travel even safer, Capone tried to avoid journeying by day. Torrio was much less security conscious. In January 1925 Torrio was ambushed and left for dead by Weiss and Moran in front of his Chicago apartment. Capone quickly took command of the situation, bunking down on a cot in Torrio's hospital room. He made sure his mentor was well-guarded at all times to prevent any future attacks. After a few weeks in recovery, a fragile looking Torrio appeared in court to hear charges against him stemming from the Sieben Brewery raid. Looking frail and ill, he received a nine month prison sentence.

In March 1925 Torrio contacted Capone from the Waukegan, Illinois, jail. He told his protégé he was retiring and wanted Capone to run the show. Torrio turned over his entire crime empire— the countless nightclubs, brothels, gambling joints, illegal breweries, and speakeasies—to Capone. Torrio wanted a cut of the proceeds, but otherwise would live abroad in peace. Unlike O'Banion, Torrio wasn't bluffing. Torrio's generosity enormously expanded Capone's wealth and power. Once he took command, Capone moved his headquarters to the swanky Metropole Hotel in Chicago. He took over a high-end suite of five rooms at a cost of $1,500 a day. Capone became one the most visible and successful crime bosses in Chicago. To reporters, Capone tried to portray himself as a slightly unorthodox businessman who was simply giving people the alcohol and vice that they wanted. As he rose in stature, Capone gained political influence. Nearly every day he went to a Chicago building complex that housed city hall and other municipal offices. Unlike his mentor, Capone made no attempt to keep a low profile.

At the end of 1925 Capone took his only child, Sonny, to New York for an operation because of the boy's chronic ear infections. Al was a devoted father who fretted constantly about his son's health. It's not clear if Capone was aware that Sonny's condition was his own fault; the boy had inherited congenital syphilis from his father. While he was in New York, Capone met with Frankie Yale to negotiate an agreement. Yale had an oversupply of alcohol, which he was happily willing to sell to Capone. If Capone could arrange transportation, he was welcome to purchase liquor in New York and bring it back to Chicago for resale. Yale invited Capone to a Christmas Day party in New York. The bash took place at the Adonis Social and Athletic Club which was, in reality, a Brooklyn speakeasy. After inviting Capone, Yale got word that a rival gangster named Richard "Peg Leg" Lonergan was going to show up with some goons. Yale suggested canceling the party, but Capone wouldn't hear of it. Capone called in some thugs, including Sicilian hit men John Scalise and Albert Anselmi. On the day of the bash, Capone and his crew went to the Adonis club and waited for the uninvited guests to arrive.

At around 3 a.m., Lonergan and his men showed up. The mobster and his crew behaved obnoxiously and made it clear they were there to raise trouble. Capone gave a signal, and his own men went into action. Lonergan's goons were gunned down before they even had a chance to draw their weapons. Lonergan himself was killed in the ambush. The event became known as the "Adonis Club Massacre" and further enhanced Capone's thuggish image.

By early 1926, Capone felt on the top of the world. He had 1,000 men on his payroll and weekly overhead costs (salaries, bribes, and bonuses) of $300,000. A huge cost, but Capone could afford it; at its peak, his organization took in $100 million a year. A strange incident in late April 1926 almost knocked him off his perch, however. The incident in question centered on McSwiggin, the same "hanging prosecutor" who couldn't convict Capone for killing Joe Howard. Apparently, when he wasn't working on a case, McSwiggin liked to have a good time. He wasn't fussy about who he partied with either, rubbing shoulders with the same kind of gangsters he opposed in court. One night in early spring, McSwiggin decided to hit the town with some cronies. Their ranks included a bootlegger named Jim Doherty. At some point in the evening, Klondike and Myles O'Donnell joined the party. This unlikely group made its way to a speakeasy located near the Hawthorne Inn, where Capone happened to hanging out. Capone was informed of the O'Donnell brothers' presence on what he considered his turf. Unaware that McSwiggin was with them, Capone gathered together a team of gunmen to deal with the obnoxious O'Donnell boys. A fleet of cars packed with thugs, including Capone, drove out to the bar where the O'Donnells had been last seen. The armed convoy braked in the parking lot and turned off their lights. Guns in hand, the men waited. Capone himself cradled a Tommy gun. Eventually, the O'Donnell brothers—along with McSwiggin and other assorted cronies—staggered out of the speakeasy and into the parking lot. The noisy crew walked right into an ambush. Capone's men cut loose at point-blank range, killing two men on the spot, one of them being McSwiggin. A third victim would die the next day. The O'Donnell brothers escaped unscathed from the slaughter. The moment the shooting started, the canny brothers dove to the ground to make themselves less conspicuous targets. Having shot up the party, Capone and company left the scene of the crime. It's highly unlikely Capone would have organized an ambush had he known McSwiggin was part of the group. He adhered to an underworld code in which cops, lawyers, judges, and journalists (Robert St. John being an exception) were not to be touched. This was to protect the underworld from the massive retaliation such a killing would surely entail.

Sure enough, McSwiggin's murder generated a storm of protest. It didn't matter that the prosecutor was chummy with gangsters, or that Capone hadn't intended on killing him. Public sympathy lay with the deceased assistant state attorney, in spite of his curious social life. To their great frustration, authorities realized they had no direct evidence linking Capone to the ambush, and therefore couldn't arrest him. Instead of booking the crime boss, police smashed up a series of Capone-operated brothels and bars, putting some to the torch. In the summer of 1926 Capone decided it would be in his best interest to lay low for a while. He went into "hiding" at a friend's house in Chicago Heights and spent time in Lansing, Michigan with friends. An estimated three hundred detectives searched for Capone across North America, but couldn't find him. Capone, however, eventually grew tired of hiding and returned to Chicago.

On September 20, 1926, Capone was nearly gunned down in one of the most audacious "drive by" shootings of the era. As Capone sipped coffee in the Hawthorne Inn, a convoy of cars drew broadside and sprayed the Inn with machine-gun fire. Police later estimated that the assailants fired over 1,000 rounds. Amazingly, no one—least of all Capone—was killed in the barrage.

Through the criminal grapevine, Capone learned that Hymie Weiss was responsible for the Hawthorne shooting. Instead of seeking revenge, Capone tried to make an alliance with Weiss. Like Torrio, Capone attempted to convince Weiss that it was pointless for leading gangsters to fight each other. Weiss wasn't swayed and turned down Capone's offers of friendship. Shortly thereafter, Weiss was shot dead by Capone assassins. He was twenty-eight years-old. In spite of Weiss' truculence, Capone was still determined to play peacemaker. He held a well publicized "peace conference" with his peers in Chicago to plead his case for cooperation. As Torrio had done before him, Capone pointed out that there was plenty of underworld business to go around. There was no reason rival gangs had to shoot it out.

Capone's words temporarily swayed the killers who had gathered for the conference. They vowed to stop murdering and maiming each other. The slate was wiped clean and past killings would not be avenged. For roughly two months, no bootleggers were killed in Chicago. The truce collapsed in January 1927, when Theodore Anton, also known as "Tony the Greek," a close friend of Capone's, was kidnapped and almost certainly murdered. When he heard the news, a teary-eyed Capone mused out loud about following Torrio into retirement. Capone held a spaghetti dinner at his house for reporters and told them he was quitting the crime business. The problem was, Capone was as addicted to the action and power just as much as the money that came with being the head of a huge organized criminal outfit. He promised to retire, but kept pushing the date further and further into the future.

In a 1927 civic election Chicago voters brought back "Big Bill" Thompson to office. By this point, Mayor Dever's reforms had largely failed. Dever was seen as well-intentioned but weak. Thompson was more entertaining, if rather idiotic. On another stage, a U.S. Supreme Court ruling in May 1927 would prove to have an enormous impact on Capone and other gangsters. In a case against a bootlegger named Manny Sullivan, the Court ruled criminals had to declare all their revenue, legally earned or not, to the government. Even if the income in question was generated by vice and corruption, it still had to be reported. Failure to file a proper income tax return could result in tax evasion charges. The ruling energized a small group of federal authorities who began to chart a new way to attack crime bosses like Capone. A dedicated civil servant named Elmer Irey worked with the Internal Revenue Service (IRS) to see if Capone could be prosecuted for not paying his taxes. Capone knew about none of these machinations. He continued to live it up and hit the town. He frequented concerts and boxing matches and struck up a friendship with famed pugilist Jack Dempsey. At Christmastime, Capone repeated his oft-stated claim that he was just a misunderstood businessman. Police and prosecutors, however, viewed him as a common, if extremely powerful, thug. Authorities kept a constant watch on Capone's house and shadowed his movements when he left home.

Under such pressure, Capone struck out for more welcoming climes. In early 1928 he traveled to Miami where he used a middleman to purchase a fourteen-room Spanish style mansion at 93 Palm Island. Capone installed safety features such as bullet proof walls made of concrete and heavy wooden doors that would give pause to anyone trying to break in. A small IRS intelligence unit, led by Irey, took note of the Miami purchase. A man named Frank Wilson was hired to document Capone's income and spending—a formidable task, given the lack of a paper trail. Buying the Miami mansion was a godsend for the law. If authorities could trace ownership to Capone, they would have proof he was earning an enormous, unreported income.

Back in Chicago, another no-nonsense official set his sights on Capone. His name was George Emmerson Q. Johnson, and he was the recently appointed U.S. attorney for Chicago. As Capone's enemies gathered, crime and mayhem continued apace in Chicago. In the spring of 1928, a violence-wracked city-wide primary election was held. Since most of the violence seemed directed at opponents of the mayor, it was assumed Big

Bill Thompson was behind the outrages, and that Al Capone, mastermind of all that was corrupt in Chicago, was pulling everybody's strings. In reality Capone, who was in Miami during the election, had little to do with the electoral mayhem. His public image was so grandiose, however, that the public assumed he had his hand in the chaos.

Big Al had more pressing worries than politics. While Mae cheerfully decorated the new Miami mansion, Capone fretted about partners. An unusually large number of trucks bearing illegal shipments of liquor for Capone's empire in Chicago were being hijacked out of New York City. Capone suspected his erstwhile ally, Frankie Yale, was responsible. Capone met with other leaders of his gang in Florida to discuss the issue. A course of action was quickly decided upon. On July 1, 1928, Yale was assassinated in his car in New York City. His killers allegedly included the prolific John Scalise and Albert Anselmi.

That same summer, Capone moved his Chicago headquarters to the Lexington Hotel. He took up two entire floors and lived like a king. He had a six-room suite all to himself, with a special kitchen just for him. He had secret doors installed so he could come and go from the hotel without being seen. Issues with his fellow gangsters continued to dominate his thoughts, however. In Chicago the Capone gang was constantly running up against crews working for Bugs Moran. Capone decided the pesky mob boss had to die. In February 1929 Capone had a meeting in Florida with "Machine Gun" Jack McGurn, a highly qualified hit man. Moran had twice tried to kill McGurn, so he was the perfect assassin to spearhead an assault on Capone's rival. Capone

told McGurn that he wanted Moran dead. McGurn could sort out the details and determine the best way to eliminate Moran and as many members of his gang as possible. McGurn returned to Chicago and assembled a team of assassins. Their ranks included Fred "Killer" Burke, James Ray, Scalise and Anselmi, Joseph Lolordo, and Harry and Phil Keywell from the Purple Gang in Detroit. Surveillance revealed that Moran used an old garage at 2122 North Clark Street in Chicago as a meeting place. The garage was housed in a one-story red brick building roughly 120 feet long and 60 feet wide. Moran received regular shipments of bootleg alcohol in the garage. McGurn decided the garage would make the perfect crime scene. He arranged to have a bootlegger offer a phony tip to Moran. The bootlegger told the mob boss he had come into some very good whisky that he was willing to sell at a reasonable price. All Moran had to do was visit the garage at 2122 North Clark Street to check out some samples. Moran agreed and told the bootlegger he would meet him there on the morning of February 14, 1929, St. Valentine's Day.

When Valentine's Day arrived, McGurn went into action. Two members of the hit team put on policemen's uniforms. Another pair pretended to be plain-clothed detectives. The four fake cops raced to 2122 North Clark Street in a stolen police cruiser. McGurn was not part of the team. Realizing he would be a prime suspect, McGurn made sure to be seen in public with his girlfriend, Louise Rolfe, on Valentine's Day. The quartet of phony law officers parked outside the garage, drew their guns, and raced inside the building, shouting that a raid was in progress. The seven men inside were surprised, but grudgingly acceded to the policemen's request, and lined up facing the wall. Of the seven, six were criminals who worked for Moran. The seventh man was a dentist with no underworld affiliation, who liked hanging out with lowlifes, much like prosecutor McSwiggin. Moran's men kept their faces to the wall, muttering threats under their breath, as the four "cops" leveled their weapons. At once, McGurn's men opened fire, raking the seven with machine gun, rifle, and pistol fire. They sprayed their victims thoroughly and administered close-range head shots to any man still moving.

With their work done, the two "detectives" put down their weapons, put up their hands, and stood in front of the two uniformed "policemen." The latter marched the former out of the building at gun point. Anyone watching the scene would assume a pair of cops had just arrested two gangsters. The presence of two policemen and a cruiser would explain the gunfire that had echoed from the garage. The four fake cops entered the stolen police car and raced away, mission accomplished— almost. Six of the men in the garage died on the spot. A seventh man, amazingly, was still alive when the real police rushed in to investigate. Although shot 22 times, the sole survivor held to the gangster's credo and refused to divulge any useful information before expiring. The canny McGurn quickly married his girlfriend, Louise. It was a good move, given that wives could not be compelled in court to testify against their husbands, even in murder cases. The "hit" had been a brilliant success, but for one thing. Moran wasn't one of the victims. The gang leader had arrived late, after the stolen cruiser had pulled up to the curb.

Moran took one look at the police car, assumed it was a raid, and took off. Thankful to still be alive, a dazed Moran blamed Capone for his near-death experience.

The St. Valentine's Day Massacre (as the press dubbed it) was front-page news across the country. Al Capone became a household name. When he was reached for comment in Miami, Capone played dumb and said he wished no ill will towards Moran and wondered who could have possibly gunned down his men. While Capone was never charged in connection with the shooting, it had severe repercussions for the Chicago crime czar. The ambush infuriated President Herbert Hoover, who was disgusted by the degree of lawlessness in Chicago. The president made it very clear to his underlings: Capone had to be stopped and put behind bars. During morning calisthenics, the president would pass a medicine ball around a circle of colleagues while questioning them on their progress against Capone.

Capone remained oblivious to the forces drawing together to bring him to justice. If anything, he became even more brutal. In the spring of 1929 Capone learned that Scalise and Anselmi planned to switch sides and work for Joseph "Hop Toad" Guinta, who had just been made president of the Unione Siciliana. The Unione was an Italian-American fraternal order dedicated to helping new immigrants that was also deeply involved in underworld activities. Guinta was an ally to Joe Aiello, one of very few rivals of any stature still opposing Capone.

On May 7 Capone held a lavish feast at a roadhouse in Hammond, Indiana, close to the state border. Roughly one hundred guests were invited to wine and dine at Big Al's expense. The guests of honor were none other than Scalise, Anselmi, and Guinta. The three men thought they were being celebrated for some sort of achievement. The gregarious Capone raised toast after toast to his honored guests. An enormous feast was consumed as feelings of good will permeated the evening. Once the meal was over, the guests sat back, bellies full of wine and food, burping with contentment. Capone rose to give a speech. Speaking in a low growl, he denounced the three main guests for turning traitor. Before the surprised trio could react, Capone's henchmen tied Scalise, Anselmi, and Guinta to their chairs. Capone produced a baseball bat and personally administered a brutal beating to each man, until most of their bones were broken and they lay limp and dying in their chairs. After reducing the trio to a pulp, Capone ordered a thug to shoot each man in the head to ensure his death. The other guests watched in horror, trying to keep down the feast they had just consumed. The corpses of Scalise, Anselmi, and Guinta were removed from the roadhouse and dumped in a field.

Shortly after the roadhouse murders, Capone attended the epochal Atlantic City Conference. This was one of the first major gatherings of crime bosses from across the country. The gangsters laid down some ground rules: under new "guidelines," mob bosses could only be "hit" with the permission of another mob boss. The gathering had another purpose: crime bosses were becoming alarmed at Capone's behavior. It was feared that his high profile was drawing undo attention to the underworld. Once the conference was over, Capone attended a movie in Philadelphia. The flick ended, and two

policemen appeared. Capone was arrested for carrying a concealed weapon and hustled off to Holmesburg County Jail. He was later moved to the Eastern Penitentiary. In his absence Capone let his brother Ralph run the show, along with Jack Guzik and Frank "The Enforcer" Nitti, a top lieutenant. It was rumored that Capone had been set up for arrest by his Atlantic City comrades, who wanted him out of the spotlight. Other accounts suggest Capone himself might have engineered his own arrest in order to lie low for a while. In either case, Capone served his time in jail as authorities plotted new campaigns against him. He was eventually released on March 17, 1930.

In Washington D.C., meanwhile, federal authorities, under pressure from the president, were coming up with plans of their own. It was decided that Capone should be attacked for two separate offences: income tax evasion and Prohibition violations. Spearheading the latter effort was a young Chicago lawman named Eliot Ness. Orders in hand, Ness put together a small team of incorruptible law officers totally dedicated to bringing Capone down. He and his team, dubbed "the Untouchables," tapped telephones and raided speakeasies and breweries to harass Capone and gather evidence of Prohibition violations. At one point, the team fixed a snowplow blade to a truck and used this vehicle to slam through the front door of Capone-run facilities. Such tactics didn't hurt his income much, but they did prove to be a major annoyance to the crime boss.

Other forces were coming together to fight Capone. In Chicago a group of esteemed citizens, fed up with the city's murderous reputation, formed the

Chicago Crime Commission. One of the Commission's most celebrated moves was to create a list of organized crime figures they called "Public Enemies." The Commission's list was published in newspapers. At the top was Al Capone. Ralph Capone, Jack McGurn, Jack Guzik and other Capone associates were also on the list. Newspapers loved the "Public Enemies" list, which proved so popular that J. Edgar Hoover, head of the FBI, stole the idea. The FBI began turning out their own Public Enemies list and were mistakenly credited with coming up with the concept. Being at the head of the list was a huge embarrassment for Capone, who craved legitimacy and respect in regular society.

Elmer Irey also continued to plague Capone. He sent undercover operatives to infiltrate Capone's gang. One of these operatives, a policeman named Graziano, uncovered an invaluable nugget of information. A Capone thug informed him that Big Al knew about the government's effort to nail him on tax charges. The police were too stupid to pin anything on Capone, however, laughed the thug. The cops didn't even realize they had a ledger book in their possession that could put the target of their campaign behind bars. The ledger contained a record of financial transactions conducted on Capone's behalf. It had been seized years before during a raid on the Hawthorne Hotel, but was overlooked in a sea of confiscated papers. Graziano even managed to get the names of the two bookkeepers responsible for the ledger: Leslie Shumway and Fred Ries. In early 1931 Irey's men tracked Shumway down to the Miami area where he worked at a racetrack. Federal officials went to Miami and brought him into custody.

Ries was located in St. Louis and likewise incarcerated. The two men eventually agreed to reveal what they knew, as long as the government protected them from mob reprisals.

As Irey worked the financial angle, Ness relied on more direct tactics against Capone. He decided to launch a psychological war on his opponent. To this end, he gathered some forty-five vehicles confiscated during raids on Capone breweries and other operations. Ness had the trucks cleaned and polished, secured drivers for all of them, and then paraded the vehicles down the street in front of the Lexington Hotel. He called the hotel and told Capone to look out the window. As Ness had hoped, Capone flew into a rage at the sight of all the impounded vehicles, and smashed up the furniture in his room.

A federal grand jury was convened to mull over tax evasion charges against Capone. On March 13, 1931, Shumway testified before the grand jury, and then was hustled off to Oregon and out of Capone's reach. The U.S. government claimed that Capone should have paid $32,488.81 in taxes in the year 1924. Spring brought more bad news for the Capone organization. On April 8 gangster-friendly mayor Big Bill Thompson was defeated in a municipal election. His replacement was a Democrat named Tony Cermak. While something of a party hack, Cermak had no great love for the Chicago underworld. With Cermak in charge, Chicago would no longer be an open city for gangsters to operate in. In June a grand jury met again to consider more tax charges against Capone. Capone was eventually hit with 22 charges of tax evasion for the years 1925 through 1929. According to the indictment, Capone earned a net income of $1.04 million over this period and thus owed the government $215,000 in back taxes. Although federal authorities had evidence that Capone had earned at least one million dollars in income, his actual revenues were probably much higher. One week later another indictment was made out against Capone and sixty-eight members of his gang for 5,000 individual Prohibition violations, some dating back to the early 1920s. Most of the charges dealt with illegal shipments of beer and had been recorded by Ness and his Untouchables. Capone appeared unworried. During the summer of 1931, he hung out in Lansing, Michigan, and feigned indifference to reporters. Capone had reason to be smug; his gang managed to get their hands on a list of prospective jurors. The Capone mob went about bribing as many of these jurors as possible. Judge James Wilkerson, who was presiding over the case, knew about the blatant jury tampering, but didn't seem concerned.

On October 6 Capone was escorted into the Federal Court Building in Chicago via a tunnel that led into the building from a freight elevator. Security was extremely tight and the courtroom bristled with armed policemen. Capone avoided putting on any flashy clothes for the day. He wore a blue beige suit that a businessman might have fancied, and didn't wear any gaudy rings or jewelery. To reporters, Capone seemed downright cocky, almost jubilant about what he was sure would be a quick trial. Judge Wilkerson strode into the courtroom and called the trial to order. In a stern voice he noted that another trial was commencing that same day in a different courtroom in the Federal Building. Having

brought everyone up to speed, the judge ordered court officials to swap jurors with the other courtroom. The jurors selected for the Capone trial would preside over another case, while a brand new jury was brought into Judge Wilkerson's courtroom. Capone's face fell. The new jury hadn't been bribed. Further, the judge ordered the jurors sequestered at night so Capone's men couldn't touch them. Once the new jury arrived, the prosecution opened its case. Almost right away, Judge Wilkerson threw out the Prohibition violations. The judge said they distracted from the government's main task, which was to prove that Al Capone was a tax cheat. Prosecutors presented Capone as a man worth millions in undeclared income. To buttress their case, bookkeepers Shumway and Ries testified against Capone, and the financial ledger seized at the Hawthorne Inn was entered into evidence. Other witnesses for the prosecution included department store merchants who testified about Capone's buying habits. According to the merchants, Capone routinely spent thousands of dollars on shirts, suits, ties and other fashion accessories. Prosecutors also pointed to Capone's enormous hotel bills and Miami mansion as proof he was living the life of a tycoon. When it came their turn, Capone's lawyers offered a weak defense. They didn't deny their client had earned a great deal of money, possibly from illegal activities. The lawyers claimed, however, that Capone had lost most of his fortune through gambling—which no one believed for a minute.

On October 17, 1931, the jury found Capone guilty on some, but not all, of the tax evasion counts. A week later he faced Judge Wilkerson for sentencing. The stern judge gave him an eleven-year sentence plus stiff fines, a brutal punishment for what was essentially a white-collar crime. The *New York Times* described the climactic moment in court:

> Capone tried to smile again, but his smile was bitter. He licked his fat lips. He jiggled on his feet. His tongue moved in his cheeks. He was trying to be nonchalant, but he looked as if he must have felt—ready to give way to an outburst of anger. It was a smashing blow to the massive gang chief. His clumsy fingers, tightly locked behind his back, twitched and twisted.

Among other sources, this vivid quote appeared in the book, *Capone: The Man and the Era* by Laurence Bergreen.

Judge Wilkerson refused to grant bail. Capone was taken directly to Cook County Jail where he would wait to be transferred to a federal penitentiary. Capone was housed in the federal penitentiary in Atlanta, Georgia, and then moved into the newly opened federal prison on Alcatraz Island in California. He was transported to Alcatraz in August 1934. Alcatraz was basically a fortress on an island surrounded by brutal currents. According to legend, no one ever successfully escaped from the prison. The few prisoners who tried generally drowned in the rough tide. Alcatraz was notoriously tough. Incoming letters were censored, and retyped by guards with large chunks of information missing. No newspapers were allowed on the island and the only magazines permitted for prisoners to read had to be half-a-year old. Prisoners could only write a single letter a week. The only visitors allowed were immediate family, who could visit twice a month. No business associates were permitted. In its first few years of operation, prisoners weren't even allowed to talk to each other. They were only allowed to address a guard in cases of dire emergencies.

Despite the harsh surroundings, Capone seemed to get along alright at first. His health began to drastically deteriorate, however. By the late 1930s, his once dormant syphilis infection was starting to affect his brain. He was confused and disoriented much of the time. His sentence was reduced to six years and five months due to good behavior. He spent the last year of his sentence in the prison hospital, where he was finally treated for syphilis. Doctors couldn't cure Capone, but they could at least halt the spread of the disease. In November 1939 Capone was released from jail and into the tender graces of his wife. Mae placed Capone in a Baltimore hospital where he received several months of additional treatment. Released from hospital on March 1940, Capone spent his remaining years in his Palm Island mansion. He was no longer an active crime boss, becoming more and more brain dead as the years went by.

On January 25, 1947, Capone died of a heart attack. Capone's family could take cold comfort in this. Unlike most of his underworld allies and enemies alike, Big Al Capone expired from natural causes.

See also: Colosimo, James "Big Jim"; O'Banion, Dion; Prohibition

Further Reading

Laurence Bergreen, *Capone: The Man and the Era*, 1994.

"Coming Out Party," *TIME* cover story March 24, 1930.

Federal Bureau of Investigation file on Al Capone. http://foia.fbi.gov/foiaindex/capone.htm.

"Glum Gorilla," *TIME*, December 19, 1927.

Nate Hendley, *Al Capone: Chicago's King of Crime*, 2006.

John Kobler, *Capone: The Life and World of Al Capone*, 1971.

"One Big Shot," *TIME*, November 3, 1930.

Gus Russo, *The Outfit: The Role of Chicago's Underworld in The Shaping of Modern America*, 2001.

Ellen Warren, "Al Capone Died Here," *Chicago Tribune*, February 15, 2007.

CASTELLANO, PAUL
(1915–1985)

Paul Castellano is best known for being the crime boss whose death propelled John Gotti to the top of the Gambino Mafia family. Castellano's ignominious end was a brutal reminder to mobsters of the dangers of trying to rise above their station.

Castellano was born in Brooklyn in 1915. As a teenager, he was arrested for armed robbery in Hartford, Connecticut. While he served three months in jail, he impressed local mobsters by refusing to inform on his criminal companions. Castellano was inducted into the Gambino crime family and quickly rose up its ranks. It helped that he was related by marriage to family boss, Carlo Gambino. Carlo married Castellano's sister, Katherine, which further cemented the family bond. In October 1976, as he was dying of cancer, Carlo appointed his brother-in-law as his replacement. The selection shocked

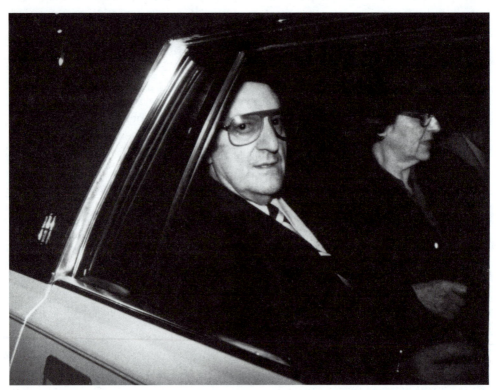

Paul Castellano in 1985, the year he was indicted on racketeering charges. [AP Photo/David Bookstaver]

other Mafia members, who figured Gambino underboss Aniello Dellacroce was next in line. The violent-tempered Dellacroce was serving time during the leadership succession, however, which made him inaccessible. Dellacroce reluctantly stayed on as family underboss, but had to be bribed into cooperation by being offered control of the Gambino's Manhattan rackets.

Standing over six feet tall and weighing 200 pounds, "Big Paul," as he was known, ruled in a very conservative manner, acting more like a businessman than a mob boss. He expanded Gambino interests in legitimate sectors such as trucking, waste disposal, and construction, while turning his nose up at the family's more sordid "street" rackets. He didn't have a problem making money off of the latter, however. Unpopular with his peers and the Mafiosi rank and file, Castellano isolated himself from his own crime family. Castellano purchased a seventeen-room mansion in one of the toniest neighborhoods in Staten Island. Castellano used his house as a headquarters, summoning subordinates to meet him at home. The residence was nicknamed "the White House" by disenchanted Gambino members. The same men began calling Castellano "the Pope"—a reflection of the boss' pompous style. Castellano didn't mingle with low-ranking "soldiers," but demanded large cuts of any profits generated by his underlings. Gambino members felt Castellano took too large a share, while doing little to advance their own interests. "He accepted fiscal tribute from his capos with the lofty dignity of an Indian raja being given his weight in gold by his subjects," noted a June 10, 1991, article in *TIME* magazine. Castellano refused to get involved in lucrative airport rackets such as stealing freight, and union

racketeering (acts he might have perceived as beneath his dignity).

Castellano did make a few strategic moves as Gambino boss. He forged an alliance with the Westies, a sociopathic gang of Irish-American toughs in the Hell's Kitchen neighborhood of New York. The Westies were used to carry out felonies at the Gambinos' request. Castellano also had close ties with legitimate entrepreneurs such as Frank Perdue, the chicken magnate. Perceived as bloodless, Castellano was capable of savagery when the occasion warranted. It is widely suspected he had his own son-in-law murdered. A low-level hoodlum, Frank Amato married Castellano's daughter, Constance. Amato proved to be a thug and wife-beater. Shortly after the couple divorced in 1973, Amato disappeared, rumored to have been killed at Castellano's bequest.

He also kept a wary eye on rising Gambino star John Gotti. Brutal, foul-mouthed, and charismatic, Gotti was everything Castellano wasn't. Castellano reinforced the old Mafiosi taboo against drugs (mob bosses were rightly terrified of the harsh penalties associated with drugs). Any Gambino family member caught trafficking would be executed, Castellano decreed. This was particularly galling to Gotti, who was heavily involved in the lucrative illicit drug trade. Gotti also faced threats on another front. In 1983 Gambino members Angelo Ruggiero, Gene Gotti (John Gotti's brother), and John Carneglia were indicted for drug trafficking. Authorities based much of their evidence from wiretaps at Ruggiero's residence. Ruggiero's lawyers had a copy of the tape transcripts, but Ruggiero refused to hand it over to Castellano. The transcripts implicated him in heroin trafficking and would also reveal that he talked about the Commission (the Mafia's ruling body) to a non-"made" member—a huge breech in protocol. The FBI also bugged Big Paul's Staten Island mansion. Castellano was oblivious, distracted by the attentions of his young, Colombian maid, Gloria Olarte. No one minded that Castellano cheated on his wife. It was that he acted like a lovesick teenager around Olarte, a humiliation for his wife that caused tongues to cluck. A rumor made the rounds that the impotent Castellano got a penile transplant in order to have sex with his winsome housekeeper. Gotti did his best to spread such rumors, and draw discontented Gambino family members to his wide.

In February 1985 Castellano was one of the top New York mob bosses indicted on racketeering charges in what became known as the Mafia Commission trial. Said indictment was brought down by Rudy Giuliani, United States Attorney General for the Southern District of New York. Giuliani slapped the leadership of the Commission with a RICO (Racketeer Influenced and Corrupt Organizations) suit, charging the bosses with operating a criminal enterprise. The indictment further unnerved Castellano's critics. They wondered how well the boss would stand up against the threat of decades in jail. Gotti and others feared Castellano would cut a deal with authorities. In early December Castellano's underboss, Aniello Dellacroce, died of lung cancer. Castellano, who was out on bail at the time, didn't attend Dellacroce's funeral, which was a huge sign of disrespect. With a trial coming up, Big Paul didn't want to be seen in public with his Mafia peers. At this point, a more aggressive mob boss would have had the rebellious Gotti and

his followers killed. Castellano did no such thing. He compounded his error by selecting Thomas Bilotti to replace Dellacroce as underboss. Bilotti was loyal, but lacked leadership skills and was more of a simple thug than a calculating Mafia chieftain.

Gotti used Dellacroce's death as a signal to make his move. On December 16, 1985, at 5:25 p.m., with the streets crowded with Christmas shoppers, Castellano and Bilotti pulled up in a black Lincoln limousine at Sparks Steak House in Manhattan. The two men were having a meeting with other mobsters inside the restaurant. As Castellano and Bilotti got out of the limousine, three assassins in trench coats and fur hats stepped forward. The trio produced semi-automatic pistols and shot the pair at point-blank range. Both men were killed on the spot. Castellano was 70 years old. Gotti and his trusted associate, Salvatore "Sammy the Bull" Gravano, sat in a car while the ambush took place. The "hit" had been orchestrated by Gotti.

In perhaps the ultimate example of his ivory tower isolation from basic Mafia mores, Castellano hadn't bothered to arm himself. Bilotti wasn't carrying a gun either. The unarmed pair didn't even go to the rudimentary caution of having bodyguards with them when they went to Sparks. They were easy prey for a wolf like Gotti, who soon seized control of the Gambino family and steered it on a very different course.

See also: Gotti, John; Mafia

Further Reading

John Davis, *Mafia Dynasty: The Rise and Fall of the Gambino Crime Family*, 1993.

John Elson, "Bugging Big Paul," *TIME*, June 10, 1991.

Federal Bureau of Investigation report on Italian organized crime. http://www.fbi.gov/hq/cid/orgcrime/lcnindex.htm.

Arnold Lubasch, "Shot by Shot, an Ex-Aide to Gotti Describes the Killing of Castellano," *New York Times*, March 4, 1992.

Selwyn Raab, *Five Families: The Rise, Decline and Resurgence of America's Most Powerful Mafia Empires*, 2005.

Thomas Reppetto, *Bringing Down the Mob: The War Against the American Mafia*, 2006.

Richard Stengel, "Slaughter on 46th Street," *TIME*, December 30, 1985.

COLL, VINCENT "MAD DOG" (1909–1932)

Vincent "Mad Dog" Coll was out of control, even by mobster standards. In addition to being extremely trigger-happy, he had an amazing ability to antagonize people and make enemies.

Vincent Coll in 1931. [AP Photo]

Born to an Irish-American family in 1909, Coll came to underworld prominence as a tough guy with Dutch Schultz's crew. After working with Schultz for a few years, Coll decided it was time he got a raise and a promotion. He wanted more money and more say in the Schultz organization. The Dutchman, however, had other ideas. Schultz thought Coll was a fine henchman, but lacked leadership potential, and told him so.

The simmering Coll struck back where his boss was the most vulnerable. In the spring of 1931 Coll was put on trial for violating the Sullivan law, which prohibited citizens from carrying concealed weapons. In a rare display of paternalism, Schultz put up Coll's bail money, which amounted to $10,000. When the case was called, however, Coll didn't show up. His absence meant that Schultz had to forfeit his bail money. Needless to say, the penny-pinching Dutchman was infuriated, and soon the former allies were at war. Coll gathered a small coterie of followers as both sides geared up for battle.

The Dutchman struck first, killing Coll's brother, Peter, on May 31, 1931. Coll retaliated by hijacking Schultz's beer trucks and murdering four of his gang members in a matter of weeks.

Just as Schultz had predicted, Coll proved totally unfit for the challenge of leadership. Coll's gang quickly ran out of money and had to come up with creative ways to refill their coffers. In typical fashion, Coll hatched upon an extremely audacious scheme to earn some fast cash. On July 15, 1931, Coll and his men drove to the Club Argonaut on Seventh Avenue. There, they kidnapped George Jean "Big Frenchy" DeMange. DeMange was close friends with longtime underworld figure Owney

"Killer" Madden. Madden paid a $35,000 ransom to release DeMange and vowed revenge against his abductors.

If Coll was worried about having aroused the animosity of a second gang boss, he didn't show it. He continued his reckless and violent course. One steaming hot night in late July 1931, Coll and his crew drove listlessly around New York, looking for potential targets. As they neared the Helmar Social Club on East 107th Street, Coll's men spotted Joey Rao standing on the sidewalk. Rao was pals with Schultz, which made him an enemy as far as Coll was concerned.

The car slowed to a crawl as it came alongside the Helmar Social Club. There was a group of children playing in the street, directly in the line of fire. This was of no matter to Coll. Coll and another thug in the vehicle drew weapons and began blasting away. Rao immediately threw himself to the sidewalk and wasn't hit. The kids playing near him weren't so lucky. A five-year-old boy named Michael Vengalli was shot and died a day later. His older brother was badly wounded. A toddler sleeping in a stroller was wounded twice in the back. Two other children were also shot and received minor wounds.

For once, police had no problem securing a witness to the crime. A man named George Brecht identified the two shooters as Coll and Frank Giordano (another former Schultz gunmen, turned traitor). The press blasted Coll as a "baby killer." They called him the "Mad Mick" or simply "Mad Dog Coll."

Following the Helmar club massacre, most mobsters wanted nothing to do with Coll. One gang boss, however, seemed to appreciate Coll's callousness. The boss was Salvatore Maranzano, victor of the Castellammarese War.

Maranzano, who was a paranoid type of person, wanted to eliminate every single ally of his former enemy, Joe Masseria. Maranzano's extensive death list included most major gangsters in New York, including Lucky Luciano, Joe Adonis, Frank Costello, Vito Genovese, and Schultz. Maranzano decided that Coll would be the perfect assassin to gun these men down. Coll agreed to take on the job, in spite of the horrible retribution that would no doubt follow from killing so many prominent gangsters.

Lucky Luciano got wind of this plot and organized a hit team of his own. This assassination squad burst into Maranzano's Park Avenue headquarters on September 10, 1931. The killers pretended to be U.S. Treasury agents and waved some fake badges in the air. The hit team disarmed Maranzano's men, and then killed the crime boss in his office. According to mob lore, the assassins bumped into Coll as they tore out of the building. Coll was just arriving to go over some murderous details with Maranzano. The fake U.S. Treasury agents shouted a warning that a police raid was in effect, and then raced away.

With Maranzano dead, Coll turned his attention back to Schultz. In early October 1931 Frank Giordano and Dominic Odierno (another former Schultz follower now working for Coll) murdered Joe Mullen, one of the Dutch's men, in the Bronx. Unfortunately for Coll, a brave witness stepped forward and identified Mullen's assailants to police. Giordano and Odierno were promptly arrested.

A couple days after Mullen's death, Coll was arrested at the Cornish Arms Hotel at 23rd Street, near Eighth Avenue. The Mad Mick had grown a moustache and dyed his hair dark, but police weren't fooled. Coll and Giordano were charged with murdering Michael Vengalli. When their case came to trial, the two men were represented by celebrated defense lawyer Samuel Leibowitz. In December 1931 Coll and Giordano were acquitted of Vengalli's murder. Coll made some appropriate noises to the press about how he wasn't a child killer and walked free. Giordano remained in custody, facing charges related to Mullen's murder. Eventually, both Giordano and Odierno would be executed for that crime.

Schultz continued to hunt Coll. On February 1, 1932, the Schultz organization got word that Coll would be playing cards in a home in the north Bronx. Four gunmen burst into the small house located on Commonwealth Avenue, and started firing. Inside, Patsy Dugan, Fiorio Basile, and Emily Torrizello, who were playing cards, were hit and killed. Basile's brother, Louis, was wounded, as was another woman. Four kids in the house (including two in cribs) were not hit; otherwise, the shooting might have been a repeat of the Helmar club slaughter.

The actual target was not at the card game, however. Mad Dog Coll arrived half an hour after his companions were shot. Coll's luck was about to run out, however.

A few days after the card game carnage, Coll stepped into a pharmacy called The London Chemist, at 23rd street near Eighth Avenue. Being cautious, Coll was accompanied by a bodyguard. Coll entered a phone booth and placed a call, allegedly to Owney Madden.

Madden had been waiting for such an opportunity for some time. He kept Coll on the line long enough to trace the call and dispatch a hit-team. Within minutes, three killers arrived on the scene. Two of the assassins stayed outside while the third entered the pharmacy, tommy gun in hand. The gunman urged customers to remain calm as he strolled up to the phone booth where Coll continued to babble into the receiver. Coll's bodyguard had vanished, slipping out of the pharmacy and past the two sentinels on duty outside. The bodyguard was most likely in on the hit.

The gunman leveled his Thompson at the phone booth and squeezed off a clip. The glass in the booth exploded as the Mad Mick took fifteen rounds at point-blank range. Satisfied with his handiwork, the gunner made an about-face and exited the pharmacy. He rejoined his comrades outside. With their mission accomplished, the three killers drove off, leaving a dead Mad Dog Coll behind.

See also: Maranzano, Salvatore; Prohibition; Schultz, Dutch

Further Reading

Nate Hendley, *Dutch Schultz: The Brazen Beer Baron of New York*, 2005.

Thomas Reppetto, *American Mafia: A History of Its Rise to Power*, 2004.

Paul Sann, *Kill the Dutchman! The Story of Dutch Schultz*, 1971.

COLOSIMO, JAMES "BIG JIM" (1877–1920)

Big Jim Colosimo was one of the first major Italian-American crime bosses in Chicago. He could have ruled the Windy City for decades, but was undone by love and the good life. Born in Cosenza, Italy in the 1880s, Colosimo immigrated with his family to Chicago in 1895. Like many immigrants, Colosimo had to settle for a series of menial jobs. He was primarily employed as a street sweeper, but showed a flair for labor organizing. Colosimo organized the city's sweepers, and helped set up social and athletic clubs for their benefit. Colosimo, who had no moral compunctions about breaking the law, moonlighted as a pimp and pickpocket.

Colosimo's organizational abilities and criminal hustle soon drew the attention of two powerful and extremely corrupt city aldermen, Michael "Hinky Dink" Kenna and "Bathhouse" John Coughlin. The pair represented the First Ward, which is where the city's red-light district (called the Levee) was based, and took a cut from vice operations in the area. Kenna and Coughlin started giving Colosimo patronage appointments, making him a precinct captain charged with getting the vote in a given area. He also ran a poolroom and a saloon, and then became a "bagman" for Kenna and Coughlin. It was his job to make the rounds of local brothels and collect money from the pimps and madams for the two aldermen. In 1902, while performing these duties, Colosimo encountered a plump, middle-aged madam named Victoria Moresco. She was drawn to Colosimo's swarthy good looks and Mediterranean charm. He, in turn, was attracted to her wealth and position as a top procurer of flesh. Colosimo and Moresco entered into a whirlwind romance. Within weeks, the brothel keeper (who was twice her paramour's age) and the bagman were married.

Moresco gave her new husband a job as manager of her relatively upscale brothel. Colosimo quickly opened up a series of new, cut-price establishments in the Levee. These were dives where the going rate for a quick encounter with a prostitute was $1 or $2. Colosimo also launched a few classier bordellos. Colosimo didn't neglect his mentors, and made sure Kenna and Coughlin got a cut of his proceeds. Having a good eye for marketing, he established gambling dens and saloons near his brothels, so patrons could enjoy multiple vices in one convenient location. Prostitution, however, remained the mainstay of the burgeoning Colosimo/Moresco empire. The pair soon owned dozens of brothels across the city.

At the time, prostitution was even less glamorous than it is today. Penicillin hadn't been invented and sexually transmitted diseases (STDs) were rife. Effective contraception didn't exist (and in some jurisdictions, was illegal); for many prostitutes, illicit abortion was their main form of birth control. Being a prostitute was a very short-term vocation. Most girls only lasted a few years, their physical and mental decline abetted by drugs, drink, abuse and STDs. Because turnover was so high, a constant supply of fresh talent was required. Colosimo and his fellow pimps relied on "white slavers" to bring in new hookers. These were unscrupulous businessmen who lured naïve country girls and new emigrants with fake ads for housekeepers and nannies. Girls who responded to the ads would be abducted, raped into submission, and then sold to pimps and madams. Prostitutes were kept in line by threats, physical beatings and the occasional murder of one of their colleagues.

Colosimo grew hugely wealthy off such misery. He took to encrusting himself in expensive stones. He wore diamond rings, diamond-studded belts and suspenders, and diamond cuff links. People started calling him "Diamond Jim." He was also fond of finely tailored, all-white suits. Lured by these riches, a few brazen criminals tried to extort money from Colosimo. Annoyed, Big Jim contacted Moresco's cousin, a young striver named Johnny Torrio. A rising star in New York City's gang firmament, Torrio was cunning and cold-blooded. He moved from New York to Chicago in 1909 and quickly took the situation in hand, arranging for a death squad to murder the Black Handers, who were bothering Colosimo. Impressed, Big Jim asked Torrio to stick around. Put in charge of a brothel, Torrio proved to be an excellent manager. Unlike most gangsters, Torrio didn't smoke, drink, curse, or avail himself of the flesh he peddled each day. Colosimo kept ceding more authority to Torrio until the up-and-comer was managing Big Jim's empire. By this point, Colosimo and his wife owned two hundred brothels and employed hundreds of people. Big Jim also set up a nightclub at 2126 Wabash Avenue and named it after himself. Colosimo's Café was a high-end establishment with a full orchestra. The café attracted famous celebrities of the day such as opera singer Enrico Caruso and legendary defense attorney Clarence Darrow. The glitzy club served gourmet food and fine wine and was Colosimo's personal playground.

In 1912 pressure from civic groups lead to the closure of the Levee. Colosimo simply opened new brothels in the suburbs outside the city. Two years later, William Hale "Big Bill" Thompson was elected mayor of Chicago. Reviled as the most corrupt mayor in American history, Thompson turned a blind eye to vice. The Levee soon reopened for business. Torrio continued to prove to be an effective manager. He expanded Colosimo's domain, opening new broth-

els, gambling dens, and saloons. Torrio hired new recruits as well. One of his finds was a young gangster he'd known in New York named Al Capone. Capone was brought to Chicago and given lowly tasks at first, such as standing outside brothels and pitching the services found inside.

Colosimo paid little attention to Torrio's staffing decisions. He was content to sit back and enjoy the fruits of his labors. In 1918 Colosimo fell in love with Dale Winter, a young winsome singer who appeared at Colosimo's Café. Big Jim started squiring Winter about town, openly treating her as his escort. Moresco was told to pack her things and leave the family home. Colosimo's fellow gangsters were appalled. As violent as they were, the gangsters held themselves to a certain standard. Family values were greatly honored. While it was perfectly acceptable to cheat on your wife, this was generally done in private. It was considered a shocking breech of underworld etiquette to humiliate your wife by accompanying a young siren in public. Deeply in love, Colosimo paid no mind. He also stopped paying any attention to business. Prohibition was scheduled to come into effect in mid-January 1920. Far-seeing gangsters such as Torrio realized that Prohibition represented a bonanza for organized crime. People would still want to drink despite the law. If they couldn't buy alcohol from a legal source, they would buy black-market booze sold by criminals. Despite Torrio's pleading, Colosimo didn't want to make a major investment in bootlegging. He was content with the way things were. Colosimo was also nervous about federal Prohibition enforcement, and more interested in his new girlfriend anyway.

In March 1920 Colosimo divorced his wife, giving her a $50,000 settlement. One month later, Big Jim married Winter. The marriage only lasted a few weeks. As his boss enjoyed his nuptials, Torrio schemed. He decided Colosimo had to be eliminated. Torrio would take over Big Jim's empire once he was gone, and go into bootlegging in a big way. Torrio met with other city crime bosses and got their approval (more or less) for his plan. On May 11 Torrio called Big Jim and told him a big whisky delivery would be arriving at Colosimo's Café at precisely 4 p.m. that day. Torrio insisted that his boss be there for the delivery. Colosimo reluctantly agreed, but when he showed up, no one knew anything about the shipment. Colosimo chatted with a few befuddled staffers, and then wandered near the cloakroom, where a gunman was waiting. The gunman fired twice and Big Jim was killed instantly. Many accounts cite Al Capone as Colosimo's assassin. This is false; Capone was still a lowly pimp at the time, not someone who could be relied upon for a top-level "hit." The actual killer was Frankie Yale, a seasoned thug from New York City. He had almost certainly been hired by Torrio.

Colosimo left the earth in the same way he lived—in a tawdry haze of flash and sparkle. "Big Jim had the first of the gangland funeral extravaganzas of the twenties—a $50,000 affair," wrote journalist Paul Sann in the book, *The Lawless Decade*. As part of the funeral procession, Colosimo's bronze casket was taken to the very café where he'd been murdered. Some 2,000 mourners crowded outside to pay their respect, as two brass bands performed appropriately somber music. A funeral service was held at Colosimo's house and all present appeared sufficiently mournful. Everyone knew Colosimo was a pimp, but that didn't stop plenty of respectable people from attending his funeral, including judges, a congressman, several city aldermen, a district state attorney, and countless other worthies. Thousands of mourners and spectators alike turned out on the street to see Colosimo's bronze casket go by.

Torrio, of course, denied having any clue who would want to harm his boss. He appeared appropriately shaken and distraught. Torrio's mourning was brief; he quickly took the reins of power and appointed himself head of Colosimo's vast empire. There was a new crime boss in Chicago and unlike his predecessor, he wasn't about to be sidetracked by women or a love of luxury.

See also: Black Hand; Capone, Al; Prohibition

Further Reading

John Kobler, *Capone: The Life and World of Al Capone*, 1971.

Thomas Reppetto, *American Mafia: A History of Its Rise to Power*, 2004.

Gus Russo, *The Outfit: The Role of Chicago's Underworld in the Shaping of Modern America*, 2001.

Paul Sann, *The Lawless Decade*, 1957.

CRIPS

The Los Angeles–based Crips gained their first major blast of notoriety in March 1972, when members of the street gang beat a young black teenager to death to steal his leather jacket. The crime, which took place at the Hollywood Palladium, shocked Los Angeles and brought the once obscure youth gang into the city's consciousness.

Members of the Crips gang display their signs for a photographer in 1988. [AP Photo]

Primarily made up of young, African-American men, the Crips were founded by Raymond Lee Washington in 1969. Described by *LA Weekly* reporter Michael Krikorian as "a fearless and mighty 5'8 sparkplug who loved to fight and loathed guns," Washington was born in Texas but raised in poverty-stricken South Central Los Angeles. A talented football player, Washington was also a gifted street pugilist, well-respected for his prowess in bare-knuckle brawls. The exact nature of Washington's reputation is open for debate, with some people claiming he protected kids in his neighborhood from bullies, and others suggesting he was a bully himself. The community Washington grew up in swarmed with youth gangs. Then, as now, most gang members were young

men looking for camaraderie, action, and excitement.

In the late 1960s, Washington decided to form his own street gang. He was inspired, in part, by the fledgling Black Panther organization, which took off during this period. A brazen group with a radical political agenda, the Panthers led armed street patrols in black communities and fought the police. Washington apparently had a vague plan of setting up something similar. Washington's gang was originally called the Baby Avenue Cribs, crib being slang for someone's residence. The name soon morphed into "Crips." There are several tales explaining how this name change came about. Anecdotal evidence suggests one of Washington's older brothers suffered a leg injury at some point and walked with a limp. His brother wrote the word "crip" (for "cripple") on his sneakers and the name caught on. Another integral aspect of Cripdom came about by accident. The California Youth Authority provided blue handkerchiefs to incarcerated youth gang members in correctional facilities. Crips started using the blue hankies as an identifier. Their rivals, who had coalesced into a street gang of their own called the Bloods, responded by claiming red for their own use

In any case, the Cribs/Crips soon blossomed under Washington's leadership. According to a 2006 report by Detective Wayne Caffey of the Los Angeles County Sheriff's office, "Washington was a great recruiter and his group . . . was growing like wildfire." One of his most famous recruits was Stanley "Tookie" Williams, a charismatic weight lifting fanatic who joined the gang in the early 1970s. While the Crips rapidly expanded, any ideals of protecting black neighborhoods were soon abandoned. Throughout the 1970s, the Crips battled other gangs (and each other), mugged people, committed robberies, sold drugs, and pursued other felonious activities. If street gangs had been content to fight with fists and knives in the 1950s and 1960s, they moved on to cheap handguns, called "Saturday Night Specials," and shotguns by the late 1970s. This was in spite of Washington's antipathy to firearms. Crip star Tookie Williams certainly had no qualms about arming himself. In 1979, Williams committed a pair of brutal robberies in which he killed several people with a shotgun. As Williams' reputation rose, Washington faded into the background. It was rumored that he was disillusioned with the very gang culture he had helped spawn. The street fighter felt

his young charges were too crazy and out of control, and too quick to use guns to settle their differences. Washington believed true gangbangers should fight face-to-face, without weapons. Ironically, Washington was shot to death in August 1979. His murder has never been solved.

The escalation in violence associated with the Crips continued after Washington's death, and Tookie's incarceration in 1981. The advent of crack cocaine in the early 1980s led to a massive influx of profits for drug-dealing gangs in L.A., including the Crips. Profits were funneled into weaponry, as gang bangers began toting arms more commonly seen in the hands of soldiers. These included Uzi and Mac-10 machine pistols and the deadly AK-47 assault rifle. If high-powered automatic weapons became the guns of choice for street gangsters, rap music (which also exploded in the 1980s) became their urban soundtrack. Crips and other gang bangers eagerly embraced rap songs glorifying "thug life."

The Crips continued to expand along with their rivals. "Sets in the Crip and Blood communities have increased nearly twenty-fold—so that there is literally a gang on every street," wrote Crip member turned introspective author Sanyika Shakur, also known as "Monster Kody Scott," in the early 1990s. "Also, there are huge conglomerate sets spanning hundreds of city blocks at a time, extending themselves into other cities and counties." It is a misnomer to suggest that the gang Washington founded works as a unified whole. Crip factions spend as much time warring with each-other as with rival gangs. The "Crips" label is something of an umbrella term, encompassing a loosely knit association of neighborhood thugs living throughout a huge metropolitan area. Within the Crip gang, there are countless smaller "sets" (or small groups of gang members). Sets operate on a more or less independent basis, to the extent that warfare between different sets within the Crip organization is not uncommon.

The Crips continue to thrive. Originally based in L.A., there are now Crip gangs nationwide. The U.S. Department of Justice estimates that there are currently 30-35,000 members of the Crips across the United States, most of them African-Americans. In addition to ruthless violence, the Crips have also become astute street businessmen. "The main source of income for Crips gangs is derived from the street-level distribution of powdered cocaine, crack cocaine, marijuana, and PCP," states a U.S. Department of Justice essay. "The Crips are also involved in other criminal activities, including assault, auto theft, burglary, and homicide."

The Crips have come a long way from Raymond Lee Washington's original concept of a fist-fighting crew of neighborhood kids protecting their turf from other gangs.

See also: Bloods; Mara Salvatrucha (MS-13); Shakur, Sanyika; Williams, Stanley "Tookie"

Further Reading

Leon Bing, *Do or Die*, 1991.

Detective Wayne Caffey, Los Angeles County Sheriff's Office, "Crips and Bloods," 2006

Michael Krikorian, "Tookie's Mistaken Identity: On the Trail of the Real Founder of the Crips," *LA Weekly*, December 15, 2005.

Sanyika Shakur, *Monster: The Autobiography of an L.A. Gang Member,* 1993.

U.S. Department of Justice, Street Gangs—Crips. http://www.usdoj.gov/criminal/gangunit/gangs/street.html.

D

DALTON GANG

The Dalton gang is largely famous for the grim failure of their last heist. Related by blood to members of the James-Younger gang, the Daltons achieved a solid reputation as crack train robbers. In trying to outdo the legacy of the James-Younger gang, however, the Daltons overreached and in one brief gun fight were largely decimated. Ironically, the Daltons' final doomed mission echoed a very similar robbery by Jesse James that also failed miserably.

The family patriarch, Louis Dalton, was originally a farmer living in Missouri. In 1851 he married Adeline Younger, who was the half-sister of Colonel Henry Washington Younger. The colonel was father to Jim, John, Bob and Cole Younger, all of whom rode with Jesse James. Thus, Mrs. Dalton was an aunt of the Younger boys. When the Civil War broke out, Dalton moved his family to Coffeyville, Kansas. It seemed safer than Missouri, which was home to a bitter, internal battle between pro- and anti-

Emmett Dalton, member of the Dalton Gang, in 1931. [AP Photo]

Union forces. Louis and Adeline had 13 children. Eight sons and three daughters survived into adulthood.

For a brief period it appeared that the Dalton boys would follow a different path than the Youngers. Frank Dalton became a deputy U.S. marshal. He was killed on the job in 1884 in an altercation with a horse thief in what was then Oklahoma Territory. Three other sons—Charles, Henry and Littleton—appeared to have no outlaw inclinations. The same was not true about the rest of the males in the clan. Bob, Emmett, Grattan (who usually went by Grat), and William all had a streak of wildness about them. That said, Bob, Emmett, and Grat all followed in Frank's footsteps and served for a time as U.S. marshals. Grat was wounded in 1888 in the course of his duties as a lawman. Bob Dalton was the most reckless and daring of all the boys, killing a man before he was twenty years old. The deceased was named Charles Montgomery. Grat claimed he caught the man stealing horses. Rumor had it, however, that Montgomery fancied a woman Grat had his eye on. By killing Montgomery, Grat removed a potential rival. As a marshal, Grat's take on the murder was accepted.

In 1889 the Dalton family got caught up in the land rush into Oklahoma Territory. Adeline Dalton set up a homestead near Kingfisher, Oklahoma. Charles, Henry and Littleton used the opportunity to establish their own farms and work the land. The rest of the boys had other ideas. Louis Dalton, who might have offered a restraining hand to his more daredevil sons, died one year after the family moved to Oklahoma Territory. Meanwhile, son William decided to head farther west to check out opportunities in the gold field. He prospected around Montana, and then moved to California where he settled down and got involved in politics. William was soon elected to the state assembly. The remaining Dalton boys stayed behind in Oklahoma, pondering their prospects. Their pay as U.S. marshals was miserable. Perhaps to augment their low wages, the Daltons took to thievery. They were accused of stealing some horses, which had vanished from Oklahoma Territory only to reappear in Kansas where they were sold. At the time, frontier justice reigned in the territory. Stealing horses could get a man lynched. Grat Dalton was arrested for skulking around property belonging to Charles McLelland. Authorities couldn't pin anything on him, however, so they had to let Grat go.

At this juncture, Bob, Grat, and Emmett decided it would be a good time to leave Oklahoma Territory and visit their brother in California. They had given up trying to enforce the law as marshals, and were looking for new opportunities. On the evening of February 6, 1891, a Southern Pacific passenger train traveling from San Francisco to Los Angeles stopped after someone lit a red lantern near the tiny station of Alila, California. The train ground to a halt, at which point a group of masked men surrounded it. With much whooping and firing of shots into the air, the bandits ordered the fireman George Radliff out of the locomotive car. At gunpoint, they told Radliff to take his coal pick and use it to break open the door to the express car where large amounts of money were stored in a safe. Radliff did as he was told, but for unclear reasons, he was shot dead after opening the express car door. With Radliff expiring by the railway track, the express messenger used the opportunity to exit the train from the express car and hide in some bushes. The express messenger had the combination to the safe and a key. Without these two things, the safe could not be opened. The masked bandits stole what they could from the passengers, and then left.

The Southern Pacific robbery was almost certainly carried out by the Daltons. In hitting a train the brothers might have been trying to emulate their famous relatives, who as part of the James-Younger gang, also robbed trains. The Southern Pacific holdup, however, was extremely unprofitable, resulting in the senseless death of fireman Radliff. Detectives began tracking the outlaws. Grat Dalton had fallen from his horse during the getaway, which left him injured. Detectives followed the wounded Grat to the home of Assemblyman William Dalton. There, they arrested both brothers. William gave a solid alibi and tried to use his political pull to help his brother. This wasn't sufficient. While Grat stoutly denied having anything to do with the Southern Pacific holdup, he was identified as one of the train robbers. He wasn't convicted of killing Radliff, but he was found guilty of armed robbery and sentenced to twenty years in Folsom Penitentiary.

Grat was put on a train at Fresno, under the guard of two deputies. He was physically manacled to one of the deputies. The day was very hot and all the windows in the train car Grat was traveling in were kept open. At some point during the journey, the deputy who was manacled to Grat fell asleep in his chair. The other deputy became preoccupied, likely chatting with other passengers. As the train rattled over a bridge, Grat jumped to his feet. Before either deputy could react, he had leapt headfirst through an open window. Had he fallen on the ground, Grat would have been killed. As it was, he splashed into a river and landed safely in water. Grat let the strong current take him downstream. In this manner Grat managed to reconnect with his brothers in Oklahoma. It is believed that Grat waited until the deputy he was manacled to fell asleep, and then stole the key to his chains. He presumably unlocked himself before taking his dive out the window.

The reunited Dalton brothers decided to form a gang along the lines of the James-Younger band. They would rob trains and banks. Bob Dalton was something of the de facto leader of the group by virtue of being the most daring, and he recruited a few other non-family members to augment the gang's ranks. His recruits included Bill Doolin, Dick Broadwell, Bill Powers and a fourth man with the intriguing nickname, Blackface Charley Bryant. Bryant had acquired this nickname by virtue of a powder burn on his visage. By this point, the Dalton brothers had cut any ties to their law-abiding, law-enforcing past. The Southern Pacific railroad was offering a reward of $6,000 for members of the Dalton clan. On May 9, 1891, the gang struck again. A train from Santa Fe was held up in Wharton, located in Oklahoma Territory. The express car was robbed, of roughly $1500. The gang's modus operandi was similar to the previous robbery. They stopped the train, held the passengers and crew up by gunpoint, and forced the fireman to open the express car. As they made their escape, the Dalton gang passed by a group of eight to ten strong, lively horses on a ranch. The gang decided to steal them. A posse was quickly formed among ranchers to get the horses back. The Daltons, realizing they were being followed, set up an ambush in a heavy growth of trees along the bank of a creek. The posse approached, and then began to cautiously enter the thick brush. A flurry of rifle shots crackled through the pines and one member of the posse fell dead. The man's comrades retreated and debated about what to do next. As the posse dithered, the Dalton gang quietly made their escape, along with the stolen horses.

The Dalton's exploits began to attract attention from the press. A *New York Times* article, dated October 12, 1891, from Guthrie, Oklahoma, stated that deputy marshal Heck Thomas and some California detectives had cornered the gang on an Indian reservation. According to the newspaper, the Dalton gang sent the marshal a note threatening to kill anyone who tried to capture them.

In any event, marshal Thomas did not manage to capture anyone from the Dalton gang. The Daltons struck again on June 1, 1892. They held up another Santa Fe train, this time at a tiny station in Red Rock. The pattern was the same as previous heists. The train was stopped at the station and two gang members, Blackface Charley Bryant and Broadwell, entered the locomotive with drawn guns. As they held the engineer and fireman hostage, Bob and Emmett Dalton and Powers entered the passenger cars to rob the travelers. Meanwhile, Doolin and Grat went to the express car, where they found the door open. The two outlaws drew guns on the express messenger and a guard who were both inside the car. The gang seized the small safe from the express car and tossed it outside. Blackface Charley, meanwhile, spotted the young station telegraph operator in the station office, frantically sending out a distress message. Bryant aimed his gun and shot the man dead. The safe was opened while this was going on, but the gang only got a few hundred dollars for the heist.

Following the train robbery, the Dalton gang split up as usual. Bryant decided to lay low at a ranch near Hennessey, where a deputy marshal named Ed Short happened to be stationed. Bryant had worked at the ranch on and off and was somewhat well-known in the area. The fireman and engineer from the robbed Santa Fe train gave authorities as many details as they could about the hold-up. While the robbers had worn masks, the two train men both mentioned that one of the bandits had a powder burn on his face. As Short knew, Blackface Charley Bryant also had a powder burn. He also knew that Daisy Bryant (Blackface Charley's sister) was on friendly terms with the Dalton gang. With this in mind, deputy marshal Short decided to keep an eye on Blackface Charley.

Accounts vary as to what happened next. In one version Short found Bryant at his sister's house and arrested him. Another more elaborate account stated that Bryant had become ill after arriving at the ranch. The bandit decided to go into Hennessey to recuperate. He took a room at the Rhodes Hotel and was being looked after by Daisy (in other versions, the nursemaid was the hotel manager's sister). When quizzed by Short, Daisy disavowed any knowledge of the whereabouts of any Dalton gang members. Deputy marshal Short was still suspicious. He took off his boots, and then hid in the hotel, waiting for Daisy to take a tray into the room where he believed the bandit lay. Short snuck behind the woman and tip-toed into the room on stocking feet. Sure enough, Bryant was on the bed, revolver and Winchester rifle by his side. Standing triumphant in his socks, deputy marshal Short aimed his own weapon and captured the stunned outlaw. Short put Bryant in handcuffs and decided to take him to Wichita, Kansas, which boasted a federal jail. A rail line ran from Hennessey to Wichita. Short put his handcuffed prisoner in the baggage car as the train got rolling. There was a third man in the car who worked as the baggage car guard.

With Grat's example in mind, deputy marshal Short should have been more cautious about transporting a Dalton via train. Instead, he didn't even bother manacling Bryant to a chair or some other fixture inside the baggage car. Bryant looked sad and miserable, so perhaps the deputy marshal thought he was no longer a threat. The train chugged along and Bryant appeared to be half-asleep. At some point, the train stopped for a brief halt at a station. Short decided to step outside the baggage car to stroll about. He handed a revolver to the baggage car guard and told him to stand watch on Bryant. Then, Winchester rifle in hand, deputy marshal Short stepped out onto the platform. The baggage car guard took the pistol and put it down on a desk inside the baggage car. He was soon occupied with work. Bryant, who had only been pretending to be drowsy, was waiting for just such an opportunity. He jumped up, dashed over to the desk, and grabbed the revolver in his manacled hands. Fortunately for Bryant, his hands were cuffed in front of him, not behind. The bandit ordered the startled baggage man to leave the car. This he did, exiting onto the opposite platform from Short. Bryant jumped out of the car to confront the deputy marshal. Aiming the revolver as best he could with his imprisoned hands, he fired three or four quick shots, one of which hit Short. Grievously wounded, the deputy marshal managed to get off a shot of his own with his rifle. Bryant was hit and crumpled to the station platform dead. Short himself collapsed and died soon after.

The Dalton gang didn't let the death of one of their members slow them down. On the evening of July 15, 1892, they decked themselves out with heavy weapons, and then headed to a tiny train station in Adair, in what was then called "Indian territory." They were eager to rob a Missouri, Kansas and Texas express train that carried $17,000 in cash. To forestall any attempt at robbery, the railway company had included several armed Indian policemen and some train detectives on the journey. For unclear reasons the guards were placed in a passenger car towards the rear of the train. The Dalton crew easily took over the tiny train station. They ransacked the station for money and valuables, and then sat down on the platform and calmly waited for the train to arrive, rifles in hand. The train came into the station and stopped, at which point two men held up the engineer and the fireman. When other members of the gang headed to the express car, they discovered the express manager had barricaded the doors. The bandits threatened to blow up the door with dynamite unless the express manager opened it. Thoroughly intimidated, the express manager did as ordered. The Daltons clambered on board and used dynamite to open the safe. At this point, one of the policemen decided to see what was going on. There were men outside running around with lanterns and this looked suspicious. The policeman leaned out the window only to attract a flurry of gunshots. He quickly ducked back into the car.

Captain J.J. Kinney, the leader of the train guards, ordered his men to fire back. He told them to remain in the passenger car, however, which was probably not the best strategy. The policemen and train detectives began to exchange gunfire with the Daltons farther up the track. The guards would stick a head and gun out a window and rattle off a couple quick shots before ducking back in. The Daltons fired back at the guards, who looked like gophers cautiously peering out of holes in the ground, and then darting back down. A total of 200 shots were fired in this melee, few of which hit their intended targets. At some point, the guards came up with the idea of exiting the train, going up the side opposite to where the bandits stood, and trying to shoot at their legs from under the car. This plan of attack failed. By this point, Captain Kinney had been wounded in the shoulder. A policeman had been hit in the leg. Two stray bullets from the gun fight slammed through a drug store located near the station where two local doctors sat, oblivious to the raging battle outside. Doctors Youngblood and W.L. Goff were both shot, with the latter physician eventually succumbing to his wounds. The Daltons, meanwhile, backed up a wagon against the express car and put their stolen money on it. The gang was cocky, almost insolent to the Indian policeman and train detectives who were peppering them with shots. The outlaws gathered up their loot, then quickly made their escape from the train. A July 16, 1892, report in the *New York Times* estimated the haul at a cool $40,000.

The Times also speculated that at least some of the Daltons were likely hiding out at the farm of their mother in Oklahoma Territory. Mrs. Dalton, an August 1, 1892 newspaper article noted, ". . . is living on a homestead claim, not far from El Reno, and this place bids fair to become as noted as the James farm in Missouri, occupied by Mrs. Samuels, mother of the notorious James boys."

The Daltons would have appreciated the comparison. Always eager to outdo their legendary relatives, the gang was talked into pulling off a new, spectacular heist by Bob Dalton.

Bob decided that the gang should set their sights on a double robbery. He wanted to hold up two banks at the same time in broad daylight. As far as he was aware, no one—not even Jesse James and the Youngers—had ever tried such a thing before. The two banks Bob had in mind were the First National Bank and the C.M. Condon Bank in the boys' old hometown of Coffeyville, Kansas. Bob was eager to "lower Jesse James' record," as Emmett put it in a later interview with the *New York Times*. Emmett and Doolin had reservations about Bob's plan, but agreed to go along with it. Coffeyville had been selected because its two banks were situated close together. Plus, having grown up there, the Dalton brothers were familiar with all the streets and buildings. The vague intent of the robbery was to secure enough cash for each member of the gang to retire, at least for a while. In trying to outdo their outlaw relatives, the Daltons should have paid more attention to the history of the James-Younger gang. The latter was also a highly successful band of bandits, holding up trains at will. The James-Younger gang eventually overreached, however, in trying to pull off a daring daylight robbery of a bank in Northfield, Minnesota. That event in September 1876 ended in total disaster with the gang shot to pieces at the hands of the courageous townspeople. Being somewhat egotistical in nature, Bob Dalton was sure a similar fate would not befall his own band of marauders in Coffeyville.

On October 2, 1892, six members of the Dalton gang set out. Over the next couple days, they rode closer to their target. On the night of October 4, within a few miles of Coffeyville, the Dalton gang set up camp. They arose the next morning, made food and coffee, and then everyone shaved. The gang was well-prepared. They all had good, thorough-bred horses and new, expensive saddles. Each man wore a black, broad-rimmed cowboy hat. They all had long coats on, buttoned to conceal a brace of revolvers. Each man had a scabbard (i.e., a pouch) on their left leg, which held a Winchester rifle. The six men saddled up and started riding towards Coffeyville. They hadn't traveled far when Doolin noticed his horse had gone lame. The horse would be useless if the bandits had to make a quick getaway. Doolin announced his intention to steal another horse, and said he spotted one in a pasture on the ride to Coffeyville. With a new horse, Doolin would ride hard and catch up with the rest of the gang. Bob Dalton thought that was a good idea and told his comrade to go ahead.

At 9 a.m., the Dalton gang, minus Doolin, rode into Coffeyville. They trotted along Eighth Street, went down Maple and headed towards an alley. There, they dismounted and tied their horses to a fence. At this point, the Daltons attempted to disguise themselves. Given that the brothers had grown up in the town, they were afraid they might be recognized. So, Grat and Emmett put on fake beards, colored jet-black, while Bob fashioned a fake moustache and goatee on his face. For some odd reason the gang waited until they were actually in the town before disguising themselves. Broadwell and Powers weren't known in Coffeyville, so they didn't put on any fake whiskers. The disguises selected by the Dalton brothers weren't particularly impressive. As the five strode down the alley, holding their Winchester rifles, they passed a local merchant named Alex McKenna. McKenna ran a local dry-goods and grocery store. He thought the facial hair on three of the men looked awfully phony. He wondered why a group of men bearing rifles would feel the need to disguise themselves. Cautiously, he observed three of the men (Grat, Powers and Broadwell) head into the Condon Bank. The other two (Bob and Emmett) went through a vacant lot and stepped into the First National Bank, which was situated down the street opposite the Condon Bank.

McKenna crept forward and looked through the window of the Condon Bank. He saw the men pointing their rifles at the startled cashiers and sounded the alarm. McKenna raced up the street, shouting that the Daltons were robbing the bank. The gang was so well known by this point that it was assumed they were the ones pulling off the heist. Alerted by McKenna, the men of Coffeyville grabbed rifles and pistols and took up positions. While some of the timid citizens of the town hid under porches or behind rails, their more determined counterparts leveled their guns at the Condon Bank. Inside the bank Grat, Broadwell and Powers worked quickly. Grat produced a grain sack and ordered the cashiers to fill it with money. A banker obliged and stuffed $1,000 in cash and $3,000 in silver into the sack. Grat then ordered the man to open the bank safe. This, the cashier claimed, he could not do. He said the safe was set to a time-lock and was supposed to open at 9:45 a.m.—a few minutes away. In truth, the safe had been open for over an hour, but Grat foolishly believed the cashier and didn't check it himself. Making a second foolhardy decision, Grat announced that he and his companions would wait for the safe to open. Just when they should have been working lightning fast, the three outlaws stood around waiting. When three minutes had gone by, a bullet shattered the bank window. Coffeyville residents began pouring rounds into the bank. Broadwell took a minor wound in the arm. At this point, Grat decided that the silver was too heavy. With bullets flying around the inside of the bank, he wasted more time removing the silver from his grain sack and having a cashier refill it with money from the safe.

Things at the First National Bank were going more to plan. Bob Dalton knew the cashier, Thomas Ayers, and addressed him as "Tom." At gunpoint, the two Dalton brothers ordered Ayers to open the safe and grab the cash. Hearing gunshots from the other bank, Ayers tried to work as slowly as possible. Bob Dalton grew impatient, however, and followed him into the vault, grabbing a couple packages filled with money and gold. He tossed these valuables into his sack. By this point, the gunfire from the townspeople had reached a crescendo. Just as in Northfield, the locals were heavily armed and weren't cowed by a gang of bank robbers. All manner of pistol, rifle and shotgun were fired en masse.

Inside the Condon Bank Grat asked if there was a back door. There was, and Grat and his group rushed through it. They ran across the street, heading to the alley where their horses were stationed, trying to elude the deadly shots from the townspeople. Meanwhile, at the other bank, Bob and Emmett took some hostages and pushed them outside in front of them. This tactic failed when Coffeyville residents began shooting at the Dalton brothers regardless of human shields. Bob and Emmett jumped back into the bank and demanded to be let out a back door. The two brothers ran to the back, and then raced outside. Townspeople covering the back entrance opened fire on them. Lucius Baldwell, a young man who worked as a clerk at a local hardware store near the bank, got caught up in the moment. He grabbed a revolver from the store's inventory and loaded it. He looked out the back door and saw Bob and Emmett racing down the alley. Baldwin began running after the bandits, taking wild pot shots with the revolver. Bob Dalton yelled a warning at the youth, which wasn't heeded. Baldwin wouldn't turn back, so Bob shot him with his Winchester rifle. The young man died a few hours later.

Bob and Emmett raced north, and then went west on Eighth Street past a grocery store. Glancing south, they saw Coffeyville residents peppering the Condon Bank with gunfire. Figuring the townspeople might not notice them in all the confusion, Bob and Emmett hit the open street, racing with the money sack to their horses. A resident named George Cubine, armed with a pistol, spotted the two brothers. Cubine was standing on the street with Charles Brown, an older man who did not have a gun on him. Cubine fired at the two Dalton brothers and missed. Bob and Emmett both fired back and killed the man. Brown tried to retrieve Cubine's revolver but was shot dead by Bob. The gunplay with Cubine and Brown drew the attention of the townspeople who had been firing on the Condon Bank. Cashier Ayers, his son, and a third man ran into the hardware store and grabbed weapons. Ayers secured a rifle, which he positioned through the door jamb, aiming at Bob and Emmett down the street. Bob spotted the cashier and reacted first. He fired a shot that hit Ayers in the head, seriously wounding him.

Bob and Emmett kept running. A clerk named Reynolds jumped out from the front door of the hardware store. Looking south, he missed Bob and Emmett (who were heading north). Reynolds aimed his rifle at the three men rushing from the Condon Bank. He leveled his weapon and fired, hitting Bill Powers. Critically wounded, but still upright, Powers cursed and shot back at Reynolds, wounding him in the foot. Grat, Broadwell and the badly wounded Powers raced down the alley where they had left their horses. There was a livery stable connected to the alley owned by Coffeyville resident John Kloehr. Hearing the commotion, Kloehr grabbed a rifle and began rushing towards the spot where the Dalton gang had tied their horses. A group of men stood on the porch of the hardware store, shooting down the alley at the bandits. Broadwell was hit in the back. He collapsed and started crawling towards his horse. Another townsperson took aim at Broadwell with his pistol, but Powers, who was still alive, lifted his rifle and shot the man in the wrist. During the entire raid, the Dalton crew only used their Winchesters. The revolvers hidden behind their buttoned coats were not touched during the double robbery.

Bob and Emmett connected with Grat and Powers, the latter of whom was having difficulty walking. A bullet hit Grat and he staggered into a shed near the alley. Still on his feet, the severely wounded Grat gripped his Winchester and tried to cover the retreat of the rest of the gang. The town marshal, Charles Connelly, was waiting by the gang's horses. Not realizing Grat was inside, marshal Connelly rushed towards the shed. Grat was too badly wounded to raise his rifle to his shoulder. He did manage to fire from his hip, stopping the lawman in his tracks. The marshal collapsed on the dusty street, dying. Kloehr, meanwhile, had taken up a position behind a board fence. He had a good view of the alley. He was accompanied by a barber named Carey Seaman who had a shotgun loaded with buckshot.

The Dalton gang members weren't the only ones in the alley. Someone was trying to drive a team of horses down the alley. The horses were pulling an oil tank. When shooting broke out, the driver got scared and raced off to hide. The horses began rearing up, which blocked Kloehr and Seaman's view. Kloehr shot the horses down, just as the Dalton gang were about to reach their own mounts. Aware he was dying, Grat walked out of the shed on very unsteady feet. He fired a couple shots from the hip at Kloehr and Seaman. Kloehr aimed and shot the outlaw through the throat. Grat fell dead on the street, next to marshal Connelly who was drawing his last breaths. The expiring Powers managed to make it to the horses. Despite his wounds, he climbed onto his horse, only to be knocked off by a barrage of shots. He fell off his mount, dead.

The incapacitated Broadwell suddenly showed up at the scene. He had managed to drag himself through the lumber yard. He reached the horses and in terrible pain, tried to climb on to his mount. Kloehr and Seaman spotted him and opened fire. Broadwell was hit again, but managed to stay in the saddle.

His horse, untied from the fence, went berserk and started racing. Broadwell remained in the saddle as his horse stampeded out of town. The horse was found about a mile outside Coffeyville, next to Broadwell's lifeless corpse. Bob and Emmett tried to get on their horses. Emmett had the money bag, which he tied to his saddle as Bob covered him with his rifle.

From an upper floor of a building, a town resident fired at the two brothers but missed. Bob shot back, thus giving his presence away to the sharp-shooting Kloehr. Bob spotted Kloehr, just as Kloehr fired a round at him. Bob got off a wild shot of his own, but was hit in the bowels. He staggered about, going down the alley. In a daze Bob sat down on some stones, rifle still in hand. Then he came to his senses and stood up and staggered some more. He careened towards the shed where Grat had been killed and leaned against it for support. Bob fired a couple more shots that didn't hit anything. Kloehr took aim and pulled the trigger of his rifle. Bob fell down, mortally wounded.

By this point, Emmett was the last man standing. He had managed to mount his horse, but didn't realize his brother, Bob, was dying. The horses on either side of Emmett were both shot and killed, but he stayed mounted. Emmett took a round in the arm, and then another bullet pierced his hips. It was only as he started to ride out of town that he noticed Bob wasn't with him. Emmett turned his horse and raced to where Bob lay by the shed. He leaned over his critically injured brother just as Seaman let loose with both barrels of his shotgun. Emmett was hit in the back and fell off his horse, landing next to his dying brother. At this point, the gunfire finally ceased. Four bandits had been killed and it was presumed Emmett would die as well. In addition to his other wounds, Emmett had a dozen pieces of buckshot in his back. Coffeyville residents cautiously emerged from their hiding and shooting places. Emmett was given a look-over. He seemed to be dying, which was the only reason the townspeople didn't lynch him.

Once the gunfight ended, some townspeople mounted their horses and began racing out of Coffeyville, spreading the news of their great victory. These riders breathlessly announced to everyone they came by that the Dalton gang had been wiped out. After hearing this news, a rider who had been heading into Coffeyville turned his horse around in the other direction and left in a hurry. The rider was Bill Doolin, who had managed to find a new horse and fix his saddle on it. Doolin was riding to meet his comrades. Instead, he became the only member of the Dalton gang who wasn't killed or captured during the ill-fated double robbery. Doolin was killed a few years later.

The wounded Emmett was shown the bodies of the four dead gang members. He identified his brothers, gave fake names for the other two men, and then wept. He was moved into a bed as enterprising townspeople put the Dalton gang's corpses on display at the city jail. As news of the disaster spread, hundreds of people started pouring into Coffeyville to view the bodies and crime scene. They were accompanied by curious reporters. "Last of the Dalton Gang–the Band of Desperadoes Practically Exterminated–Four of them Killed and a Fifth Dying" read a headline from the October 6, 1892, *New York Times*.

Emmett didn't die, however. He gave an interview which explained the purpose of the foolish attack on the town ("To Surpass Jesse James—Why the Daltons Made the Coffeyville Raid" blared a headline in the October 7, 1892, *New York Times*). After recovering, Emmett was put on trial and given a life sentence. He served 14.5 years then managed to get pardoned. Out of jail, Emmett wrote a book about the Dalton's exploits that was later turned into a movie. He died at age 65 in Los Angeles, the sole survivor of a daring robbery gone spectacularly wrong.

See also: James, Jesse

Further Reading

"After the Dalton Gang," *New York Times*, August 1, 1892.

"An Outlaw Band Surrounded," *New York Times*, October 12, 1891.

"Another Train Robbery," *New York Times*, October 14, 1892.

"Held Up an Express Train," *New York Times*, July 16, 1892.

"Last of the Dalton Gang," *New York Times*, October 6, 1892.

"To Surpass Jesse James," *New York Times*, October 7, 1892.

Paul Wellman, *A Dynasty of Western Outlaws*, 1961.

DEAD RABBITS

The Dead Rabbits emerged from the same squalor and filth that produced countless other New York street gangs in the 19th century. The gang came into existence in the 1840s in Manhattan's horrid Five Points district, a slum of terrible repute.

At first, the Dead Rabbits were part of another gang called the Roach Guards. The Roach Guards suffered from internal dissension. According to legend, someone tossed a dead rabbit into a room where Roach Guard factions were arguing. Breakaway Roach Guard members decided to adopt this animal as their emblem. At the time, "rabbit" was street slang for a rowdy person, with "dead rabbit" meaning someone who was very rowdy. The Dead Rabbits would proudly head into battle, led by a standard bearer toting a dead bunny on a stake. In an interesting foreshadowing of the color war to come between contemporary gangs such as the Crips and Bloods, the Dead Rabbits painted red stripes on their pants, while their arch rivals, the Roach Guards, wore blue stripes.

Brawls between the Dead Rabbits and Roach Guards, or other gangs such as the Bowery Boys, happened frequently. These wars were no small affair. Brawls could last for days, as members erected street barricades and fought it out with guns, knives, stones, bricks and blackjacks. Some of the fighting took on a political or ethnic dimension. The Dead Rabbits supported the corrupt local political machine named Tammany Hall. Tammany's power base lay with the poor Irish immigrants, who were entering the city in waves at the time. American-born citizens of Anglo-Saxon descent were alarmed by this Celtic flood. Gang leaders such as Bill "the Butcher" Poole, a former Bowery Boy who broke off to form his own crew, were strongly anti-Tammany Hall and anti-Irish. In an 1850 New York election, Irish-American political leader John Morrissey was hired to supervise voting in one of the city's poorer districts. Morrissey, in turn, paid fifty members of the Dead Rabbits to guard the polls. Poole arrived with thirty of his own street warriors, intent on smashing up the polling station. They had a brief face-off with the Dead

Rabbits. Then, seeing they were outnumbered, Poole's men retreated.

If they were pro-Tammany, the Dead Rabbits were also equal opportunists when it came to mayhem. One of their most prominent early members was a woman known as "Hell-Cat Maggie." She allegedly filed her teeth into points and wore sharp brass fingernails (the better for cutting and stabbing). She would go into battle screeching like a wildcat and tearing at unlucky men with tooth and claw. Other women would also accompany the Rabbits during riots, carrying supplies of ammunition and encouraging their men with shrill taunts.

The Dead Rabbits were prime instigators of the Fourth of July riots of 1857. Along with an allied gang called the Plug Uglies, the Dead Rabbits descended on the Bowery, home turf of the Bowery Boys. The Bowery Boys, backed by the Atlantic Guards, met the invaders and a huge brawl erupted that lasted for hours. Clubs, paving stones, and bricks were used as weapons, along with knives, blackjacks and guns. At the time, New York law enforcement was divided between two separate police forces—one controlled by the mayor, the other controlled by commissioners appointed by the state governor. The end result was chaos, as the two police departments spent more time squabbling than arresting felons. During the Fourth of July riots, the municipal police refused to help their peers on the state-controlled force restore order. On July 5 a huge collection of roughly 5,000 gangsters from all over the Five Points neighborhood congregated and marched en masse to the Bowery. There, they locked in battle with an equal number of Bowery thugs. During a lull in the fighting, Dead Rabbits stormed the rooftops of several local buildings in order to hurl down missiles in the form of bricks and stones at the municipal police. The riot finally ended when the National Guard showed up in full force. With the municipal police as a spearhead, the Guard pushed the now exhausted rioters back to their own neighborhoods.

The Fourth of July riots killed anywhere from eight to 100 people. These riots pale in comparison, however, with the apocalyptic Draft Riots that razed New York in July 1863. The Draft Riots were triggered by federal legislation to conscript men into military service. The Civil War had been grinding on for three bloody years by this point, and few New Yorkers, patriotic as they were to the northern cause, wanted to join the fray. Apparently, fighting on the streets of Manhattan was more appealing than fighting the Confederates. The Dead Rabbits, along with every other gang in town, participated in the Draft Riots with great enthusiasm. The riot soon turned into a pogrom against Blacks (whose promised freedom was seen as the cause of the Civil War, in rioters' eyes). African-Americans were beaten and lynched on the streets, with some of them tortured, then doused in oil, hung up on posts, and set ablaze. Rioters looted and burned houses at will, including an orphanage for African-American children. The Draft Riots ended when President Lincoln sent in federal troops. Soldiers used rifle fire, bayonets, and artillery to subdue the raging mob. Some sources claim that hundreds of people were killed in the Draft Riots. An exact casualty figure is unknown. These 1863 urban uprisings are still the most destructive riots in American history—far greater in scope and intensity than the Rodney King riot that shook Los

Angeles in 1992, or the ghetto uprisings of the 1960s.

For all their ferocity in the Draft Riots, the Dead Rabbits were largely gone by the late 1800s, replaced by newer, younger gangs. The Rabbits left behind a legacy of bloodshed, street violence and collusion with local politicians. Decades after they vanished from the scene, the Dead Rabbits were featured prominently in Martin Scorsese's film version of *Gangs of New York*.

See Also: Kelly, Paul; Osterman, Edward "Monk" Eastman

Further Reading

Herbert Asbury, *The Gangs of New York*, 1927.

Helena Katz, *Gang Wars: Blood and Guts on the Streets of Early New York*, 2005.

"Riot in the Sixth Ward: The Feuds of the Dead Rabbits," *New York Times*, February 14, 1859.

"Rioting and Bloodshed the Fourth and Fifth of July," *New York Times*, August 6, 1857.

Joe Sharkey, "Word for Word/New York Gangs; The Dapper Don and Company Were a Bunch of Copycats," *New York Times*, May 3, 1998.

DRUG TRADE

Charles "Lucky" Luciano was one of the first gangsters to get involved in the illegal drug trade. In 1915 the 18-year-old mobster-in-training purchased a supply of drugs, either opium or morphine according to varying accounts, which he

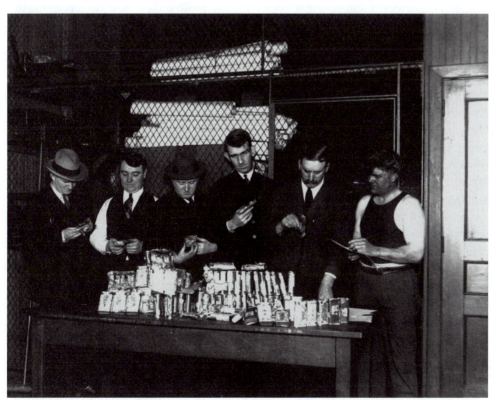

Smoking opium valued at $25,000, seized on a ship in Brooklyn, New York, by members of the Surveyors' Searching Squad of New York, 1925. [AP Photo]

sold to addicts in his neighborhood. Luciano was caught and spent six months in a reformatory. He was something of a pioneer, given that non-medical use of opiates had only recently been banned by federal law. As it happened, Luciano was one of the first in a line of criminals to recognize the vast potential in selling illegal drugs.

Initially, organized crime had little to do with drug trafficking. This was largely because in the decades after the Civil War, opiates, cocaine, marijuana and other drugs were legally available and cheaply priced. "The Consumers Union Report on Licit and Illicit Drugs," published in 1972, has described 19th century America as "a dope fiend's paradise." Drugs could be purchased legally from doctors, over-the-counter in drugstores, in grocery and general stores, or even by mail. Hard drugs could also be found in "patent medicines," compounds of dubious medical merit, sold as cure-alls for vague ailments. Some of these medicines were "soothing syrups" designed to quiet crying babies. Patent medicines usually didn't contain a list of ingredients, or even a hint that they contained heavy drugs or alcohol. As a result, many people inadvertently became hooked.

Even legitimate doctors regarded opium, the parent drug for heroin, morphine and codeine, as a miracle drug. Physicians referred to opium and morphine as "God's Own Medicine." Addiction was not well understood at the time, and some doctors even recommended that alcoholics switch to morphine, which they considered less destructive. In a time of medical care that seems primitive compared to today's advances, pain-killing drugs were something miraculous. Patients might still die from various illnesses and infections, but at least now their sufferings could be lessened. Opium was grown legally across the U.S. in the 19th century, and two or three grains of morphine could be purchased for mere pennies, an astonishingly cheap price for hard drugs by today's standards.

The typical 19th-century drug user was very different from today's. Consumers Union cites an 1878 study of 1,313 opiate drug users living in Michigan. The survey determined that 61.2 percent were female. Likewise, an 1880 Chicago survey found 169 of 235 habitual opium users were female. These results were not surprising: opiate drugs, particularly laudanum (a tincture of opium and alcohol) were freely given to women to ease the pain of childbirth. This gender skew would change drastically over the years. By the 1960s, male addicts outnumbered female by a ratio of five to one.

Cocaine-laced products were fashionable in the late 1800s. A popular beverage called Vin Mariani (named after the chemist who made it) consisted of a mix of wine and cocaine. This cocaine-laden wine was popular with Pope Leo XIII and Queen Victoria. The success of this wine might have influenced the launch of Coca-Cola, a soft drink that originally contained coca leaves.

Marijuana was commonly grown in the Victorian era, although few people were smoking it. The fiber from hemp (a non-intoxicating cousin of marijuana) which is used for making ropes and clothes) was cultivated extensively, particularly in Kentucky. Marijuana itself was used for medicinal purposes. It was listed in the United States Pharmacopeia from 1850 to 1942. Marijuana use as an intoxicant was very rare, however.

While it wasn't a crime to take drugs, their use was not encouraged. Drug-taking was seen as a disreputable vice, on par with gambling, drinking, smoking, or being sexually promiscuous. The earliest laws against drugs were generally rooted in racism. In 1875 San Francisco banned opium smoking in the city. Smoking opium was a common habit among Chinese workers, who were brought into the U.S. to help build railroads. The ban only applied to smoking (which is how the Chinese consumed it), not eating or taking opium in other ways.

Exact totals are hard to come by, but it's estimated that about three out of 1000 people were drug addicts at the turn of the 20th century. In 1905 *Collier's* magazine ran a famous expose on patent medicines, pointing out the harmful and addictive nature of many of these products. The U.S. Congress responded one year later with the Pure Food and Drug Act. The Act required medicine manufacturers to clearly label the ingredients of their products. Sales of patent medicines crashed when consumers realized what was actually in them.

The move to ban drugs began to pick up steam in the early 1900s. The anti-drug campaign stemmed from two different motivations: genuine concern about addiction and base racism against minority groups associated with drug use. Newspaper headlines tell the story. "Drug Crazed Negroes Start a Reign of Terror and Defy Whole Mississippi Town," reads a September 29, 1913, piece in the *New York Times*. Another story, from February 8, 1914, was tagged, "Negro Cocaine 'Fiends' Are a New Southern Menace." An April 30, 1905, *Times* article with the headline "Cocaine Habit's Horrors" noted that "In the south, some of the worst crimes committed by the negroes result from the use of cocaine."

Racism was not limited to African-Americans. A March 15, 1906, article in the *New York Times* with the headline "Patent Medicine Bill to Curb Drug Users" stated, ". . . of the 250 white girls, some no more than 14 years old, now living in Chinatown, New York, 60 percent of them were cocaine and opium fiends." Cocaine was associated with African-Americans, opium with Asians, and marijuana with Mexicans. All three groups were said to go berserk when on these drugs. Minorities were also accused of using drugs to seduce unwitting white girls.

Individual states began to clamp down on hard drugs. In March 1907, for example, the New York state assembly unanimously passed a law requiring a prescription from a doctor in order to purchase cocaine.

A few well-known gangsters were caught up in early drug raids. Monk Eastman, head of a notorious gang of thugs in New York City, was arrested for smoking opium in 1912. He was jailed for eight months.

In 1913 California became the first state to prohibit marijuana, though it was unclear if anyone noticed, as the ban attracted virtually no media attention. One year later, Utah banned the use of marijuana, a habit brought into the state from Mormons returning from Mexico.

On December 17, 1914, partly to fulfill international treaty obligations, Congress approved the Harrison Narcotics Act. The Act came into force on March 1, 1915. On the surface, the bill didn't appear to ban non-medical drug use at all. It merely called for tax and registration requirements on the part of people who sold or prescribed "opium or coca leaves, their salts, derivatives or preparations." Doctors were allowed to keep prescribing drugs within "the course of professional practice only."

Physicians thought this meant they simply needed to get a license and keep strict records if they wanted to recommend opiate or coca-based drugs, for whatever reason. Law enforcement took a narrower view. In their opinion, giving drugs to addicts just to maintain their habit didn't constitute "professional practices." Once the Harrison Act was imposed, doctors who continued to prescribe maintenance doses to addicts found themselves under arrest. Physicians got the hint and stopped prescribing to people already addicted.

No one was really sure how many addicts there were in the United States at the time. Estimates ranged from 100,000 to one million. A study by the United States Public Health Services in the 1920s figured there were probably around 215,000 opiate addicts in the U.S. prior to the Harrison Narcotics Act.

The federal government continued to impose tough laws. In 1924 it became illegal to import heroin (basically, a stronger version of morphine), even for medical reasons. Penalties became harsher. While the Harrison Act called for a five-year maximum sentence for violations, this was beefed up to ten years in the early 1920s.

If doctors wouldn't help them, the underworld was more than happy to supply addicts with drugs. After his release from the reformatory, teenage Luciano went to work for Arnold Rothstein, the grey eminence of organized crime. Rothstein didn't directly run rackets, but provided seed money for other criminals to get various illicit projects off the ground. In addition to bootlegging, Rothstein

funded drug smuggling operations. He sent emissaries to Europe and Asia in the 1920s to purchase opium and other drugs. These, in turn, were smuggled back to the United States. In this way, Rothstein became one of the first major criminal traffickers of illegal drugs.

The money to be had in drug sales was impressive, even in the early days. For example, Federal Narcotics Commissioner Harry Anslinger noted that heroin, which cost $25–$50 an ounce in the 1920s, was retailing for $3,000 an ounce by the 1950s. As drugs became less available, their value shot up dramatically in price.

Anslinger was largely responsible for the federal ban on marijuana (also called pot). Authorities knew very little about pot, except that Mexican immigrants were fond of it. It was thought that marijuana gave Mexicans superhuman strength and made them criminally insane. By the late 1930s, every state but two had passed laws prohibiting marijuana. Anslinger set his sights on getting a federal law against pot. To this end, he testified before Congress about pot's allegedly dreadful impact. He relied heavily on gory anecdotes about hideous murders and rapes supposedly committed by marijuana users. Congress was appropriately horrified and responded with the Marijuana Tax Act in 1937. Modeled after the Harrison Narcotics Act, the legislation imposed a tax for medical use of pot and banned non-medical, non-taxed use of the drug.

For several decades, Anslinger was the main federal bureaucrat fighting the illicit drug trade. Interestingly enough, J. Edgar Hoover, director of the Federal Bureau of Investigation (FBI) didn't want to get involved in drug cases. Just as Hoover denied there was such a thing as the Mafia, he insisted that drug offences were better handled by state and local authorities. It is believed Hoover worried that his agents might be prone to bribery or addiction if they pursued undercover drug cases.

From the 1940s to the early 1960s, state and federal penalties on drugs continued to get tougher. By early 1970, second-time offenders in Missouri could get life sentences for possessing marijuana. Judges in Texas could impose life on first-time offenders, while possession of marijuana in Louisiana netted a mandatory five -year sentence to hard labor for anyone over the age of twenty-one.

These penalties had an impact, and were likely the reason why the Mafia opposed trafficking (in theory, at least). This anti-drug stance had little to do with morality. Top Mafia bosses correctly summarized that stiff penalties might induce lower-ranking mobsters to talk if they were arrested on narcotics charges. Faced with the prospect of decades in jail, arrestees might start spilling secrets to police in order to get lighter sentences. To prevent such an unthinkable violation of "omerta" (the Mafia code of silence), family bosses counseled against drug dealing.

"No narcotics. You are in serious trouble if you were arrested for narcotics. After (Mafia boss Albert) Anastasia died in 1957, all families were notified—no narcotics," Mafia turncoat Joseph Valachi said in testimony before the Senate in the early 1960s.

Of course, some Mafia crime families simply ignored this stricture. The Lucchese family was involved in drug trafficking, as was the Magaddino family, based near Buffalo. In Senate hearings, Valachi admitted that many Mafia members couldn't resist the enormous profits involved in selling drugs. Valachi himself was arrested in the mid-1950s on drug charges and given five years in jail (dropped when his conviction was reversed). Released from prison, Valachi promptly got arrested again on drug charges in November 1959, and drew a fifteen year sentence to be served at a federal penitentiary in Atlanta.

In the early days, the Mafia didn't really need to impose a ban on trafficking, because demand for illegal drugs was very low. Opiates, marijuana and cocaine were only used by a fringe minority, including jazz musicians, artistic types and a few daring rebels. Illicit drug use didn't become mainstream until the mid-1960s, when young people began experimenting with marijuana and LSD en masse.

As drug use exploded, the underworld stepped up to provide a supply for boosted demand. In 1973, for example, Harlem mobster Leroy "Nicky" Barnes organized drug dealers into a city-wide syndicate called "the Council." Barnes received his supply of drugs from Mafia wholesalers, who were happy to let African-Americans retail their product on the streets of New York City.

Certain drugs, such as powder cocaine, took on a hip status. Cocaine was expensive and the preferred treat of the rich and hip. Coca plants (the raw ingredient for cocaine) grew extensively in South America. Traffickers would pay farmers to grow coca, which was then processed into cocaine and smuggled to the United States. By the mid-1970s, Miami had become "the drug capital of the Western Hemisphere" due to its geographical location, notes a report on the Drug Enforcement Administration (DEA) Web site. South Florida teemed with violent Latin American drug traffickers. In 1970, the U.S. Customs service seized 108 pounds of cocaine, a total that leapt to 729 pounds in 1975. By 1979, the illicit drug trade was Florida's largest industry, worth $10 billion per year on the wholesale market, states the DEA.

As use of drugs, particularly marijuana, became more common, most U.S. states modified their drug laws. In the 1970s, several states, including California and New York, "decriminalized" small amounts of pot (that is, removed the threat of jail—but not necessarily a fine or a record—for simple possession).

President Ronald Reagan reignited the so-called "war on drugs" in the early 1980s. This call to arms was marked by the sudden emergence of crack cocaine in 1985. Crack cocaine is simply powder cocaine that has been mixed with baking soda and water to turn it into a solid. The word "crack" comes from the crackling sound the drug makes when smoked. It provides a very short, very intense high that is extremely addictive. Whereas powder cocaine was primarily used by wealthy Whites, crack became popular among poor, inner-city Blacks.

By the late 1980s, over 10,000 gang members were dealing crack in fifty U.S. cities, reports the DEA. Brutal violence was one of the most significant features of this new drug market. A 1988 study by the Bureau of Justice Statistics found that crack use played a role in 32 percent of all homicides and 60 percent of drug-related homicides in New York City.

Crack gangs used the proceeds of their crimes to invest in heavy weaponry. By the late 1980s, it was common to see gangsters armed with Mac-10 and Uzi sub-machine guns or AK-47 assault rifles. A similar phenomenon occurred during Alcohol Prohibition. Money from bootlegging was used to purchase military style firearms such as machine guns and automatic rifles. Crack dealers, just like bootleggers of the Roaring Twenties, began shooting it out in public for market share.

The 1990s saw the emergence of methamphetamine as a major public health threat. Methamphetamine (meth) is basically just a stronger version of amphetamine, a stimulant. Invented in 1919, meth was used for years by soldiers, blue-collar workers, farmers, bikers, students, and truck drivers to stay awake. A combination of new cooking methods and downloadable recipes on the Internet led to a resurgence of methamphetamine use in the 1990s. Like crack, methamphetamine is extremely addictive and destructive. Unlike crack, methamphetamine is largely popular with poor, rural White users who use it for recreational purposes or simply to work harder.

Made in clandestine labs, meth was initially sold and distributed by bike gangs. The drug was nicknamed "crank" because bikers allegedly stored the drug in the crankcases of their motorcycles. As methamphetamine became more common, other organized crime groups began to muscle the bikers aside.

"In the mid-1990s, trafficking groups from Mexico became deeply involved in the methamphetamine trade, replacing domestic outlaw motorcycle gangs as the predominant methamphetamine producers, traffickers and distributors," reads a DEA history.

Today, the drug war continues to grind on. As the main federal department enforcing drug laws, the DEA made 26,425 arrests in 2008, up from 19,884 in 1986. FBI data indicates there was a total of 1,841,182 arrests for drugs by federal, state and local authorities in 2007. A little under half of these arrests were for simple marijuana possession.

In 2008 the DEA seized 49,823.3 kilos of cocaine, 598.6 kilos of heroin, 660,969.2 kilos of marijuana, 1,540.4 kilos of methamphetamine, and 9,199,693 dosage units of hallucinogens. These seizures are up sharply from 1986, when DEA seized 29,389 kilos of cocaine, 421 kilos of heroin, 491,831 kilos of marijuana, 234.5 kilos of meth, and 4,146,329 dosage units of hallucinogens. As with Alcohol Prohibition, authorities only manage to stop a small fraction of total drugs coming into the country.

The National Drug Threat Assessment 2009 report, by the U.S. Department of Justice, focuses heavily on the dangers posed by Mexican drug trafficking organizations (DTOs).

"DTOs represent the greatest organized crime threat to the United States," reads the document. Mexican DTOs have established transportation routes and affiliations with street gangs across the United States. The majority of cocaine available in the U.S. is smuggled over the border with Mexico by DTOs. Mexico is also "the primary foreign source of marijuana in the United States," adds the report. Roughly 15,500 metric tons of cannabis were produced in Mexico in 2007, largely for export to the U.S., estimates the Department of Justice.

By contrast, the Royal Canadian Mounted Police (RCMP) estimates that crime groups produce about 1,399 to 3,498 metric tons of marijuana in Canada each year, destined primarily for the U.S.

According to the National Gang Threat Assessment 2009 by the U.S. Department of Justice, if Mexican based DTOs are the main "wholesalers," or those responsible for bringing in huge amounts of drugs, then street, prison and motorcycle gangs are the main retailers, making sales to users.

Street gangs involved in drug trade include:

- Almighty Latin King and Queen Nation (founded 1960s in Chicago mostly Mexican and Puerto Rican men, 2,200–7,500 members in 15 cities)
- Asian Boyz (founded 1970s in southern California, mostly Asian composition, 1,300–2,000 members nationwide, one of the largest Asian street gangs in the United States)
- Black P. Stone (Chicago-based, primarily Black members, 6–8,000 members arrayed in a federation of "Seven highly structured street gangs with a single leader and a common culture," according to the Gang Threat Assessment 2009)
- Bloods (formed early 1970s in Los Angeles to oppose the Crips, mostly African-American male followers, with 5–20,000 members in 120 cities)
- Crips (founded 1969 in Los Angeles, primarily African-American membership, with 30–35,000 members nationwide)
- Gangster Disciples (founded in the mid-1960s in Chicago primarily African-American composition with a membership of 25,000–50,000 in 110 cities)

- Latin Disciples (founded in Chicago in the late 1960s, primarily Hispanic membership, 1,500–2,000 members, mostly in the Great Lakes and Southwest regions)

- Mara Salvatrucha (founded in Latin-America, primarily Hispanic membership, 10,000 members in the United States, also called MS-13, this gang is noted for its level of violence)

- Vice Lord Nation (Chicago-based, mostly African-American composition, 30–35,000 members, collection of gangs governed by a national board)

Prison gangs involved in drug trade include:

- Aryan Brotherhood (primarily based in Southwest and Pacific regions, mostly white membership, noted for its levels of violence)

- Barrio Azteca (violence-prone gang primarily-based in Texas and the Southwest regions, mostly Hispanic composition, 2,000 members)

- Black Guerrilla Family (founded 1966 in San Quentin State Prison, California, mostly Black membership, 100–300 members, organized along paramilitary lines)

- Mexican Mafia (founded in late 1950s, mostly Hispanic membership, 200 members, also known as La Eme, Spanish for letter "M")

Outlaw motorcycle gangs involved in drug trade include:

- Bandidos (founded in Texas, currently most active in Pacific, Southwest, Southeast, West Central regions, 2,000–2,500 members around the world, regarded as one of the largest outlaw biker gangs in the United States)

- Hells Angels (founded late 1940s in California, 2,000–2,500 members around the world, best known outlaw biker gang in world)

- Mongols (primarily based in Pacific and Southwest, mostly Hispanic membership, 800–850 members, extremely violent gang that has brawled with Hells Angels)

- Outlaws (predominant in Great Lakes region, 1,700 members in 176 chapters around world, rival to the Hells Angels)

- Sons of Silence (250–275 members in 12 U.S. states)

The old Italian-American Mafia also has its hands in the drug trade. Part of the conflict in the 1980s between rising mob boss John Gotti and Gambino crime family boss Paul Castellano was due to the former's heavy involvement in drug operations. Henry Hill, long-time Mafia associate, was also a major drug trafficker.

In the mid-1980s, mobster Rosario Gambino of the crime family that bears his name, was found guilty of a conspiracy to sell heroin and sentenced to forty-five years in jail. Gambino was linked to the "Pizza Connection" probe, which centered on a heroin and cocaine smuggling operation that used pizzerias as fronts. He was deported to Italy in May 2009.

The allure of drug trade remains obvious. According to the United Nations 2008 World Drug Report, a gram of heroin was retailing at $172 in the U.S., while cocaine was going for $119 a gram. The DEA pegged methamphetamine prices at a mean of $237.99 a gram in mid-2008. A pound of meth was wholesaling for $16,500–19,500 in Los Angeles in mid-2008. The wholesale price of marijuana in Los Angeles in the same time period ranged from $750 a pound for middling quality pot, to $2,500–6,000 for a pound of high-quality dope.

The 2007 National Survey on Drug Use and Health by the Substance Abuse and Mental Health Services Administration (SAMHSA) found that twenty million Americans twelve years of age or older had recently used illegal drugs. This works out to around 8 percent of the population.

SAMHSA estimated the number of recent marijuana smokers at 14.4 million, versus 2.1 million for cocaine, 529,000 for methamphetamine, and one million for hallucinogens. Opiate drug use, meanwhile, is common among about 0.6 percent of the U.S. adult population, according to other reports.

The Centers for Disease Control and Prevention (CDC) estimates roughly 438,000 Americans die each year from tobacco, while 80,000 die from alcohol. The number of "drug induced deaths" was estimated at 38,396 in 2006 by the CDC. The latter has increased considerably from 1990, when the CDC recorded 9,463 drug-induced deaths, rising to 15,973 by 1997.

There are considerable economic costs from drug use as well. The National Institute on Drug Abuse (NIDA) pegged health, crime, and lost productivity costs caused by illegal drugs at $181 billion a year. Tobacco costs came in at $168 billion, and alcohol at $185 billion.

Drug policy is one of the most hotly debated topics in North American political discourse. Some critics say the drug war has failed; they point to the unsuccessful Prohibition on alcohol as an example of the negative consequences of trying to ban popular intoxicants. Drug law reformers believe that criminalizing drugs keeps their price artificially high (thus making them a desirable commodity for gangsters) while providing zero quality controls or health warnings.

Drug war supporters think this is nonsense and that any move towards loosening drug laws would increase addiction. They argue that if mobsters stopped selling drugs, they would simply move to other rackets (as what happened after Prohibition was repealed in 1933). Tougher enforcement and greater drug education, they believe, is the answer. It is unlikely this debate will be settled any time soon.

See Also: Mafia; Prohibition

Further Reading

"Anti-Cocaine Bill Passed," *New York Times*, March 29, 1907.

Dan Baum, *Smoke and Mirrors: The War on Drugs and the Politics of Failure*, 1996.

Edward M. Brecher and editors, "The Consumers Union Report on Licit and Illicit Drugs," *Consumer Reports Magazine*, 1972.

Centers for Disease Control and Prevention Quick Stats—General Information on Alcohol Use and Health

"Cocaine Evil Among Negroes," *New York Times*, November 3, 1902.

"Cocaine Forbidden in the U.S. Mails," *New York Times*, July 17, 1908.

"Cocaine Habit's Horrors," *New York Times*, April 30, 1905.

Ariel David, "U.S. Deports Gambino Mafia Boss to Italy," *Yahoo! News*, May 23, 2009.

Mike Gray, *Drug Crazy: How We Got Into This Mess and How We Can Get Out*, 1998.

National Drug Threat Assessment 2009, National Drug Intelligence Center, U.S. Department of Justice

National Gang Threat Assessment 2009, National Gang Intelligence Center, U.S. Department of Justice

National Survey on Drug Use and Health, Substance Abuse and Mental Health Services Administration, 2007.

"Negro Cocaine Evil," *New York Times*, March 20, 1905.

"NIDA InfoFacts: Understanding Drug Abuse and Addiction," National Institute on Drug Abuse

"Patent Medicine Bill To Curb Drug Users," *New York Times*, March 15, 1906.

David Robbins, *Heavy Traffic: 30 Years of Headlines and Major Ops From the Case Files of the DEA*, 2005.

"10 Dead, 20 Hurt in a Race Riot: Drug-Crazed Negroes Start a Reign of Terror and Defy Whole Mississippi Town," *New York Times*, September 29, 1913.

Evan Thomas, "America's Crusade," *TIME*, September 15, 1986.

2008 World Drug Report, United Nations Office on Drugs and Crime

U.S. Drug Enforcement Administration http://www.usdoj.gov/dea/index.htm and http://www.usdoj.gov/dea/history.htm.

Edward Huntington Williams, "Negro Cocaine 'Fiends' Are a New Southern Menace," *New York Times*, February 8, 1914.

E-G

EASTMAN, EDWARD "MONK"

See: Osterman, Edward "Monk" Eastman

GENNA BROTHERS

They were called the "Terrible Gennas" for their violent tendencies and perhaps the quality of the bootleg liquor they peddled. The six fierce Genna brothers—Sam, Angelo, Mike, Jim, Antonio (Tony) and Peter—were all born in Sicily. The clan moved to Chicago in 1910 where the Gennas' father took a job in a railway yard. The boys grew up tough in Little Italy, a neighborhood they came to dominate.

The Genna brothers moved through various rackets while coming of age, including pimping, extortion and running brothels. They didn't become rich, however, until the advent of Prohibition in 1919.

After Prohibition came into effect, the Gennas somehow acquired a government license to make industrial alcohol (which was still legal). They redistilled this poisonous product to produce batches of bootleg liquor. The latter was doused in chemicals and coloring to make it look and taste more like real whisky. That said, the product was still highly dangerous. It could potentially kill someone who drank it or leave them blind, two side effects that didn't bother the Genna boys one bit. Despite the noxious quality of their brew, the Gennas couldn't keep up with demand for illegal alcohol.

To expand their bootlegging empire, the Genna brothers hired hundreds of poor Italian families to produce cheap liquor in their residences. The Gennas paid these "alky cookers" $15 a day (a princely sum at the time) to turn their residences into mini-distilleries. Each alky cooker could distil roughly 350 gallons of vile alcohol a week. The Gennas sold this product wholesale for $6 a gallon. The brothers were soon earning $350,000 a month from their liquor operations.

The Gennas established a reputation for extreme violence and corruption. They hired scores of policemen to escort their liquor-laden trucks. The Genna brothers made little effort to hide their bootleg facilities, or the fact that they kept hundreds of policemen on their payroll.

In the early 1920s Johnny Torrio was the major underworld figure in Chicago. A businessman at heart, Torrio arranged a truce among the top bootleggers in the city, a group which included the Gennas. Each gang agreed to stick to a given territory and not impede each other's business.

The Gennas were the biggest power in Little Italy. In addition to Torrio (and his protégé, Al Capone), the Gennas were erstwhile allies of Dion O'Banion, leading mobster in Chicago's North End. A wily Irishman, O'Banion headed a loyal gang of hundreds of thugs. He ran a flower shop when he wasn't busy ordering beatings and killings.

While they respected Torrio, the Genna boys despised O'Banion, which was understandable given that the Irish gang leader was prejudiced against Italians, openly calling them "greaseballs" and "dagos."

Needless to say, Torrio's truce didn't last long. The Gennas got greedy and began flooding their allies' territories with cheaply priced, low-quality liquor. Genna representatives beat up North Side bar owners to induce them to stock their vile product.

O'Banion was deeply offended, and not just because the Genna brothers were breaking the terms of the truce. He was personally affronted by the Gennas' rotgut spirits. O'Banion's bootleg brew was more expensive but of considerably higher quality. To underline his annoyance, the Irish gang boss arranged the hijacking of a $30,000 shipment of Genna liquor. Given the Gennas' propensity for extreme violence, the audacity of this move astonished O'Banion's fellow gangsters.

The Genna boys demanded that O'Banion be killed. Torrio insisted on abiding by the truce, however, and tried his best to appease both sides.

At this juncture, O'Banion pulled his notorious practical "joke" on Torrio, setting the gang boss up for arrest at the Sieben brewery (a facility jointly owned by Torrio, Capone and O'Banion) on the evening of May 19, 1924. After this "prank" Torrio changed his mind about keeping the peace. He agreed that O'Banion should be killed.

If O'Banion was aware of these machinations, he didn't care. In fact, the gang boss soon compounded his problems with the Genna clan.

By early November 1924 Angelo Genna had run up a $30,000 IOU at a gangster run casino. Capone was willing to overlook the debt for the sake of keeping the Gennas happy, but O'Banion wasn't. O'Banion placed a snarky phone call to Angelo, giving him one week to pay up. He threatened the volatile mob boss as if he were a lowly, anonymous gambler who was behind on his tab.

On November 10, 1924, O'Banion was shot dead in his flower-shop by three assailants. It is believed two of the assassins were John Scalise and Albert Anselmi (a pair of highly skilled hitmen). The third man was thought to be either Frankie Yale (who had murdered gang boss "Big Jim" Colosimo earlier in the decade) or Mike Genna. If the Gennas weren't directly involved in the killing, they certainly supported it.

Eccentric as he was, O'Banion inspired intense loyalty in his followers. After O'Banion died his second-in-command, George "Bugs" Moran, took over the gang and vowed revenge.

Oblivious, the Genna brothers decided the time had come to expand their operations. Angelo Genna became the head of the Unione Siciliana (a fraternal, mob-controlled association representing Sicilian-Americans). He didn't have long to enjoy his new position, however. On May 25, 1925, Angelo departed in a roadster from the luxury Chicago hotel he was staying at. A sedan containing "Bugs" Moran and two other O'Banion stalwarts, Vincent "the Schemer" Drucci and Earl "Hymie" Weiss, began to follow. Angelo spotted the sedan and tried to outrace it. He ended up smashing his roadster around a lamppost. The sedan pulled up and raked the wrecked roadster with gunfire. Angelo, who was trapped behind the wheel, was hit and killed.

One month later, Mike Genna was driving around Chicago with Anselmi and Scalise. A police car spotted the men and started off in pursuit. As with Angelo, the car containing Mike Genna crashed. The three occupants leapt out, guns in hand. They began shooting at the police, killing one officer. Anselmi and Scalise got separated from Mike, who was hit in the leg and taken prisoner. As he lay on a stretcher, Mike tried to kick an ambulance attendant with his good leg. His defiance was short-lived; the bullet in his leg had severed an artery. Mike Genna bled to death before doctors could save him.

With Angelo and Mike dead, Tony Genna became head of the family organization. Understandably paranoid, Tony surrounded himself with armed guards and refused to leave his hotel residence. On July 8, 1925, Tony took a phone call from Giuseppe "the Cavalier" Nerone, his top enforcer. Tony allegedly told the man he was planning on fleeing Chicago with his remaining brothers. Nerone said he had information linking Capone (who had taken over Torrio's rackets after he retired) to Mike Genna's death. Underworld rumor had it that Capone wanted to eliminate the Genna brothers as a source of competition.

Nerone told Tony that he wanted to meet in person to discuss retaliatory action. Tony agreed and drove to the meeting site. Looking cautiously up and down the street, Tony got out of his vehicle and stepped over to Nerone, who was waiting for him. Tony shook Nerone's hand, at which point two assassins jumped from the shadows and shot the unfortunate Genna brother dead. Apparently, Nerone had switched sides and was working for Capone.

Jim, Peter, and Sam Genna could see the writing on the wall. The three surviving brothers abruptly left Chicago, their power and morale shattered. According to some accounts, the three stayed in Sicily for a while, eventually returning to America to run a legitimate olive oil and cheese importing firm, but studiously avoiding any underworld activity.

In the Gennas' absence, Capone and "Bugs" Moran seized the brothers' mighty bootlegging empire and continued to battle for supremacy in Chicago.

See Also: Capone, Al; O'Banion, Dion; Prohibition

Further Reading

Laurence Bergreen, *Capone: The Man and the Era*, 1994.

Nate Hendley, *Al Capone: Chicago's King of Crime*, 2006.

John Kobler, *Capone: the Life and World of Al Capone*, 1971.

Gus Russo, *The Outfit: The Role of Chicago's Underworld in the Shaping of Modern America*, 2001.

GOTTI, JOHN (1940–2002)

The best-known gangster in America since Al Capone, John Gotti, was called the "Dapper Don" for his taste in expensive clothes, and the "Teflon Don" for his ability to duck convictions. Nevertheless, his high media profile and demands for regal deference made it easier for authorities to eventually convict him. Gotti violated several unwritten mob rules and in the process, managed to undermine one of the largest Mafia families in America.

Gotti was born October 27, 1940, in the South Bronx, the fifth of thirteen kids. His parents, John and Fannie Gotti, hailed from the Naples region of Italy. Gotti grew up poor and somewhat resentful; his father seemed incapable of keeping even the most basic of jobs, from construction to factory work. The Gotti family moved around quite a bit. By the time he was twelve, the Gotti family had settled in Brooklyn.

A tough kid, Gotti routinely got into fist-fights with other youths in his neighborhood. While still in his youth, Gotti began working for local mobster named Carmine Fatico, a capo in what would eventually become the Gambino family. Gotti ran errands and did other small chores for Fatico. As a teenager, Gotti worked as a car thief, mugger and small-time burglar. He was relatively bright, but had a desultory school record. Gotti was frequently in trouble for mouthing off to teachers and fighting other

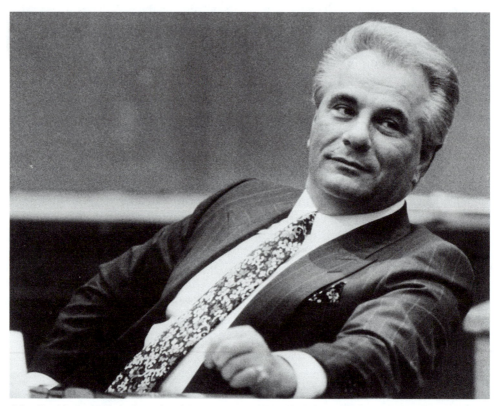

John Gotti leans back during a break in testimony in New York Supreme Court in Manhattan, 1990. [AP Photo/Daniel Sheehan]

students. Gotti's undistinguished academic record came to an end at age sixteen. The high school drop-out worked a series of low-end jobs, from trucker's helper to pants presser in a garment factory. He also took up another more steady vocation as an enforcer for Fatico. After the notorious Albert Anastasia was murdered in 1957, the crew Fatico belonged to became part of the Gambino crime family. Gotti admired the thugs who lounged at Fatico's club, who seemed to have plenty of cash and lots of leisure time on their hands, in sharp contrast to his ne'er-do-well father. Gotti noted how the "wise guys" at Fatico's place had the respect of everyone in the neighborhood. He set his sights on becoming a mobster.

In March 1962 at the age of 22, Gotti married Victoria DiGiorgio, a half-Jewish nineteen-year-old with whom he'd already had a child, a daughter named Angela. It was not a smooth relationship, and in the early years Gotti wasn't bringing in much money as a fledgling mobster and blue-collar worker. Victoria had to take him to court a few times for non-support of his child. The two eventually reconciled, and their family expanded to include three sons and two daughters. The Gotti clan moved into an apartment in Howard Beach, a middle-class neighborhood in the borough of Queens.

Gotti continued to commit robberies, steal cars and fist-fight on the street with assorted miscreants. Under Fatico's tutelage Gotti also hijacked cargo trucks leaving nearby John F. Kennedy airport. On these jobs he often worked with his brother, Gene, and Angelo Ruggiero, a heavy-set young man who hung out at Fatico's clubhouse. Like Gotti, Ruggiero dreamed of entering the underworld big-

leagues. At the time, Kennedy airport handled $200 million in freight each year and employed thousands of workers. For a gangster like Fatico, the airport presented vast opportunities for theft, not to mention loan-sharking and book-making with staff.

Gotti's progress up the Mafia's hierarchy was slow and interrupted by arrests. On the last day of March 1965, a policeman caught him in the act of using a crowbar to gain entry to a locked tavern. Gotti ended up serving two-and-a-half years for the offence. By the time Gotti was released, his patron, Fatico, had moved his headquarters from Brooklyn to Ozone Park in the borough of Queens. The mobster wanted to be nearer to Kennedy airport, and farther away from the Black and Hispanic families moving into his old neighborhood. Fatico established a base of operations on 101st Street, and took over some storefronts to create a hooligan hangout dubbed "The Bergin Hunt and Fish Club." Gotti resumed his chores for Fatico, stealing cargo from Kennedy airport. He sometimes worked with Ruggiero or Gene Gotti.

In 1968 the FBI arrested Gotti, his brother Gene, and Ruggiero for stealing airport cargo. Gotti was also slapped with additional hijacking charges for some capers in New Jersey. Gotti was incarcerated at Lewisburg Federal Penitentiary in Pennsylvania, where he attracted the notice of another imprisoned Mafiosi, Carmine Galante. A member of the Bonanno family, Galante was the top Mafia leader at Lewisburg. At some point during his incarceration, Gotti approached Galante with a complaint. Galante made sure his crew was well supplied with contraband steak and whisky. Although Gotti was not yet a "made" man, meaning that he hadn't been formally inducted into the Mafia's ranks, he complained he wasn't receiving his fair share of liquor and meat. Galante was impressed by the upstart's moxie. He invited Gotti to join the Bonanno family when he was released. Gotti appreciated the offer, but decided to rejoin Fatico instead.

Gotti was released from Lewisburg in 1972 after serving three years. When Fatico began to experience legal woes, Gotti was appointed acting capo with the firm endorsement of Aniello Dellacroce, a well-placed Gambino family member. The promotion was slightly unusual in that Gotti still wasn't "made." Gotti got along well with Dellacroce, who served as another mentor to the striving young gangster. Both men enjoyed gambling and had no qualms about using violence to get their way. Dellacroce would become underboss of the Gambino family, second only to Carlo Gambino. Dellacroce used a locale called the Ravenite Social Club, located in Manhattan's Little Italy, as a headquarters and hangout.

Roughly a year after Gotti got out of Lewisburg, Manny Gambino, nephew of Carlo, was kidnapped. His abductors demanded $100,000, which Carlo Gambino paid. His nephew was murdered anyway and buried in a dump in New Jersey. The FBI took two suspects into custody. A third suspect, named James McBratney, remained at large. McBratney was a career criminal, but had no affiliation with the Mafia. Carlo Gambino put a contract on his life, which Gotti decided to collect.

A clever assassin would have spent time getting to know McBratney's movements—where he lived, worked and played. Only then would the assassin determine an appropriate time and place for a "hit." Gotti took a more direct approach. On May 22, 1973, throwing caution to the wind, Gotti, Ruggiero and a third man named Ralph Galione, barged into a Staten Island bar that McBratney patronized. The trio flashed some phony badges, said they were policemen, and that McBratney was under arrest. They planned on hustling McBratney to some lonely locale and torturing him to death. The problem was that McBratney didn't believe for an instant that Gotti, Ruggiero, and Galione were real cops. The threesome looked, talked and walked like gangsters, not policemen. McBratney began to struggle as the trio of fake cops seized him. With the bar patrons cheering on McBratney, Gotti and his accomplices attempted to regain control of the situation. In frustration, Galione produced a pistol and shot McBratney dead in the middle of the bar. Shortly after, Galione himself was murdered, most likely as punishment for the fumbled hit. Gotti laid low for a year after the botched assassination. Thanks to a tip, FBI agents eventually caught up with Gotti at a bar, no less, and arrested him.

Despite the sloppy way Gotti's men had carried out McBratney's murder, Carlo Gambino was delighted that his nephew's death had been avenged. To show his appreciation, Gambino hired notorious lawyer Roy Cohn to represent Gotti and Ruggiero (who had also been picked up) at trial. A courtroom deal was cut. Gotti pled guilty to attempted manslaughter and got a four-year sentence. Gotti stayed at the Green Haven Correctional Facility in upstate New York and was treated as a privileged prisoner, befitting his status as an up-and-coming mobster.

By the mid-1970s, Gambino was in ill health. It was widely assumed the family boss would appoint Dellacroce as his successor. Instead, Gambino shocked his coterie by choosing Paul Castellano as his replacement. The choice almost certainly reflected family favoritism; Gambino was married to Castellano's sister, Katherine. Selecting his brother-in-law over the more experienced Dellacroce would have devastating repercussions for the Gambino family. Gambino himself died of cancer in 1976, and Castellano took over the family. "Big Paul" Castellano was widely regarded as weak and ineffectual, more concerned with personal wealth than extending the Gambino family's power. Gotti disliked Castellano, and the feeling was mutual. The two managed to put their differences aside for the sake of business. Castellano even presided over Gotti's induction ceremony as a "made man" once he got out of prison in 1977. Gotti didn't have to toil as a lowly soldier; he was formally appointed as capo of the Bergin crew. As an official Gambino chieftain, Gotti earned a reputation for ruthlessness that was startling even by underworld standards. He threatened minions with instant death unless they obeyed his every command. Gotti's crew engaged in typical mob money-making pursuits such as loan-sharking, theft and gambling, but also dealt drugs, which was technically a violation of Mafia rules. Gotti didn't care as long as his men cut him in on their drug profits.

Gotti's violence spilled over into his personal life. In March 1980, for example, Gotti's twelve son Frank rode his bicycle into the path of a car driven by neighbour John Favara and was killed. By all accounts, Favara was a quiet family-man with no mob connections.

His children played with Gotti's children. Frank's death was a tragic accident, but Gotti and his wife didn't see it that way. Favara started to receive threatening phone calls and was shocked to see the word "murderer" spray-painted on his car. Frightened, Favara put his house up for sale, and planned to flee the community. In July 1980, as he left his shift as a service manager at a furniture plant, Favara was forced into a car by a group of men. He disappeared and his body was never found. Rumour had it that Favara was murdered with a chain saw, and then placed in a car, which was in turn, placed in a demolition machine that pounded it into a one-square foot block. John and Victoria Gotti made sure they were in Florida when their neighbour disappeared, and claimed they knew nothing about Favara's disappearance when asked by police. Frank's death remained an open wound in Gotti's life. He regularly visited the crypt where his son was buried. Each year on the boy's birthday, Gotti ran an In Memoriam ad in the *New York Daily News*.

In 1981 authorities managed to bug two phones in the office of the Bergin Hunt Club. Later that same year, the FBI got a court order permitting them to bug Ruggiero's home phone. Ruggiero had a tendency to gossip about mob business, a trait that earned him the less-than-flattering nickname "Quack Quack" from his peers. Ruggiero thought he was safe from electronic eavesdropping because he used his daughter's pink Princess phone, which was on a separate line from his home phone. The court order extended to this phone as well, however, and the FBI gleefully recorded all his conversations. When Ruggiero moved to Cedarhurst, Long Island, federal authorities planted listening devices in his new home. A microphone was placed in the dinette. As luck would have it, this was the precise location where Ruggiero liked to confer with fellow gangsters.

Once a week, Ruggiero had a face-to-face meeting with Big Paul at the latter's regal Staten Island estate . After returning home Ruggiero would immediately call Gotti and relay what Castellano had told him. On the basis of information gathered from the Ruggiero bug, the FBI got court permission to plant listening devices in Castellano's and Dellacroce's residences. Among other details, they discovered that Ruggiero served as Gotti's unofficial valet. Like many gangsters, Gotti was a night owl, spending late evenings eating, drinking, partying and meeting with his fellow gangsters. Ruggiero would call on Gotti around noon at his home to wake the groggy Don up.

On May 6, 1982, Ruggiero's brother, Salvatore, was killed in a plane accident off the coast of Georgia. Salvatore was a major heroin trafficker. Via wiretaps the FBI determined that Ruggiero inherited his brother's drug connections. The same bugs also revealed that Gotti's brother, Gene, was deeply implicated in drug deals. In August 1983, the United States District Attorney indicted Ruggiero, Gene Gotti, and a third man named John Carneglia on drug charges. The indictments infuriated Castellano, who had pretensions of being accepted as a legitimate businessman. Ruggiero's lawyer had FBI transcripts of his client's bugged conversations. Castellano demanded to see the transcripts, threatening Gotti (who as crew capo was held responsible for the acts of his underlings) with dire punishment if they weren't handed over. Among other threats, Castellano said he would demote Gotti to the rank of

"soldier," disband his crew, and transfer his men to other crews. Ruggiero and Gotti had good reason not to give up the transcripts. The bugs revealed that Ruggiero and other Gambino family members disliked their boss and called him names behind his back. These midlevel mobsters were also angry that Castellano banned them from selling narcotics, but apparently had no problem accepting cash from drug dealers. Ruggiero also blabbed at length about the ultra-secretive Commission, a grave offence for a Mafiosi. Founded decades earlier, the Commission was the leadership body of the Mafia that set policy and settled internal disputes within the mob.

Castellano continued to regard Gotti with suspicion, viewing him as a base thug. This opinion was reinforced by a strange incident in 1984. On a street in Queens a motorist named Romual Piecyk found himself blocked in by Gotti's double-parked and unattended Lincoln. Piecyk began honking his horn, which drew the attention of one of Gotti's men in a nearby tavern. The Gotti soldier stepped out of the tavern and started to brawl with Piecyk on the street. Gotti appeared on the scene and instead of breaking up the fight, joined in. Piecyk was beaten by the two mobsters and robbed of $325 in cash. Unaware of Gotti's underworld connections, Piecyk called police. The police went to a restaurant frequented by Gotti's crew, where they arrested the capo and his fellow thug for assault and theft.

Throughout the spring of 1985, Gotti continued to stonewall, refusing to hand over the transcripts. Gotti sought advice from Dellacroce, who was chronically ill with cancer. His old mentor urged him to surrender the incriminating documents.

Gotti had other plans. He began scheming against Castellano. He drew a select crew of loyalists to his side who were equally displeased with Castellano's rule. These loyalists included Salvatore Gravano, nicknamed "Sammy the Bull." Sammy was short, squat, extremely muscular, and very violent. He killed his first man at age 25 and proceeded to murder several others. Gravano marched to the beat of his own drummer. At one point he transferred his allegiance from the Colombo family to the Gambino family. Gravano had his boss' permission to switch families, but his lateral move, which was highly unusual in Mafia circles, still raised eyebrows.

As Gotti plotted, the pressure on Castellano increased. In February 1985, Big Paul was one of several New York mob bosses indicted on racketeering charges in what became known as the Mafia Commission trial. Dellacroce was also indicted, but Gotti was solely focused on Castellano. Given that he was dying of cancer and had a reputation for toughness, it was unlikely that Dellacroce would cut a deal with authorities for more lenient treatment. Mobsters were less sure about Castellano, who was a senior citizen and widely perceived as soft. No one knew if Castellano had it in him to uphold the tradition of silence, called omerta, and keep his mouth shut.

As if Castellano's position wasn't tenuous enough, the Gambino boss proceeded to make some questionable staffing decisions. He boosted a crony, Thomas Bilotti, to the position of capo, which made him Gotti's equal. Mob gossip suggested Bilotti would be promoted to underboss once Dellacroce died. Then, if Castellano had to serve time, Bilotti would become the acting family

boss. Gotti would be left out in the cold, a mid-level capo with no chance of further advancement. Other mid-level mobsters also had issues with Castellano. He was perceived as greedy, someone who made a huge amount of money, but wouldn't share it among his lieutenants. The circle of opponents united against Castellano began to expand. In addition to Gravano, a capo named Frankie DeCicco gravitated to Gotti's side.

On December 2, 1985, Dellacroce died of cancer. Castellano did not attend the funeral. Being under indictment, he didn't want to be seen in public with known mobsters. It was a good legal move, but bad Mafia politics. Not attending the funeral was seen as a shocking violation of underworld etiquette. In the eyes of his Mafia family, Castellano had again proven to be a distant, cowardly leader. A tougher mob boss would have used Dellacroce's death as an occasion to clean house, and eliminate annoying subordinates such as John Gotti. Castellano did no such thing, even as Gotti gathered a crew of traitors around him. Just under a dozen mobsters joined Gotti's side.

In mid-December 1985, Gotti informed his fellow conspirators that they were going to take part in a major hit. He was vague about the target. DeCicco, meanwhile, arranged a meeting with Castellano and Bilotti for Sparks Steak House in Manhattan on December 16, at 5 p.m. Shortly before this meeting, Gotti gathered his team together. He informed them their target was none other than Castellano, then got his men in place. Gotti and Gravano got into a car and drove to Sparks. Around 5:25 p.m., Bilotti steered a car through heavy Manhattan traffic for the scheduled rendezvous with DeCicco. His only passenger in the vehicle was Castellano. Streets swarmed with holiday shoppers. Both Bilotti and Castellano were unarmed, evidence of their willful naivety.

At one point, Bilotti drew up alongside the car containing Gotti and Gravano. The latter were astonished to see their target so close by, but Castellano didn't turn his head and didn't notice the two conspirators. Bilotti steered the vehicle to the sidewalk and stepped out along with Castellano. As the two mob bosses exited their car, three assassins wearing identical white trench coats and fur hats (to confuse witnesses) stepped forward and opened fire on the pair with semiautomatic pistols. Another team of killers lurked nearby in case the trio of gunmen screwed up. The second team was unnecessary; Castellano and Bilotti went down in a broadside of bullets and collapsed on the street. Gotti and Gravano cruised by the murder scene to make sure both men were dead and then drove off. The fur-hatted assassins slipped out of the area on foot.

Following this killing, the most extravagant take down of a mob boss since Albert Anastasia's murder, Gotti took the reins of the Gambino family. Gotti feigned shock and promised to lead an internal investigation into Castellano's death. In mid-January 1986, Gotti held a meeting with twenty Gambino capos (all of whom probably had a good idea who murdered Castellano). The capos unanimously selected him as the next Gambino boss. Gotti made Frank DeCicco underboss and Gravano a capo. Gotti began hanging out at the Ravenite Social Club, which had been Dellacroce's domain.

The hit on Castellano propelled Gotti from mid-level mobster to the most famous gangster in New York City. His visage began regularly turning up on the front page. Unlike most mob bosses who never spoke to the press, Gotti was happy to chat with reporters. He seemed eager to flaunt his Mafia pedigree, dressing in attention-grabbing double-breasted silk suits and expensive accessories. Gotti's surge in status had some unintended benefits. When his assault and theft case came to trial in March 1986, Piecyk, who by then was well aware who Gotti was, refused to testify. Gotti's lawyer in the case was Bruce Cutler, a bald, abrasive former high school wrestling champion and college football star. Cutler claimed his client was a plumbing goods salesman with no connections to the underworld and had the charges dismissed.

Some of Gotti's peers weren't impressed by his rapid rise. Vincent "the Chin" Gigante, head of the Genovese mob family, was annoyed that Gotti hadn't asked for permission to kill Castellano. According to long-standing Mafia protocol, hits against a family boss had to be approved in advance by the Commission. Gigante worked with the Lucchese family to come up with a suitable plan of revenge. On April 13, 1986, Gambino underboss DeCicco opened the door to his parked car and was blown to pieces by a bomb. At the moment of his death, DeCicco had been standing next to a mobster who resembled John Gotti. The bomb had been remotely-activated, which suggested the real target was Gotti himself. Gotti was alarmed by this close call, but not unduly worried. He was more focused on the fabulous wealth that suddenly came his way as family boss. To his surprise, he discovered the Gambinos were involved in several white collar rackets, from pornography to a gas excise tax scam. As boss, Gotti was entitled to a cut of the proceeds.

In early 1986, a restaurant in lower Manhattan called Bankers and Brokers was vandalized at the behest of John O'Connor, corrupt vice-president and business agent of the United Brotherhood of Carpenters and Joiners of America, Local 608. O'Connor was annoyed that the Mafiosi running the restaurant had the temerity to hire non-union laborers to work on the place. O'Connor was offered $5,000 to overlook this breech in union etiquette, but he felt this wasn't sufficient. The union boss unleashed his goons to smash up the restaurant. Gotti found out and told Ruggiero, now one of his chief lieutenants, to take care of O'Connor. In May of 1986 Ruggiero hired four members of the Westies, a violent Irish street gang, to assassinate the truculent labour leader. The Westies bungled the job, however, and only ended up wounding O'Connor. For unclear reasons, Gotti decided to let the matter drop and didn't plot any new violence against the wily O'Connor.

Gotti held to a regular schedule. He slept in late each morning, then got picked up in a chauffeur driven Mercedes-Benz. Clad in a track suit, he would be transported to the Bergin Club for lunch. After eating he spent the afternoon hanging around with his crew at the club. A backroom at the Bergin was turned into a one-person grooming station for Gotti. A stylist came in every day to wash, cut and blow-dry his silvery pompadour. Gotti also did daily sun lap treatments to maintain an even tan. In addition to hair care products, Gotti kept a vast collection of expensive suits, shirts, ties, shoes and underwear at the club. He would select an appropriate outfit at around 5 p.m., and then would head over to the Ravenite Club. Dinner would be conducted in a high profile restaurant. Afterwards, Gotti would go clubbing. He drank expensive brandy and champagne, and had regular sexual encounters with women drawn to his gangster celebrity.

Once a week, all high-ranking Gambino members had to report to the Ravenite Club to update the boss on their activities. Gotti would frequently conduct "walk-talks" with his men. In a walk talk, gangsters discussed business while briskly strolling on the sidewalk to foil any attempt at police eavesdropping. Gotti began to attract a following of young aspiring gangsters who dressed and acted like he did. These admirers wore Armani jackets, gray colored turtleneck sweaters, and gold chains after their idol.

Even though he was now boss of a rich Mafia family, Gotti remained in his old Howard Beach home. Every July 4, he acted as benevolent neighborhood patron and arranged a huge party for area residents, complete with free carnival rides, card games, music, and food. These parties would climax with a thundering fireworks display. Gotti never bothered to get a permit for his pyrotechnics. Police typically stood around and gawked at the festivities. Needless to say, Gotti was a popular figure in his clannish, blue-collar neighborhood. His neighbors were pleased to see someone from their own ranks become rich and powerful, even if it was through organized crime. Ironically, Gotti was frequently broke, despite earning millions a year. An obsessive but losing gambler, Gotti lost much of what he made in bad bets. In 1982 alone Gotti blew $90,000 in losing bets on college football games.

In the spring of 1986 Gotti was hit with federal racketeering charges. The trial started in Brooklyn in August 1986 and lasted until March 1987. Gotti and a handful of co-defendants were prosecuted by Diane Giacalone, Assistant U.S. Attorney in the federal Eastern District. Giacalone didn't have much experience dealing with the Mafia, and her case was further weakened by a lack of cooperation among authorities. Gotti and his co-defendants were charged with three murder conspiracies, among other racketeering offences. The prosecution had 30 hours of evidence gleaned from listening devices and ninety witnesses, but the case was still weak. Several of these witnesses were former gangsters themselves who left a bad impression on the jury. Acting as Gotti's defense attorney, Cutler tore up these witnesses on the stand. In a powerful opening statement Cutler lambasted the whole trial, denied the existence of the Mafia, and theatrically tossed the indictment into a wastepaper basket, saying it made him sick. These dramatics worked, and the jury found Gotti and his associates not guilty.

During the late 1980s, Gotti and Gravano became close. Gravano was heavily involved in the construction trade and prided himself on his technical knowledge of the field. Gravano found himself elevated to the position of family consigliere (advisor). Unlike his boss, Gravano shunned the spotlight. He dressed down in blue jeans and wouldn't accompany Gotti on his nightly partying rounds. In spite of his exalted position with the Gambino family, Gravano occasionally carried out murders himself. This was a huge departure from Mafia tradition, in which top leaders generally had underlings do their dirty work.

Gotti continued to be a media celebrity. The press called him the "Dapper Don" after his extensive wardrobe or the "Teflon Don," a reflection of the seeming inability of authorities to successfully convict him. The FBI, however, were methodically building a case against Gotti. The FBI established a secret viewing post near the Ravenite Club, where Gotti had more or less established his permanent headquarters. Every time a Mafia leader came by to pay homage to Gotti, the two were photographed by FBI agents.

In the spring of 1988 the FBI planted bugs in the Ravenite Club, but sound problems rendered them useless. A year later, the FBI caught a lucky break. In late 1989 federal authorities discovered that Gotti used an apartment above the Ravenite for meetings. The apartment belonged to Nettie Cirelli, the former wife of a dead Gambino soldier. While wary of potential bugs in the Ravenite itself, Gotti apparently thought he was safe to talk business in Cirelli's apartment. Whenever Gotti felt like holding a meeting, Cirelli would go out shopping for a few hours, and her residence became a temporary Gambino family nerve center.

On November 19, 1989, an FBI surveillance team spotted Cirelli leaving her apartment with a suitcase, almost certainly going on a Thanksgiving vacation. Seeing their chance, the FBI cautiously broke into Cirelli's residence and planted listening devices. To their delight, the bugs picked up crystal-clear conversations featuring a chatty Gotti and his underlings. Gotti completely let his guard down in Cirelli's residence, and openly talked about murder, Mafia intrigue, and problems with employees. He frequently criticized Gravano for allegedly building up his own power base and murdering anyone with whom he had business problems. On the surface, however, Gotti remained on good terms with Gravano, promoting him to underboss in early 1990.

Gotti began the 1990s on a high note. On February 9, 1990, he was found not guilty in a trial stemming around the assault on John O'Connor. A crowd of 1,000 people greeted Gotti as he walked out of the courthouse like a conquering hero. To celebrate Gotti's win residents in South Ozone Park festooned the area with balloons and banners.

The government wasn't through with Gotti, however. The listening device in Cirelli's apartment was picking up extremely valuable information. Federal authorities carefully put together another slate of charges against Gotti and his top leadership. On December 11, 1990, the FBI struck. They burst into the Ravenite as Gotti presided over a meeting with Gravano and thirty other associates, soldiers, and capos. Gotti, Gravano, and a third man named Frank Locascio (who had served as underboss before Gravano took the job) were arrested and taken to FBI headquarters in downtown Manhattan.

One day after the raid, the trio got to hear the charges against them. The three were indicted as leaders of a criminal association. They were slapped with thirteen counts under the RICO (Racketeer Influenced and Corrupt Organizations) Act. These counts included murder, conspiracy, illegal gambling, income tax evasion, loan-sharking, and obstruction of justice. Gotti was also indicted for taking part in the murder of Castellano and Bilotti. A few days before Christmas, Gotti received a shock. To prevent the judge from granting bail, prosecutors

played snippets of the Cirelli tapes in court. For the first time, Gotti realized some of his most private conversations had been recorded by the FBI. Federal District Court Judge Leo Glasser listened to the tapes and denied bail.

Gotti faced setbacks on another front. Federal prosecutors managed to get four lawyers working for Gotti and Gravano disqualified. Their ranks included the pugnacious Bruce Cutler. The attorneys had been picked up on bugs giving advice to Gotti. As a result of these recorded conversations, the lawyers might be called as witnesses. This would create an impossible conflict of interest for the attorneys, so they were disqualified. In court the Cirelli tapes proved devastating. Gravano was shocked to hear Gotti put him down and complain about not giving him a fair share of Gravano's proceeds from construction operations. Prior to their arrest, Gravano had been feeding Gotti $2 million a year, but this wasn't enough to satisfy the greedy Don. The tapes also revealed that Gotti seemed somewhat jealous of Gravano.

Gravano became rapidly disenchanted. He was annoyed by Gotti's constant self-aggrandizing in court and in lockup. Despite Gotti's reassurances, Gravano began to suspect his boss was setting him up, trying to make him the fall-guy for Gambino family violence. Realizing he faced, at best, a life sentence behind bars, Gravano did the unthinkable. In early fall 1991, he turned traitor and decided to reveal what he knew about the Gotti organization to authorities. On November 8, 1991, Gravano was removed from the prison where he was staying with Gotti and transferred to protective custody in a secret locale. Gravano was then taken to the FBI training academy in Quantico,

Virginia, where he was questioned extensively. Gravano revealed the inner workings of the Gambino family, including the plot to murder Castellano and Bilotti. For the first time, authorities now knew the motivation and strategy behind the mob coup. Gravano also confessed to an extensive criminal record that included involvement in nineteen murders. In January 1992, jury selection began in what was now a case against Gotti and Locascio. It was a case the federal government absolutely had to win. Were they to lose again, Gotti would gain a reputation as untouchable. Gotti put up a defiant front in court, whispering insults about the judge and prosecutors that reporters overheard. Judge Glasser was no pushover, however, and ordered Gotti to stop the outbursts.

Instead of the steadfast Bruce Cutler, Gotti was defended by Albert Krieger, an able but less blustery trial attorney from Florida. The jury, meanwhile, was sequestered and billeted under guard at hotels to prevent bribery or intimidation. As a further precaution, the identities of the jurors were kept secret. The courtroom atmosphere verged on circus-like at times. Fans and family of Gotti routinely showed up to show their support. Sometimes, groups of pro-Gotti demonstrators picketed outside the courthouse. Celebrities such as Mickey Rourke and Anthony Quinn dropped by to watch the proceedings. The prosecution continued to play the damning tapes from the Cirelli bug. To underline Gotti's importance, the prosecution screened blown up photographs of Mafia leaders coming and going at the Ravenite.

The tapes alone might not have been enough to convict Gotti. Combined with Sammy the Bull's testimony, however, Gotti had no chance. Gravano testified for the prosecution under tight security. He spent a total of nine days on the stand, offering minute details about the Gotti organization. As part of the deal he made with the prosecution, Gravano had to reveal his full criminal history to the court. This was a small concession on Gravano's part, given that he'd been promised a 20 year sentence in return for cooperating. Sammy the Bull was the most significant Mafia turncoat ever. He was much higher placed than Joe Valachi, a lowly soldier who told authorities what he knew about the underworld in the early 1960s. While most of his testimony centered on murder plots and felonies, Gravano also took the time to explain arcane Mafia slang and gestures and detail day-to-day life as a mobster. The longer Gravano testified, the more unnerved Gotti became. He was dismayed by his lawyer's inability to shake Gravano's composure, and by Gravano's comprehensive memory of Gambino family business.

On April 2, 1992, the Teflon Don was found guilty on all thirteen RICO counts. His co-defendant, Frank Locascio, who was almost entirely overlooked by the media in the proceedings, was also convicted of most charges. Two months later, a smirking Gotti appeared before Judge Glasser for sentencing. To no one's surprise, Gotti received life in jail without parole. Locascio, who had been serving as family consigliere when he was arrested, got the same. When the verdict was announced, a crowd of several hundred people outside the courthouse began a small riot. Cars were overturned amidst cries of "Free John Gotti!" Members of his group of supporters were from the Bergin Hunt and Fish Club or from Gotti's old neighborhood.

Gotti arrived in shackles at the Marion Federal Penitentiary in Marion, Illinois on June 24, 1992. After being processed, Gotti was placed in a tiny cell, where he was kept twenty-two hours a day. Meal trays were slid into his cell through a slit in the door. The only visitors allowed were lawyers and relatives, and they were separated by a glass wall and had to communicate via telephone. For entertainment, Gotti was allowed a small black and white television set in his cell. For exercise, he was periodically allowed to walk the tier outside his cell in shackles.

At first, Gotti believed he could still run the family from behind bars. He put members of his kin, his brother Peter and eldest son, John Gotti Jr., in charge of family business. Thanks to his father, John Gotti Jr. had enjoyed a spectacular rise up the Mafia hierarchy. The fact that he was even in the mob was contrary to longstanding Mafia tradition, in which family bosses tried to steer their sons into legitimate professions. Exceptions were continually made for John Junior; he became a "made man" at 24, despite not having a pure Italian lineage due to his mother being partly Jewish. Two years later, his father made him a capo.

Officially, John Jr. was a businessman who owned successful trucking and real-estate firms. Unofficially, he was made acting boss of the Gambinos by his imprisoned father. John Jr., would be assisted in day-to-day operations by three capos, whose ranks included Peter Gotti. John Jr., was not well-liked by the Mafia rank and file. They resented his fast promotion and the obvious nepotism that put him at the front of the family. Mafiosi doubted his leadership abilities and disliked his perceived arrogance

and inept handling of business. The Genovese family outright refused to negotiate with John Jr., regarding him as a joke.

Authorities were determined to make John Jr.'s ascension to family boss as trying as possible. In 1998 he was slapped with a RICO indictment. John Jr. was accused of running gambling, loansharking and extortion rackets. Among evidence seized by police was a list found in John Jr.'s office of soldiers who had been inducted into the New York Mafia from 1991 to 1992. Such information was never supposed to be written down and saved for the very reason that authorities might use it against the mob. The discovery of this piece of evidence further diminished John Jr.'s reputation. Eventually, the Mafia son accepted a plea bargain and in September 1999 was sentenced to six years and five months imprisonment, plus a fine of $750,000.

The Ravenite Club, meanwhile, was seized by the government on the grounds that it was a major center for illegal racketeering. The building was auctioned off by authorities and purchased by a new landlord who turned it into a store for women's accessories. Back in Marion, John Gotti remained in virtual isolation, cut off from the family he had led. In the late 1990s, he came down with neck and head cancer. In June 2002, the cancer killed him. Gotti had an appropriately splashy, $200,000 funeral. His bronze casket was coated in gold and transported through Queens with twenty-two limos and hundreds of private cars in its wake. Some nineteen vehicles alone were needed just to transport flowers.

The elaborate funeral could not cover up the fact that Gotti's reign had been disastrous. He had taken over the biggest, most powerful Mafia family in

America and left it a wreck. Gotti ignored the fact that the mob's very strength depended on secrecy and stealth. Keeping out of the spotlight was a major Mafia tenet, then and now. Gotti violated other Mafia commandments, such as the unwritten rule that mob bosses are chosen on the basis of merit, not family connections. Making his son the boss of the Gambinos merely confounded Gotti's mistakes. If Gotti senior was a weak leader, his son was outright incompetent and widely disliked.

In 2004, as John Jr. was about to be released from prison, he was hit with new RICO charges. After three trials, John Jr. was set free, only to be arrested again in August 2008 on conspiracy charges in Florida. The charges related to large-scale cocaine trafficking and the murder of three men in New York City. John Jr. was moved to New York for trial in late 2008. He is currently incarcerated in New York City, awaiting trial. As his father once did, John Gotti Jr. faces the prospect of much of his adulthood behind bars.

See Also: Castellano, Paul; Mafia

Further Reading

"A Thug in a Great-Looking Suit," CNN backgrounder on John Gotti. http://www.cnn.com/CNN/Programs/people/shows/gotti/profile.html.

John Davis, *Mafia Dynasty: The Rise and Fall of the Gambino Crime Family*, 1993.

Alan Feuer, "The Curious and the Police Abound at a Wake for Gotti," *New York Times*, June 14, 2002.

"John Gotti Jr. Arrested on Murder Conspiracy Charge," *Chicago Tribune*, August 5, 2008.

Arnold Lubasch, "Jury Hears Gotti Discuss Organization on Tapes," *New York Times*, February 18, 1992.

Gene Mustain and Jerry Capeci, *Mob Star: The Story of John Gotti*, 1988.

Selwyn Raab, *Five Families: The Rise, Decline and Resurgence of America's Most Powerful Mafia Empires*, 2005.

Selwyn Raab, "John Gotti Dies in Prison at 61; Mafia Boss Relished the Spotlight," *New York Times*, June 11, 2002.

Thomas Reppetto, *Bringing Down the Mob: The War against the American Mafia*, 2006.

Timothy Williams, "For the Third Time, a Jury Fails to Convict Gotti," *New York Times*, September 28, 2006.

H

HELLS ANGELS

They are the biggest outlaw motorcycle gang in the world, a crew of freedom-loving road warriors (in their own eyes) or a violent band of gangsters on two-wheels (according to police). The Hells Angels Motorcycle Club (HAMC) currently boasts 800 members in ninety-two chapters throughout the United States, and a reputation for wanton violence. The HAMC traces its origins to the late 1940s, when bored U.S. Army veterans started to buy motorcycles and band together to relive the camaraderie and stimulation of wartime. The first HAMC chapter was established in San Bernardino, California on March 17, 1948. The club's founding fathers did not invent their name. There were U.S. bomber formations in World War II that dubbed themselves "Hell's Angels." A unit of the Flying Tigers, mercenary pilots who flew missions for China against Japan in World War II, used the same nickname. Hell's Angels was also the title of a well-known 1930 film about aerial combat. Motorcycles themselves have a war-like precedent. In World War I both Germany and the United States used motorcyclists as couriers and scouts. The Germans came up with the idea of putting a sidecar onto a motorcycle and equipping it with a machine gun. These armed, two-man motorcycles were used for patrols and direct combat roles.

HAMC chapters in San Francisco and Oakland, California, were established in the 1950s. Rapid expansion, thanks in part to sensationalized media coverage, followed in the late 1960s. California proved to be ground zero for post-war motorcycle culture. Part of this was a reflection of southern California's generally sunny weather and warm climate, which allowed bikers to ride all year round.

From the start, the Angels cultivated a vile public persona. Dirty jeans, battle-scarred leather jackets, and unkempt hair and beards were the norm. The Angels were among the first North American subcultures to grow their hair long. Some members sported shoulder length locks in the early 1960s, years before long hair became common among the mainstream.

Members of the Hells Angels motorcycle club and their guests line up their Harley-Davidsons at chapter headquarters in Oakland, California, 2007, to celebrate the 50th anniversary of the Oakland arm of the international club. [AP Photo/Dino Vournas]

This hirsute image was complemented by Nazi paraphernalia, from swastikas and iron crosses to vintage Germany army helmets. Heavy drinking and drug use was accompanied by vulgar rituals, such as earning your "wings." HAMC members could earn "red" wings by performing oral sex on a woman having her period or "black" wings by orally pleasuring a female African-American.

In addition to being expert motorcycle riders, the HAMC quickly established a reputation for brutality. The Angels adopted the belligerent pose of elite fighting units, in which the slightest insult or assault is followed by massive retaliation by all available members. "When you fight with one Hells Angel, you fight us all. We stick up for our own, right or wrong," noted Ralph "Sonny" Barger, a prominent HAMC leader from Oakland, California, in his memoirs. Writing in the *Nation* magazine in March 1965, "gonzo" journalist Hunter S. Thompson described the Angels as "tough, mean and potentially as dangerous as a pack of wild boar." In addition to being keen brawlers, the HAMC earned a reputation as dedicated sex offenders, with a fondness for group sex between multiple Angels and one female. Some of the earliest media coverage of the club concerned their alleged penchant for gang rape—an accusation the club denies.

According to the Department of Justice, the HAMC requires that joining members be male, at least twenty-one years old, own a Harley Davidson motorcycle, and be of Caucasian, Asian, or Hispanic descent. Barger has written there is no rule that members have to ride Harleys, though most Hells Angels do out of habit. Only American-made motorcycles are acceptable in the HAMC community. There are other common denominators in the gang. "The vast majority of motorcycle outlaws are uneducated, unskilled men between 20 and 30, and most have no credentials except a police record," wrote Thompson, in his *Nation* piece, an observation that remains as true today as did in the mid-1960s. The Hells Angels have a strict hierarchy and membership protocol. Bikers who want to join the club start off as a "hangaround," doing lowly tasks for "full-patch" members. After a year or two of service, the hangaround becomes a "prospect" and continues to perform menial duties on behalf of the club. Eventually, a vote is held among chapter members on whether to elevate the prospect to full member status. Hangarounds and prospects often do the club's dirty work, from selling drugs to administering beatings and killings.

According to Thompson, the Angels practice a unique initiation ritual. New members are given a pair of jeans and a denim jacket with the club's death head logo on the back. Initiates put these items on, and then stand in front of their colleagues as a bucket of urine and feces is dumped on them. The jeans are further decorated with motor oil and left to dry, or placed under a motorcycle at night to sop up crankcase emissions. Thus decorated, these jeans and jacket become a new member's "originals"—an official uniform worn until it literally falls apart. Barger, for his part, has denied the authenticity of this ritual and blasted Thompson as a teller of lies.

One thing that is certain is the seriousness with which the Angels take their logo. Called a "patch" or "colors" in biker lingo, the HAMC logo consists of a stylized drawing of a winged skull (called a Death's Head). This drawing is accompanied by a "top rocker," which is a white patch with the name "Hells Angels" written in red letters placed above the winged skull. A "bottom rocker," a white patch with the city the chapter is based in, written in red letters, is placed beneath the skeletal visage. Some Angels also wear "one percenter" patches, an ironic reference to the American Motorcyclist Association's assertion (which some sources say is apocryphal) that 99 percent of American motorcycle owners are peaceful, law-abiding citizens. "HAMC is a sophisticated organization that was incorporated as a non-profit entity in California in 1967. HAMC Corporation owns the rights to the words 'Hells Angels' and the winged Death Head, the symbol of HAMC and vigorously defends those rights . . . the Death Head is trademarked in over 50 countries," notes a U.S. Department of Justice profile of outlaw biker gangs. Motorcyclists caught wearing Hells Angels' "colors" who aren't actually HAMC members are typically brutalized.

Sometimes the Hells Angels do a bit of recruiting. The HAMC will align itself with a smaller motorcycle club. If the smaller club does the HAMC's bidding, then members are allowed to "patch over" and join the Angels. This happened recently in Arizona, a place that had no Hells Angels presence until the late 1990s, when the HAMC absorbed a violent, statewide club called the Dirty Dozen (DD). Despite their name, the DD actually ranked over 120 members. The Angels fast-tracked the membership process, allowing Dirty Dozen members to only serve six months as HAMC prospects, not the usual twelve. Once the Angels had swallowed the club, they culled its ranks to about forty-five core members.

HAMC chapters are grouped into regions. Regional executives meet regularly to discuss business and internal issues. A typical HAMC chapter consists of a president, vice president, secretary/treasurer, road captain, and sergeant-at-arms. The president has veto power over the whole executive. The vice-president steps in when the president is busy. The secretary/treasurer records the chapter minutes and takes care of finances while the sergeant-at-arms keeps order and makes sure everyone follows the rules. It's against HAMC regulations, for example, to spike members' drinks with drugs or toss live ammunition into bonfires at motorcycle runs (events similar to car rallies, in which bikers from across the U.S. congregate in one locale). "Drug burns" are also prohibited. In other words, if a HAMC member sells drugs, they are supposed to carry through with the deal and not rip off their clients. The road captain, meanwhile, is in charge of coordinating and organizing chapter runs. Barring illness, injury, or incarceration, attendance at major runs is mandatory.

Unlike members of the Mafia, who traditionally keep a low profile, HAMC members and other bikers flaunt their outlaw status by their manner of dress, attitude and mode of transportation. It's hard to stay under the radar when you're in a line of Harleys tearing up the highway at 80 mph. Boisterous partying and public rowdiness are an essential part of the HAMC lifestyle. Hells Angels and other outlaw bikers have also exhibited few qualms about committing murders and assaults in front of police, civilians, and security cameras, placing greater importance on club reputation than legal consequences. In spring 2002, for example, the Angels clashed violently with a rival gang called the Mongols in a casino in Laughlin, Nevada. The brief but deadly battle involved hundreds of bikers bearing guns, knives, hammers, wrenches, and other instruments of mayhem. Within minutes, three bikers were killed and a dozen others seriously injured. What was remarkable about the Laughlin clash was that it took place in a public venue, in plain view of countless security cameras, not to mention casino staff and patrons. That their images were being captured on camera for future posterity—and identification purposes by police—bothered neither the HAMC, nor their hated enemies, the Mongols.

Once purely a southern California phenomenon, the Hells Angels now boast members from around the world. The first HAMC chapter outside the USA was launched in New Zealand in 1961. In 1967 the HAMC established their first chapter on the eastern seaboard in Lowell, Massachusetts. A chapter in London, UK was founded in 1969. A chapter was launched in Zurich, Switzerland one year later. The HAMC boasts a worldwide membership of 2,000–2,500 bikers in twenty-six countries, including Germany, Spain, Finland, Canada, Brazil, and

South Africa. As the U.S. Department of Justice succinctly notes, "the Hells Angels pose a criminal threat on six continents."

While biker apologists portray the HAMC as a benign social club for motorcycle enthusiasts, authorities accuse the gang of financing its operations through the proceeds of crime. The FBI claims the HAMC generates $1 billion a year around the world through drug sales alone The U.S. Department of Justice briefing on Outlaw Motorcycle Gangs reports:

The Hells Angels are involved in the production, transportation, and distribution of marijuana and methamphetamine. Additionally, the Hells Angels are involved in the transportation and distribution of cocaine, hashish, heroin, LSD, ecstasy, PCP and diverted pharmaceuticals. The Hells Angels are also involved in other criminal activity including assault, extortion, homicide, money laundering and motorcycle theft.

While eager to portray itself as a club of rowdy but law-abiding motorcyclists, the HAMC's website indicates otherwise. The site contains a page listing deceased members and another page listing members behind bars. Both pages contain a plethora of names, a reflection of the occupational hazards of belonging to the world's most notorious motorcycle club.

See also: Barger, Ralph "Sonny"; Outlaw Motorcycle Gangs

Further Reading:

Ralph "Sonny" Barger, with Keith and Kent Zimmerman, *Hell's Angel: The Life and Times of Sonny Barger and the Hell's Angels Motorcycle Club*, 2001.

Canadian Broadcasting Corporation, "Biker Gangs in Canada," April 21, 2009. http://www.cbc.ca/canada/story/2009/04/01/f-biker-gangs.html.

Drugs and Crime: Outlaw Motorcycle Gang Profile—Hells Angels Motorcycle Club, National Drug Intelligence Center, U.S. Department of Justice, October 2002.

Federal Bureau of Investigation report on Hells Angels. http://foia.fbi.gov/foiaindex/hellsang.htm.

Hells Angels Motorcycle Club. http://www.hells-angels.com.

Yves Lavigne, *Hells Angels at War*, 1999.

William Marsden and Julian Sher, *Angels of Death: Inside the Bikers' Global Crime Empire*, 2006.

Hunter Thompson, *Hell's Angels: The Strange and Terrible Saga of the Outlaw Motorcycle Gangs*, 1966.

Hunter Thompson, "The Motorcycle Gangs: Losers and Outsiders," *The Nation*, May 17, 1965.

U.S. Department of Justice, Outlaw Motorcycle Gangs in the United States. http://www.usdoj.gov/criminal/gangunit/about/omgangs.html.

HILL, HENRY (1943–)

Henry Hill, a former associate of the Lucchese crime family, helped engineer the 1978 Lufthansa heist at JFK airport—one of the largest robberies in U.S. history. He is best known as the primary subject of Nicholas Pileggi's book *Wiseguy*, the inspiration for the movie *Goodfellas*. He later testified in court about his involvement and is one of the most famous of all underworld turncoats.

Hill was fascinated by gangsters as a boy. Born in 1943, Hill grew up in a working class section of Brooklyn. His father was Irish-American, his mother Sicilian-American. He had several

Former mobster Henry Hill in 2005, at the Firefly restaurant in North Platte, Nebraska, where he worked as a chef. [AP Photo/Nati Harnik]

brothers and sisters and little interest in leading an ordinary, respectable life. Hill was drawn to a cabstand near his parents' apartment where mobsters ("wiseguys" in Mafia lingo) congregated. The stand was owned by Paul Vario, a capo in the Lucchese crime family. As a young boy, Hill started doing odd jobs for Vario. In 1955 he dropped out of school for good, to hang out full-time at the cab stand and rub shoulders with gangsters. Besides admiring their clothes, money, and attitude, Hill had one other reason for liking gangsters so much—they treated him decently, unlike his father, who beat him after discovering his son was consorting with criminals. Ironically, Hill was not eligible to join the very organization he so admired. His half-Irish ancestry precluded him from ever becoming "made," or formally inducted into the Mafia. An all Italian-

American group, the Mafia had no problem with letting people from another ethnicity serve in supporting roles now and then. These auxiliary members are known as "associates" and this was the niche Hill set his sights on.

After serving a stint in the army in the early 1960s, Hill returned to New York City where he began working closely with Jimmy Burke, a fellow Irish-American Mafia associate, and Tommy DeSimone, an extremely violent, mentally unstable gangster. In concert with other associates and made Mafia members, the three men pursued various felonies, including loan-sharking, book making, and dealing in stolen goods. Burke's main specialty was hijacking cargo-laden trucks as they left John F. Kennedy Airport. Burke typically gave the driver of each hijacked truck $50 for his trouble, a gesture which earned him the nickname "Jimmy the Gent." In addition to hijacking trucks, Hill took part in an infamous 1967 robbery at JFK airport, in which nearly half-a-million dollars was stolen from an Air France storage room. The heist greatly raised Hill's reputation in New York crime circles.

By the mid-1960s, Hill had acquired a cover job—he had a union card with a local bricklayers association in case officials got nosy about what he did for a living. He had also begun dating a Jewish-American girl named Karen. Karen was impressed with Hill's bon vivant lifestyle, which included top tables at leading nightclubs, expensive restaurant meals, and premium-priced liquor. Shortly after she met Henry, Karen went for a drive with a boy from her Long Island neighborhood. The boy tried to grope her, Karen slapped him, and the boy ended up ditching her miles from home. Karen called Hill, who stormed over to the boy's house and pistol-whipped the overly amorous youth. After beating the boy bloody, Hill stomped to Karen's house, handed her his soiled gun, and asked her to hide it for him. Such macho displays didn't turn Karen off, and she and Hill were married on August 29, 1965. They briefly lived with Karen's parents. Eventually, the newlyweds moved to an apartment in Island Park, New York. They quickly produced two children, Gregg and Gina.

Hill continued to work closely with Burke. At one point the two men traveled to Florida, to collect a large debt from a gambler. The gambler was savagely beaten by Burke and Hill, who ended up getting arrested and charged in federal court for the incident. Hill received a ten-year sentence on federal charges of extortion (the case went federal because he had crossed state lines to commit the assault). Hill served six years, during which time he dealt drugs and did relatively easy time in the company of other Mafia members and associates. He was paroled on July 12, 1978, after Vario promised authorities he would give Hill a job in a nightclub he owned. The position was, in fact, a "no-show" job, somewhat like Hill's faux membership in the bricklayer's union.

Two days after he was paroled, Hill bribed an official at his halfway house in New York and flew to Pittsburgh in violation of his parole conditions. In Pittsburgh he met with a man named Paul Mazzei who owned him money. In lieu of cash Mazzei gave Hill two suitcases filled with marijuana to sell. Too wary to bring this luggage on a plane, Hill took a bus back to New York and started selling pot, thus violating the tenets of both the parole board and the Mafia. Vario had a standing rule that no members or associates of his family were allowed to deal drugs. He feared that the harsh sentences handed down for drug crimes could induce his underlings to cut deals and reveal family secrets if they were ever arrested. Hill wasn't hemmed in by such strictures. He established a big drug operation covering several states. He dealt marijuana, cocaine, heroin, and Quaaludes, and dipped frequently into his own supply. Soon, Hill was snorting cocaine each day, on top of taking Quaaludes, and consuming copious amounts of alcohol.

The infamous Lufthansa heist at JFK airport was Hill's most notable criminal achievement. On December 11, 1978, six or seven men wearing masks and toting guns broke into the Lufthansa cargo building at the airport, tied up the guards, and absconded with $5.8 million in cash and jewels. Hill helped set up the heist. A cargo agent, who also happened to be an avid gambler, had heard that the Lufthansa warehouse wasn't very secure and could be robbed with ease. The cargo agent told a bookie, and the bookie introduced the cargo agent to Marty Krugman, an underworld associate and acquaintance of Hill who owned a men's hair salon and ran gambling operations on the side. Krugman talked to Hill, who passed the information on to Jimmy Burke. Burke met with Krugman, and then arranged the robbery. Hill didn't participate in the actual theft. Shortly after the Lufthansa heist, Burke began killing all the partners who'd helped him pull it off to cover his tracks. In January 1979, Krugman disappeared likely murdered by Burke. By spring 1979, six people with connections to the Lufthansa robbery had been murdered or disappeared.

Tommy DeSimone dropped out of sight roughly around the same time

Marty vanished. It is believed DeSimone was lured into a house under the assumption he was being formally inducted into the Mafia. Instead, he was shot in the head and killed. The criminal grapevine suggested this was in revenge for DeSimone's previous murder of a made Gambino family member named Billy Batts. In the Mafia's strict code of conduct, "made" members are only supposed to be killed with the sanction of higher up bosses.

In the late 1970s, Hill cooked up a point shaving scam with Mazzei, involving the Boston College basketball team. Hill and Mazzei bribed a couple Boston players to miss a few easy baskets, in order to alter the point spread. Hill found bookies who could handle large bets, made sure debts were paid, and generally served as the background organizer of the scheme. Hill involved Burke and other underworld contacts in the scam.

On April 27, 1980, Hill was arrested in Nassau County, New York, on drug trafficking charges. He made bail, only to be arrested again as a material witness for the Lufthansa heist. Hill began to suspect his former colleagues were planning on murdering him. Vario and Burke both had a reason: for breaking the no-drugs rule, and to maintain silence about the Lufthansa heist, respectively. Hill was drinking and drugging heavily during this period, which exacerbated his paranoia. He decided to make a deal with authorities. Shortly after his arrest, Hill and his wife, Karen, and their two kids, entered the federal Witness Protection Program. In return for testifying against former business partners, Hill would be relocated somewhere in the United States, given a monthly stipend, a new name,

and a clean criminal record. His family was included in the deal. Hill testified in several trials which resulted in dozens of convictions. In early 1982 Burke received 20 years for his involvement in the point shaving scam. Two years later, Burke got a life sentence for murder. He died in jail at age sixty-nine on April 13, 1996. Hill also helped convict his old mentor, Vario. The Lucchese capo received four years for lying to federal authorities about the "no-show" job that helped win Hill's parole. In between court appearances, Hill continued to drink and take huge amounts of drugs. His family was moved around quite a bit, from Nebraska to Kentucky, finally ending up in the state of Washington. Even while receiving a regular state stipend, Hill ran scams, sold drugs, and generally burned through any money he had. He would spend his days and nights in barrooms drinking and watching sports, or at home, making deals over the phone. Instead of keeping a low profile, Hill would typically befriend a coterie of drinkers, drug-takers, hustlers and petty criminals in whatever locale he ended up in. More seriously, as far as the federal government was concerned, Hill seemed incapable of keeping silent. He gave interviews to *Sports Illustrated* magazine that resulted in a cover story on the Boston College point shaving scandal. In September 1981 Hill signed a book deal. He worked with a crime writer to come up with the autobiographical tale that would be released under the title *Wiseguy*. In Washington State, Hill racked up several new arrests for drunk driving and burglary, among other offenses. These arrests occurred in 1984. That same year, Hill was dismissed from Witness Protection, due to his inability to remain out of trouble and out of sight. During this same period, Hill began using heroin on top of other drugs and alcohol. More arrests on drug charges followed. In the late 1980s, Hill and Karen divorced.

Hill's children were extremely displeased with his career trajectory: "My father was a cheating, wife-beating, drug-dealing, thieving, gambling, alcoholic ex-con drug addict. I had nothing to rebel against. My only rebellion was to behave," wrote Gregg Hill. Gina Hill was a little more forgiving at first, but later she also soured on Hill. Both Gregg and Gina attended public schools in the communities they were placed in, and had to regularly concoct cover stories to explain their father's behavior to their friends. Their mother's relationship with Hill was equally strange, veering from extreme adoration and forgiveness to towering rages.

Even if his personal and professional life was a mess, Hill found himself becoming famous. The book *Wiseguy*, came out in December 1985 and was a huge bestseller. Director Martin Scorsese turned the book into the well-received 1990 movie *Goodfellas*, which offered a brutal depiction of low-ranking Mafia members and their associates. The book and the movie turned Hill into a mob celebrity, and in-demand interview subject.

Henry Hill has taken up art and sells his amateur paintings on eBay. An avid cook, he has also peddled a Sunday Gravy pasta sauce and worked as a chef in an Italian restaurant. Hill is a regular guest on the Howard Stern Show and continues to run into problems with the law. He was arrested twice for public intoxication in May 2008, for example. He has a fiancée named Lisa Caserta, and lives in southern California.

See Also: Mafia

Further Reading

Heather Alexander, "Mafia King on the Straight and Narrow," *BBC News*, February 29, 2008.

"Ex-Mobster of 'Goodfellas' Fame Wanted in California," *Yahoo! News*, May 17, 2009.

Gregg and Gina Hill, *On the Run: A Mafia Childhood*, 2004.

Henry Hill personal website. http://henryhill 90290.tripod.com.

Nicholas Pileggi, *Wiseguy*, 1986.

J

JAMES, JESSE (1847–1882)

Given his reputation as a folk hero of the Old West, it's ironic that Jesse James always regarded himself as son of the South. Throughout his short life, James fought tenaciously for the Confederate States of America. Even after the Civil War ended, James and his compatriots continued to attack pro-Union individuals and institutions. In fact, James' most famous bank robbery—in Northfield, Minnesota—was conceived as a way to punish a former Northern general turned military governor in occupied Dixie. Contrary to popular legend, James was not a Robin Hood like wraith, striking at the rich to feed the poor. Nor should he be seen as a symbol of the fight against the rising power of corporations, as exemplified by railroad, express companies, and banks. The true burning cause that motivated James was that of Southern secession, an issue that ripped apart the border state of Missouri, where he was raised.

Jesse Woodson James was born on September 5, 1847, in Clay County, Missouri. His mother, Zerelda, was

Jesse James, around the date of his marriage in 1874. [Library of Congress]

strong-willed and pro-South. His father, Robert James, was a wealthy, slave-owning hemp farmer and Baptist minister who migrated to Missouri from Kentucky. Zerelda and Robert had an older son named Frank, and a handful of slaves. Clay County, where James grew up, was called "Little Dixie" after the

103

wave of immigrants from Southern states who settled there. Fully a quarter of the population in Little Dixie was black slaves, versus 10 percent for the state as a whole. Missouri also had a fairly substantial population of immigrants from the North who opposed slavery and supported the Union. Jesse never got to know his father; Robert died when he was three after going to minister to gold miners in California. Widows in 19th century America faced a precarious existence at best, so it's no surprise that Zerelda quickly married again. Her second husband was Benjamin Simms, a wealthy farmer who died two years after the wedding in early 1854. Zerelda had better luck with Dr. Reuben Samuel, a mild-mannered physician whom she married in September 1855. Dr. Samuel moved into Zerelda's existing home, which became known as the Samuel farm.

When the Civil War broke out a bitter internal struggle commenced in Missouri between pro- and anti-Union factions. Southern sympathizers banded together in guerrilla formations. They called themselves "bushwhackers" and targeted civilians and soldiers alike. The bushwhackers were opposed by "Unionists" (people who supported the northern and border states that stayed in the Union). Unionists also formed militias and committed atrocities of their own. The war forced Zerelda and her husband to switch to tobacco farming, as markets for hemp, primarily purchased by Southern interests to make rope for binding cotton bales, were cut off. Zerelda wasn't concerned about any potential loss in commerce, however; she was fanatically pro-South and was delighted when her oldest son, Frank, joined the bushwhackers.

On May 25, 1863, a pro-Union militia called the Enrolled Missouri Militia (EMM) raided the Samuel farm in search of Frank. The Unionists put a noose around Dr. Samuel's neck and threatened to hang him unless he revealed the hiding spot of his stepson. It's believed the EMM also beat or whipped young Jesse, still a teenager. In the end, Frank managed to elude the militia. The EMM had good reason to hunt for Frank, who had joined forces with the notorious William Quantrill. Quantrill's Raiders, as they were called, were bushwhackers of extreme brutality, even by Civil War standards. Three months after the EMM visited the Samuel farm, Quantrill sacked Lawrence, Kansas. The Raiders burned the town down and murdered every man and boy they could find. The final death toll was anywhere from 140 to 200 people. Frank James was believed to have been involved in the carnage.

Unlike a regular army, the bushwhackers didn't have a permanent roster of members. When Frank returned to Clay County in late 1863 after a sojourn in Texas, he teamed up with a different guerrilla unit, this one led by a bushwhacker named Fletch Taylor. Even though he was only sixteen, Jesse James joined as well. It was a brutal apprenticeship for the young Missourian. Taylor's group essentially served as a death squad, going from homestead to homestead murdering pro-Union farmers. On August 8, 1864, Taylor was badly wounded in action, so the James brothers joined a guerrilla band led by Bloody Bill Anderson. Long-haired, charismatic Anderson had been with Quantrill, but broke off to lead his own bushwhacker formation. If possible, Anderson was even more violent than Quantrill. He was in the habit of scalping his victims and hanging their bloody skin and hair on his saddle. Anderson set up camp near the Samuel farm. Zerelda was so taken by the guerrilla leader she made meals for Anderson and his men. She reveled in tales of their worst atrocities. Dr. Samuel was horrified, but remained under his wife's spell and kept up a polite facade before their gruesome house guest.

In mid-August 1864, while riding with his brother, Jesse was wounded in the saddle by a farmer with a rifle. Frank immediately came to his aid, stealing a wagon to transport his injured sibling. Frank took Jesse to the home of a Confederate sympathizer. A doctor was called and Jesse took a month to recover. Jesse was well enough to rejoin Bloody Bill in late September. It's not known for sure if Frank and Jesse participated in the notorious Centralia Massacre, which happened around the same time. In the latter incident, bushwhackers forced twenty-two unarmed Union soldiers off of a train near Centralia, Missouri, shot them dead, and mutilated their bodies. It is believed Jesse and Frank were on hand a few days after the Centralia Massacre, when bushwhackers ambushed a column of Union soldiers. Roughly 100 troopers were killed in this engagement, some of them cut down while trying to surrender. Bloody Bill Anderson himself was ambushed and killed in October 1864. Following his death, Frank rode with Quantrill to Kentucky while Jesse went to Texas with Archie Clement, a former lieutenant of Bloody Bill. Like his mentor, Clement enjoyed scalping his victims and displaying their hairpieces on his saddle.

Jesse and Frank's activities did not go unnoticed. On January 29, 1865, Union authorities ordered Zerelda and Dr. Samuel out of Missouri. They were part of a wave of pro-Southern families exiled from the state in order to deprive the bushwhackers of bases of support. Zerelda and her husband ended up in Rulo, Nebraska. The Civil War officially ended on April 9, 1865, with the surrender of Robert E. Lee at the Appomattox Courthouse in Virginia. Confederate die-hards, such as Jesse and Frank James, refused to give up. The James brothers joined a ragtag group of about 150 guerrillas who worked their way from Texas to Missouri, burning farmhouses belonging to Union supporters, murdering civilians, and ignoring Lee's surrender.

The reality of defeat began hitting home, however, and some bushwhackers gave up. On May 10, 1865, Quantrill himself was ambushed and killed. A few days later, Jesse and Clement tangled with a Union cavalry patrol in rural Missouri. Jesse was badly wounded in the skirmish, shot through the right side of his chest near his previous injury. With his horse killed, Jesse staggered into the woods, bleeding heavily. His fellow bushwhackers stole a carriage and rode Jesse into Lexington, Missouri. He was placed in a hotel where he lay in bed, near death. In later years, Jesse would claim he was trying to surrender when he was shot, and that drunk Union troops ignored a truce flag in his hands. None of this was true. Jesse's recuperation was slow, and it wasn't until October 1865 that he was well enough to return to the Samuel farm in Missouri, to which his parents had been allowed to return when the war ended. He couldn't mount a horse until the next spring. His lengthy convalescence did have one positive benefit; Jesse spent part of his recovery in a boarding-house run by his uncle, John Mimms. Jesse's cousin, who was named Zerelda, after his mother, helped him recover. The two fell in love and proceeded to have a long courtship.

The Civil War had been a shattering experience for the United States, with some 620,000 dead (360,000 Union soldiers and 260,000 Confederates). Missouri was hit worse than some states; the population decreased by 300,000 people from 1861 to 1865. The freeing of the slaves and the abrupt change to the Southern way of life provoked a huge backlash among whites. In the post-war period, the Ku Klux Klan rose to power in several former Confederate states, terrorizing freed blacks and their white allies. Post-war politics in Missouri consisted of a brutal struggle between Republicans (also called Radicals) and Democrats (also called Conservatives). The Republicans wanted to extend full civil rights to African-Americans, prevent Confederates from voting, and make everyone take a loyalty oath to the United States of America. They viewed Confederates as traitors. The Democrats supported the Union, but wanted to put the old social order back in place. They had no problem letting former Confederates take office, viewing them as simply misguided, not traitorous. While opposed to slavery, Democrats were virulently racist, and harbored little good will towards freed African-Americans. Like many bushwhacker veterans, Jesse was horrified by the thought of former slaves winning rights of any kind. His family, in fact, continued to retain the services of some of their slaves, even after they had been technically set free. In addition to being outraged by postwar politics, Jesse was bored. Peacetime couldn't measure up to the action, danger, and camaraderie of being guerrillas in an epic struggle.

Other former bushwhackers felt the same. Clement and his men, for example, continued to run wild. On February 13, 1866, a group led by Clement committed the first ever daylight robbery of a bank in U.S. history. The target—the Clay County Savings Association—was based in Liberty, Missouri, and run by Republicans. During the robbery, an innocent bystander named George Wymore was shot dead. Banks had been robbed in America before, but generally by burglars operating in the dead of night, or white collar criminals pursuing financial scams. Clement's crew robbed a few more banks and in late 1866, launched an audacious raid on Lexington, Missouri. A force of about 100 bushwhackers took over the town only to withdraw, as a pro-Union militia sent by the governor approached. On December 13, for unclear reasons, Clement and a couple dozen bushwhackers re-entered Lexington. Clement went to a local bar and started drinking. When Union troops arrived to arrest him, a gunfight ensued and Clement was killed. Jesse was extremely upset. Some reports indicate Jesse and Frank took part in some of Clement's bank robberies, although the record is unclear on this.

A group of colleagues began to coalesce around Jesse and Frank. They were mostly ex-bushwhackers, and they included Clell Miller, Wood and Clarence Hite, George and Ol (Oliver) Shepherd, Bill Ryan, Charlie Pitts, Jim Cummins, Tom Little, and Payton (Payne) Jones. These men were used to guns, violence, horses, and quick escapes. A quartet of brothers—Cole, John, Jim and Bob Younger—rounded out this loose-knit group. By dint of charisma, zeal, and determination, Jesse became the de facto leader of the band. His more phlegmatic older brother Frank apparently had no problem with this leadership arrangement. At some point, this ragtag group of former guerrillas decided to follow Clement's example and start robbing banks. It's unclear which was the first bank robbed by the fledgling James-Younger gang, as they came to be called. On March 20, 1868, for example, bandits made off with $9,000 in paper money and $3,000 in gold coins in a bank robbery in Russellville, Kentucky. Jesse and Frank were involved in the heist, though not in a key way. The robbers didn't get away unscathed; George Shepherd was arrested and received three years in jail for his troubles, while his brother Ol, was shot dead by lawmen.

Jesse James didn't achieve notoriety until December 7, 1869, when he and Frank held up the Daviess County Savings Association in Gallatin, Missouri. The robbery didn't net much money. What made the event infamous was a cold-blooded murder committed by Jesse. Jesse mistook cashier Captain John Sheets for Samuel Cox, the Union militia officer who killed Bloody Bill Anderson, and shot the man dead. Jesse and Frank ran outside the bank as townspeople, alerted by the gunfire inside the bank, began shooting at them. The shots startled Jesse's horse, which reared and knocked him off the saddle. His boot was still trapped in the stirrup, however, and Jesse was dragged about thirty feet before he could free himself. Frank circled back on his horse and picked up his younger brother. Just out of town, the pair came across a mount tied to a fence, which they stole at gunpoint, giving each man his own horse. The Gallatin robbery

was committed during an extremely bitter period in American history. In response to violence in the South directed at ex-slaves, Radical Republicans in Congress passed the Reconstruction Act of 1867. The South was divided into five districts under military control. The Republicans vowed to keep a military presence in the South until the former Confederate states passed new constitutions that allowed blacks to vote. Ironically, the man Jesse murdered in the Daviess County Savings Association was a Democrat, who opposed the Radical Republican agenda.

Jesse ventured to Texas in August 1870. When he returned to Missouri in the following year, he began to court Zerelda Mimms (better known as "Zee") while Frank went about courting a schoolteacher named Anna or Annie Ralston. On June 3, 1871, four men on horseback—believed to be the James brothers, plus Clell Miller and Cole Younger—rode to Corydon, Iowa. Almost the whole of that small community had turned out to hear famous orator Henry Clay Dean, who was giving a talk in the yard of a Methodist church. The town was nearly empty as the quartet of strangers rode to the local bank and robbed it of about $6,000. After relieving the bank of cash, the four rode by the churchyard. One of their members couldn't resist interrupting Mr. Dean to announce they had just robbed the bank. With that announcement hanging in the air, Jesse and his comrades sauntered off, laughing.

The James-Younger gang had no formal structure or permanent roster of members except for Jesse and Frank. The gang came together to commit robberies, with members often going their own way once the heist had been pulled. While their main goal was profit, not murder, the James-Younger gang had no scruples about killing anyone who got in their way. During an April 29, 1872, robbery at a Columbia, Kentucky, bank, for example, the gang murdered cashier R.A.C. Martin because he wouldn't give up the keys to the vault. If lethal, the James-Younger gang was also audacious. On September 26, 1872, three men (sources differ as to whether it was Jesse, Cole and John Younger or Jesse, Frank and Bob Younger) robbed a ticket booth at the Kansas City Exposition. Given that thousands of people were in attendance, it was a pretty daring move. In the course of the robbery, one member of the gang accidentally shot and wounded a little girl. For all their gall, the gang collected less than $1,000 for the robbery. Had they made their appearance half an hour earlier, they could have gotten ten times that amount, as the treasurer of the fair had arrived at that time to get the take.

Around this time, Jesse formed an informal alliance with John Newman Edwards, a newspaper editor with a strong pro-Confederate bias. Edwards' paper, the *Kansas City Times*, lauded Jesse and his comrades for the Kansas City heist in a glowing editorial called, "The Chivalry of Crime." Edwards compared the trio to King Arthur's Knights of the Roundtable, and praised their courage, while glossing over their careless gunplay. A couple weeks after the Kansas City robbery, Edwards published a letter, believed to have been penned by Jesse James. It was signed with the names of three famous outlaws from Europe, and tried to vindicate the Kansas City robbers. "It is true I shot a little girl, though it was not intentional and I am very sorry that the child was shot; and if the parents will give me

their address, through the columns in the *Kansas City Weekly Times*, I will send them money to pay for her doctor's bills," wrote Jesse. The letter also touched on politics: "Just let a party of men commit a bold robbery and the cry is to hang them, but Grant and his party steal millions and it is alright." This was a reference to Republican president Ulysses S. Grant whose administration was notoriously corrupt. The letter claimed that the James-Younger gang only ever killed in self-defense. The gang's definition of "self-defense" seemed rather broad, however, given that the missive stated, "a man who is damned enough fool to refuse to open a safe or vault when he is covered with a pistol ought to die." The same letter also claimed the gang robbed from the rich and gave to the poor, which was totally untrue. Jesse James' mob never shared their loot, except with fellow gang members and their families.

On July 21, 1873, the James-Younger gang carried out their first train robbery. The gang pulled a pair of spikes from a track near Council Bluffs, Iowa, and derailed a train. The engine was thrown off the track which caused the boiler to burst, scalding engineer John Rafferty to death. The train was heavy laden with precious metal bullion, which express companies shipped across the country between financial institutions, but the gang didn't touch it. Bullion was far too bulky to transport. It was much easier to concentrate on the train safe and make off with cash, which is what the gang did, taking a total of $2,337.

In January 1874 bandits robbed stagecoaches in Bienville Parish, Louisiana, and Malvern, Arkansas. The James-Younger gang was believed responsible for both hold ups.

At the end of the same month, the gang held up another train near the tiny village of Gads Hill, Missouri. After riding into town, the James-Younger gang robbed money and valuables from the town's leading merchant, and then herded all the residents of the small community to the local train platform. When the train arrived, Jesse's men flagged it down to get it to stop and then threw a switch, forcing the train into a side platform. After the train came to a halt, the gang stepped on board, drew their guns, and robbed the passengers. The crew treated the heist almost as a lark. Jesse announced he didn't want money from workingmen, but only wealthy passengers. In total, the gang collected about $2,000.

As the James-Younger gang rose in notoriety, the clamor to do something about them grew louder. In early 1874 the Adams Express Company hired the famous Pinkerton National Detective Agency to crush Jesse's gang. The Chicago-based Pinkertons were best known for tracking down big-city criminals in urban environments. They were slightly out of their league dealing with rural felons like Jesse James and his crew. The Pinkertons also faced another major problem in that many residents of Missouri were strongly sympathetic towards the James-Younger gang, seeing them as allies in the Confederate cause. The Pinkertons were game, however, and in mid-March 1874 an agent named Joseph or John Whicher suddenly showed up in Clay County. Whicher tried to pass himself off as a farm hand looking for work—a ploy that was not hugely believable, given the lack of calluses on his hands. His plan was to infiltrate Jesse's community, and observe the James brothers, with an eye to eventually arresting them. The brave but foolhardy Whicher knocked on the door to the Samuel farm one night, and that was the last time he was seen alive. Historians speculate that Jesse and Frank saw through his weak disguise and murdered the man forthwith.

Whicher wasn't the only agent trying to track down the James-Younger gang. Two other Pinkertons—Louis Lull and John Boyle—enlisted the help of a former deputy sheriff named Edwin Daniels, and set out on the same quest in the same region at roughly the same time. Lull and Boyle pretended to be cattle buyers. Riding around rural Missouri, the trio managed to attract the attention of two of the Younger brothers, John and Jim. The two brothers rode after the three lawmen and caught up with them near a crossroads. As the Youngers came into view, Boyle spurred his horse and rode away at a gallop. Lull and Daniel were taken prisoner. Still mounted on their horses, the men were ordered to drop their pistol belts to the ground. Lull, however, had an extra pistol behind his back. As John Younger covered the men with a shotgun, Lull whipped out his backup gun and fired a round that caught the bandit in the throat. John managed to pull the trigger on his shotgun, shredding Lull's arm, before collapsing. In fury, Jim Younger also fired at Lull, then at Daniels, killing him. Lull's horse panicked and raced away, with its badly wounded master still in the saddle. Lull hit a tree branch and fell from his horse. He managed to stumble through the woods, despite his terrible injuries. He was helped by a farm laborer and led to safety. Lull managed to live for three more days, during which time he gave a sworn account of the gunfight to a coroner.

Jesse was annoyed but not alarmed at being targeted by the Pinkertons. On April 24, 1874, he finally married his cousin, Zee. The happy couple ended up having two children who survived childhood, a boy and a girl. The James-Younger gang had, however, made themselves bitter enemies of Allan Pinkerton, founder of the private detective agency that bore his name. Crushing Jesse James became something of an obsession for the dedicated sleuth. Pinkerton sent more men into the fray, who worked closely with pro-Union farmers who also detested Jesse and company. One of these farmers, Daniel Askew, happened to own land that abutted the Samuel homestead, which was extremely convenient for the Pinkertons.

On the night of January 25, 1875, the Pinkerton agents made their move. They had received a tip that the James brothers were planning on visiting their mother at the Samuel farm. Unfortunately, when the Pinkertons crept onto Zerelda's property, her two sons weren't home. The Pinkerton men stealthily made their way up to the Samuel farmhouse then tossed either a bomb or an incendiary device inside. The Pinkertons would later claim they merely wanted to illuminate the interior of the house in order to carry out a raid. Unsure what the strange device was, Dr. Reuben Samuel scooped it up with a shovel and tossed it in the fireplace. The object overheated and, as the Samuel family stood watching, exploded. Jesse's eight-year-old half-brother, Archie, was killed in the blast. The matriarch of the James clan lost her arm and nearly died. The botched raid was a public relations nightmare for the Pinkerton Agency. The bomb plot made the Pinkertons look both sinister and incompetent. Jesse and Frank soon had their revenge. Askew was shot dead in April 1875, as were other area Union supporters who had assisted the Pinkertons.

By this point, Jesse could be forgiven for feeling over-confident. The armed robberies he led had been successful for the most part. He was receiving highly congratulatory press coverage, thanks to John Newman Edwards (an important consideration for an avid newspaper reader like Jesse) and so far, the law had proven totally unable to stop his gang. With this in mind, Jesse organized what was to become his gang's most famous—and least successful—armed robbery. The target was the First National Bank of Northfield in distant Minnesota. While the James-Younger gang was eager to steal cash, they also wanted to punish one the bank's main customers: former Civil War general Adelbert Ames. Ames had fought bravely for the North and was deeply sympathetic to black ex-slaves. Ames served as military governor of Mississippi from 1873 to 1876, and tried to protect African-Americans from the Ku Klux Klan and other white supremacists. After only a few years in office, Ames desperately wanted to escape the madness of the Deep South. He quit his position and moved to Northfield, where his father and brother John lived, and ran a flour mill. Ames joined the family business and expected no more trouble from die-hard Confederates.

In later years, Cole Younger wrote a description of the Northfield raid during his stay in Minnesota's Stillwater Prison. The report was published by *The Northfield News* on November 26, 1915. "We had been informed that ex-Governor Ames of Mississippi and General

Benjamin Butler of Massachusetts had deposited $75,000 in the National Bank of that place, and it was the above information that caused us to select the bank of Northfield," wrote Cole. Butler was Ames' father-in-law. He too had been a Union commander, but the James-Younger gang was mistaken. Butler had no connection to the First National Bank.

A total of eight men set out on horseback from Missouri to Northfield. Led by Jesse and Frank, the men purchased good horses for their trip and made sure they were well stocked with weapons, including new Smith & Wesson revolvers. If anyone asked, the men pretended to be cattle buyers. At 10 a.m. on the morning of September 7, 1876, four of the bandits made a leisurely scouting mission around Northfield, and then retired to a local restaurant for breakfast. After eating their fill, the James-Younger gang went to work. Jesse divided the men into three groups. The first group, made up of three men, would go into the bank and perform the robbery. Two men would stay outside the bank to act as guards while a third group positioned themselves at a bridge near an adjacent square. Jesse, Frank and Charlie Pitts rushed into the bank, brandishing pistols. The plan almost immediately became unglued. Far from being cowed, cashier Joseph Heywood refused to open the safe. Even with a knife pressed to his throat and threatened with death, Heywood remained defiant. He lied and claimed the safe had a time lock and couldn't be opened. In frustration one of the bandits pistol-whipped Heywood and fired a shot next to his head to intimidate him. It didn't work. Using the commotion as cover, another clerk named A.E. Bunker rushed out the bank's back door. Pitts

chased after the man and shot him, but the clerk kept running until he reached safety.

The two bandits outside the bank began shooting their weapons in the air to frighten the townspeople. The group of three posted by the bridge began riding their horses up and down the street in front of the bank, shooting and hollering. Instead of frightening Northfield residents, the shooting emboldened them. Quickly grasping that a bank robbery was in process, townspeople grabbed their guns and returned fire. Many of the townspeople had rifles, which they used to hunt deer. Some were veterans of the Civil War on the Northern side. They were familiar with guns and weren't scared to stand up to the James-Younger gang. Residents took cover and blasted the bandits without mercy. Clell Miller screamed as he was hit in the face with birdshot fired from a shotgun. His horse was killed, and he flopped to the ground. Cole Younger leapt off his horse and raced to his comrade. Seeing that Miller was dying, Cole took his gun belts, correctly reckoning that the extra firearms would soon be necessary. Then Cole got back on his horse and continued shooting.

In the middle of the battle, a messenger rushed to the flour mill to inform Adelbert Ames about the raid. Ames bravely decided to investigate the situation for himself. He stood behind a hardware store owner who was firing away with a rifle. Ames noticed that the man's hands were trembling, affecting his aim. He spoke reassuring words to the store owner, just as a general might do to encourage a private in the heat of war. The former Union commander's presence helped settle the store owner, and his hands became steady as he worked his rifle. The store owner took aim and fired, and a bandit named Bill Chadwell (also known as William Stiles) dropped dead in the street. Bob and Jim Younger dismounted and used one of their horses for cover. The horse was shot and killed, and then Bob took a round in the right elbow. With his right arm hanging uselessly, Bob transferred his pistol to his left hand and fired wildly. Realizing they were in a desperate situation, Cole kicked in the bank door and shouted at Jesse to leave. As the bandits raced out of the bank, Jesse turned and shot the cashier, Heywood, dead. Now that they were all outside, the gang continued to draw fire. As Jesse, Frank and Charlie Pitts leapt on their horses, Jim Younger was hit in the shoulder. The badly wounded Bob Younger saw his comrades fleeing on horseback and cried after them. Cole Younger swung around, grabbed his brother and pulled him onto his own mount. Then they raced out of town with the remaining men in the gang.

The raid had been a total disaster—the James-Younger gang left behind two dead and didn't get a single dollar. Ironically, the gang was a victim of its own success. Accounts of their previous robberies had been major news. Small towns became familiar with their modus operandi and Northfield residents didn't fall into paralyzed shock when the gang came raiding. Jesse and his compatriots fled the town in disarra, as a massive posse began chasing them. The gang paused very briefly outside of Northfield to clean and bandage their wounds and take stock of the situation. Almost every member of the gang had been badly wounded. Jim Younger had been hit in the shoulder and upper jaw. His mouth bled profusely, despite the best efforts of

his friends to stem the flow. Bob Younger had his elbow wound to deal with, while Frank had taken shots in his legs. Jesse was the least injured of all the men. They had no time to contemplate medical intervention, however. Other towns had been telegraphed about the robbery and now the whole state was on high alert. Moving very slowly, the gang only managed to travel fifteen miles from Northfield in four days.

With hundreds of men searching for them, Jesse made a brutal command decision. The group would have to split off. Jesse and Frank would head back to Missouri. The badly wounded Younger brothers would have to fend for themselves. Charlie Pitts had the choice of staying with the Youngers or taking off with the James brothers. He chose to stay with the Youngers. Frank and Jesse split from the group. They hid in the forest by day and rode on one horse at night. While they managed to escape from the main body of the posse pursuing them, both brothers were wounded in an altercation with a farmer. The farmer fired a shotgun blast that killed their horse and injured both brothers—Jesse in the knee and Frank in the thigh. The bleeding brothers stumbled into a cornfield where they remained for several hours. The posse after them wasn't eager to search for the two killers amidst crowded rows of corn. Jesse and Frank waited until nightfall, and then slipped away. They stole two horses from another farmer and kept going.

On September 17, 1876, the James brothers crossed the state border into Dakota Territory. They pressed on, wearing the same clothes they'd had on for days, and stealing food from farms to eat until they reached Iowa. On September 20, 1876, near Sioux City, Iowa, they encountered a doctor on horseback who stopped to ask them directions to a patient's farm. Jesse and Frank produced pistols instead. The doctor was forced to re-bandage their wounds and exchange clothes with Jesse. The brothers also took the physician's horse, leaving him one of their broken down mounts in return. Then they departed, safe from Minnesota posses. The Youngers and Charlie Pitts weren't quite so lucky. The four men continued to hobble through the forest, the wounded among them in great pain. The quartet's morale wasn't helped by their growing hunger (by this point, the men were reduced to stealing corn and potatoes from farm fields to survive) and the torrential rain which soaked them. Meanwhile, a huge posse was determined to hunt them down.

On September 21, 1876, one of the four hungry bandits tried to buy bread and eggs from a farmhouse in Madelia (150 miles southwest of Northfield). The farm boy he approached sensed something about the man was suspicious. The youth followed him into the forest, where he discovered three other men by a campsite. The boy made it out of the woods without being spotted. He raced to inform local sheriff James Glispin of his find. Glispin grabbed his rifle, organized a posse, and then went searching in the woods where the boy said the men were hiding. The Youngers and Pitts were trapped. The posse, numbering about 150, stood outside the woods, blasting the trees with shotguns and rifles. They hoped to flush the bandits out, or even shoot them dead at long distance. Sheriff Glispin and seven other brave men stepped into the forest. The group walked cautiously in a line. After going about 50 yards into the woods, Glispin spotted Pitts. The two men shot

at each other at almost the same time. Pitts missed, but the sheriff didn't. Pitts tried to run, but fell over dead. The eight man detachment quickly located the three wounded Younger brothers. The trio tried shooting it out but it was hopeless. Cole and Jim were shot again. Bob Younger fired back with his left hand, and then called out in surrender. The posse entered the woods en masse, took the Youngers prisoner, and removed Pitts' body. Doctors in Madelia were amazed at the extent of the Youngers' wounds. Cole Younger had been shot eleven times, including once under his right eye. Jim had accumulated eight buckshot wounds, one rifle wound, and a smashed upper jaw. Doctors didn't expect Jim to live, but he pulled through.

On December 11, 1876, the Youngers pled guilty to robbery and being accessories to murder. The three were placed in a penitentiary at Stillwater, Minnesota. Bob died in jail of tuberculosis on September 16, 1889. Cole and Jim served out twenty-five-year sentences, and were then released. Jim Younger committed suicide in a St. Paul, Minnesota hotel, depressed over his inability to get a normal job and an unrequited infatuation with a young lady. Cole Younger outlasted his siblings, and died in Lee's Summit in Missouri, on March 21, 1916.

The masterminds behind the disastrous Northfield raid laid low. It was rumored that Jesse and Frank lived in Mexico for a while. At some point, they moved to the Nashville, Tennessee area where they adopted fake names; Frank called himself B.J. Woodson while Jesse went by J.D. Howard. In Nashville they were joined by two old members of the James-Younger gang who hadn't accompanied them to Northfield: Bill Ryan (who called himself Tom Hill) and Dick Liddil (who went by Charles Underwood). Frank used the respite to abandon the outlaw life. He became a hard-working farmer and even started attending church. His more impulsive younger brother found it harder to adjust to a normal life, however. Jesse was extremely bored and itched for action, in spite of the Northfield fiasco. Jesse had been immersed in outlaw activity since he was sixteen years old. It was practically all he knew. He wasn't interested in settling down like Frank and farming the land. Jesse moved his family into Frank's home in 1879, and then went about recruiting a new gang. On October 8, 1879, Jesse's new gang held up a train in Glendale, Missouri. Six men in total took part in the heist. The gunmen herded the town's small population into the train station, and then ordered the station agent to signal for the train to stop. Once stopped, the bandits boarded the train and removed $35,000 in cash and valuables from the safe. A good haul, except that only $6,000 of this amount was in cash.

While initially successful, Jesse's new outfit couldn't hold a match to the original James-Younger gang. While the latter was made up of disciplined, battle-hardened veterans of the Civil War, the latest version of the James gang consisted largely of inexperienced youths and simple thugs. New members included Tucker Basham, a none-too-intelligent young farmer, and Ed Miller, younger brother of Clell Miller who had been killed at Northfield. The gang also included Wood Hite, Dick Liddil and Bill Ryan. In the spring of 1880 Jesse was introduced to the Ford brothers, Bob and Charley, another pair of potential gang recruits. The two young men lived with their sister, a widow named Martha Bolton, who kept a farm near Richmond, in Ray County, Missouri. Martha's homestead was called the Harbison place. Jesse started using the Harbison place as a hideout, which no doubt pleased Dick Liddil, who had his eye on the widow Bolton.

Jesse continued his outlaw pursuits, oblivious to the forces coming together to bring him down. On January 10, 1881, Thomas Crittenden was inaugurated as the new governor of Missouri. A pro-Union Democrat, Crittenden was determined to crush Jesse James and bandits like him. Crittenden spent much of his inaugural address attacking banditry and lawlessness in Missouri. In mid-March, Jesse and company robbed an engineering crew who were doing work on the Muscle Shoals canal in Alabama. Jesse stole $5,240.18 in gold and silver coins and bills. Assisting him on this adventure were Ryan and, most likely, Wood Hite.

It quickly became evident that Ryan was an unreliable member of the gang. Shortly after the Muscle Shoals robbery, Ryan got drunk in a bar near Nashville. He unwisely started spouting off about what a daring outlaw he was, which attracted the attention of the law. Ryan was arrested and tossed in jail. His bad luck didn't end there. A robbery victim identified Ryan as one of the gunmen who had pulled off the Muscle Shoals job. After learning about Ryan's arrest through the newspaper, the James brothers decided it would be a good idea to leave Nashville. It was not a prospect Frank looked forward to. He was happy being a farmer and a family man, and had no desire to be an outlaw again. Above all else, however, Frank remained loyal to his brother and grudgingly accompanied Jesse to Kentucky, where they hid out.

Having convinced Frank to leave his farm, Jesse managed to entice his older brother back into the criminal life. Frank reluctantly agreed to take part in a train robbery, which the James gang pulled off in mid-July 1881. Frank, Jesse and a third man boarded the Rock Island & Pacific Train in Cameron, north of Kansas City. All three men had beards (Jesse had dyed his black, to throw off anyone trying to identify him). Near Gallatin, Missouri, four other men boarded the train. The quartet proceeded to order the engineer to stop the train. Once the train halted, the three bearded men leapt up and brandished revolvers at the startled passengers. Jesse fired a few warning shots into the ceiling of the passenger car. Either by accident or deliberate intent, Jesse shot and killed the train conductor, William Westfall. Another innocent civilian—a man named Frank McMillan—was also killed in the robbery. All the James gang got for two murders was about $600 in cash.

There has been speculation that Westfall was specifically targeted for death. According to one theory, Westfall happened to have been the conductor on the train that sped the Pinkerton agents to Clay County back in 1875 for their disastrous raid on the Samuel farm. The implication was that Westfall knew about the Pinkerton's secret mission, and therefore was an accessory to the crime as far as Jesse was concerned. Regardless of Westfall's possible involvement in the ill-fated Pinkerton foray, the train shootings turned public sentiment against the new James gang. On July 25, 1881, Governor Crittenden met with executives from railway and express companies in St. Louis. He convinced them to put up a huge reward for the capture of Jesse, Frank and all their accomplices. For turning in Jesse or Frank, a citizen could expect a reward of $10,000. The rest of the gang was valued at $5,000 apiece. These were staggering sums for the era. The potential reward money caught the attention of many erstwhile allies of the James gang, including Bob and Charley Ford.

In September 1881 a determined prosecutor named William Wallace convicted James gang member Ryan, who was sent to a Missouri penitentiary for 25 years. The conviction came as a huge blow to Jesse, who was convinced no jury in Missouri would ever convict one of his men. Even more disheartening was the fact that former gang member Tucker Basham, who had been arrested back in July 1880, testified against Ryan. Basham had turned on his comrades in return for the promise of a lighter sentence. Ryan's trial and Basham's betrayal unnerved Jesse, who became increasingly paranoid. He started having doubts about every member of his gang, with the exception of Frank. In a paranoid rage he murdered Ed Miller, convinced the man was disloyal as well.

As it turned out, Jesse had good reason to be paranoid. Martha Bolton was secretly communicating with Governor Crittenden. She told the governor she might have information about the James gang. She wanted an assurance however, that gang members who voluntarily turned themselves in wouldn't be punished too harshly. Governor Crittenden assured the widow that any member of the James gang other than Jesse and Frank could expect to receive clemency if they surrendered. Of course, they would also have to provide helpful information about the gang's movements. At the widow's urging, Dick Liddil turned himself in. With Liddil's assistance, authorities arrested Clarence Hite, who was jailed for taking part in the Winston train robbery. Clarence proceeded to get tuberculosis while in jail, and was subsequently released to go home and die.

Liddil wasn't through with the Hite family yet; on December 4, 1881, Liddil and Wood Hite got into a ferocious, close-quarters gun duel inside the Harbison place. The two men were most likely fighting over Martha Bolton, though Liddil himself later claimed otherwise. Wood was killed, and Liddil was wounded. It has been speculated that Bob Ford might have heard the commotion and joined the fray, shooting Hite himself for good measure. With Hite dead and Liddil bound for jail, Jesse would have two less men by his side if and when the Ford brothers decided to collect the reward on his head. On January 6, 1882, Liddil was arrested again. He agreed to testify against the James brothers in exchange for not being prosecuted for various violent offenses.

Charley and Bob Ford arranged to meet with Governor Crittenden in Kansas City, on January 13, 1882. The Ford brothers were led to believe (so they later stated) that the reward money would be handed out regardless of whether Jesse and Frank were brought in alive or killed in action. Crittenden also suggested that the Ford brothers would receive pardons for any crimes committed in the quest to bring down the James brothers. Charley and Bob were in an excellent position to carry out the governor's wishes. Running low on recruits thanks to murder, jail, and betrayal, Jesse

had accepted the Ford brothers into his gang. By this point, Jesse was residing in St. Joseph, Missouri. Charley Ford had been living with Jesse since the previous fall. Bob joined the household in March of 1882. Apparently Jesse wanted to keep his remaining gang members close to his side.

On April 3, 1882, Jesse and the Ford brothers had breakfast at the James residence. A robbery had been planned for later that day, which Charley and Bob were scheduled to take part in. An unseasonably warm day, Jesse removed his coat, and also took off his guns. Noticing some dust on a picture hanging on a wall, he stood on a chair and swiped at the offending grime with a feather duster. With his back turned to the Ford brothers, he didn't see Bob's gun aimed at his skull. Bob shot twice, hitting Jesse at point-blank range in the back of the head. He was likely dead before he hit the floor. Jesse's violent death caused a huge commotion in St. Joseph, with startled residents pouring into the James residence to view the slain bank robber. The Ford brothers made no attempt to cover up their crime, and even took credit for Jesse's assassination. To their surprise, Charley and Bob found themselves under arrest. The brothers plead guilty to murder, were sentenced to die, and received pardons from Governor Crittenden all on the same day.

Jesse James was buried on the grounds of the Samuel farm in Clay County. He was thirty-four years old. The inscription on his grave-marker, (written by Zerelda) highlighted Jesse's violent end. According to his tombstone, Jesse had been "murdered by a traitor and a coward whose name is not worthy to appear here." While they managed to elude jail, the sniveling Ford brothers met a barrage of criticism from the public. The manner and method of Jesse's murder was seen as cowardly in the extreme. After receiving a bit of reward money, the brothers wisely left Missouri. There was also public outrage over what appeared to be a blatant sanction of the murder a citizen on the part of Governor Crittenden. It was never clear if the governor directly ordered the assassination of Jesse James, but that was how the affair was perceived. Already a folk hero, Jesse now became a martyr to the Confederate cause.

Zerelda James and Frank James's wife, Anne Ralston, approached prosecutor Wallace with an eye to saving Frank's life. They arranged for Frank to surrender peacefully without being murdered. Frank kept his part of the deal and gave himself up to Governor Crittenden in October 1881. Frank was put on trial for murdering Frank McMillan during the Winston train robbery. The courthouse battle, which commenced in mid 1883, took on shades of the Civil War. The topic of Southern rights was discussed alongside the mechanics of murder, as if Frank's support for the former exonerated him on the latter count. Certainly, the jury was sympathetic; even though Dick Liddil testified against him, Frank was acquitted. Frank was tried in federal court for the Muscle Shoals, Alabama robbery, but he had nothing to do with that crime, and was acquitted again. Another trial in February 1885 for the Missouri Pacific Train robbery was discontinued after a key witness died. The case was dropped and Frank lived out his life free from jail. He died peacefully at age 72 in 1915.

The Ford brothers met more violent endings. On May 8, 1884, sick with tuberculosis and addicted to morphine, Charley Ford killed himself in Richmond, Missouri. Bob Ford, meanwhile, was shot dead on June 8, 1892, in Creede, Colorado.

Soon after his death, Jesse's life was heralded in a series of "dime novels" about Wild West characters. Later, many films were made about Jesse, usually portraying him in a sympathetic light as a Robin Hood-like folk hero. These films generally played down his Confederate sympathies and Civil War activities. Today, along with Billy the Kid, Jesse James remains a well-known bandit of the American West. Although his name is famous, very few people are aware of the political convictions that actually inspired Jesse to rob, raid, and murder.

See Also: Dalton Gang

Further Reading:

"An Old Accomplice's Comment: An Interview with Cole Younger, in Jail, in Minnesota," *New York Times*, April 5, 1882.

"A Train Robber's Story: Confession of a Man Who Was Connected with Jesse James and his Party," *New York Times*, April 1, 1882.

"Jesse James's Death," *New York Times*, April 6, 1882.

"Jesse James Shot Down," *New York Times*, April 4, 1882.

T. J. Stiles, *Jesse James: Last Rebel of the Civil War*, 2002.

T.J. Stiles, "The War on Terror, 1865: The Civil War in Missouri and the Rise of Jesse James." http://www.tjstiles.net/work7.htm.

Primary source Archive One, T.J. Stiles. http://www.tjstiles.net/work2.htm.

Paul Wellman, *A Dynasty of Western Outlaws*, 1961.

JEWISH GANGSTERS

Today, the term "Jewish gangster" seems like an oxymoron. Jews are not typically associated with organized crime in the public's mind, as are (fairly or not) Italian-Americans and other groups.

For the first half of the 20th century, however, Jewish gangsters such as Dutch Schultz, Meyer Lansky, and Louis ("Lepke") Buchalter were among the most prominent crime bosses in America. Many of the assassins in Murder, Inc. were Jewish, as was Benjamin "Bugsy" Siegel, the mobster who created the template for modern Las Vegas.

There were Jewish members in late 19th and early 20th century New York street gangs, such as Edward "Monk" Eastman's loose-knit organization.

The first truly prominent Jewish gangster, however, was likely Arnold Rothstein, who rose to infamy in New York in the 1910s and 1920s. Rothstein was an underworld financier who provided start up money for promising criminal enterprises. Rothstein was such a seminal figure that he served as the basis for the character Meyer Wolfsheim, the mysterious mob boss at the center of the classic American novel, *The Great Gatsby*.

The stereotype of Jews being good with money also applied to Meyer Lansky, who was close friends with Mafia boss Charles "Lucky" Luciano. Born Meyer Suchowljansky in Grodno, Poland in 1902, Lansky was widely hailed as a financial genius whose criminal net worth came to $300 million. While the latter figure represented a wild exaggeration, Lansky did have a well-deserved reputation for being a cool businessman who preferred to negotiate

Jewish gangster Louis "Lepke" Buchalter, handcuffed and with cigar in his free hand, is led into a police van transporting him to the New York Court of Appeals Building in Albany, New York, 1936. [AP Photo]

with rivals and potential allies, rather than just kill them.

Like Rothstein, Lansky was immortalized in fictional format as the duplicitous character "Hyman Roth" in *The Godfather Part Two*. In real life Lansky was somewhat less than an all-powerful puppet master. In the late 1950s he spent millions on a luxury hotel/casino in Cuba, only to have it seized by the government when Fidel Castro took power.

Other prominent Jewish gangsters weren't satisfied with merely being financiers. Detroit's Purple Gang, for example, simply murdered everyone who stood in their way, including hapless truck drivers shipping bootleg liquor for rival gangs. A loosely knit organization run by brothers Abe, Ray, Izzy and Joe Bernstein, the Purples emerged from Detroit's old Jewish neighborhood. Their rise as a top bootlegging gang during

Prohibition was accompanied by ferocious violence.

At one point, some Purple members left the gang to set up something called the "Little Jewish Navy" with thugs from Al Capone's crew. The Navy was a collection of fast boats that sped bootleg alcohol across the Detroit River from Canada to the United States.

The Purple's affiliation with Al Capone didn't end there; Purple Gang members Phil and Harry Keywell took part in the notorious St. Valentine's Day Massacre, in which Capone's thugs murdered members of a rival gang in a cold Chicago garage.

Abraham "Kid Twist" Reles was another Jewish thug who murdered a group of his peers (Irving, Meyer and Willie Shapiro) in the early 1930s. Reles and his partner, Buggsy Goldstein, worked closely with Lansky and his partner, Bugsy Siegel. Lansky and Siegel provided Reles and Goldstein with slot machines (then illegal in many locales), which were placed in New York City bars.

Reles went on to become a charter member of the assassination team known as Murder, Inc. Largely made up of Jewish and Italian killers, Murder, Inc. was an underworld death squad which dispatched their prey with cold, professional detachment. The nominal boss of Murder, Inc., was Louis ("Lepke") Buchalter, another fellow Jew. Murder, Inc., was responsible for scores of deaths.

Dutch Schultz (born Arthur Flegenheimer) was one of few Jewish gangsters who took a keen interest in spiritual matters—albeit, from a Christian perspective. In the mid-1930s, Schultz made a sudden dramatic conversion to Catholicism. As a Catholic convert, he continued to run his underworld empire with violence and fear. His peers took the conversion as another sign of Schultz's alleged mental instability.

Bugsy Siegel, meanwhile, managed to inject a note of suave urbanity into the Jewish-gangster milieu. Handsome and self-assured, Siegel partied with Hollywood celebrities such as actor George Raft, as he went about building a huge Las Vegas casino/hotel called the Flamingo in the late 1940s. A charismatic charmer, Siegel also had a hair-trigger temper that he unleashed at the slightest provocation (hence the nickname "Bugsy"—bugs being slang for "crazy" at the time).

As with their Irish and Italian-American counterparts, many Jewish gangsters ended up dying violently. Rothstein was shot dead in 1928, while Dutch Schultz was shot and killed seven years later. Abe Reles fell from a Coney Island hotel window in a mysterious "accident" in 1941, shortly before he was set to testify against his brethren in Murder, Inc. In 1944 Buchalter managed to become the only top mob boss ever executed by the state. Three years later, Siegel took two bullets to the head and died as he sat in the Beverly Hills living room of his mistress. Other groups, such as the Purple Gang, faded into obscurity.

Lansky, supposed financial wizard of the underworld, suffered a more humiliating fate. He spent his declining years in the 1970s and 1980s trying to outrun the U.S. government and become a citizen of Israel, two goals at which he failed miserably.

By the time Lansky died of cancer in 1983, the image of the Jewish gangster had almost completely vanished from the cultural landscape.

There are several reasons for this. Jewish gangsters did not encourage their offspring to enter the world of organized crime. Likewise, Jewish mobsters didn't establish crime "families" along the lines of Mafia clans—enduring organizations designed to last into perpetuity. Community derision was another factor. Unlike Mafiosi like John Gotti and black mobsters such as Leroy "Nicky" Barnes, Jewish gangsters were not hailed as heroes in their communities. The larger Jewish community was revolted by the likes of Schultz, Lansky and Siegel. They rightly worried that such men would encourage anti-Semitism in the greater society.

Ironically, some contemporary Jewish writers have embraced Jewish mobsters of days past out of a perverse sense of ethnic pride

"For people like me, who grew up hearing only of the good Jews, fundraisers and activists, the gangsters offer a glimpse of a less stable time, like the Ice Age, when a greater variety of species thrived on earth," wrote author Rich Cohen in his book, *Tough Jews*, which chronicles the Jewish underworld. Cohen continues:

> The Jewish gangster has been forgotten because no one wants to remember him . . . because he is something to be ashamed of. Well, to me, remembering Jewish gangsters is a good way to deal with being born after 1945, with being someone who has always had the Holocaust at his back, the distant tomtom: *six million, six million, six million*. The gangsters, with their own wisecracking machine-gun beat, push that other noise clear from my head. And they drowned out other things too, like the stereotype that fits the entire Jewish community into the middle-class, comfortable easy-chair Jews with nothing but morality for dessert.

See Also: Lansky,Meyer; Purple Gang; Reles, Abraham "Kid Twist"; Schultz, Dutch

Further Reading:

Rich Cohen, *Tough Jews: Fathers, Sons and Gangster Dreams*, 1998.

Robert Lacey, *Little Man: Meyer Lansky and the Gangster Life*, 1991.

David Southwell, *The History of Organized Crime: The True Story and Secrets of Global Gangland*, 2006.

JOHNSON, ELLSWORTH "BUMPY" (1906–1968)

Ellsworth "Bumpy" Johnson's criminal legacy is controversial. One of the first well-known African-American gangsters, he has been mythologized as a Harlem folk hero who bravely stood up to white mobsters encroaching on his territory. Other sources describe Johnson as a tool of the white underworld, doing its bidding while maintaining a facade of independence.

Johnson was born around the turn of the 20th century in Charleston, South Carolina. As a young teenager in 1919, his father sent him to New York City to better himself. Johnson's timing was excellent; after the World War I, Harlem blossomed as a mecca for black business and culture. Its population exploded as thousands of black migrants, like Johnson, fled the South to live there. At first, Johnson acceded to his father's wishes and led a respectable life. He was educated at Boys High in Brooklyn and briefly attended City College, where he studied pre-law. The lure of the streets, however, was too powerful for Johnson to ignore. He dropped out of school to become a thug, performing burglaries and becoming proficient at knife fighting. Johnson quickly gained a reputation for absolute fearlessness and courage. It's not entirely clear how Johnson acquired his nickname "Bumpy." It might have been a reference to a bump on his head, or his habit of "bumping people off" (i.e., killing them) as a rising mobster.

Well-dressed and dapper, Johnson caught the eye of Stephanie St. Clair, the top female "banker" in the Harlem numbers racket. Also called "policy," the numbers racket was essentially an illegal lottery. For mere pennies, people bought slips of a paper that contained a three-digit number. If their number "hit," they received a cash prize of a few dollars. Winning numbers were taken from objective sources such as sports scores or stock market prices, so no one could accuse the bankers of cheating. Born in the French Caribbean island of Martinique, St. Clair spoke with a French accent and had been running numbers since the early 1920s. At first, white mobsters shunned the numbers racket, considering it too small time to get involved with. The players might have been poor, but their pennies added up to a considerable sum. At her peak, St. Clair was making $100,000 a year and owned fine cars, dresses, and brownstone residences.

By the early 1930s, the established white underworld began waking up to the potential numbers presented. Prohibition was on its last legs (it would be rescinded in 1933) and mobsters were casting about for new sources of revenue. Jewish gangster Dutch Schultz was one of the first white crime bosses to start moving in on the Harlem numbers scene. Through a combination of threats, intimidation, and negotiation, Schultz took over the operations of black policy

bankers, one by one. Bankers were allowed to stay in business, as long as they gave Schultz a sizeable cut of their profits and let him make all leadership decisions.

With Johnson by her side, St. Clair at first resisted this encroachment. She complained to both police and the press to no avail. Johnson took a more realistic approach to the crisis. He secretly met with white mobsters, who convinced him it would be in his best interest to work with them, not against them. Johnson encouraged his boss to give in, and eventually she did. St. Clair began paying off Schultz for the privilege of staying in business. As St. Clair faded into the background, Johnson's star rose. In addition to numbers, he ran pimping and robbery operations and became a prominent underworld figure. He acted as a middleman between Harlem street hustlers and white mobster kingpins. "Bumpy was the only Negro who dealt with the Italian mob as if he were their equal," stated his former wife Mayme, whom he married in the 1940s, in a recent memoir. It's not clear if this was actually the case, however. Some historians say Bumpy was little more than a figurehead, carrying out the white mob's wishes. Figurehead or not, Bumpy became the best known black gangster in New York. He always carried a large wad of money and contributed to local churches and schools. Johnson also arranged free food giveaways for the poor, somewhat like Al Capone, who opened soup kitchens in Chicago during the Depression to feed the unemployed.

According to crime historians, Johnson served as something of a "go to" man. Black street hustlers who wanted to start selling drugs, pimping, or robbing in a given territory, for example, would approach Johnson first to receive his blessings and support. In return, they kicked back a slice of their profits to him. Johnson didn't operate without opposition. He was jailed three times on drug charges, and ended up spending about a quarter of his life behind bars. In June 1952 he was shot and nearly killed by Robert "Hawk" Hawkins, a black pimp and wannabe gangster. Johnson survived and continued to oversee criminal activities in Harlem. Arrested again in 1967 for alleged involvement in a drug operation, Johnson died of a heart attack before going to trial. He expired in Well's, a popular Harlem restaurant, in July 1968.

One of Johnson's later assistants was Frank Lucas, whose life story formed the basis of the 2007 movie, *American Gangster*. Johnson also featured prominently in this film to the disgust of his widow. Mayme Johnson blasted the movie for factual inaccuracies and said it incorrectly portrayed Lucas as her husband's right-hand man. Johnson was also the main subject of the 1997 film, *Hoodlum*, which focused on Dutch Schultz's attempt to take over the Harlem numbers racket. As played by Laurence Fishburne, Johnson was depicted as heroically fending off Schultz's minions. The actual truth was no doubt murkier, though it's inarguable that Johnson was the biggest African-American mobster in his day.

See Also: Barnes, Leroy "Nicky"; Mafia

Further Reading

Nate Hendley, *Dutch Schultz: The Brazen Beer Baron of New York*, 2005.

Mayme Hatcher Johnson and Karen E. Quinones Miller, *Harlem Godfather: The Rap on My Husband Ellsworth "Bumpy" Johnson*, 2008.

Denise Millner, "From Harlem to 'Hoodlum,' Meet the Black Mobster Whose 'Bumpy' Life of Crime Is Now a New Movie," *New York Daily News*, August 24, 1997.

K

KELLY, PAUL (1871–1927?)

The *New York Times* referred to Paul Kelly as "perhaps the most successful and the most influential gangster in New York history." Since that assessment was made in 1912, other mobsters have surpassed Kelly in terms of power and influence in the Big Apple. For his day, however, Kelly was indeed one of the top gang leaders in New York, and among the first criminals to recognize the importance of having political support.

Kelly's real name was Paulo (or Paolo) Antonio Vaccerelli. Born in Sicily, his parents were part of the vast Italian Diaspora to the New World. Vaccerelli changed his name to the more Irish sounding Paul Kelly in the 1890s, when he fought as bantamweight boxer. At the time, it was traditional for Italian athletes to assume Celtic names to better ingratiate themselves with fans and fight promoters. This made sense given the strong anti-Italian prejudice of the day. Kelly was relatively successful as a boxer. He channeled his winnings from the ring into a series of bordellos in the Italian neighborhood around the Bowery in Manhattan. Profits from these brothels were used to set up "athletic clubs" made up of young goons not involved in any kind of sporting activity. Rather, these thugs served to do Kelly's bidding, and served as shock troops in his rise to the top of the criminal hierarchy. His embryonic crew was called the Five Points Gang, and was built on the legacy of previous street gangs in the city, such as the Whyos, Plug Uglies, and Dead Rabbits.

Soft-spoken and charming, Kelly was astute enough to realize that prominent crime bosses required political connections to survive. Kelly made himself useful to Big Tim Sullivan, a boss in Tammany Hall, the corrupt Democratic political machine that ran the city. In a primary election for the Second Assembly District held in September 1901, Kelly threw his support behind Tom Foley, the candidate favored by Sullivan. Foley was pitted against Patrick "Paddy" Divver in the primary. Divver was also connected to Tammany Hall, but had a reformist bent that concerned his political masters. More to the point, Divver opposed the expansion of brothels into the district, something Kelly, Foley and Sullivan supported. Come electionday, Kelly's thugs, who numbered around 1,500, beat up Divver supporters, caused chaos at polling stations, and voted repeatedly under false names. Police stood by and did nothing as the Five Points Gang helped steal the election for Foley.

Kelly didn't have long to celebrate Foley's victory; shortly after the primary, he was arrested for assault and robbery. His political connections proved their worth, however, and he received a lenient nine-month sentence. Big Tim Sullivan put the fix in to make sure Kelly wasn't punished too harshly. Kelly dutifully served his time, and was given a hero's welcome upon his release by Tammany Hall supporters and his army of thugs. He promptly launched a new organization, called the Paul Kelly Association, to put a semi-respectable face on his growing army of goons. The Sicilian turned pseudo Irishman set up his headquarters in a café/dance hall called the New Brighton Dance Hall. He wore a tuxedo and black tie while conducting business and put on gentlemanly airs. His territory on Manhattan Island ran between Broadway and the Bowery, and 14th Street and City Hall Park.

Apparently, Kelly could speak Italian, French, and Spanish, had good manners, and possessed a certain magnetism. "He resembled a bank clerk or a theological student more than a gang chieftain," wrote crime historian Herbert Asbury. The same could not be said about his archrival, Edward "Monk" Eastman, who had his own powerbase in the Lower East Side. A former bouncer, Eastman was an out-and-out thug who enjoyed inflicting pain, and scoffed at Kelly's "man of the manor" pose.

Eastman had his own crew of goons, cutthroats, and petty criminals. Lacking a proper name, the gang—who counted 1,200 men as members—was simply referred to as the Eastmans.

Kelly and Eastman began bumping up against each other. Their squabbles were primarily territorial in nature. Kelly felt the border of his crime empire extended to the Bowery, while Eastman placed it at the Pelham, a vile bar on Pell Street. Eastman refused to negotiate a truce that would have left both gang bosses happily ensconced in their own territories. The Eastmans and the Five Pointers began to fight a low intensity war of attrition with lead pipes, blackjacks, knives, and pistols. Members of each gang would routinely make armed expeditions into the other side's territory, which naturally resulted in violence. By some accounts, thirty men were killed in the early 1900s during the struggle between the two sides.

In September 1903 a huge brawl broke out between the Eastmans and the Five Points Gang that brought simmering tensions to a broil. A *New York Times* story published September 17, 1903, reported that the battle began as a bar brawl in a saloon around First Avenue and First Street. Shooting broke out around 9:30 p.m. between Eastman and Kelly's men. The gunfire climaxed with a huge firefight around Rivington Street underneath an elevated train. "They shot up the town in regular wild west style," a police detective told *the Times*.

The gunfight beneath the elevated train infuriated Tammany Hall. While New York had seen bigger, more destructive riots, rarely had so many guns been used in one urban battle by so many men. The intensity of the clash terrified city residents who, like their contemporary counterparts, refused to give any evidence that would have helped police investigating the shoot-out. Foley was ordered to set up a cease-fire between the two gang leaders. Kelly and Eastman met in a restaurant surrounded by heavily armed followers. There, Foley laid down the law and told the men to stop warring and stick to their own territories. A rough truce was declared, with a patch of turf around the Pelham club declared neutral territory. At a dance held to celebrate the truce, Eastman and Kelly shook hands as members of their gangs mixed and mingled and whooped it up. Of course, a truce between gangsters is an inherently volatile thing. After it was declared, an Eastman thug got roughed up by a Five Pointer thug named Ford. Eastman demanded that Kelly turn Ford over to him for punishment, a demand Kelly refused. Instead, Kelly challenged his opponent to a boxing match. Incredibly, Eastman agreed. The two men squared off in a ring in a Bronx saloon (some sources say the fight was held in an old barn), with hundreds of armed supporters in attendance. Kelly was a technically more proficient boxer, but Eastman was larger and very tough. The fight lasted two hours and ended in a draw, when both men were too exhausted to continue. The war between the two gang leaders continued.

While Kelly generally stayed out of the day-to-day street operations of his thuggish army, Eastman enjoyed having a direct hand in felonious activities. In February 1904 Eastman was nabbed by a policeman after trying to rob a drunk. Leaders at Tammany Hall were fed up and washed their hands of the man. Eastman's political support evaporated and he was sent to jail for several years.

In November 1905 an attempt was made on Kelly's life. The official newspaper version of the near-assassination stated that members of a rival set called the Jack Cirocco gang entered Kelly's territory (identified either as the New Brighton Dance Hall or Little Naples in press coverage—evidently the place underwent a name-change at some point). The Cirocco gang was angry because their leader had been gunned down by Kelly's men. Bent on revenge, the Cirocco crew stepped into the saloon and began shooting. Kelly was unhurt, but a Five Points Gang member named William Harrington was killed in the melee.

Crime historians paint a slightly different story. They posit that two thugs named James "Biff" Ellison and Razor Riley, so-called because of his skill using old-fashioned razors as weapons, harbored a grievance against Kelly. Ellison was mad because Kelly wouldn't make him the chief bouncer at the New Brighton. Riley was sore because Kelly had humiliated him by personally tossing him out of the same saloon. The two men got drunk in a low-end bar on Pell Street, and then tried to kill Kelly. They walked into the New Brighton and pulled out pistols. William Harrington spotted them and called out a warning to his chief. As Kelly dove under a table, Harrington took a bullet from Ellison or Riley for his pains. Kelly emerged from under the table, blazing away with a pistol in each hand. The lights were extinguished and a fire-fight erupted in the darkness. When police arrived thirty minutes later, they found Harrington's corpse but no one else on the scene. The gangsters had departed.

Kelly, who was wounded in the attack, went into hiding after the clash. Police were eager to locate him in order to question him about Harrington's death. Media accounts state that the gang boss was subsequently captured in December 1905. "The credit for the capture of Kelly . . . is due to Assistant District Attorney Michael Cardozo Jr., whose familiarity with the idiosyncrasies of the Italian race enabled him to frighten those hiding Kelly into revealing his place of refuge," read an article in the *New York Times*. Kelly was arrested at the home of his cousin, James Vaccarelli, on Park Avenue. The gang boss was apparently smoking a cigar and dressed in evening clothes when police picked him up. Police questioned him about Harrington's murder, but naturally Kelly had little to say. At a subsequent trial in 1911, "Biff" Ellison was found guilty of manslaughter. Razor Riley escaped punishment by conveniently dying of pneumonia before police could catch him.

While Kelly managed to avoid any major trouble with authorities over the Harrington shooting, his time in the sun was starting to end. Police closed the café/dance hall he was using as a headquarters, and he began to fade into the background. Membership in the Five Points Gang dwindled. Kelly moved the center of his operations to an Italian neighborhood in Harlem. In subsequent years after the Harrington shooting, Kelly hired his goons out as strikebreakers during labor strife, and ran a shifty real estate business. He tried to open a new club but it failed. It is believed that Kelly retired from criminal life and died in his bed in 1927, though some sources place Kelly's death later, sometime in the mid-1930s. Regardless, he was one of few prominent gang leaders to expire in such a peaceful fashion.

See Also: Dead Rabbits; Osterman, Edward "Monk" Eastman

Further Reading

"An East Side Vendetta," *New York Times*, September 17, 1903.

Herbert Asbury, *The Gangs of New York*, 1927.

"Ellison Convicted of Manslaughter," *New York Times*, June 9, 1911.

"Gangsters Again Engaged in a Murderous War," *New York Times*, June 9, 1912.

Helena Katz, *Gang Wars: Blood and Guts on the Streets of Early New York*, 2005.

"Paul Kelly Found in Cousin's House," *New York Times*, December 2, 1905.

L

LANSKY, MEYER
(1902–1983)

Meyer Lansky's life offers a vivid example of the difference between perception and reality in the underworld. Born Meyer Suchowljansky to a Jewish family in Grodno, Poland in 1902, Lansky was lionized by the media as the financial "brains" behind the Mafia. Hailed as a wizard of criminality, his net worth was pegged at $300 million. In truth, Lansky left his family almost nothing and his crippled eldest son was reduced to living in a welfare hospital before he died. Lansky himself spent his declining years trying to outrun the U.S. government.

Lansky's father moved to the United States in 1909, worked for two years, and then brought the rest of his kin over. The family lived in the Brownsville area of Brooklyn, and then moved to Manhattan when Meyer was eleven years old. Along the way, Suchowljansky Sr., anglicized the family name to the more pronounceable "Lansky." Meyer Lansky was a short, slightly built, studious

Meyer Lansky, after surrendering in 1952. He was named in an indictment on charges of conspiracy, gambling, and forgery. [AP Photo]

young boy who enjoyed school and was good at math. While he was quiet and introverted, Lansky was also street smart from an early age. After losing money in street corner dice games, Lansky came to realize that in gambling, the true winner is the person who controls the game. The odds are always with the house, regardless of whether the game is held in a plush casino or on a street corner.

As a boy, Lansky became acquainted with future mob superstars Benny Siegel and Charles "Lucky" Luciano. According to legend, Lansky met Siegel at a street fight between two craps players. During the struggle, one of the players dropped a pistol on the sidewalk, which was scooped up by a good-looking young boy. With police whistles blasting, Lansky slapped the gun out of the boy's hand and urged him to run. There was no sense in being caught in possession of someone else's weapon. Once they were safe, the two boys introduced themselves. The wannabe gunslinger was a fellow Jew named Ben Siegel. Unlike Lansky, Siegel was impulsive, erratic, and highly charming. Despite their different temperaments, the two boys became friends. Shortly thereafter, Lansky met Charles "Lucky" Luciano. Luciano was part of a gang of Sicilian boys who terrorized individual Jews they encountered on the streets. As the story goes, Luciano and his crew descended upon Lansky, demanding money or else. Rather than give up his cash, Lansky swore at the Sicilian wolf pack and refused to back down. Impressed by his moxie, Luciano became friends with the slight, but spirited, Jewish kid.

Despite his obvious intelligence, Lansky left school before he turned fifteen and took a position as a mechanic in a tool and die shop, a job arranged by his father. At night, he worked as a lookout for illegal craps games. Lansky began attracting the attention of the police. In 1918 he was arrested for felonious assault, but the case was dismissed. He quit working as a mechanic in 1921. The previous year, Prohibition had become the law. To young hustlers like Lansky, Siegel, and Luciano, it was like winning a lottery. All three went into the bootlegging business.

Lansky, the quiet kid who loved to read, impressed his coworkers with his photographic memory. While other mobsters had to write down their deals on paper, lest they would forget the details, Lansky could recite complicated financial transactions and figures from memory. In this manner, he avoided creating a paper trail that might land him in jail.

Lansky earned respect in another crucial way. Unlike most up-and-coming gangsters, Lansky wasn't greedy. He didn't cheat his partners. He had no problem offering a generous "share out"—a division of profits among underworld allies. Lansky was aided in some of his business deals by his younger brother, Jake. Jake lacked any of his older brother's mathematical acumen, but he was stolid, loyal, and dependable. As he rose in the criminal underworld, Lansky developed a reputation as a cool businessman who preferred diplomacy and negotiation over brute force. He had no problem threatening clients with violence if need be, but preferred to take care of business in a calm, rational manner, more like a corporate boss than a crime boss. This aspect of Lansky's personality might have also been a reflection of his physical condition; as an adult, he never reached beyond five foot four inches tall and remained slightly built.

Lansky's reputation for relying on brains over brawn didn't spare him from the occasional arrest. On March 1928, for example, Lansky and another gangster named Samuel Levine were arrested for assaulting a fellow criminal named John Barrett. Charges were later dropped and the case did not proceed.

In the late 1920s Lansky attracted a girlfriend named Anne Citron. The two were married in spring 1929 and had their first child in early 1930. The parents were shocked when it was discovered that their son, Bernard, whom they called "Buddy," had cerebral palsy, which would drastically limit his mobility. Some sources claim Lansky went into a brief period of mourning, nursing his sorrow with whisky. Buddy's affliction was something he couldn't fix or change with a deal. Once he got his bearings, Lansky started reading up on cerebral palsy and arranged excellent medical care for his son. At this time, Lansky and his family lived in an apartment called the Majestic that overlooked Central Park. While the building was classy, Lansky took pains not to live it up, like his pal Lucky Luciano. As Luciano gained power and money, he ensconced himself at the Waldorf-Astoria and surrounded himself with luxury. Lansky preferred to stay low key and keep out of the public eye. His wife didn't share these scruples, and spent his money freely. Lansky moved his family, which now included a son named Paul born without any physical defects, to Boston in the early 1930s. The move was made to be closer to a Boston physician who offered new ways of treating cerebral palsy. The Lanskys employed a butler and a cook. Not a strict father by any means, Lansky shuttled back and forth between his family in Boston and his business concerns in New York. He bought his boys expensive toys, presents, and kept his eye on new opportunities in fields such as illegal gambling.

With the exception of Nevada, which legalized casino gambling in 1931, gambling for money was illegal across the United States. Just as with alcohol, however, the gambling ban spawned a huge, thriving subculture in which gangsters provided the means for people to enjoy themselves. Swanky Saratoga Springs, New York, was a hub in the world of illicit gaming. High-end gamblers were attracted to the racetrack and to Saratoga's private casinos, called "lake houses." These casinos featured ornate gaming rooms, but also offered dining and dancing facilities and live entertainment.

Lansky first ventured to Saratoga Springs in the 1920s as a sideline to bootlegging. He picked up some valuable pointers. The casinos in Saratoga were high class and "honest" in that the games weren't rigged; any money lost by gamblers was due to either bad luck or bad strategy, not loaded dice and marked cards. Lansky realized smart gamblers could tell when a game was rigged. Once word got out, gamblers would stop patronizing a club or street corner game that cheated. Lansky picked up on the importance of maintaining good relations with local police, politicians, and judges through timely bribes. He also noted that the well-heeled elite at Saratoga wanted luxurious accommodations, high-end food, and classy entertainment along with games of chance.

Even as he diversified into gambling, Lansky avoided any involvement with prostitution or drugs, two rackets he viewed with distaste. He had no problem associating with mobsters who were pimps and dealers, however. His pal, Luciano, for example, would eventually be brought down on charges of running a massive prostitution operation in New York City.

In 1932, with the election of Franklin Roosevelt as president, the end of Prohibition became a certainty. Before the ban on alcohol was lifted, Lansky became a partner in a molasses company. The plan was to provide molasses to the distilling industry once the latter was allowed to distill again. For a variety of reasons, the venture was a flop and the molasses company went out of business. When Prohibition was officially lifted in early December, 1933, the public no longer needed to purchase alcohol from bootleggers. Lansky complained that his income had been reduced to "only" $10,000 a year. Although this was several times what the average family made at the time, it wasn't a particularly huge income for a gangster. Lansky began to expand his gambling interests to make up for lost bootlegging profits.

World War II brought new opportunities. Lansky had always been a staunch anti-fascist; during the Depression, he organized goon squads to violently break up meetings of Nazi sympathizers in New York. After the United States joined the war in December 1941, German U-boats moved in on the east coast and began sinking huge numbers of American ships. It was suspected that the U-boats were receiving assistance from pro-Hitler Americans. U.S. Naval Intelligence had a slew of agents throughout New York, but found it difficult to glean information from the waterfront. The Italian longshoremen and fishermen who worked the area weren't eager to share their insights with government agents. U.S. Naval Intelligence turned to underworld figures, including Lansky, for assistance. At the government's behest, Lansky visited Luciano, who had been incarcerated since the mid-1930s. Luciano didn't control the New York waterfront, but knew the people who did. Lansky continued to visit his comrade in prison, who in turn

instructed his own multiple waterfront contacts to keep their eyes open for sabotage and suspicious activity. In June 1942 the FBI arrested eight German spies who had landed in the U.S. from U-boats and were bent on sabotage. Luciano's exact role in this affair is murky. It is speculated that he passed on information from his waterfront sources which helped lead to the arrests. In any case, Luciano was released from prison when the war ended and deported to his native Italy. Officials acknowledged that Luciano was sprung in recognition for his contributions to the war effort.

Lansky was also in close contact with another old friend during this period. In the mid-1940s the flamboyant Benny Siegel decided to build a huge casino/hotel in Nevada to take advantage of legal gambling in the state. One of several investors, Lansky put $62,500 of his own money into the casino/hotel, which bore the name "the Flamingo." Under Siegel's unsteady leadership, the Flamingo went massively over budget. The gang boss ordered extremely expensive materials and kept his work crews toiling around the clock, which added up to a lot of overtime. The Flamingo finally opened in late 1946, but Siegel's backers were fed up. Siegel was shot dead on June 20, 1947, at the home of his mistress, Virginia Hill. Lansky always denied having anything to do with Siegel's death, but it's almost certain he knew who killed his childhood friend.

Other matters also occupied Lansky's time in the late 1940s. He began experiencing family difficulties. Anne was getting temperamental. She was not able to adjust well to life as a gangster's "moll." She and Lansky started having physical fights. Anne also began to deteriorate mentally. The two were divorced on February 14, 1947. By this point, they also had a daughter named Sandra in addition to the two boys. Lansky remarried on December 16, 1948. His new bride was Thelma "Teddy" Schwartz, who was loud and loyal, and seemingly unconcerned with Lansky's underworld status.

Lansky continued to watch his business operations. He was involved in illegal gambling operations in Florida and also in the jukebox business for a time. He maintained his disdain for drugs and prostitution. Lansky faced constant stress and developed ulcers as a result. His ulcers grew worse when he found himself at the receiving end of a government probe and a grand jury. In the early 1950s Tennessee Senator Estes Kefauver launched a nation-wide investigation into organized crime. Kefauver and other Senators would travel from city to city and interrogate local criminals and law officials. Lansky was subpoenaed and testified before the Kefauver Commission on October 11, 1950, in New York City. While he freely admitted knowing several mobsters, Lansky offered no details of his business relationships with these men. When Senators demanded more information, Lansky pled the Fifth Amendment. The one topic he did cheerfully touch on was his war work with Luciano. In the summer of 1952 a grand jury began investigating gambling operations in Saratoga. That September, Lansky and a handful of others were indicted on charges involving conspiracy, gambling, and forgery. The last thing Lansky wanted was a trial that might stir up unwanted publicity. He pled guilty in early May 1953, and was given a fine of $2,500 and a three-month jail term to be served in the Saratoga area. He behaved amicably and got a month off of his sentence for good behavior.

Outside the United States, developments were taking place that would have a major impact on organized crime. In March 1952 Fulgencio Batista became president of Cuba for the second time; he had also served from 1940 to 1944. At the time, Cuba was a hugely popular party spot—providing women, music, alcohol, great weather, and gambling for wealthy tourists. Batista's return proved to be good fortune for Lansky. The Cuban leader took note of Lansky's reputation for running "honest" gambling operations. Batista put the mobster on his payroll at $25,000 a year to advise him on how to clean up Cuba's notoriously corrupt casinos. Under Lansky's guidance, Batista "reformed" gambling in Cuba and made the games less fixed.

In 1955 Lansky opened a casino operation in the Nacional Hotel in Cuba. He installed his brother Jake as the casino floor manager. Lansky began to dream of building his own brand-new casino in Cuba. His plan was to open an opulent gaming palace called the Riviera, which would stand twenty-one stories high and contain 440 rooms. Work began on the Riviera in January 1957 and was finished in less than one year. Lansky wanted the casino/hotel as swanky as possible. It became, for example, the first big building in Havana with central air conditioning. The interior was lavish and richly decorated. The hotel opened on December 10, 1957, and proved to be a big hit. Lansky ran the Riviera in a disciplined manner and again proved to be a generous boss, never one to skimp on bribes and the share-out.

The Riviera might have been a jewel, but Lansky's timing was miserable. On New Year's Eve, 1958, leftist rebels led by Fidel Castro seized power in Cuba. Batista fled the nation on a plane. Suffering from ulcers and a swollen knee that left him barely able to walk, Lansky stayed in Cuba after the revolution to make sure his pampered hotel guests got back to the United States in one piece. After a few days of this, Lansky himself left Cuba for Miami. One month later, he was back in Cuba trying to work out an arrangement with the new political order. He wasn't successful. Castro decided to close the casinos that had generated so much wealth for the underworld. The Riviera was seized by the government in October 1960. Lansky estimated he lost $14 to $18 million thanks to Fidel.

Lansky suffered a heart attack after the Riviera fiasco. While recuperating in August 1962, he visited Israel for the first time.

By the mid-1960s, Lansky's reputation had been exaggerated beyond all logical measure. A December 1965 story in the *Miami Herald* pegged his personal wealth at an astronomical $300 million—a wild exaggeration that became widely accepted as fact. The media made Lansky out to be a sinister criminal puppet master on par with the evil villain "Blofeld" from the James Bond movies. The FBI put wiretaps on Lansky to pick up his private conversations. Through a wiretap, Lansky was caught comparing the size of the underworld with legitimate American corporations. As the book *Little Man: Meyer Lansky and the Gangster Life*, explains, this off-hand comment was turned into one of the most famous mob quotes ever: "We're bigger than U.S. Steel." This quote was attributed to Lansky in a September 1967 issue of *Life* magazine, and has been forever associated with him since. It's unclear if these were Lansky's exact words, however. When the *Godfather*

Part II was released, a Lansky-like character named Hyman Roth uttered this very same line to the rising Don played by Al Pacino.

Lansky traveled to Israel in July 1970 with his second wife, Teddy. The two went to Tel Aviv, partly to escape law authorities in the U.S. who were investigating "skimming"—the siphoning of undeclared profits from casinos by mobsters—at the Flamingo hotel. Lansky enjoyed himself in Tel Aviv. He tried to take advantage of Israel's Law of Return, which allowed any Jew to take out Israeli citizenship. The Law of Return defined a Jew as anyone born of a Jewish mother. Exceptions were made, however, for criminals. The U.S. government wasn't eager for Lansky to get sanctuary in Israel. He was subpoenaed to show up in Miami and give testimony to a grand jury investigating skimming at the Flamingo. When he failed to appear before a grand jury, he was hit with a contempt of court charge. In the spring of 1971 the U.S. Embassy in Israel contacted Lansky. They informed him that the U.S. State Department had revoked his American passport and that he should return to the United States to face criminal charges.

By this point, Lansky's inflated reputation continued to expand. He acquired the wholly undeserved nickname "Chairman of the Board" of the so-called national crime syndicate that allegedly ran all rackets in the U.S. Although Lucky Luciano did set up a loosely knit organized crime hierarchy, it had nowhere near the power or authority bestowed on it by inflated media accounts. Throughout 1971, Lansky continued to wrangle with his lawyers and government officials in Israel, who were less than thrilled to have a wanted mobster in their country. In an attempt to mollify authorities, Lansky claimed he had retired from most of his business operations in 1959 and now lived off of proceeds from investments in real estate and oil. He pegged his annual pre-tax income at $60,000. Lansky tried to portray himself as a put upon Jew who did fundraising for Israel and organized violent disruptions of neo-Nazi meetings in the 1930s. Israeli authorities were unimpressed. In September 1971 the Israeli government decided Meyer wasn't a good candidate for citizenship. His application for citizenship was denied and his tourist visa was not renewed.

Lansky appealed his case to the Israeli Supreme Court, which in September 1972 ruled in the government's favor. Lansky would have to go. Israel gave Lansky a "laissez-passer"—that is, a document he could use to travel to any country that accepted him. A close friend booked airline tickets for himself and Lansky in November 1972. The plan was to fly from Zurich to Paraguay via Rio de Janeiro and Buenos Aires. Ticket reservations were made under the name "Mr. Meyer." Lansky arrived in Switzerland and was allowed to fly to South America. When his plane eventually landed in Paraguay, however, authorities refused to let him disembark. He was hustled out of Paraguay and onto a flight that wound up in Miami. Knowing he was cornered, Lansky asked his friend to look after his money. Lansky had bank accounts in Switzerland. Were he to die, Lansky wanted to make sure Buddy and second wife, Teddy, were taken care of. Lansky's friend was astonished to discover that the "Chairman of the Board" had under a million dollars in the bank. The plane landed in Miami on November 7, 1972. FBI agents came on board and told Lansky he was under arrest. His hapless thirty-six-hour flight

around the world had been totally in vain. Reporters and photographers hounded Lansky as he arrived in America. He went to a hospital where doctors monitored his heart.

Lansky's ill-fated global trek should have shattered his image as a financial mastermind of the underworld. Had Lansky really been worth $300 million, he surely could have found shelter somewhere. The mid-1970s were a blur of court dates for Lansky, who was now complaining about his strained finances. His court cases were draining him, and he was also paying for the medical care of the increasingly ailing Buddy. Lansky was no longer a power in the underworld. A senior citizen, he spent most of days playing gin rummy with his cronies and reminiscing about the old days.

By the early 1980s, Buddy had become almost totally paralyzed and required assistance just to eat. Lansky also had his own medical problems. He developed lung cancer, the result of a lifelong habit of heavy smoking. Doctors removed part of Lansky's lung, but the cancer spread. He died on January 15, 1983, and was buried in west Miami. Lansky's obituaries inevitably cited his position as a financial wizard of organized crime. His treatment of his family casts doubt on that image. By the time of his father's death, Buddy was a quadriplegic who needed twenty-four-hour medical care. He was being looked after in a low-end private nursing home near North Miami.

Lansky left no great fortune to his heirs. His investments in oil and gas soon petered out, leaving little for his children. Buddy suffered the most. He was moved into a charity facility in Miami for indigents. Totally helpless, Buddy's horrendous situation improved somewhat when he was approved for

Medicare payments, which would have hardly been necessary had he inherited a share of the $300 million his father was allegedly worth. Buddy was moved back into private care, but died shortly after Christmas in 1989.

Buddy's pathetic finale was an apt reminder of the mythology of the mob. Lansky himself ruefully admitted before he died that he probably could have made more money if he'd stayed "straight." He could have avoided lawyer's bills and the cost of hiding out in Israel for a start. He also could have invested his money without fear of it being seized by the U.S. government as proceeds of crime. In the end the smart little boy from Brownsville who was good with numbers managed to outsmart himself.

See Also: Jewish Gangsters; Luciano, Charles "Lucky"; Mafia; Siegel, Benjamin "Bugsy"

Further Reading

Edna Buchanan, "Criminal Mastermind," *TIME*, December 7, 1998.

Rich Cohen, *Tough Jews: Father, Sons and Gangster Dreams*, 1998.

Robert Lacey, *Little Man: Meyer Lansky and the Gangster Life*, 1991.

"*Meyer Lansky Is Dead at 81; Financial Wizard of Organized Crime*," New York Times, January 16, 1983.

"Non-Returnable Lansky," *TIME*, September 25, 1972.

Thomas Reppetto, *American Mafia: A History of Its Rise to Power*, 2004.

LUCIANO, CHARLES "LUCKY" (1897–1962)

"Lucky" Luciano became the first head of the Genovese family, still one of the most powerful of the five New York

Lucky Luciano in 1936. [Library of Congress]

families. He solidified the current organizational structure of the American mafia, and is considered the father of modern organized crime. *TIME* magazine called him "Horatio Alger with a gun, an ice pick and a dark vision of Big Business." The FBI credited him with "making the American (Mafia) what it is today." He was jailed for vice crimes, but escaped punishment for murder. He killed two mob bosses to seize their empires and might have killed a third in order to save a crusading prosecutor.

Salvatore Lucania was born in 1897 in Lercara Friddi, a village near Palermo, Sicily. In 1907 his family joined the Sicilian exodus to America, settling in a mixed Italian/Jewish neighborhood in New York's Lower East Side. Salvatore was an ugly child with a pockmarked face due to bad acne. While proud of his heritage, he was eager to be seen as American. Like a lot of sons and daughters of first generation immigrants, he changed his name. Luciana became the easier to pronounce "Luciano." Salvatore was dropped for the more American "Charlie" or just plain "Charles." The "Lucky" tag would come in later years.

Little Charlie grew up wild and tough. He was part of a gang of Sicilian-American urchins who terrorized their neighborhood. Among other activities, the gang liked to swarm individual Jews, whom they perceived as cowardly, beat them, and take their money. This was allegedly how Luciano came to meet a fellow criminal-in-training named Meyer Lansky. According to mob legend, Luciano and his snarling horde confronted Lansky on the street and demanded money. Lansky was a wispy, frail Jewish boy, but he didn't lack for confidence. He told Luciano off and wouldn't back down. Far from being angered, Luciano was impressed by Lansky's courage and befriended the boy. In another tale Luciano came across a girl having sex with a young Jewish runaround named Benjamin "Bugs" Siegel. The girl was apparently from Luciano's stable; he was her pimp, and he was outraged that Siegel was getting the benefit of her charms for free. Luciano stormed up and attacked the couple with his fists. A slight, but tough boy named Meyer Lansky interrupted, breaking up the fight by smacking Luciano on the head with a wrench. Whatever the actual truth of their first encounter was, Luciano became lifelong pals and business associates with Siegel and Lansky. Such cross-ethnic friendships were unusual in an era that was much more parochial than today, especially in new immigrant communities.

Luciano dropped out of school at fourteen and took a factory job, which he hated. He started hanging around poolrooms and continued to hustle on the side. An enterprising lad, Luciano at one point purchased a supply of opium or morphine, which he proceeded to dole out to local addicts for a price. He was caught and served six months in a reformatory as punishment. Like a lot of delinquents, Luciano would have most likely remained a petty criminal were it not for Prohibition. Luciano, Lansky, and Siegel rejoiced when alcohol became a banned commodity in early 1920. As street criminals realized, the public wasn't about to change their drinking habits just because alcohol was banned. If citizens couldn't buy liquor from legitimate sources, they would get it from criminals, who were more than happy for the business. Working with Lansky, Luciano became a major bootlegger. The two young mobsters sold liquor to speakeasies throughout the city. This booze was brought into New York by sea. A mother ship containing a large cargo of liquor purchased from Canada or Europe, where it was legal to manufacture spirits, would drop anchor a few miles off the coast. Smaller, faster boats would rendezvous, and then bring the precious cargo to shore.

Luciano's life as a budding gangster was not without a few scrapes with the law. In 1923 federal agents caught him selling cocaine and opium to a police informer. To avoid arrest Luciano sheepishly led authorities to a larger stash of drugs, setting up another dealer for arrest. Luciano was much embarrassed when this sleazy incident was revealed in court years later. Under the code of the streets, arrested criminals were expected to stay mute, not turn in their peers.

During this formative period, Luciano made the acquaintance of several rising mobsters, including Jack "Legs" Diamond and Arnold Rothstein. Rothstein was a major underworld player who preferred to fund other people's criminal operations instead of running rackets himself. Rothstein was more financier than gang leader. He convinced Luciano to tone down his flashy wardrobe and to wear sober, conservative men's suits. The most influential mobster Luciano met as a young man was Giuseppe "Joe the Boss" Masseria, who commanded a vast criminal organization. In 1927 Masseria asked Luciano to join his growing empire as a lieutenant. The highly ambitious gangster happily agreed. Masseria put his new hire in charge of criminal activities in lower Manhattan.

As Luciano soon discovered, Masseria had some major shortcomings. He was Sicilian-born, like Luciano, but the similarity ended there. Masseria was clannish and narrow-minded. He behaved like an Old World Mafia chief, demanding fealty and tribute from his minions while obsessing on points of honor. Masseria wouldn't do business with non-Italians. By contrast, Luciano would work with anyone who could make him money. Masseria's main enemy was another Sicilian-American mobster named Salvatore Maranzano. One year after Luciano joined the Masseria mob, his boss went to war with Maranzano. Gunmen representing each boss fought it out on the streets or wrecked each other's businesses. At stake was who was going to lead the Italian-American underworld in New York.

It was around this time that Luciano acquired the nickname "Lucky." As Luciano told it, he was standing idle on a sidewalk in midtown Manhattan in October 1929 when a car pulled up. Three armed men forced Luciano into the vehicle and slapped tape over his lips. The trio took Luciano to a deserted beach on Staten Island and proceeded to hang him by his fingers from a tree while torturing him with lit cigarettes, among other painful implements. Luciano was burned, beaten, and slashed. In the middle of this brutal punishment, he passed out and was left for dead. While terribly injured, Luciano was still alive. After coming to at around 2 a.m., he staggered around the beach and almost ran into a policeman on patrol. The officer took the bloodied gangster to a hospital. While Luciano survived, his face retained scars from the incident. His left eye acquired a permanent droop. Nonetheless, this was a small price to pay for the extremely rare feat of being "taken for a ride" and surviving. It was unclear who Luciano's attackers were. Some historians point to a rival gang boss who wanted Luciano to reveal where he'd hidden some drugs. Other sources suggest that he was tortured by Masseria's enemies in order to take out one of Joe the Boss' top men. His assailants could have even been police officers, who put Luciano through a rather harsh interrogation in the hope he'd reveal mob secrets.

Luciano didn't have time to dwell on the identity of his shadowy attackers. Masseria was still caught up in his vendetta with Maranzano. The press called it "the Castellammarese War," after the small Sicilian town both men came from. By the early 1930s, the Castellammarese War had taken dozens of lives with no end in sight. Luciano found the whole thing utterly pointless. He wanted to get rich, not settle scores. Luciano had a lot of ideas. He wanted to modernize the mob, raise it above simple clannish thuggery. Luciano saw no reason why Italian and Jewish gangs couldn't work together. Though he wasn't a U.S. citizen, Luciano had been raised in

New York and considered himself an American, not a transplanted Sicilian. He contemptuously dismissed traditional Mafia chiefs like Masseria as "Moustache Petes." The sobriquet was a put-down of old-style mob bosses, whose backwardness was supposedly epitomized by their unfashionable facial hair. Masseria was clean-shaven but it didn't matter; it was the perception of his old-fashioned ways that concerned up-and-coming gangsters such as Luciano.

On his own initiative, Luciano went behind Masseria's back and struck a deal with Maranzano. Luciano would arrange for Masseria to be killed. In exchange, Maranzano promised to bring the Castellammarese War to a close. Masseria remained oblivious to these machinations. When Luciano asked if he felt like a meal at a Coney Island restaurant on April 15, 1931, Joe the Boss readily agreed. The two men, plus Masseria's three bodyguards, repaired to a restaurant called Nuova Villa Tammaro (some accounts say they met at a place called Scarpato's). Once the sumptuous meal was over, Luciano suggested a card game was in order. Feeling mellow and sedated from the vast quantities of food, Masseria happily played cards with his top lieutenant. At some point, Luciano excused himself to use the bathroom. Masseria's bodyguards suddenly disappeared and a death squad of four men came rushing into the restaurant. The squad, whose members included Ben Siegel and Albert Anastasia, a rising underworld sadist, shot Masseria to death at close range. When police arrived, Luciano expressed complete shock. He said he hadn't witnessed the shooting, being in the bathroom at the time, and had no idea who or why anyone would shoot Masseria.

Maranzano quickly took over Masseria's rackets and took command of his gang members. He kept his end of the bargain and ended the Castellammarese War. Maranzano had a grand vision of organizing crime in New York City, which Luciano heartily endorsed. Maranzano wanted to divide the main Italian gangs into five families, each with a boss, underboss, capos, soldiers, and associates. Capos were the rough equivalent of Mafia middle managers. Soldiers were gangsters who were formal members of the Mafia, while associates were gangsters who weren't formal members but worked with the Mafia. Only full-blooded Italian Americans would be allowed to formally join the Mafia, though associates could come from any background. Under this command structure, leaders at the top were insulated from the actions of their minions on the street. Bosses gave orders to underbosses, who passed the orders on to capos, who carried out the orders with a team of soldiers and associates.

At a mass meeting of mobsters shortly after Masseria's death, Maranzano outlined his vision. The five families would be led by Luciano, Joe Bonanno, Joseph Profaci, Vincent Mangano and Thomas Gagliano. Luciano would take over what used to be Masseria's gang. Luciano might have gone along with the plan, except Maranzano added a twist. He wanted to be supreme leader (capo di tutti capi, or "boss of the bosses"). His word would be law and all other gangsters would be expected to obey him unconditionally. Luciano didn't care for this idea and began plotting against his new boss. As capo di tutti capi, Maranzano proved to be extremely paranoid. He arranged for the mentally unstable Vincent "Mad Dog" Coll, who acquired his nickname after shooting a bunch of children during a botched "hit," to murder his rebellious underlings. Maranzano drew up a death list and Luciano's name featured prominently on it. Through contacts, Luciano caught wind of the plot and decided to launch a counter attack. On September 10, 1931, a group of gunmen disguised as U.S. Treasury agents burst into Maranzano's Park Avenue headquarters. They held up Maranzano's guards, and then stabbed and shot the gang leader to death.

In a little under half of a year, Luciano had arranged the assassination of the two biggest mob bosses in New York City. To smooth things over with his peers, Luciano put out the word that Maranzano was power-mad and was preparing to murder a slew of gangsters. Killing Maranzano, in other words, had been an act of self-defense. New York gangsters could appreciate this kind of logic and didn't try to avenge Maranzano's death.

Luciano retained Maranzano's concept of an underworld made up of crime families, each with their own specific territories, rackets, and hierarchy. Luciano's refinement was to create the position of "consigliere" (advisor) to the bosses. He also added a top level called "the Commission." The Commission would act as a board of directors, settling disputes between families and sanctioning high-level hits. To sit on the Commission, you had to be a high-ranking boss. The Commission's purview would extend beyond New York City. Essentially, it would oversee Mafia rackets throughout America. All five New York families had representation on the Commission. Luciano also made sure there was room reserved for families from other cities, especially Chicago, which was dominated by Al Capone at the time.

The Commission has been depicted as an underworld nerve centre, with a cabal of mob bosses plotting schemes of national importance. This image is false. The Commission largely dealt with territorial disputes, such as which branch of the underworld would handle a particular vice in a given area, and had far less power than the media credited it with. Luciano wanted organized crime to work like a corporation, not a village clan. To this end, he placed great stress on cooperation, negotiation, and amassing political power. While Luciano didn't hesitate to use violence to eliminate anyone in his way, he didn't kill out of spite or sadism. To further distance himself from Masseria and Maranzano, Luciano eliminated the "boss of bosses" position and refused to accept cash tributes from fellow mob leaders. That said, Luciano's modesty was a bit of a facade. While there was no single supreme leader of the U.S. Mafia any more, Luciano was treated as the de facto boss of bosses throughout his career. For all of Luciano's innovations, the American Mafia remained a fluid entity, with a constant churn of new members, new alliances, and new deals. It had an amorphous quality, in which secrecy, guile, and deceit were inherent. The Mafia was never simply the mirror image of General Motors or any other huge U.S. corporation. The underworld created by Luciano did not issue annual reports or hold public stockholder meetings to discuss expansion plans. Unlike legitimate companies, the Mafia avoided all publicity and did not actively solicit new members.

Luciano's own crime family consisted of roughly 500 front-line soldiers ready to do his bidding on the streets. His men ran rackets in New York Harbor and at the Fulton Fish Market in Manhattan. Luciano's ally Tommy Lucchese ("Three Finger Brown") controlled the huge kosher poultry sector, while Louis Buchalter, another ally, ran the garment district in New York. Although Luciano refused to accept the boss of bosses title, he had no problem living in luxury. He had a private plane at his disposal and a suite at the extremely swanky Waldorf-Astoria. His apartment cost $7,600 a year in rent, roughly equivalent to $100,000 in contemporary figures. To avoid any hassles with hotel management, Luciano registered under the name "Charlie Ross."

Even as he moved in the top tier of organized crime, Luciano retained his old street smarts. He was very circumspect about talking on the phone for fear it would be tapped, and didn't keep a paper trail; he maintained details of deals in his head. He was also canny enough to operate his business in the shadows. He didn't rub his position in the public's face as John Gotti did decades later. If anyone asked, Luciano claimed he earned his keep through sports gambling, craps, and "bookmaking," or taking wagers. He was always on the prowl for new money-making opportunities. With the repeal of Prohibition in 1933, all gangsters had to find new rackets. Luciano expanded his operations in bookmaking, prostitution, drugs, loan sharking, robbery, and labor racketeering, among others.

In June 1935 New York Governor Herbert Lehman appointed vigorous, straight arrow attorney Thomas Dewey as a Special Prosecutor, with a view to cleaning up organized crime in the Big Apple. Dewey's first target was maverick Jewish mobster Dutch Schultz, who had built an empire on beer bootlegging,

labor racketeering, and the "numbers" racket, which was essentially an illegal lottery for poor people. Schultz was in a vulnerable position. The federal government was trying to jail him on charges of income tax evasion, the same offense that had brought down Al Capone. While his first tax trial had ended in a hung jury, Schultz faced a second trial that summer. The Dutchman, as he was called in the press, had been more or less hounded out of New York City by authorities as he sorted out his tax problems.

Fearing that his boss was going down, one of Schultz's top men—a thug named Bo Weinberg—decided to defect. Weinberg approached New Jersey gangster Abner "Longy" Zwillman for assistance. Zwillman arranged a meeting between Weinberg and Luciano. At this meeting, Weinberg outlined what he had in mind. He was prepared to give Luciano inside information that would allow him to take over Schultz's crime empire. In return Weinberg wanted a cut of any profits. Luciano called a gangster summit at his Waldorf-Astoria headquarters. Mobsters present included Zwillman, Joe Adonis, Frank Costello, Luciano's old chum Meyer Lansky, Lepke Buchalter, Tommy Lucchese, and Vito Genovese. The men listened as Luciano explained Weinberg's proposal. Being a collegial sort, Luciano invited his peers to join him in the wholesale looting of Schultz's empire. The gangsters at the Waldorf-Astoria liked what they heard. Schultz had always been an erratic, unpopular leader who dressed like a slob and had little time for mob etiquette.

At this juncture, Schultz himself asked for a meeting with Luciano. The meeting was granted, and Schultz used his time to ramble at length about his legal problems and his recent conversion to Catholicism. Apparently, Schultz figured that Luciano, a Catholic by birth, would be interested in his religious transformation. If anything, the meeting made Luciano wonder about Schultz's mental state. Luciano might have also worried that in his newfound Catholic zeal, Schultz might make a confession to police and give away secrets that would implicate other mob bosses. Catholic convert or not, Schultz remained a dangerous thug. When he learned of Weinberg's betrayal, he quickly had his traitorous lieutenant eliminated. Mob legend has it that Weinberg's feet were encased in cement, and then he was unceremoniously dumped into the Atlantic Ocean while still alive.

Schultz's reach extended beyond the underworld. He became obsessed with Special Prosecutor Dewey. He openly announced his intention to have the man murdered. This would violate a major Mafia tenet; killing authorities was forbidden for fear that it would bring about massive retaliation. Albert Anastasia was reportedly asked to spy on Dewey for Schultz's benefit. The future mob boss put the prosecutor under surveillance to figure out his daily routine and determine an appropriate place and time where he could be assassinated. There are several versions of what happened next. In one version Luciano convened a meeting of top mobsters in which the murder of Dewey was the main topic of discussion. Anastasia offered up the results of his spy mission, stating that the prosecutor visited a pharmacy every morning before going to the office. This would be the perfect place to kill him, Anastasia reasoned. The general feeling around the table, however, was that

assassination would be ill-advised. The murder of Thomas Dewey was called off. Another take suggests Schultz himself was at the meeting, and put in a personal plea for Dewey's death. When the assembled mobsters expressed strong reservations, Schultz angrily announced he would murder the Special Prosecutor himself, and stormed off. The remaining mobsters reconvened and decided that Schultz had to die, ironically, in order to save the very man who was doing his best to expose New York's underworld. A hit was arranged, and on October 23, 1935, Schultz and three of his accomplices were gunned down in a restaurant in New Jersey. The Dutchman and his underlings all succumbed to their wounds shortly after the attack.

Luciano might have been less eager to murder Schultz had he been more aware of the Special Prosecutor's agenda. At first, Dewey and his office were mainly concerned with industrial racketeering and mob control of the "numbers" racket. As almost a side issue, Dewey launched what he thought would be a limited probe into corruption and case-fixing at New York's Women's Court. What his investigators found was evidence of a massive prostitution ring allegedly run by none other than Lucky Luciano. Wiretaps in brothels revealed that an outfit called "the Combine" or "the Combination" controlled prostitution in New York City. The Combination managed about 300 brothels (some of which were tiny one- or two-woman operations) and 2,000 prostitutes. Dewey's investigators estimated that the organized sex trade in New York brought in about $12 million a year in revenue. Dewey's team discovered that Dave "Little Davie" Betillo was the mob's overseer of prostitution. Betillo happened to be one of Luciano's trusted lieutenants.

In January 1936 Dewey's agents raided 80 brothels simultaneously across New York City. While this mission was supposed to be top secret, roughly half of the brothels were empty when investigators stormed inside, indicating that someone had tipped off management. Nonetheless, authorities arrested hundreds of working girls, madams, and brothel managers, called "bookers." Ordinarily, a prostitute who worked for the Combination followed a set script when arrested. They would inevitably give police a sob story about being from out of town and visiting a friend in an apartment, which through some terrible coincidence happened to be a brothel. Bail would be set at around $300, which a bail bondsman who worked for the Combination would pay. When the case came to court, prostitutes were usually given a small fine or told to get out of town. Dewey took a considerably tougher tack. He had bail set at $10,000 for each arrested girl, and threatened to keep each in pre-trial custody for a lengthy period of time. His staff could also play nice, taking some of the arrested women to movies or buying them treats like ice cream. The "good cop-bad cop" routine worked, and soon some of the suspects were talking. They told Dewey they knew Luciano was directly involved in prostitution.

Feeling the noose tightening, Luciano fled New York for Hot Springs, Arkansas, a very corrupt town that was something of a resort/hide-out for gangsters. Dewey got an extradition order to force Luciano back to New York City. He was poised to charge the mob boss with ninety counts of aiding and abetting compulsory prostitution. At first, it looked like Luciano

wouldn't have to worry about facing Dewey's wrath. He was let out of jail on only $5,000 bail (extremely low for a major mobster wanted in connection with a top-level investigation) after only spending a few hours in lockup. New York authorities took this as another indication of the level of municipal corruption in Hot Springs. Upon his release, Luciano angrily denounced Dewey's charges and denied having anything to do with prostitution. Dewey decided more drastic measures were necessary to bring Luciano to justice. Convinced that Luciano's lawyers would keep him in Hot Springs forever, Dewey sent agents down south to fetch him. Working with state troopers, these agents more or less kidnapped Luciano and hustled him back to New York.

The trial of Luciano and twelve of his underlings began in May 1936. About sixty-eight witnesses testified, most of them being prostitutes, pimps, bookers, or madams. On the stand they freely admitted they had been promised more lenient sentencing in return for their testimony. Only three of these witnesses offered any evidence directly linking Luciano to the sex trade. One was a heroin addict with the intriguing nickname, Cokey Flo Brown. Ms. Brown claimed to have been present at meetings between Luciano and her pimp, during which time the gang boss talked business. Another prostitute spoke of being sent to the Waldorf-Astoria to have sex with Luciano himself. After the sex was over, the prostitute allegedly overhead the mob boss discuss the prostitution racket with his colleagues. In damning testimony, staff at the Waldorf-Astoria said they had seen the witness and other prostitutes in Luciano's company. The trial revealed the degree of organization

Luciano had imposed on the prostitution racket. Jurors were told that the prostitutes working for the Combination typically put in a twelve-hour shift per day, with one day off a week. The average working girl made $300 a week, not a bad salary for the time. Of this, $150 went to her madam (plus an additional $30 for meals and medical care), leaving each woman with a bit over $100. This would be divided between the girl and her pimp.

Mob lawyers typically discourage their clients from testifying on their own behalf. Gangsters on the stand have a tendency to unnerve juries. Plus, if they lie (which was more or less a given) they opened themselves to charges of perjury. In a brave move, Luciano decided to take the stand. In response to softball questions from his lawyer, Luciano insisted that he earned his keep through gambling and bookmaking. He denied meeting any of the witnesses who said they'd been with him. When the cross-examination took place, Luciano's confidence collapsed. Dewey quickly had him sweaty and squirming. Luciano became evasive, claiming vaguely that he couldn't remember certain details about his business dealings. Luciano's case was not helped when Dewey introduced phone records indicating a series of calls from the Waldof-Astoria to a parade of known gangsters, including Al Capone. Dewey also introduced Luciano's tax records from 1929 to 1935. The records pegged Luciano's highest annual income at a mere $22,500, a ridiculously low figure considering his extravagant lifestyle. When pressed, Luciano was unable to come up with a convincing explanation as to how he managed to live like a tycoon on this income.

Luciano and all his co-defendants were found guilty. Ironically, the mob boss might have beaten the charge if he hadn't testified. The evidence against him was shaky at best and not terribly substantial, with only three witnesses claiming direct knowledge of Luciano's involvement in prostitution. In truth, Luciano was probably not directly involved in the sex trade. A smart mob boss like Luciano knew it would be folly to micromanage 300 separate brothels.

Convicted on 62 counts, Luciano received a sentence of thirty to fifty years in jail. He was imprisoned in Clinton Penitentiary, a maximum-security state facility in Dannemora, New York. Luciano did not serve hard time. He used his position, as well as bribes of food and money, to get fellow prisoners to look after him by cleaning his cell, taking on his work duties, and cooking him meals in a special kitchen. The guards largely left Luciano alone. Emboldened by his conviction of Luciano, Dewey became a national hero. He was eventually elected governor of New York State and ran unsuccessfully for president on the Republican ticket in 1944 and 1948.

Luciano might have remained in jail for the rest of his life, were it not for the advent of World War II. When the U.S. jumped into the fray in late 1941 following the bombing of Pearl Harbor, the federal government became extremely worried about infiltration and sabotage along the unguarded east coast. German submarines, called U-boats, began sinking dozens of American ships, giving rise to fears that fascist sympathizers on shore were revealing nautical secrets to the enemy. This sense of paranoia reached new heights in February, 1942, when the French liner, Normandie, which was being refitted as a troop ship, caught fire and sank in the Hudson River in New York City. The fire was later determined to be accidental, but for the moment, authorities were convinced the ship had been sunk by sabotage.

Feeding Washington, D.C.'s paranoia was the fact that many Italian-Americans worked as longshoremen, dock laborers, and fishermen along the east coast. Would these new immigrants remain loyal to America, or would their sympathies lie with the fascist powers, as Italy was an ally of Nazi Germany? U.S. government agents tried to penetrate this mysterious world of Italian-American docksiders, but failed miserably. Italian-Americans had little interest in talking to nosy government officials.

In despair, the U.S. Naval Intelligence settled on an unconventional plan. Naval Intelligence approached Luciano's friend, Meyer Lansky, with an eye to helping the government. Lansky was induced to visit Luciano in jail and explain the situation to him. Luciano did not have direct command of all waterfront activities in New York or anywhere else. He did, however, have plenty of contacts and a reputation as a well-respected mob boss. Through Lansky, Luciano agreed to spread the word among his contacts that it was alright to speak freely to U.S. Intelligence agents. Luciano encouraged his countrymen to report any suspicious activity on the coast. In June 1942, when Nazi Germany landed eight spies on American soil via U-boat, the FBI caught them quickly, thanks in part to tips from the public.

It's important not to overestimate Luciano's wartime role. The Normandie aside, there were no incidents of sabotage along the east coast during the World War II. Most Italian-Americans remained loyal to the United States and did nothing to encourage the Axis powers. That said, Luciano's efforts were deemed sufficient

to set him free. In January 1946 Dewey (now governor of New York State) approved Luciano's release from jail on the condition that he be deported back to Italy. In a terse statement to the press, gangbuster Dewey praised Luciano for providing information to the U.S. government, "Although the actual value of the information procured is not clear."

On February 10, 1946, a ship containing Luciano left the dock in Brooklyn. He was taken across the ocean to his native village of Lercara Friddi in Sicily. Although Luciano was given a hero's welcome, he didn't care to hang around his hometown. He departed, first for Palermo, then for Naples. By the late 1940s, Luciano was living in a luxury apartment in Rome, with a blonde mistress in her late twenties. He ran a small bakery as a front business and got involved in drug operations. Luciano lived well in Italy, but was quite homesick. *TIME* magazine quoted him as saying, "I'm a city boy. Italy's dead—nice, but dead. I love movement. Business opportunities here are no good. All small-time stuff." In early 1947 Luciano traveled to Cuba in a failed attempt to run his U.S. crime interests offshore. The U.S. government found out and applied pressure until Cuba kicked their unwanted guest out.

In the fall of 1950 Meyer Lansky testified before the Kefauver Committee that was looking into organized crime. The Committee was led by Senator Estes Kefauver of Tennessee. Lansky didn't answer many questions, though he did happily discuss Luciano's work during World War II.

Luciano spent the rest of his life in genteel exile. He helped set up some drug rings, but mostly just strolled about, sat in cafes, read the paper, and ate in good restaurants. He talked about writing his memoirs or having a feature film made about his life. He even allowed reporters to interview him. The proposed memoir and feature film never got off the ground. Luciano died of a heart attack on January 26, 1962, in Italy, a country he disdained compared to his adopted homeland in America.

See Also: Lansky, Meyer; Mafia; Maranzano, Salvatore; Schultz, Dutch

Further Reading

"Bawdy Business," *TIME*, May 25, 1936.

Edna Buchanan, "Criminal Mastermind," *TIME*, December 7, 1998.

"City Boy," *TIME*, July 25, 1949.

Robert Lacey, *Little Man: Meyer Lansky and the Gangster Life*, 1991.

Selwyn Raab, *Five Families: The Rise, Decline and Resurgence of America's Most Powerful Mafia Empires*, 2005.

Burton Turkus and Sid Feder, *Murder, Inc: The Story of the Syndicate*, 1951.

LUPO THE WOLF

See: Saietta, Ignazio "Lupo the Wolf"

M

MAFIA

According to an FBI report on Italian organized crime, Giuseppe Esposito "was the first known Sicilian Mafia member to emigrate to the United States." Esposito made the trek in 1880 "after murdering the chancellor and a vice-chancellor of a Sicilian province and 11 wealthy landowners," continues the report. Other accounts don't mention anything about wealthy landlords and murder, but merely state that Esposito was eager to escape one of the periodic crackdowns on the Mafia in his homeland.

Esposito first journeyed to New York City, then went to New Orleans, which had a burgeoning Sicilian American population. The emigrants liked the warm climate and the city's Catholic ambience. Esposito was captured in 1881 and extradited back to Sicily.

A decade after Esposito's visit, New Orleans was the site of what the FBI called "the first major Mafia incident in this country." On October 15, 1890, New Orleans police chief David Hennessy was shot, execution-style. Before he died, Hennessy blamed "the dagos" for his shooting, "dago" being a derogatory name for anyone hailing from a Mediterranean nation. Police found four "luparas" (double or single barreled, sawed-off shotguns, often with retractable stocks) near the scene of the crime. Such weapons were extremely common in Sicily.

At the time, two prominent Sicilian American factions in New Orleans—one led by Charlie Matranga, the other by Joe Provenzano—were feuding over who would win the right to unload fruit boats at the docks. Hennessy (who was rumored to favor the Provenzano side) had been investigating this low-intensity conflict. In the aftermath of Chief Hennessy's death, scores of Sicilians were arrested. A total of 19 men (from the Matranga faction) were indicted for murder, but only nine ended up going on trial.

When the case came to court, six of the defendants were acquitted outright. As for the other three, the jury said it couldn't make up its mind. In a city already tense with racial strife and

FBI agents escort unidentified associates of the Gambino crime family to a police vehicle in New York City in 2008, when American and Italian authorities arrested dozens of people in a takedown of the remnants of New York's Gambino crime family, also meant to cripple a trans-Atlantic drug trafficking operation run by the Mafia. [AP Photo/Jin Lee]

rumors about a mysterious group called "the Mafia," the verdict triggered an explosive reaction. A mob of several thousand people stormed the prison where the six acquitted defendants (who were still in jail, pending the outcome of some other minor matters), plus the other 13 men from the original indictment were being held. Prison staff let the Sicilians out of their cells and told them to hide. The mob surged inside the prison and grabbed as many of the Sicilians as they could find. Two were hung and nine shot dead. The other eight men managed to get away. It was one of the worst mass lynchings in American history. It's unclear whether any of 19 men indicted for killing the chief were actually connected to the Mafia (or had anything to do with Hennessy's murder). No

matter; the assassination of Chief Hennessy and subsequent lynching of his accused killers marked the first time Americans faced the specter of Mafia violence on their home soil.

The actual origins of the Mafia, in sunny Sicily, are shrouded in legend and myth. A strategically placed island in the Mediterranean, Sicily has been repeatedly conquered by foreigners. At different times in its history, Sicily was ruled by Greeks, Arabs, Romans, Normans, Byzantines, Austrians, the French, and the Spanish. Most of these groups ruled badly and treated the island's peasantry like slaves, fit only for generating wealth for the ruling class. Making things even more inhospitable was the island's geography. Western Sicily in particular is mountainous with many isolated villages. The climate is hot and bare survival is a struggle.

Not surprisingly, the Sicilian population began to develop certain cultural traits to endure foreign occupation. Sicilians learned to distrust all forms of government and anyone in authority. The rule of law meant nothing in Sicily; citizens were encouraged to take personal revenge for crimes against kin and clan rather than seek justice in court. This of course, led to a never-ending series of blood feuds (vendettas). Helping authorities in any way was taboo. It was considered far better to remain silent than to assist the police, even if someone in your family had been murdered.

There is no consensus on the origins of the word "Mafia." "Scholars disagree on whether the term came from 'maehfil' meaning union in the language of the 9th century Arab conquerors of Sicily or from the Tuscan word 'maffia' signifying poverty or misery," states an October 15, 1984, article in *TIME* magazine. One legend suggests that in 1282, Sicilians rebelled against French rule. As their battle cry, these rebels used the slogan, "Morte alla Francia Italia anela" ("Death to the French is Italy's cry"). The first letters in each word of this slogan spell out "Mafia." Another legend posits that in the 13th century, a French soldier raped a Sicilian maiden on her wedding day. The hysterical mother ran around the streets shouting, "Ma fia! Ma fia!" ("my daughter, my daughter).

Sicily was freed from foreign oppression in 1860 with the unification of Italy. The central Italian government was weak, however, and generally ignored the poor south, including Sicily. Conditions were perfect for the rise of a violent underworld. Accounts vary as to how exactly this underworld came to be.

In one version, organized bands of armed men (who were primarily related by blood) were formed in the 19th century to fight off various oppressors. Although these groups were initially founded for self-defense, they quickly resorted to blatant thuggery. These armed bands practiced something of a protection racket. They demanded money from landowners and businessmen to guard their properties and ensure their personal safety while in Sicily. They also started extorting merchants, insisting on a share of their profits. These criminal organizations became something of a quasi-government in parts of Sicily, doling out raw justice and controlling the economic lives of the peasantry. Such brigands were lumped under the generic term "Mafia."

A different story points to absentee landlords, particularly in isolated western Sicily. These absentee landlords would typically let an overseer actually run their property. The overseer would collect rents from the peasantry, keep some himself and forward the rest to the absentee landlords. The overseers typically relied on a clutch of toughs with guns to enforce their rules and guard the landlord's property. In addition to guarding rich people's property, these toughs began to terrorize the population. In this manner, the Mafia was born.

In Italy, the Sicilian Mafia was merely one of several organized crime groups. Other groups included the Camorra or Neapolitan Mafia, based in Naples, which first emerged in the mid-1800s as a prison gang. The 'Ndrangheta or Calabrian Mafia was also formed around the same time in Calabria. The fourth major organization was the Sacra Corona Unita or United Sacred Crown, based in the Puglia region. Generally, all these groups shared a proclivity toward violence, avarice, and thuggish behavior.

Mafia clans in Sicily were not united. There was no single, monolithic "Mafia" organization with a central command and supreme leader. Various Mafia factions fought each other as much as the police or carabinieri (paramilitary peace officers). Needless to say, when the opportunity to emigrate arrived, millions of people took advantage of it. By the end of the 19th century, the trickle of Sicilian and other Italian immigrants to America turned into a flood. Within a few years, an estimated four million immigrants from southern Italy and Sicily settled in the United States. Among their ranks were a handful of criminals.

In this environment, the "Black Hand" racket thrived. Very common in Italian American communities, the Black Hand racket was a crude but extremely effective extortion scheme. A person would get an anonymous note demanding money. The note would threaten all manner of violence if the victim didn't comply. These notes typically bore the inky handprint of the person who sent them.

At the turn of the 20th century, New York police lieutenant Joseph Petrosino headed an "Italian squad" that dealt with issues in that community. Petrosino made hundreds of Black Hand arrests and wasn't above beating up Black Hand suspects in the street. In March 1909, Petrosino traveled to Palermo, Sicily, to investigate Black Hand links with the Sicilian Mafia. On March 12, 1909, he was murdered, almost certainly by Mafia assassins. He remains the only New York City police officer killed on assignment in another country.

As Petrosino fought against the Black Hand in New York City, "Big Jim" Colosimo rose to notoriety in Chicago as the biggest Italian American crime boss in the city. Colosimo's empire was largely based on prostitution. Colosimo was much bothered by pesky Black Hand extortionists. To deal with them, he brought in his wife's cousin, Johnny Torrio, from New York. A rising gangster, Torrio quickly took care of Colosimo's problem by murdering the Black Handers who were bothering him. Colosimo and Torrio aside, Italian organized crime in America remained relatively small-scale for decades. In the 1920s, two things gave the U.S. Mafia a major boost: Prohibition and a brutal crackdown in Sicily on Mafia groups. "Mafia operations in the United States were still comparatively limited at the time the 18th Amendment to the Constitution became effective in 1920. The advent of Prohibition brought the Mafia to fruition," reads an FBI report. "The wealth and influence achieved by Mafiosi before 1920 were insignificant compared to what they had achieved by the end of Prohibition. To Mafiosi, the manufacture and sale of illegal liquor was the ring on which they cut their teeth."

Prohibition, which came into effect in early 1920, also served as something of a demarcation line for Italian organized crime. In Chicago, Torrio was frustrated by his boss's reluctance to jump into the bootlegging racket. As Torrio correctly perceived, the attempt to ban liquor by law presented incredible opportunities for gangsters. Colosimo wasn't interested, however, so Torrio had him murdered on May 11, 1920. A good judge of criminal talent, Torrio brought his protégé, Al Capone, from New York to help him run rackets in Chicago. The pair soon controlled one of the largest underworld gangs in the country.

In the mid-1920s, newly installed Fascist dictator Benito Mussolini launched a vicious campaign to crush the Sicilian Mafia. Hundreds of Mafiosi found themselves behind bars. Hundreds of others fled to America. One Mafiosi who made the trek to the New World had a vision and a plan. His name was Salvatore Maranzano, and initially he was an emissary for Sicilian Mafia boss Don Vito Cascio Ferro. Ferro had a dream of uniting the Italian American underworld and putting himself in command. By the late 1920s, however, Ferro found himself languishing in a Fascist prison cell. His emissary, Maranzano, decided to co-opt his boss's plan for himself. Maranzano established himself in New York City and forged alliances with leading gangsters.

Maranzano quickly butted heads with a fellow countryman, Joe "The Boss" Masseria, who regarded himself as top mobster in New York. The ensuing conflict between Maranzano and Masseria was called "the Castellammarese War" after the Sicilian town from which many of the participants came.

Masseria was murdered April 15, 1931, after being betrayed by his lieutenant, Charles "Lucky" Luciano. Maranzano organized a mass meeting of

MUSSOLINI: A BRUTAL CRACKDOWN SENDS AN EXODUS OF MAFIOSI TO AMERICA

Fascist dictator Benito Mussolini seized power in Italy in the early 1920s. Shortly thereafter, he launched a brutal crackdown on the Sicilian Mafia, which he viewed as a threat to his total control of the country. Mussolini ordered Cesare Mori, prefect of Palermo, to root out the Mafia by any means necessary. An accomplished henchman, Mori set about his task with great energy. To achieve his mission, Mori relied on a huge army of police and paramilitary security forces. Mori's campaign featured the widespread use of torture, preventive detention, mass arrests, violence, and public humiliation (arrested Mafiosi were displayed in cages during their trials). This crackdown was highly successful, largely because the Fascists, like their Mafiosi opponents, didn't hesitate to break the law to achieve their goals. In the end, over 1,200 Mafia members were convicted for terms ranging from a few years to life behind bars. The downside to this brutal crackdown was that an estimated 500 to 1,000 Mafiosi left Sicily for the more welcoming climes of America. Salvatore Maranzano, emissary of Sicilian master Mafia boss Don Vito Cascio Ferro, helped arrange for scores of his kin to settle in the United States. Fleeing Mafiosi typically entered America in one of two ways: via Marseilles, where they would ship out to Canada or New York, or via Tunis then Cuba, then Miami or other southern cities. Mori's campaign ended in 1929. Although he hadn't fully eradicated the Mafia, his campaign was an enormous success. Unfortunately, invading American forces treated imprisoned Mafiosi like political prisoners. When they liberated Sicily in 1943, the U.S. military released Mafia members from jail, which allowed them to quickly reassume power.

Sources: Thomas Reppetto, *American Mafia: A History of Its Rise to Power*, 2004; Denis Mack Smith, *Mussolini: A Biography*, 1983; David Southwell, *The History of Organized Crime: The True Story and Secrets of Global Gangland*, 2006.

Italian gangsters at which he laid down the template for a formal, American-style Mafia. The New York underworld would be divided into five Mafia "families." Each family would have its own specific territory and rackets. The families would be led by a boss and an underboss. Bosses would be in charge of a group of capos or caporegimes (middle managers). Each capo, in turn, would control a "regime" (a "crew" in modern-day Mafia lingo) of about 10 soldiers (i.e. front-line workers). Soldiers could count on the assistance of countless "associates" (people who worked for the Mafia but were not formal members). The decision-making process in each family was filtered through several layers of staff. That way, if a soldier or an associate was arrested, they would not be able to implicate the family boss.

Maranzano introduced an element of ritual into the Mafia, borrowed from organized crime groups in Italy. In testimony before the U.S. Senate in 1963, Mafia turncoat Joseph Valachi described an elaborate induction ceremony that involved making oaths over pistols and knives and having a piece of paper burned in his hand (to symbolize how he was supposed to "burn" if he betrayed Mafia secrets). These rituals underlined the two main prerequisites of Mafia membership: total obedience to superiors and total silence, "omerta", to police. Members also had to be white males of Italian descent. Associates, however, could come from any ethnicity.

The contemporary Mafia still puts an enormous stress on being "made" (i.e., becoming a formal member of the organization). Typically, an associate is abruptly told to come to a certain location, dressed formally. The associate has to feign ignorance of what the meeting is all about. At the locale, the associate meets made members who take him to another location, usually someone's house. There, the associate is asked if he has any idea why he had been summoned. The only correct answer is "no." At this point, the associate is inducted formally into the ranks of the Mafia. A party or feasting often follows.

Maranzano's organizational talents were solid, but he made the mistake of appointing himself "capo di tutti capi"— "boss of the bosses." The mobsters under him didn't like the idea of having a tyrant in charge of all Mafia operations, so they had him killed in September 1931. The wily Luciano once again organized the hit.

With Maranzano out of the way, Luciano took command. He retained Maranzano's family structure but added a few new elements. Luciano eliminated the "boss of bosses" position and in its place created a "board of directors" called the Commission. The Commission would act as a ruling body for Mafia activities all over the United States. It would be made up of the bosses of each of the five New York families, plus membership from Chicago and elsewhere. In practice, the Commission has been more of a regulatory then an administrative body, dealing with territorial disputes and settling "beefs" (i.e., issues) between families. The Commission has always had far less power than it's been credited with. Luciano also added one new position in the Mafia hierarchy, that of "consigliere." Loosely translated as "counselor," the consigliere would serve as an advisor to the family boss and underboss.

The emergence of a formal, structured American Mafia gave rise to conspiratorial musings in some quarters. Harry

Anslinger, Commissioner of the Federal Bureau of Narcotics (FBN), was convinced the U.S. Mafia was controlled by its Sicilian counterpart. Anslinger was wrong. The American Mafia has always acted independently of crime groups in Sicily. This was particularly true in the 1930s to mid-1940s, when most Sicilian Mafiosi were in jail.

Under Luciano, the Mafia thrived. With the end of Prohibition in 1933, the underworld found new sources of revenue in prostitution, drugs, labor racketeering, extortion of businesses, and, especially, gambling. That said, it is a mistake to view the Mafia as the mirror image of corporate America. In most corporations, profits flow from the top down. The workers at the bottom of the chain benefit from the industry of the leaders at the top. This is not the case in the Mafia, where all money flows upwards. Soldiers and associates handle the dirty work and are expected to share their profits with their superiors. The boss and underboss do the least amount of work and take the fewest chances, but reap the most rewards. Members have to accept this system without complaint; making waves about greedy bosses is a good way to get yourself killed.

Other unwritten rules apply to all Mafia members: always deal in cash, never purchase anything in your own name (houses and vehicles should be registered to wives or relatives), always be available for Mafia work, never engage in sex with a member's spouse or daughter, and remain silent in the face of arrest.

Though bound by strict rules, "made" Mafiosi also have extensive privileges. They have an array of illicit business opportunities at their disposal and can boss around associates any way they see fit. Most importantly, made members benefit from the political pull of their family bosses. They can operate without fear of arrest because local police, judges, and politicians have been paid off by their family. And in case they do get arrested anyway, made men know they can count on legal counsel, courtesy of the family. In theory, made men can't be killed or harmed by other made men except with the express approval of a higher ranking Mafiosi. Although this rule isn't always honored, associates who kill or injure a made man run a huge risk of being killed themselves.

Luciano was jailed on prostitution charges in the mid-1930s, and organized crime somewhat fell off the public's radar. The advent of World War II made Americans more concerned about foreign than domestic enemies. The public was also reassured by FBI director J. Edgar Hoover, who insisted there was no such thing as a U.S. Mafia. He didn't deny there were gangsters; he just thought they were all just local, small-time hoods. In stark contrast, FBN Commissioner Anslinger readily acknowledged a domestic Mafia but thought it was controlled by global cabal.

There are many theories to explain Hoover's detached view, from the conspiratorial, the Mafia had compromising pictures of Hoover, a confirmed bachelor, to simply bureaucratic, it was easier to focus on simple investigations into car theft and bank robbery, which made the FBI look good. Investigations into organized crime might take years and produce scanty results. Hoover might have had practical considerations too: investigating organized crime would have opened FBI agents to corruption. Hoover remembered Prohibition and how the agents in charge of enforcing the law were paid off to look the other way. It was safer to focus on common criminals who didn't have the money to bribe their way out of trouble. Hoover's stance was a little hypocritical, given that FBI agents did, in fact, keep close watch on gangsters throughout the 1940s and 1950s. Their efforts, however, were primarily focused on surveillance, not making cases.

If Hoover was complacent, others weren't. In the early 1950s, Tennessee Senator Estes Kefauver led televised hearings into organized crime that were broadcast around the country. In total contradiction to Hoover's stance, Kefauver acknowledged the existence of a domestic Mafia.

While authorities argued about whether a U.S. Mafia existed, the underworld continued to rumble. On October 25, 1957, Gambino crime family boss Albert Anastasia was murdered in a barber chair in Manhattan's Park-Sheraton Hotel. In November 1957, a group of Mafia bosses having a conference in bucolic Apalachin, New York, were interrupted by the arrival of police. Mobsters went crashing through the woods, in expensive leather shoes and tailored suits. Though no one was jailed for any length of time as a result of the police raid, the botched conference was a humiliation for the underworld. It also marked conclusively that organized crime was active in America. Police estimated at the time that the U.S. Mafia boasted 4,000 to 5000 formal members in 24 crime families across the country. The Mafia could also field 10 "associates" (non-Mafia members who assist the organization) for each formal member.

Thanks to Apalachin, Hoover could no longer deny the existence of the Mafia. The FBI director managed to save face by simply changing the Mafia's name: Hoover began calling it "La Cosa Nostra" (which roughly translates as "this thing of ours"), and claimed it was a newfound organization. The precise meaning of the term La Cosa Nostra (LCN) is open to dispute. In his Senate testimony, Valachi said this was the term Mafia members used to describe the organization they belonged to. It wasn't clear, however, if La Cosa Nostra was a formal title or just simply a bit of gangster slang.

Shortly after Apalachin, the FBI introduced a "Top Hoodlum Program" (THP). Each FBI office was instructed to come up with a list of exactly 10 (no more, no less) "top hoodlums" in their region. Once identified, these hoods would be subjected to greater FBI scrutiny. Though it was at least a start, the THP had obvious flaws. FBI offices in New York and Chicago had hundreds of gangsters to choose from, but bureaus in rural locales and under-populated states had difficulty filling their quota of hoods. THP was useful, however, in gathering information that was later put to good use in future crackdowns on the mob.

The late 1950s saw two other major developments: in 1957, a U.S. Senate Select Committee launched an investigation into labor racketeering. The purpose of the probe was to determine whether the Mafia and certain unions—particularly the Teamsters—were working in collusion. These hearings are primarily remembered today for the epic clash between Robert Kennedy, on the investigator's side, and Teamster leader Jimmy Hoffa on the defense. The probe did, however, alert the public to the dangerous inroads the Mafia had made into legitimate labor organizations.

One year after the Select Committee was launched, the FBI published a top-secret internal report called the "Mafia Monograph." The report brought the FBI up to speed on the history of the Sicilian Mafia and the establishment of a formal American Mafia under Maranzano/ Luciano. The report pulled no punches. It stated, "The Mafia persists in Sicily as the most vicious and extensive racket ever to have been foisted and imposed upon the public. To law enforcement, the Mafia presents the most deeply entrenched and monstrous challenge ever to have crept forth from the under-world." The FBI also correctly ascertained the Mafia's amorphous quality, "The traditional Mafia is not a compact centrally organized society or party such as the Communist Party, but a collection of gangs autonomous in their own territories and loosely federated when federated at all."

In the early 1960s, Mafia secrets became public knowledge following the Senate testimony of former mobster Joseph Valachi. Among other intriguing details, Valachi pointed out that Mafia members don't receive a salary (although some do collect wages through "no show" or "no work" jobs in mob-infiltrated companies). Membership alone is considered remuneration enough. Valachi has been criticized for hyperbole, describing the Mafia as akin to "a second government" and overstating the organization's power. Though Valachi couldn't have known, the Mafia's power was about to be seriously curtailed by legal developments.

Cracking the Mafia's tradition of secrecy had always been a source of frustration for law enforcement groups. The Mafia didn't hold public meetings at which they discussed their plans for the future. Meetings were private, plans were clandestine. To find out what the Mafia was talking about, police had to either slip an informer into the mob's ranks (difficult but not impossible), rely on the occasional traitor such as Valachi to come forward (a rare occurrence), or plant listening devices in underworld locales. The problem was, listening devices, better known as "bugs," were illegal to use.

Back in 1934, legislation was passed prohibiting "wiretapping"—that is, inserting a bug on a telephone to record conversations. The logic was, in order to plant a bug you had to trespass on private property, and that was against the law. The same applied to bugs planted in walls, light fixtures, or elsewhere.

Prior to World War II, the U.S. Attorney General said the FBI could plant wiretaps in cases involving national security. In 1954, Attorney General Herbert Brownell reaffirmed this ruling, and said it was fine to bug subversive groups if national security was at stake. The Attorney General had the Communist Party in mind, but according to some accounts, FBI director Hoover took a broader view. He decided the ruling also applied to investigations of organized crime groups. The Top Hoodlum Program, for example, relied heavily on electronic surveillance. Despite the Attorney General's assurances, evidence gathered through bugs still fell into a legal grey area and wasn't admissible in court.

Electronic surveillance was finally legalized in June 1968 with the passage of the Omnibus Crime Control and Safe Streets Act. The Act permitted authorities to plant bugs and wiretaps, provided they got a court order first. Police and federal agencies now had a powerful weapon to use against the underworld. Words spoken in private by Mafia bosses could be surreptitiously recorded and used in court to secure convictions.

Authorities had also been long frustrated by their inability to hold family bosses to account for crimes committed on their behalf. Because most bosses were smart enough to let low-echelon members handle the family's dirty work (bosses rarely participated in hits, for example) gathering evidence against them was difficult. Even if authorities did successfully prosecute the odd Mafia boss, such as Luciano, another mobster simply took his place.

This situation was largely rectified by the advent of the Racketeer Influenced and Corrupt Organizations (RICO) Act. Included in the Organized Crime Control Act of 1970, RICO was designed to attack underworld leaders and the groups they belonged to. It no longer mattered if a crime boss didn't directly take part in murders and mayhem. As long as they headed an association that broke the law, they could be put in jail.

A March 4, 1985, story in *TIME* magazine explained:

> Under the statute, the leaders of any organization can be prosecuted when the group's members commit crimes that show a pattern of racketeering. Prosecutors do not have to prove that the leader personally committed the illegal acts, only that he supported the specific crime in some way, such as approving them or sharing in any illegal profits.

Thanks to RICO, untouchable family bosses could finally be brought down. RICO also attacked mobsters on the financial front, where they were most vulnerable. RICO allowed authorities to launch civil suits for damages and freeze suspects' assets even before they were convicted. Needless to say, this made mounting a defense quite a bit more difficult and lessened the possibility of bribed jurors and judges. Unfortunately, RICO was complicated and burdensome and was largely ignored for years. Some prosecutors wondered whether it was even constitutional: it did, after all, make free association a crime.

While the federal government was preparing new tools that would eventually devastate the underworld, the Mafia was enjoying a resurgence in public interest. Valachi's testimony and the memoir he wrote while serving time were used as the basis for the 1968 book *The Valachi Papers*. This best-seller was followed a year later by Mario Puzo's novel *The Godfather*, which offered a romanticized view of Mafia life at the top. *The Godfather* was a runaway sensation and was turned into a blockbuster movie with Al Pacino and Marlon Brando in 1972. A well-regarded sequel followed two years later.

The Godfather books and films borrowed elements from real life events. Some gangsters, however, weren't impressed. To combat what he viewed as prejudicial pop culture portrayals of the mob, Colombo crime family boss Joseph Colombo Sr. founded the Italian American Civil Rights League in 1970. Among other activities, the League picketed FBI offices for harassing Italian Americans and complained about media depictions of the Mafia. Colombo organized an Italian American Unity rally in 1970 in New York that attracted 50,000 people and a slew of prominent politicians. Colombo's fellow gangsters were not pleased.

Successful Mafia bosses generally kept a low profile, avoiding publicity and never speaking to the press. Colombo by contrast, was turning himself into a media spokesperson. Given that Colombo was the head of an organized crime family, his new persona as civil rights defender was all the more bizarre. His moment in the spotlight didn't last long, however. At a second Italian American Unity rally on June 28, 1971, Colombo was shot and badly wounded. His assailant was a man named Jerome Johnson, who was almost certainly working on the behalf of an aggrieved Mafia family. Johnson himself was shot dead after firing at Colombo. Colombo lingered in a vegetative state for years before dying.

A 1977 *TIME* magazine cover story on the Mafia pegged the organization's annual earnings at around $48 billion a year, more than most major corporations. If this figure is correct, it represented something of a high-water mark for the Mafia. The mob's fortunes soon took a downward trajectory. Under President Ronald Reagan, the U.S. government's war on organized crime was drastically beefed up. New, hard-driving prosecutors such as Rudolph Giuliani came to the fore. From 1983 to 1988, Giuliani served as United States Attorney for the Southern District of New York. Giuliani was firmly committed to attacking the Mafia with all available legal weapons at his disposal, including RICO.

As a U.S. Attorney, Giuliani was a prime mover in the effort to incarcerate every New York Mafia Family boss. In February 1985, federal authorities indicted all the leaders of the New York Mafia on RICO charges involving labor racketeering, extortion, and murder. Those indicted included Paul Castellano of the Gambino family, Carmine Persico of the Colombo (formerly Profaci) family, Anthony "Tony Ducks" Corallo of the Luchesse family, Philip "Rusty" Rastelli of the Bonanno clan, and Anthony "Fat Tony" Salerno of the Genovese family. The Family underbosses were indicted as well. This unprecedented sweep was designed to cripple "the Commission"—the Mafia board of directors set up by Lucky Luciano.

Not all the bosses who were indicted ended up in court. On December 16, 1985, Castellano and his underboss, Thomas Bilotti, were gunned down in front of the Sparks Steak House in Manhattan. Their murders had been carefully arranged by rising capo John Gotti, who then seized control of the Gambino clan. It was the most audacious hit on a mob leader since the 1957 death of Albert Anastasia, also in New York.

The so-called Commission trial began in September 1986. Rastelli was severed from the trial because he had charges pending elsewhere. A key government witness was FBI agent Joseph Pistone, who, as "Donnie Brasco," had successfully infiltrated the Mafia in New York. In November 1986, all the defendants were found guilty and received huge sentences (in some cases, upwards of 100 years in jail). In later testimony before the U.S. Senate, Pistone identified gambling, not drugs, as the Mafia's main source of income in the post-Prohibition era. "Although narcotics trafficking may be a major money-maker for various members of the mob, not every member of the family may be involved in it. On the other hand, every Mafia member was involved in gambling and used the profits from it to sustain other activities," noted Pistone, in testimony before the U.S. Senate in 1988.

In a 2004 book entitled *The Way of the Wiseguy*, Pistone elaborated on this theme. According to Pistone, the advent of legal gambling has done little to curtail the Mafia's involvement in the gaming industry. Casinos require winners to pay taxes on their earnings and file paperwork. This is generally too much hassle for so-called "degenerate" (i.e., addicted) gamblers, explained Pistone. The latter generally prefer to take their chances with Mafia-run games, where the winnings aren't taxed and no paperwork is required, he stated. The Mafia also makes money from legal gambling through the practice of "skimming"— squirreling away part of a casino's revenue before it can be declared as taxable income. Hand-in-hand with gambling is the age-old underworld racket of loan-sharking, Pistone continued. Also known as "shylocking," loan sharking involves providing loans at exorbitant rates of interest. Interest rates might work out to be more than the actual principal of the loan, in the end. Fear of incurring a beating or worse generally encourages people to pay off their loans.

Gambling aside, the Giuliani era marked a severe decline in Mafia power. Family bosses weren't the only ones targeted by authorities. "During the 1980s, some 1,200 Mafia operatives were convicted," noted a *TIME* magazine article published September 3, 1990. The 1980s were also a transitional period, with new modes of business and a new generation of mobsters. At 1988 Senate hearings, Angelo Lonardo, former acting boss of the Cleveland Mafia, bewailed the changing times. He told the Senate:

I have been in the Mafia most of my adult life. I have been aware of it ever since I was a child in Cleveland. It has changed since I first joined in the 1940s, especially in the last few years with the growth of narcotics. Greed is causing younger members to go into narcotics without the knowledge of the families. These younger members lack the discipline and respect that made "this thing" as strong as it once was.

Greed, combined with lack of discipline and respect, certainly applied to Gotti. He made money dealing drugs (a fact he barely bothered to hide, in spite of mob strictures against trafficking) and clearly had little respect for his boss. Gotti didn't care for mob protocol either—he didn't consult the Commission or get permission from other family bosses before he murdered Castellano. Gotti also lacked self-discipline: he eagerly courted media attention and seemed incapable of keeping his mouth shut. In meetings he assumed were private, Gotti routinely spilled family secrets and named names. Many of these conversations were recorded by the FBI. These recordings helped convict Gotti on racketeering charges in April 1992. Gotti was also brought down by his own second-in-command, Salvatore "Sammy the Bull" Gravano, who ignored decades of Mafia tradition and told all to police. Two months after being found guilty, Gotti appeared for sentencing. He received life in prison without parole. Gotti died behind bars in 2002.

By the time Gotti passed away, some observers were ready to write the Mafia off: "The combined federal and state campaigns [of the 1980s and 1990s] were arguably the most successful anti-crime expedition in American history. Over a span of two decades, 24 mob families, once the best organized and most affluent criminal associations in the nation, were virtually eliminated or seriously undermined," wrote Selwyn Raab in his book, *Five Families*. Indeed, family boss Joseph Massino, put on trial in 2004, was referred to as "the last Don" by the press. "Mr. Massino, 61, is often portrayed as a model of old-style mobsters who are fading from the scene," noted the *New York Times* magazine on March 23, 2004. The article quoted Benjamin Brafman, a New York lawyer who represented imprisoned Genovese family boss Vincent Gigante. Brafman stated, "Most of the people in that world who were household names for the last 30 years have either passed away, are incarcerated or have retired."

It should be noted that Gigante was also described as the last great Mafia boss. Known as "The Chin," Gigante was certainly one of the more colorful bosses of the modern-era. He spent decades pretending to be mentally ill, in the hope that this would fool police into leaving him alone. Gigante would wander around New York City in a ratty bath-robe, acting strange and seemingly oblivious to his surroundings. The media labeled him "The Odd Father." Authorities didn't buy the "crazy" act, however. Following an FBI investigation, Gigante was convicted on racketeering and murder charges in December 1997 and received a sentence of 12 years. Following another FBI probe, he was indicted January 17, 2002, on charges of running the Genovese family from prison. Gigante pled guilty to obstructing justice in 2003, and died in prison two years later. Gigante expired in the same federal hospital where Gotti died.

Though no one is totally discounting the Mafia, they have been superseded to a degree by other rising organized crime groups, including the Asian and Russian mobs, African American street gangs, outlaw motorcycle gangs, and Mexican crime associations. A 2009 report by the National Drug Intelligence Center of the U.S. Department of Justice cited Mexican "drug trafficking organizations" (DTOs) as the biggest organized crime threat to America. "Today the old mobs are but a shadow of what they once were," stated crime writer Thomas Reppetto in his book, *American Mafia*. A report submitted to the United Nations by the International Center, National Institute of Justice, pegged current U.S. Mafia membership at 1,100 nationwide, roughly 80 percent of whom operate in the New York metropolitan area. These members can count on roughly 10,000 associates for help. The report also noted that the Mafia has lost almost all of its former political power and influence over courts and police. While La Cosa Nostra has been forced out of several areas where it used to dominate (such as the Teamsters and other labor unions, New York's garment district and Fulton Fish market, Las Vegas casinos, etc) the underworld has moved into new rackets, such as credit and telephone card fraud, counterfeit consumer goods, computer fraud, and pirating CDs and DVDs.

"Anyone who thinks the Mafia is dead is engaged in wishful thinking. There are still functioning crews ready, willing and able to take advantage of human foibles. And there are still young hoods who want to emulate and perpetuate the gangster lifestyle," stated Daniel Castleman, a prosecutor specializing in organized crime with the Manhattan District Attorney office, in *Five Families*.

See Also: Drug Trade; Luciano, Charles "Lucky"; Maranzano, Salvatore; Pistone, Joseph

Further Reading

Richard Behar, "Special Report: Organized Crime," *TIME*, September 3, 1990.

Patricia Blake, "Blood, Business, Honor," *TIME*, October 15, 1984.

Pierre de Champlain, *Mobsters: Gangsters and Men of Honour*, 2004.

Federal Bureau of Investigation, Mafia Monograph, 1958. http://foia.fbi.gov/foiaindex/mafiamon.htm.

Federal Bureau of Investigation, Organized Crime: Italian Organized Crime—Overview. http://www.fbi.gov/hq/cid/orgcrime/lcnindex.htm.

James O. Finckenauer, "La Cosa Nostra in the United States," National Institute of Justice, 2007.

William Glaberson, "An Archetypal Mob Trial: It's Just Like in the Movies," *New York Times*, May 23, 2004.

David Greenberg, "Civil Rights: Let 'em Wiretap!" History News Network, October 22, 2001. http://www.hnn.us/articles/366.html.

Angelo Lonardo, Testimony before the U.S. Senate Permanent Subcommittee on Investigations of the Senate Committee on Government Affairs, April 4, 1988.

Peter Maas, *The Valachi Papers*, 1968.

"The Mafia: Back to the Bad Old Days?," *TIME* cover story, July 12, 1971.

"The Mafia: Big, Bad and Booming," *TIME* cover story, May 16, 1977.

Ed Magnuson, "Hard Days for the Mafia," *TIME*, March 4, 1985.

National Drug Intelligence Center, U.S. Department of Justice, National Drug Threat Assessment, 2009.

Officer Down Memorial Page—Chief of Police David Hennessy. http://www.odmp.org/officer/6389-chief-of-police-david-c.-hennessy.

Officer Down Memorial Page-Lieutenant Joseph Petrosino. http://www.odmp.org/officer/10600-lieutenant-giuseppe-(joseph)-petrosino.

Joseph Pistone, Testimony before the U.S. Senate Permanent Subcommittee on Investigations of the Committee on Government Affairs, 1988. http://www.americanmafia.com/pistone_testimony.html.

Joseph Pistone, *The Way of the Wiseguy*, 2004.

Selwyn Raab, *Five Families: The Rise, Decline and Resurgence of America's Most Powerful Mafia Empires*, 2005.

Thomas Reppetto, *American Mafia: A History of Its Rise to Power*, 2004.

MARANZANO, SALVATORE (1868–1931)

Salvatore Maranzano established the internal structure of the American Mafia, but was too tyrannical to enjoy the benefits of his creation. In addition to creating the template for organized crime, Maranzano's life serves as a cautionary tale for wannabe mobsters on how not to behave.

Equal parts visionary and megalomaniac, Maranzano was born in 1868 in Castellammare del Golfo, Sicily, a part of the world that has birthed an unusually large number of crime bosses. It is rumored that Maranzano studied in a seminary to become a priest or even attended college. He never served as a man of the cloth, however, preferring to plunge into Sicily's thriving criminal culture.

Maranzano came to America in 1927 as an emissary of Sicilian mob boss Don Vito Cascio Ferro. Ferro had dreams of organizing the United States underworld and putting it under his command. Once established in New York, Maranzano became more interested in bootlegging than empire-building for a distant boss.

He allied himself with rising gangsters such as Joseph Bonanno, Joseph Profaci, and Stefano Magaddino. Ferro, meanwhile, had other problems to contend with. In the 1920s, Italian Fascist dictator Benito Mussolini launched a brutal crackdown on the Sicilian Mafia. Countless Mafiosi—including Ferro—disappeared into the dictator's prison system. Hundreds of Mafia members fled the island. Maranzano was quick to profit from his mentor's misery. In addition to bootlegging, he got involved in the people trafficking business—smuggling his Mafia comrades into the United States.

There are opposing views on Maranzano's personality and character. The recent book *American Mafia* offers a flattering description of the man:

> The first thing [people] noticed about Maranzano was his physical appearance. He was tall for a Sicilian and powerfully built giving the impression that he could snap a man's neck with his fingers. But his greatest asset was his voice. According to Bonanno, it was clear and pleasant with an "echo like" quality. A former seminarian who spoke five languages and could quote the Latin poets, he held audiences in rapt attention.

It was also said that Maranzano was an amateur historian who was fascinated by tales of Imperial Rome. Other descriptions are considerably less flattering. They describe a man who could barely speak a word of English, much less master five languages. Turncoat Mafia soldier Joseph Valachi certainly wasn't awed by Maranzano. "He looked just like a banker. You'd never guess in a million years that he was a racketeer," Valachi wrote in his memoirs.

If there are discrepancies about his character, no one disputes that Maranzano had nerve. Not only did he spurn the instructions of his mentor, he blatantly encroached on the territory of fellow Sicilian gangster Giuseppe "Joe" Masseria in New York City. Joe liked people to refer to him as "The Boss." He was a powerful mobster who was not pleased by Maranzano's cheek. Maranzano remained defiant, in spite of Masseria's growing wrath. His men began hijacking trucks containing illicit liquor belonging to the Boss and taking over speakeasies Masseria controlled. Not surprisingly, the rivalry between the two hot-headed Sicilian American gangsters soon erupted into outright warfare. The struggle was dubbed "The Castellammarese War" in honor of the town from which most of the men involved came.

At the outset of the war, in 1928, it appeared that Masseria was bound to win. He had more gunmen and clout, but was hobbled by an unlikeable personality. In the eyes of the Young Turks in Masseria's organization, the Boss was a "Moustache Pete"—a contemptuous term for an old-fashioned, old-world style underworld leader. Moustache Pete's were clannish and closed-minded. They refused to do business with non-Sicilians, were dismissive of new ideas, and were more concerned with preserving "honor" then making money. As the War ground on, younger members of Masseria's gang quickly grew disenchanted. The younger soldiers didn't see any point in pursuing a personal, bloody vendetta for the benefit of "the Boss." They were primarily interested in getting rich, not getting even. Charles "Lucky" Luciano—one of Masseria's youngest, most able lieutenants—was particularly annoyed. Luciano was chums with Meyer Lansky, a Jewish criminal mastermind. Luciano and his peers had no problems doing business with Jews or Irish gangsters—something Masseria frowned upon. They resented Masseria's narrow worldview and obsessive bloodlust. Luciano contacted Maranzano and struck a deal. Luciano would arrange for his boss to be killed. In exchange, Maranzano would end the costly Castellammarese War.

On April 15, 1931, Masseria was murdered in a restaurant in the Coney Island section of Brooklyn. Luciano, who was conveniently in the washroom when a hit team burst into the eatery and shot his boss, told investigators he had no idea why anyone would want to kill Masseria. Maranzano quickly took charge of Masseria's troops following the death of Joe the Boss. True to his word, Maranzano ended the Castellammarese War. The strife had resulted in an estimated 50 deaths, though an exact total would be difficult to calculate. Maranzano's newly expanded gang was unhappy to discover that their new leader shared many of the same traits as the despised Masseria. Maranzano was perceived as arrogant and pretentious. If it is true that he barely spoke English, Maranzano would have faced a massive communications gap with the mobsters under his command. Like Masseria, Maranzano was clannish, set in his ways, and more interested in amassing personal power than in making his followers rich.

For all his faults, Maranzano was a man with big ideas. He borrowed Ferro's grandiose vision, of a united underworld, and put a historical twist on the notion. Maranzano's concept was to organize the New York mob like a military unit, with clear chains of command. Maranzano divided the main gangs in New York City into five "families." Each family would have a boss and underboss. He appointed five of his closest allies—Luciano, Bonanno, Profaci, Vincent Mangano, and Gaetano ("Tommy") Gagliano—to lead these families. These bosses would command a handful of capos or caporegimes—the equivalent of Mafia middle-managers. Each capo was in charge of a regime (i.e., a unit) of roughly 10 "soldiers" (low-ranking Mafia gunmen and thugs). Soldiers could rely on associates (non-Mafiosi who helped the organization) for assistance. Mafia membership was only open to Italian males. This orderly structure was designed to provide maximum protection for the leaders at the top. Family bosses would only deal with capos and underbosses. They would have no personal relationship with the men who did the family's dirty work. Any felonious activity within the family would be performed by disposable soldiers and associates.

Maranzano outlined his vision at a mass meeting of several hundred mobsters held two weeks after Masseria's death. The mobsters met in a banquet hall in upstate New York (Valachi said it was a rented hall in the Bronx and estimated that 400–500 gangsters were in attendance). In his remarks, Maranzano defended Masseria's assassination on the grounds that Joe the Boss was out of control and killing people for no good reason. It was a hypocritical stance, but no one challenged Maranzano on it. During his speech, Maranzano used the expression "Cosa Nostra" ("our thing" in

Italian) to refer to the criminal organization he envisioned. He avoided using the word "Mafia" (a loaded term that referred specifically to the Sicilian underworld).

Maranzano laid down several operating principles. Talking about Cosa Nostra to outsiders was forbidden and punishable by death. Random killings of family members were out (all major hits were supposed to be cleared by the bosses first), as was having sex with another member's wife. Adultery among the ranks of Cosa Nostra would be a capital offence. In the organized family structure he put together, Maranzano envisioned himself as "capo di tutti capi"—"Boss of the Bosses." It was the same role that Ferro had wanted for himself. Like Caesar, Maranzano wanted to rule without any checks or balances.

Though gangsters readily agreed to Maranzano's organizational model, they resented his position at the apex of power. It didn't help that he bossed around his subordinates as if they were serfs and refused to countenance any views but his own. Maranzano suspected that his subordinates were unhappy with his tyrannical leadership and were plotting against him. He hired notorious hit man Vincent "Mad Dog" Coll to eliminate his rebellious underlings. Maranzano wanted Coll to murder Luciano and Vito Genovese. He later expanded his death list to include Dutch Schultz (Coll's former boss), Al Capone, Frank Costello, Willie Moretti, and Joe Adonis, among others.

Before Coll could do any killing, however, Luciano caught wind of Maranzano's plans and hatched a plot of his own. On September 10, 1931, in mid-afternoon, four men pretending to be U.S. Treasury agents burst into Maranzano's headquarters, which was located on the ninth floor of the Eagle Building on Park Avenue. A sign outside the offices said "Real Estate" to conceal the actual nature of the transactions that went on inside. The hit team disarmed the bodyguards on the scene. Two of them stood watch over the bodyguards while the other pair burst into an inner office. Inside the inner office they found Maranzano sitting behind a desk. The two assassins shot and stabbed the gang leader to death. Then, all four members of the death squad raced out of the building. Legend has it that the foursome ran into Mad Dog Coll, who was arriving for a meeting. The four men yelled a warning that a police raid was taking place and Coll took off.

Maranzano had served as "Boss of Bosses" for only four months. After his death, Luciano emerged as top New York Cosa Nostra leader. Luciano wisely refused to take on the capo di tutti capi position. He retained the basic structure of the organization Maranzano had put into place, but made the top level more egalitarian. Luciano thought the Mafia should be run as a corporation, with a board of directors setting policy rather than one dictatorial boss. Though an arguably ineffective leader, Maranzano was still an enormous influence on organized crime. His Five Families structure (now expanded to include a sixth family, based in New Jersey) remains intact today. The hierarchical structure he set up also remains in place.

See Also: Luciano, Charles "Lucky"; Mafia

Further Reading

Federal Bureau of Investigation, Mafia Monograph, 1958. http://foia.fbi.gov/foiaindex/mafiamon.htm.

Nate Hendley, *Dutch Schultz, the Brazen Beer Baron of New York*, 2005.

Peter Maas, *The Valachi Papers*, 1968.

Joseph Pistone, Testimony before the U.S. Senate Permanent Subcommittee on Investigations of the Committee on Government Affairs, 1988.-Thomas Reppetto, *American Mafia: A History of Its Rise to Power*, 2004.

Burton Turkus and Sid Feder, *Murder, Inc: The Story of the Syndicate*, 1951.

MARA SALVATRUCHA (MS-13)

Mara Salvatrucha, or simply MS-13, is a relatively new and extremely violent street gang with roots in Latin America. MS-13 handles all the usual street gang vocations such as contract killing, drug smuggling, gun trafficking, auto theft, and home invasions, among other activities. The gang was founded in Los Angeles in the 1980s by refugees fleeing the brutal civil war in El Salvador that pitted left-wing guerrillas against a right-wing government. The initial purpose of the organization was to protect El Salvadorians from other Hispanic street gangs. MS-13 soon turned into a criminal organization, however. Many of the original gang members were former guerrilla fighters or army soldiers who were used to working with guns and committing acts of violence. The gang is loosely structured, with no single boss giving directives. Members of MS-13 organize themselves into "cliques" that operate independently of each other. There are different accounts to explain the origins of the MS-13 name. It has been suggested that "13" simply refers to the letter "M" which comes from "mara"—a slang term in El Salvador for a group of people or a gang.

Geography also helps explain the etymology of MS-13. Unlike most street gangs, MS-13 is not solely based in urban centers. Hispanic workers, who travel across the rural United States looking for farm jobs, represent a convenient recruitment pool for MS-13. There have been reports of MS-13 activity in small towns and rural communities across the United States. "Hispanic gangs in California have separated into two rival factions, the Nortenos, which are primarily found in northern California and the Surenos, found in the south," explained Chris Swecker, assistant director of the FBI's criminal investigative bureau, in Congressional testimony April 20, 2005. "Hispanic gangs aligned under the Nortenos will generally add the number 14 after their gang name, while gangs aligned under the Surenos will generally add the number 13." Another explanation suggests the word "mara" is short for "marabunta," a South American term that refers to deadly army ants. The second part of the Mara Salvatrucha tag most likely stems from the name of the guerrilla movement involved in El Salvador's civil war.

The FBI estimates MS-13 has 10,000 members in the United States, and perhaps five times that number in El Salvador, Guatemala, Honduras, and Mexico. Numerically, MS-13 is not the largest gang in the United States, but it does have a fearsome reputation. In 2003, a pregnant teenage girl accused of being a federal informer was stabbed to death near Shenandoah River in Virginia by MS-13 members. In Honduras, MS-13 gunmen killed nearly 30 people, several of them children, on December 23, 2004, when they opened fire on a public bus.

The United States has unwittingly helped the growth of MS-13. During the

Reagan presidency, the United States supported the government of El Salvador, which engaged in brutal measures that ensured a steady stream of refugees from the country. After MS-13 made its appearance on American soil, the federal government began deporting captured members back to their home countries—where they promptly spread the gang's influence.

Hispanic gangs have a long history in the United States, going back over a century. There was a great deal of prejudice against Hispanics on the part of white Americans in the early 20th century. Such discrimination was ironic, given that most of the U.S. southwest once belonged to Mexico, a historical grievance not lost on Hispanic immigrants. In the 1940s, Hispanic gangs in L.A. could be identified by their outlandish "zoot suits," outfits that consisted of wide-legged pants with tight cuffs, low hanging, over-sized jackets, flamboyant hats, dangling chains, and shiny shoes. During the Second World War, Los Angeles was racked with riots between Hispanics and servicemen who viewed zoot suits as unpatriotic because they used up valuable cloth and other materials that could have gone to make military uniforms. The 1950s, meanwhile, saw the birth of a notorious Hispanic prison gang called La Eme, or "the Mexican Mafia."

For now, however, it is MS-13 that has everyone's attention. The FBI launched an MS-13 National Gang Task Force in 2004. The FBI has also posted agents in El Salvador to assist local authorities in keeping tabs MS-13 activity. These agents also forward information to FBI headquarters in Washington, D.C., to help the anti-gang war on the home front. In 2006, *National Geographic* magazine aired a documentary on MS-13, which it dubbed "the world's most dangerous gang." An exaggeration perhaps, but a testament to the strength of this brutal gang.

See Also: Drug Trade

Further Reading

Matthew Brzenzinski, "Hillbangers," *New York Times*, August 15, 2004.

Federal Bureau of Investigation, The MS-13 Threat: A National Assessment. http://www.fbi.gov/page2/jan08/ms13_011408.html.

Luis Rodriguez, "A Gang of our Own Making," *New York Times*, March 28, 2005.

Chris Swecker, Assistant Director, Criminal Investigative Division, Federal Bureau of Investigation, Testimony before the Subcommittee on the Western Hemisphere House International Relations Committee, April 20, 2005.

Al Valdez, "A History of California's Hispanic Gangs," National Alliance of Gang Investigators' Associations, July 30, 2008.

"The World's Most Dangerous Gang," *National Geographic Channel,* 2006.

MURDER, INC.

Murder, Inc., was the name newspapers gave to the collection of killers who carried out assassinations for the loosely organized national crime syndicate. Headed by Meyer Lansky, Louis "Lepke" Buchalter, Charles "Lucky" Luciano, and Joe Adonis, among others, the syndicate was founded in the early 1930s to regulate vice. The syndicate was more of an advisory board then an actual administrative body. That said, the syndicate did have great power over life and death; Murder, Inc. served as the syndicate's enforcement arm, taking down anyone who aggrieved the crime

Albert Anastasia, executioner for Murder, Inc., arrives for a Senate crime hearing at New York's Federal Courthouse, 1951. [AP Photo]

bosses at the top. "These killers were not for hire. Their services were limited exclusively to the syndicate, for use when business required," explains the book, *Murder, Inc.* The organization has been credited with hundreds of homicides—no one is sure of the exact total. Members of the group included Harry "Pittsburgh Phil" Strauss, Harry "Happy" Maione (who acquired his nickname because he was always sullen), Martin "Buggsy" Goldstein, Seymour "Blue Jaw" Magoon, Frank "the Dasher" Abbandando, Albert "Tick Tock" Tannenbaum, and Dukey Maffetore.

They were an assorted bunch of Jewish and Italian thugs who dispatched their victims in a variety of ways, with gun, rope, knife, and ice-pick (stabbed through a victim's ear into his brain) as the most popular weapons of choice. Some of these killers had a great passion for their work. According to *Murder, Inc.*, "Pittsburgh Phil" Strauss was "as vicious as a Gestapo agent, as causally cold-blooded as a meat-grinding machine in a butcher shop." Strauss personally killed at least 60 people, perhaps double that number. He once unsuccessfully tried to kill a target with a fire axe in a crowded movie theatre. Frank "the Dasher" Abbandando got his nickname for his running abilities. On one occasion, he confronted a victim on the street, but his gun misfired. The victim chased Abbandando who ran around the block so fast, he came up behind the victim, got his pistol working, and shot the man dead. Murder, Inc., also introduced some now common expressions into the gangster vocabulary, such as "hit" for homicide and "putting out a contract" for targeting a victim for death. Victims were generally referred to as "bums" and other unflattering terms.

Members of Murder, Inc., used a 24-hour candy store in Brooklyn as their headquarters. When they weren't killing people, they hung out at the candy store and ran local rackets—extorting money from merchants, organizing gambling activities, and the like. Unlike most underworld members, the killer elite in Murder, Inc., were on permanent retainer and were paid $250 a week. They also received bonuses for jobs well done. In addition, members could count on the best lawyers to defend them if they were ever arrested.

The effectiveness of Murder, Inc., lay in its impersonal, business-like structure. The killers often didn't know the person they were assigned to murder. They had no strong feelings one way or the other about the people they killed. They were as indifferent as workers in an abattoir. The system worked like this: the top members of the syndicate would get together to mull over a murder. There would have to be general agreement among their ranks before going forward. Strict rules about homicide applied. The members of Murder, Inc., were not supposed to kill policemen, politicians, prosecutors, or journalists. This had nothing to do with morality and everything to do with fear of massive retaliation.

Once the top members of the syndicate were in agreement, Buchalter, the syndicate member directly in charge of Murder, Inc., would pass the orders down the line. Buchalter would speak to the sadistic Albert Anastasia, the second in command, who in turn would contact a middle manager, such as Louis Capone (no relation to Al). Capone, in turn, would provide instructions to the actual killers. "Field commanders" such as Abe "Kid Twist" Reles would actually lead the troops on the ground. This hierarchical system was designed to protect the leaders at the top. Even if an assassin was arrested, he would only be able to give away the name of the sub-boss directly above him. He wouldn't be able to implicate the syndicate commanders.

If the killing took place outside of New York, the assassin would rely on the assistance of a local thug to point out the victim and provide information on his work and play habits. Assassinations were carefully planned, with the Murder, Inc. killer studiously researching his target. Murder, Inc., members would find out where their targets lived and worked. From this information, the assassin would then find a good place to perform a hit. A car would be stolen to drive the hit man to the scene of the hit, and a getaway route would be carefully mapped. Meticulous planning was the key. Murder, Inc., members knew, after

all, they could expect little mercy if they botched an assignment. Once the hit had taken place, the Murder, Inc., gunman would leave town and head back to Brooklyn. Police would be left puzzling over a homicide for which they could discern no clear motive or any local suspects.

The decentralized nature of crime fighting at the time worked in Murder, Inc.'s favor. Most municipal police forces jealously guarded their turf and wouldn't share information with other jurisdictions. There were no computerized databases of known assassins that police could tap into to solve crimes. A murder in Sante Fe might be completely overlooked by police in Baltimore, even if a similar killing had taken place in that city. The federal agency that should have been keeping tabs on Murder, Inc.—the FBI—was preoccupied with political rather than criminal subversives.

There were occasional light moments in Murder, Inc.'s gory history. Once, the killers were told to murder Walter Sage, an underworld figure in charge of slot machines in Long Island whom the mob suspected was "skimming" from their profits. The men of Murder, Inc., induced a fellow thug named Gangy Cohen, who was friends with Sage, to lure the man into a trap. Cohen convinced Sage to take a late-night drive through the woods. Three killers— Strauss, Tannenbaum, and Abe "Pretty" Levine, waited in another car at a pre-arranged spot. The vehicle containing Cohen, Sage, and a driver cruised by, flashing its headlights. The Murder, Inc., executioners followed. Inside the first car, Sage sat in the passenger seat next to a driver. Gangy sat behind his friend, with another man in the back seat. At some point, one of the two men in the back seat reached over and stabbed Sage repeatedly with an ice pick. There was a great commotion in the car and it went out of control. The vehicle stopped and Gangy opened the door and raced out, tearing through the woods. The assassins called after him, but couldn't get Gangy to stop running. They soon forgot about him and dealt with the matters at hand. The killers took Sage's lifeless body and drove to a lake. They tied a slot machine around his corpse and tossed it into the water. The body subsequently resurfaced a few weeks later, after gases in the stomach began to expand.

A few years later, Pretty Levine and another thug decided to see a movie called *Golden Boy*. To their great surprise, one of the extras in the film was Gangy Cohen. It turned out that Gangy had left the scene of the crime after realizing he might be next. He knew too much for the other Murder, Inc., members to feel comfortable around him. Gangy had kept running until he came upon a train station in a clearing. He bought a ticket for the west coast and ended up in Hollywood, California. Cohen knew a few actors. He changed his name and became an actor himself, picking up bit parts in movies. Cohen was eventually unmasked as a killer on the run and was arrested by authorities.

Murder, Inc.'s most famous victim was the unstable gangster boss Dutch Schultz. Erratic and eccentric, he was notorious for wearing cheap clothes and generally dressing like a hobo, Schultz wanted Murder, Inc. to kill Thomas Dewey, a crusading prosecutor who was investigating his rackets. The other top members of the syndicate refused, fearful of the awesome retribution that would surely follow. Enraged, Schultz announced he would perform the hit himself. This unnerved the syndicate, who ordered his execution. Schultz and three members of his gang were gunned down in the Palace Chop House restaurant in New Jersey on October 23, 1935. Their killers were a pair of expert assassins named Charlie "the Bug" Workman and Mendy Weiss. A third man, known as "Piggy," served as getaway driver.

Murder, Inc. fell apart in the early 1940s. A criminal named Harry Rudolph, imprisoned in New York, contacted assistant district attorney Burton Turkus, offering him inside information in exchange for leniency. Rudolph stated that a hoodlum friend of his, Alex "Red" Alpert, had been killed by Murder, Inc. members Abe "Kid Twist" Reles, Buggsy Goldstein, and Dukey Maffetore in 1933. Kid Twist Reles was a repellent gangster who got his nickname because of his dexterity in strangling people. The name was also bestowed in honor of a previous New York gangster called Kid Twist. Reles was short, heavyset, and often compared to an ape. "There was something about Reles' physical bearing and a look in his eye that actually made the hair on the back of your neck stand up," states *Murder Inc*.

Reles learned through the criminal grapevine that the Murder, Inc., bosses had put out a contract on him to prevent him from talking. With this in mind, Reles decided to turn state's evidence. He gave important testimony on dozens of killings that he either committed himself or had knowledge of. As a result of Reles's damning testimony, several Murder, Inc. members were killed in the electric chair, including Strauss, Louis Capone, Weiss, Goldstein, Happy Maione, Dasher Abbandando, and Lepke Buchalter. Executed in March 1944, Buchalter is still the highest ranking crime boss ever put to death by the U.S. government.

Reles didn't live long enough to see his former boss face the ultimate punishment, however. On November 12, 1941, Reles was staying at a Coney Island hotel, guarded by several policemen. Reles was set to give more damaging testimony in court. Only Reles mysteriously went out the window of his sixth-story room before that could happen. Newspaper wits described him as the "canary that couldn't fly." Though Reles' death has never been solved, Murder, Inc., fell apart, largely due to his confessions. Not that murder itself went out of style in the underworld. Mobsters today continue to use hit men to enforce "contracts" against their victims. The difference now is that there isn't a stable of killers hanging around a candy store, waiting for random assignments anywhere in the United States.

See Also: Jewish Gangsters; Reles, Abraham "Kid Twist"

Further Reading

Pierre de Champlain, *Mobsters: Gangsters and Men of Honour*, 2004.

Rich Cohen, *Tough Jews: Fathers, Sons and Gangster Dreams*, 1998.

"Murder, Inc." *TIME*, April 1, 1940.

Burton Turkus and Sid Feder, *Murder, Inc.: The Story of the Syndicate*, 1951.

N

NUMBERS RACKET

Essentially an illegal lottery, the numbers racket first made its appearance in the United States in the late 19th century. For a small fee, often as little as a few pennies, players bought a "policy" slip from a bookie containing a three digit number from 000 to 999. Each day or week, depending on who was running the racket, a winning combination would be selected. If your three digit number "hit," you won a cash prize. Winning numbers were taken from sports scores, stock market prices, or other objective sources.

For the sake of convenience, bookies would sell "policy slips" in work places or at home. Slips were then collected at "policy banks." The gangsters controlling the operation were called "bankers." Each banker employed a large stable of "runners" whose task was to transport bets and policy slips to the bank.

Numbers offered a cheap, low-risk way to gamble. Numbers was a widely accepted vice, played by all members of the community, particularly in low-income neighborhoods. Numbers was one of the few rackets controlled by African Americans. Though white mobsters dominated other rackets, they turned up their noses at numbers, a game they sneeringly dismissed as "nigger pennies."

Dutch Schultz was one of the first white mobsters to recognize the potential of numbers. Using violent means of persuasion, Schultz took over the Harlem numbers racket in the early 1930s. He allowed African American bankers to stay in business, provided they gave him most of their profits and all of their decision-making authority.

At his peak, Schultz was making $12 million to $14 million a year just from numbers. This wasn't enough to satisfy him, however. Schultz agreed to a complicated scheme to rig the game and make it tougher to win. The plan was proposed by a professional gambler named Otto Berman. Berman went by the name "Abbadabba" because he was a mathematical genius, able to juggle complex figures in his head. Abbadabba was a highly successful gambler with a propensity for choosing winning mounts in horse races.

Bankers under Schultz's control determined their winning three-digit combinations from horse-racing results. The cash payoffs from a preselected series of races would be tallied. Bankers would take the third digit from each payoff and put them together for the winning combination. Say the payoffs were $125.09, $252.75 and $1,681.34. The winning combination would therefore be "521" (as in, 12<u>5</u>, 25<u>2</u> and 1,68<u>1</u>).

Everyone who had purchased a policy slip bearing the number "521" would be a winner. If only a handful of people played the winning number, the policy bank would earn a healthy profit. But if many people played that number, the bank would have to hand out a fortune in winnings. Policy bankers lived in dread of the day when a popular number hit.

This is where Abbadabba Berman came in. Each day, Berman would go to one of the racetracks where policy numbers were derived. These tracks were located as far afield as Florida or Ohio. Berman would watch a few races, and then phone a Schultz associate in New York to find out what the most popular numbers were that day. After receiving this information, Berman would calculate the odds in various upcoming races, then place a bunch of last-minute bets. His intention was to alter the payoffs, so that heavily played numbers didn't hit. The scheme was mind-bogglingly complex, but it worked. Berman soon increased the Dutchman's profit margin by a healthy share. Abbadabba himself became the beneficiary of a $10,000 a week salary, courtesy of Schultz. Schultz and Abbadabba Berman were gunned down together in 1935, but the numbers racket lived on.

The advent of legal lotteries and "scratch and win" cards available in convenience stores has cut into the popularity of numbers, but the game still exists in certain locales. After all, winnings are tax-free and it still costs relatively little to play.

See Also: Johnson, Ellsworth "Bumpy"; Schultz, Dutch

Further Reading

Nate Hendley, *Dutch Schultz: the Brazen Beer Baron of New York*, 2005.

Paul Sann, *Kill the Dutchman! The Story of Dutch Schultz*, 1971.

O

O'BANION, DION
(1892–1924)

Irish gang leader Dion O'Banion is arguably the only mob boss murdered over a practical joke, albeit one with very serious consequences. An amiable, charming sociopath, O'Banion inspired both fierce loyalty and intense hatred. He loved flowers, frowned on prostitution, disparaged his fellow bootleggers for the quality of their brew, and had an unerring knack for antagonizing people.

O'Banion was born in 1892 in Aurora, Illinois. O'Banion's father was a first-generation immigrant from Ireland who worked as a plasterer and house painter when he wasn't drinking. O'Banion, a blue-eyed, angel-faced boy, was generally an upbeat young man, despite a pronounced disability: his left leg was a few inches shorter than his right, which caused him to walk with a limp. He didn't dwell on his disability, however, and it certainly didn't dampen his boisterous spirits. O'Banion's mother died when he was just five years

old, and O'Banion's father moved the family to Chicago shortly afterward. The O'Banion's settled in a rundown Chicago neighborhood that was nicknamed "Little Hell." Located near Little Sicily, on the North Side of the city, Little Hell boasted a slew of factories. Flames from the chimney of a local gasworks made the night sky look red, which is how the area acquired its nickname. Needless to say, it was a violent, crime-ridden place.

As a child, O'Banion attended church regularly. He was even an altar boy and sang in the choir at Holy Name Cathedral. For a time, the church fathers hoped O'Banion might join the priesthood. When O'Banion became a teenager, he began to harbor less holy ambitions. He started running with a pack of street kids and became an accomplished petty thief and juvenile delinquent. At the age of 16, O'Banion took a job as a singing waiter in a dive called McGovern's Saloon on North Clark Street. He was a highly capable vocalist who could reduce customers to tears with sentimental Irish ballads. After entertaining the saloon patrons, O'Banion would occasionally pick their pockets (depending how drunk they were). Sometimes, he slipped customers a "Mickey Finn," a drink with knock-out drugs in it, which would render them unconscious and easier to rob. O'Banion's time at McGovern's was well spent. He met his future wife, Viola Kaniff, there and also befriended many of the youths who would become his loyal gang associates. Their ranks included George "Bugs" Moran, Earl "Hymie" Weiss, Vincent "The Schemer" Drucci, Frank and Peter Gusenberg, and Samuel "Nails" Morton.

When he wasn't spending time at McGovern's, O'Banion was expanding his repertoire of criminal skills. In addition to mugging and robbing people, he tried his hand at burglary and safecracking. O'Banion was also involved in the Chicago newspaper wars, which saw the daily papers relying on street thugs to impose market monopolies and shut down uncooperative newsstand managers and street vendors.

In 1909, O'Banion spent three months in a house of corrections for robbery. Two years later, he served another six months for either blackjacking someone or carrying concealed weapons (accounts vary). Like any number of Chicago criminals, O'Banion might have remained an obscure petty thief were it not for the federal government's decision to legislate sobriety. As of January 1920, the United States officially went dry, and it became illegal to manufacture or sell alcoholic beverages. The ban delighted fledgling mobsters such as O'Banion, who instantly sensed a new revenue source. O'Banion took to bootlegging, forming a gang with the miscreants he'd befriended at McGovern's Saloon.

At the time, Johnny Torrio was the leading gangster in Chicago (having murdered the previous leading gangster, Big Jim Colosimo). In 1920, Torrio held a meeting for Chicago mob bosses, O'Banion included, in which he laid out a vision of mutual cooperation for maximum profit. Torrio argued that it was foolish and counterproductive for bootleggers to war with each other when there was so much money at stake. He suggested dividing the city into territories and establishing peace between warring underworld factions. The basic idea was to avoid internal conflicts, so as to ensure a steady stream of income for everyone involved in bootlegging. O'Banion was promised his home turf: Chicago's North Side. He was agreeable to this, even though he disliked Italians and didn't approve of Torrio's involvement in prostitution. Bootlegging alcohol was one thing, but selling sex for money was squalid and undignified, as far as O'Banion was concerned.

Despite his status as a rising bootlegger, O'Banion still enjoyed carrying out the occasional robbery or safecracking. In 1921, he was caught red-handed, along with some accomplices, trying to open a Postal Telegraph safe with dynamite. To the policeman who stumbled onto this crime scene, O'Banion explained that he and his three accomplices were merely interested in applying for jobs as apprentice telegraph operators. The cop didn't believe it and booked the men. O'Banion didn't spend long behind bars. His $10,000 bail bond was put forward by a city alderman he was on good terms with. For another $30,000 or so in bribes, O'Banion made the case disappear.

O'Banion's bright-eyed cheer and charm covered an extremely violent, impulsive personality. He was also quite paranoid. O'Banion never shook hands with someone he didn't know. Upon meeting a stranger, he would stand, hands on hips, facing the stranger, ready to draw one of the three pistols he kept on him at all times. O'Banion could shoot accurately with either hand and became a marksman with pistols. As a bootlegger, he arranged to bring in liquor from Canada, for distribution in Illinois. He also ran gambling rackets and amassed control of a gang of roughly 200 thugs.

Politicians soon discovered that O'Banion was extremely good at getting the vote out in North Side wards. His gang would routinely stuff ballot boxes, register phony voters, escort repeat voters to the polls, and discourage anyone from voting against the candidates the gang supported. Naturally, the politicians who benefited from these tactics were very supportive of O'Banion once they got into office. O'Banion had the North Side so locked up that he became the subject of a running joke in Chicago. People asked, "Who'll carry the 42nd and 43rd wards?" The answer was, "O'Banion, in his pistol pockets." This common retort has been noted by several sources, including the book, *Capone: The Life and World of Al Capone.*

O'Banion had another diverting sideline. He loved flowers, and when he had sufficient capital, he purchased an interest in the Schofield Flower Shop on North State Street. The shop was located directly across the street from Holy Name Cathedral, where he sang as a boy. During the daytime, O'Banion could be found in the flower store, fussing over arrangements and taking orders on the phone. In this manner, O'Banion become the underworld's florist of choice, routinely providing tasteful flower displays for gangster funerals. He generally wore a suit while at the shop, with a white carnation or a sprig of lily of the valley in his buttonhole. At night, O'Banion would either spend a quiet evening with his wife, Viola, in their 12-room apartment, or he'd hit the town. He usually wore a tuxedo in the latter capacity, and encouraged his fellow gangsters to dress nattily as well. When out at a restaurant or theater, O'Banion was usually on his best behavior. Interestingly, for a major bootlegger, O'Banion didn't drink alcohol himself. He and Viola had no children, but otherwise seemed happily married.

Stories about O'Banion's trigger-happy habits began to make the rounds. In one incident, O'Banion was on the Madison Avenue Bridge in Chicago when a car backfired. Thinking he was under attack, O'Banion drew a pistol and fired at the nearest suspect. He ended up shooting a totally innocent workingman named Arthur Vadis in the leg. After reading about the shooting in the newspaper (the story said Vadis had been wounded by an unknown assailant), O'Banion sent cigars to the man as an apology. In another story, O'Banion was attending a theatrical performance at La Salle Theatre when he spotted Davy "Yiddles" Miller in the crowd. For unclear reasons, O'Banion was convinced that Miller, who worked as a referee at prizefights, had slighted him or someone in his gang. After the performance, O'Banion waited in the lobby for Miller to emerge from the theatre. When he did, O'Banion shot him in the stomach, in front of scores of witnesses. Miller's younger brother Max leapt into the fray to help his sibling. O'Banion fired a round at Max, which ricocheted off his belt buckle. O'Banion causally sauntered off, leaving the two dazed brothers behind. Yiddles Miller survived the shooting, but neither he nor his brother wanted to press charges. Even though he had shot two men in front of hundreds of witnesses, O'Banion managed to get away scot-free. His judgment in other matters was also a little odd. In May 1923, his associate "Nails" Morton was thrown from a horse and killed in Lincoln Park in Chicago. O'Banion was mortified, and had the horse assassinated.

Eccentric as he was, O'Banion was also highly successful, earning an estimated $1 million a year through bootlegging alone. He had no compunctions about augmenting his stock of spirits by hijacking liquor delivery trucks belonging to other gangs. In early 1924, O'Banion's goons broke into a West Side railway yard and moved $100,000 worth of Canadian whisky from a freight car to a truck. Shortly thereafter, O'Banion's gang also broke into a Chicago warehouse and stole 1,750 barrels of bonded liquor. The gang left behind barrels of water, to fool authorities into thinking the alcohol was still there. As he grew rich, O'Banion became more generous. He would drive into slums on the North Side of Chicago and distribute food, money, and clothing to the destitute. Poor residents in the North Side began to look upon him as a benign patron, not a violent gangster.

In theory, O'Banion was allied with Johnny Torrio and his protégé, Al Capone. In reality, O'Banion was far too much of an individualist to put up with an alliance. He was prejudiced and openly referred to Italians as "spics," "greaseballs," "dagos," and "wops." O'Banion would meet regularly with Torrio and Capone at a gambling casino called The Ship to divide up the profits from various joint operations. O'Banion constantly groused that his partners were allowing the notorious Genna brothers to lose money gambling at The Ship without ever paying up. The "Terrible Gennas" as they were called, were a gang of six fierce Sicilian American brothers. They were also a constant source of friction for the prickly O'Banion.

After Prohibition came into effect, the Gennas somehow acquired a government license to make industrial alcohol (which is poisonous to drink). The Gennas also paid countless Sicilian immigrants to brew liquor in their apartments. Regardless of where it originated, the Gennas' "whisky" was notoriously awful, possibly even toxic.

O'Banion was offended by the low quality of the Gennas' whisky. His own bootleg liquor was more expensive, but of considerably higher quality. O'Banion took a strange pride in the quality of his spirits and was outraged when the Gennas began selling their low-end product in his North Side territory. To illustrate his anger, O'Banion arranged for a $30,000 shipment of Genna liquor to be hijacked. Given the Gennas propensity for extreme violence, the audacity of this move astonished fellow gangsters.

Deanie, as he was known to intimates, had other reasons for being miffed. He had supplied some excellent thugs to Torrio and Capone for use in the bloody April 1, 1924, municipal election in Cicero, Illinois, a small city near Chicago. The election featured a wave of violence as Capone and Torrio sought to get the candidates they controlled into office. In a confrontation with Chicago police, Al Capone's older brother Frank was gunned down. O'Banion supplied the flowers for Frank's funeral, but barely got a "thank you" in return from the Torrio/Capone organization. Not only that, but Torrio unwittingly offended O'Banion's morals. At some point in early 1924, Torrio gave O'Banion a small piece of territory in Cicero in which he could sell liquor. It wasn't a very generous gift; sales of bootleg spirits in the area only amounted to about $20,000 a month (small change for gangsters). O'Banion proved to be something of a marketing genius, however. He attracted new customers by pricing his liquor lower than anyone else's. He also managed to convince about 50 speakeasies to move from Chicago to his turf in Cicero and set up shop anew. Soon, O'Banion was bringing home $100,000 in revenue each month from his Cicero holdings.

Torrio took note of O'Banion's success. He offered to give the Irishman a cut of the money he and Capone were making from prostitution if O'Banion shared some of the wealth he was generating in Cicero. O'Banion wanted nothing to do with prostitution, however, and turned the deal down flat. By May 1924, the delicate truce Torrio had imposed on Chicago was starting to unravel. The Gennas were calling for O'Banion's death, and Torrio was finding it harder and harder to keep the volatile brothers in line. Just when it appeared that open gang warfare would return to the Windy City, O'Banion came up with a surprising proposal. O'Banion announced that he was tired of being a criminal and constantly worrying about the Gennas. He wanted to retire and live off his considerable earnings. O'Banion even suggested he might leave Chicago altogether for a more tranquil locale.

All O'Banion wanted, in return for giving up the gangster life, was for Torrio to buy out his share in the Sieben Brewery. The latter was a Chicago facility co-owned by O'Banion, Torrio, and Capone. The brewery was one of several owned by legitimate businessmen who cut deals with gangsters to keep their companies in operation during Prohibition. O'Banion said he was willing sell his share for $500,000, a price that Torrio found more than reasonable. Though a bit suspicious of O'Banion's charm offensive, Torrio liked the sound of gaining more control over the Sieben Brewery. He agreed to the deal. As a show of good faith, O'Banion said he would help out with one last shipment of beer. He asked Torrio to meet him at the brewery at a precise time on the evening of May 19, 1924, to seal the bargain.

On the night in question, Torrio, O'Banion, and their entourages converged at the Sieben Brewery. Beer trucks were being loaded, as the brewery hummed with life. The two gang leaders met and began to chat. Suddenly, police broke into the facility and pointed guns at everyone. The officers were led by Chief Morgan Collins, one of a handful of incorruptible officers on the Chicago force. Torrio quickly realized this was no ordinary police raid. It was supervised by federal authorities, for one thing, with the support of reform minded Chicago mayor William Dever. The gangsters weren't locked up in a city jail, but in a federal holding tank instead. Torrio faced a big problem. He already had one federal Prohibition violation on his record. A second violation would most likely bring some serious jail time and fines. It slowly became apparent to Torrio that he had been set up. O'Banion's federal record was clean. As a first-time offender, his punishment would be relatively light. O'Banion had found out about the raid in advance from his police sources, but didn't bother to apprise Torrio of this fact. Torrio bailed himself out of federal custody but refused to put up any bail for O'Banion and his men. O'Banion didn't seem upset. He had successfully humiliated the biggest gangster in the city, a man who prided himself on his business smarts. To add insult to injury, police padlocked the Sieben Brewery and O'Banion refused to give Torrio his money back.

As if O'Banion wasn't putting himself in enough trouble, he soon compounded his situation. In early November 1924, he showed up at The Ship for the regular distribution of profits. As usual, the Gennas were into the house for a large amount of money. Angelo Genna had left behind an IOU for $30,000. Capone suggested that it was in everyone's best interest to forgive this debt. O'Banion refused. He stalked to a phone, called Angelo, and angrily ordered him to pay up, as if the Terrible Genna was some lowly, anonymous gambler. O'Banion gave Angelo a week to make good on his IOU.

A few days later, on November 8, Mike Merlo, head of Chicago's Unione Siciliana, died of cancer. The Unione had originally been founded to assist Sicilian immigrants become acclimatized to America. The Unione helped Sicilians find housing, jobs, and English language classes. The organization also had a less positive side. It was seen in some quarters as little more than a Mafia front. The Unione stood accused of being involved in prostitution, kidnapping, bank robbery, extortion, and murder.

O'Banion realized he would be kept very busy doing floral decorations for Merlo's funeral. Sure enough, a day after Merlo died, O'Banion took an order for a custom wreath, to be picked up on November 10. On the day in question, O'Banion was fiddling with floral arrangements in his shop when three men entered. They looked like ordinary customers, so O'Banion didn't seem worried. O'Banion might have even recognized the men. He asked if they were there for the custom wreath for Merlo's funeral. He held his hand out to shake— something he would only do with customers he knew. One of the three men grabbed his wrist and held it tight as the other two men pulled out pistols and shot at O'Banion at point-blank range. The shots were overheard by a black employee in the backroom. Plucking up his courage, the employee dashed into the store, to find his boss lying on the floor, bloodied and surrounded by petals and stems. O'Banion was critically wounded. He died soon after. It is believed two of the assassins were John Scalise and Albert Anselmi. The third man was mostly likely Frankie Yale (the killer of Big Jim Colosimo) or Mike Genna.

O'Banion was 32 years old when he died. His funeral was huge. Some 10,000 people took part in the funeral cortege, while another 10,000 people waited at the cemetery. Capone and Torrio took their places among the mourners, although it was almost certain they were the ones who ordered the hit. The funeral procession stretched for a mile and included three bands. Among the conspicuous displays of flowers was a huge basket of roses with a card reading, "From Al." O'Banion was placed in a casket worth $10,000. The casket was carried to a hearse by Weiss, Bugs Moran, Frank Gusenberg, and Schemer Drucci, among others.

The laughing Irish American gangster was a suspect in at least 25 murders. His death would unleash a major war between O'Banion's loyal followers and Torrio and Capone, which climaxed in the St. Valentine's Day Massacre of 1929. O'Banion would likely have been pleased by this show of fealty by his follow gang members. He also would have liked the fact that 26 vehicles alone were needed just to carry the flowers for his funeral.

See Also: Capone, Al; Genna Brothers

Further Reading

John Kobler, *Capone: The Life and World of Al Capone,* 1971.

Gus Russo, *The Outfit: The Role of Chicago's Underworld in the Shaping of Modern America,* 2001.

Paul Sann, *The Lawless Decade,* 1957.

OSTERMAN, EDWARD "MONK" EASTMAN (1873–1920)

Born Edward Osterman in 1873, New York gang leader Monk Eastman loved animals and violence. The latter was reserved for humans, whom Eastman appears to have kept in lower regard than the stray cats and pigeons that used to follow him around on the streets of New York. According to rumor, Eastman owned hundreds of pigeons and cats. He would sometimes walk the streets with a cat under his arm and a tamed pigeon on his shoulder. Kindness to animals aside, Eastman was a straight-out thug. Even a century later, his battered face leaps out of police photographs. He was bullet-headed and so bashed up and scarred he appeared deformed. His ears looked like lumps of cauliflower, and his nose was squashed and misshapen. Eastman's body was equally cut-up and scarred, evidence of countless street battles.

Encouraging an early love of animals, Eastman's father set him up in a pet store. Eastman was 20 years old at the time. Much as he loved creatures with four legs and two wings, life as a shopkeeper was too boring for Eastman's restless spirit. He soon picked up another job, as a bouncer at Manhattan's New Irving Dance Hall. While only 5'5" tall and weighing around 150 pounds, Eastman was an exemplary bouncer. He carried a big club to maintain decorum and also used brass knuckles and a blackjack when circumstances warranted the use of such weapons. In his first six months on the job, Eastman sent 50 victims to the hospital. He left the dance hall to become a gang leader, a vocation at which he thrived. Hundreds of young men, impressed by his feats as a bouncer, were happy to follow him. The gang never had an official name beyond "The Eastmans." Boys who weren't quite at adult fighting age joined an auxiliary group called the Monk Eastman Juniors.

The Eastmans came to number around 1,200 men in total. Their stomping ground was Manhattan's Lower East Side. The gang's turf went roughly from the Bowery to the East River, Monroe to 14th Street. The Eastmans headquarters was a low-end bar on Chrystie Street, close to the Bowery. In addition to burglary, Monk Eastman's goons ran gambling dens and brothels, and performed mayhem and murder for hire. Eastman also did jobs for the corrupt city political machine, Tammany Hall. His men served as "repeaters," voting repeatedly under false names come election time, and beat up people trying to vote against Tammany candidates.

Eastman's main rival was another young gang leader named Paul Kelly. Kelly was dapper and well-dressed and acted like a respectable businessman. Kelly headed a crew of 1,500 thugs called the Five Points gang and also had connections with Tammany Hall. Eastman and Kelly found themselves locked in a battle over territorial borders. Eastman insisted that Kelly's turf ended at the Pelham club on Pell Street. Kelly believed it went beyond the Pelham, into the Bowery. The two gangs found themselves locked in a war of attrition. Border raids and skirmishes were fought with revolvers, rocks, knives, and blackjacks. In April 1901, while he was walking in the Bowery, four members of Kelly's gang jumped Eastman. The gang had revolvers and blackjacks whereas Eastman only had brass knuckles and a slungshot (an improvised weapon made from rope and a weighted object that worked somewhat like a malicious yo-yo). Though outnumbered, Eastman refused to submit and managed to injure three of his attackers. The fourth man pulled out a gun and fired two quick shots that hit Eastman in the stomach. Then, the Five Pointers ran off, thinking their rival had been killed. Eastman, however, was only wounded, albeit quite badly. Eastman slowly got to his feet. Placing a hand over his wounds he stumbled his way to Gouverneur Hospital. In true gangland fashion, Eastman refused to give police any useful information about the shooting. He recovered over the course of a few weeks. Shortly after Eastman was released, the Five Pointer who shot him was murdered. He was found dead, lying in the gutter near Grand and Chrystie Streets.

Meanwhile, the war between the Five Points gang and the Eastmans continued.

The gangs raided each other's gambling operations and brawled at local dance clubs. Sometimes the police intervened, but to little avail. Both gangs had the protection of Tammany Hall, so arrests never stuck. In August 1903, for example, Eastman managed to elude punishment on what should have been an open-and-shut case. A man named David Lamar, identified by the *New York Times* as the "Wolf of Wall Street," was beaten by his coachman, James McMahon after firing the man. With two cronies, Eastman traveled to Freehold, New Jersey, and gave McMahon a retaliatory beating outside his house. Eastman was named as one of the assailants and he was charged with assault. When the case hit the courts, all charges were dropped, supposedly because of lack of evidence.

One month later, there was a massive melee between the Eastmans and the Five Points gang. A bar fight between the two factions escalated into a shooting match on Rivington Street underneath an elevated train. Both sides sniped at each other for hours. Eastman arrived to take personal command of his men. When police finally got control of the situation, Eastman was arrested. He claimed to be an ordinary citizen out for a walk, who happened to blunder into a firefight. It wasn't very believable, but he was discharged from police custody, thanks to Tammany. Up to three people were killed in the Rivington Street shoot-out, and the battle received widespread media coverage. The political masters at Tammany Hall were very displeased. Street fights were one thing, but a massive Wild West gun battle was bad for the city's image. A meeting was arranged between Kelly and Eastman to hammer out a truce. A shaky cease-fire was brokered between the two sides, with both gang leaders agreeing to keep to their particular territories. The truce was broken almost immediately. One provocation lead to another and Kelly, a former bantamweight boxer, challenged Eastman to a boxing match. Eastman accepted. The idea was that the winner would be able to dictate territorial rights to the loser. The two gang leaders fought in a ring in a Bronx saloon (some sources say it was an old barn) as hundreds of their supporters cheered them on. The men were relatively evenly matched—whereas Kelly was the more scientific boxer, Eastman was bigger and very tough. The fight went on for two hours and ended in a draw, with both boxers too exhausted to continue.

Unlike the more fastidious Kelly, Eastman enjoyed having a direct hand in criminal operations. On February 2, 1904, around 3:00 a.m., Eastman and a crony named Christopher Wallace spotted a potential victim—a well-dressed, drunk young man staggering round Times Square. The youth was followed by a sour-faced, tough-looking man. Eastman figured the tough guy was tailing the young man in order to rob him, and decided to beat him to the punch. Eastman and Wallace stuck their pistols in the young drunk's face and demanded he hand over his cash. At this point, the tough man trailing the youth pulled out his own gun and began shooting. It turned out he was a Pinkerton detective, hired by the young man's family to protect him from just this sort of situation. The two gangsters fired a few shots in return then beat a hasty retreat. While Wallace managed to escape, Eastman ran right into a police officer at the corner of Broadway and 42nd Street. The policeman knocked Eastman out and took him down to the station to be booked. Once

he came to, Eastman gave his occupation as "newspaper speculator." He wasn't worried, believing that Tammany Hall would spring him, just as they always had in the past. The politicians, however, were fed up with the violent, uncontrollable gang leader. Tammany Hall washed their hands of Eastman and refused to help. At his April 12, 1904, trial, Eastman claimed that he only wanted to protect the young drunk from the tough looking man who was following him. No one believed it. The jury deliberated for an hour and found Eastman guilty. He was sentenced to ten years in prison.

With their leader in prison, some of Eastman's lieutenants tried to hold his gang together. Kid Twist (real name Max Zweibach, no relation to Kid Twist Abe Reles) and Ritchie Fitzgerald attempted to run the gang together. The would-be leaders soon fell out, however. In the fall of 1904, Kid Twist lured Fitzpatrick into attending a "peace conference" in a Chrystie Street bar. When Fitzgerald arrived, the lights turned off and guns came out. When the lights came back on, Fitzgerald was dead. Kid Twist hung on for a few more years, but eventually succumbed to an equally violent fate. In 1908, Kid Twist and a friend named Vach "Cyclone Louie" Lewis, a circus strong man who could bend iron bars with his bare hands, got into a bar fight with a Five Points gang member at a Coney Island dance hall. The Five Pointer, Louis "the Lump" Pioggi, jumped out of a second-floor window to escape from Kid Twist and his hulking comrade. Pioggi alerted his leadership about Kid Twist's presence, and a Five Points crew rushed over to Coney Island to deal with the gang leader. On May 14, 1908, Kid Twist was shot dead.

With Eastman in jail and his two erst-while successors murdered, the Eastman gang largely fell apart. By the time Eastman was paroled, in June 1909, he no longer had much of a gang to lead. Eastman became a petty criminal, picking pockets, committing burglaries, and selling drugs. In 1912, police arrested Eastman for smoking opium and put him in jail for eight months. He was arrested again three years later, and on July 1, 1915, was sentenced to two years and eleven months for robbery.

Finally, in September 1917, Eastman got out of jail for good. Under a false name, "William Delaney," he joined the army. His timing was good: the United States was amassing a huge military force to intervene in the First World War. An army recruiting officer was astonished by Eastman's multiple scars, and asked him what battles he had been in previously. According to crime historian Herbert Asbury, Eastman replied, "A lot of little wars around New York." Eastman joined the 106th Infantry of the New York National Guard. He was shipped to France and saw combat. Apparently, he was quite a good soldier, with an excellent service record.

In 1920, out of the army, Eastman returned to New York. Prohibition had just been declared, and astute gangsters were getting into the booze business. Around Christmastime, Eastman went drinking with a business partner, Jeremiah "Jerry" Bohan, who happened to be a Prohibition agent. Bohan found it more profitable to work with criminals than against them. Eastman and Bohan were involved in a bootlegging racket. The two men went drinking at the Blue Bird Cafe at number 62 East 14th Street near Fourth Avenue. Around 4:00 a.m., the men left the bar and proceeded to get into an argument on the street. Bohan pulled out a gun and shot Eastman several times at point-blank range. Eastman's corpse was found on December 26. He was buried with full military honors at Cypress Hill Cemetery in Brooklyn.

See Also: Kelly, Paul

Further Reading

"An East Side Vendetta," *New York Times*, September 17, 1903.

Herbert Asbury, *The Gangs of New York*, 1927.

Helena Katz, *Gang Wars: Blood and Guts on the Streets of Early New York*, 2005.

"'Monk' Eastman Caught After Pistol Battle," *New York Times*, February 3, 1904.

"'Monk' Eastman, Gangster, Murdered; Found in Union Square Shot Five Times; His Partner in Bootlegging Suspected," *New York Times*, December 27, 1920.

OUTLAW MOTORCYCLE GANGS

Outlaw motorcycle gangs first entered the public consciousness in 1947, when the small California community of Hollister hosted a motorcycle rally as part of its Independence Day celebrations. Some 2,000 motorcyclists attended, far more than the small town was expecting or could accommodate. A lot of boisterous public drinking ensued, as the bikers partied, brawled, and staged motorcycle races up and down Hollister's main street. Press accounts of the Hollister incident veered towards sensationalism: according to a report in *the San Francisco Chronicle*, "The motorcyclists drove their vehicles into bars and restaurants, tossed beer bottles over upper-floor windows and raced through traffic

Christopher Horlock

Bernard Russell Ortman

Two Federal ATF "wanted" posters in Seattle in 2005 show suspected Bandidos Motorcycle gang secretary Christopher Horlock, left, and suspected Missoula, Montana, chapter president Bernard Russell Ortman, right. Both were named in two federal indictments after busts in three states netted arrests on charges related to racketeering, drug trafficking, theft and weapons violations. [AP Photo/Ted S. Warren]

signals and defied the [local] seven-man police force."

The colorful media reports of the Hollister "biker invasion" were highly exaggerated. A famous photograph published in *Life* magazine, of a scruffy biker lying on his motorcycle, surrounded by beer bottles, was apparently faked. In reality, the local Hollister force had been reinforced by police from other jurisdictions, and a little over two-dozen police officers managed to get the "riot" under control by noon, July 5. A total of 50 arrests were made, most for public intoxication, disturbing the peace, and drunk driving.

This true-life event was used as the basis for a controversial 1953 movie called *The Wild One*. Featuring Marlon Brando and Lee Marvin as rival motorcycle gang leaders, the film depicted the travails of a small town facing an onslaught of bikers. As exaggerated as it was, *The Wild One* did highlight the real-life split between outlaw bikers and mainstream bikers. The former lived outside the law, whereas the latter tried to present an acceptable face to society. Mainstream bikers were often members of the American Motorcyclist Association (AMA), a national organization that disavowed any connection with scofflaw types. The AMA insisted that 99 percent of motorcyclists were clean-cut, law-abiding types who simply enjoyed the speed and freedom that their unique mode of transportation entailed. Outlaw bikers took this to heart, and began wearing "1%" badges, proudly indicating their status as brigands in the eyes of the AMA. There are suggestions that the AMA's comments were actually apocryphal; even so, outlaw motorcycle gangs remain devoted to the concept of being "one percenters."

Outlaw bikers were still a tiny fringe until the late 1960s, when increased media coverage and the emerging hippie counterculture led to a rapid expansion in their ranks. Outlaw bikers were closely associated with the latter (despite their fierce antagonism towards peace protesters and radical left politics). As illicit drugs became more popular, some outlaw bikers took to trafficking and dealing. This was so common that the Hells Angels Motorcycle Club (HAMC) even included a clause in their constitution banning "drug burns," the practice of ripping off clients in drug deals. The stimulant methamphetamine acquired the nickname "crank," allegedly because bikers hid the product in the crankcases of their motorcycles.

The U.S. Department of Justice currently estimates that there are over 300 Outlaw Motorcycle Gangs (OMG) in the United States, "ranging in size from single chapters with five or six members to hundreds of chapters with thousands of members worldwide." The Justice Department pegs total OMG membership in the United States at around 20,000 bikers.

The Hells Angels are the best-known and most-feared OMG. The HAMC was founded in the late 1940s, as army veterans started buying motorcycles and banding together to relieve the boredom of postwar life. The first HAMC chapter was launched on March 17, 1948, in San Bernardino, California. The Angels currently boast 800 members in 92 chapters throughout the United States. There are an estimated 230 HAMC chapters worldwide, with a total membership around 2,000 to 2,500. The Department of Justice claims the Angels routinely engage in all manner of felonious behavior, including drug trafficking, murder, assault, extortion, money laundering, and motorcycle theft.

Other major motorcycle gangs include the Bandidos. Founded in Texas in 1966, the Bandidos currently boast 2,000 to 2,500 members in the United States and 13 other countries. They are most active in the Pacific, Southeastern, Southwestern, and west-central parts of the United States and, according to the federal government, are involved in the same kind of felonies favored by the HAMC.

Another gang, called the Outlaws, were founded in a bar near Chicago, Illinois, in 1935. The Outlaws count 1,700 members in 176 chapters in the United States and 12 foreign countries. "The Outlaws are the dominant OMG in the Great Lakes region," states the U.S. Department of Justice, citing the gang's involvement in drug trafficking, arson, assault, explosives, extortion, fraud, homicide, intimidation, kidnapping, money laundering, theft, prostitution, and weapons violations. "The Outlaws compete with the Hells Angels for both members and territory," notes the Department of Justice. Harry "Taco" Bowman, president of the Outlaws, made the FBI's 10 Most Wanted list for a while. He was captured in the Detroit area in 1999 and convicted two years later of a variety of offences, including murder. Randy Michael Yager, regional president of the Outlaws, was featured on the Bureau of Alcohol, Tobacco, Firearms and Explosives "most wanted" list in February 2009 for violations of the RICO (Racketeer Influenced and Corrupt Organizations) statute.

A relatively obscure OMG called the Mongols have come to pose "a serious criminal threat to the Pacific and Southwestern regions of the U.S.," in the words of the Department of Justice. Branded as "an extremely violent OMG," the Mongols have allied themselves with the Bandidos, Outlaws, and other groups in opposition to the HAMC. The Mongols and the Angels engaged in a spectacular brawl at a casino in Laughlin, Nevada in the spring of 2002 in which three people were

---

OUTLAW MOTORCYCLE GANGS WORLDWIDE: EXPORTING BIKER VIOLENCE

Although outlaw motorcycle gang culture was born in the United States, biker violence is now a global phenomenon. Quebec, for example, was the scene of a brutal biker war between a Canadian branch of the Hells Angels Motorcycle Club (HAMC) and a rival gang called the Rock Machine.

The long-lasting feud, over control of the drug trade, started in the mid-1990s. The war resulted in 150 deaths, including innocent civilians. Canadian Hells Angels have not hesitated to target law officers and journalists, two groups the underworld traditionally leaves alone, for fear of massive retaliation. In the late 1990s, Quebec HAMC leader Maurice "Mom" Boucher was arrested for allegedly arranging the murder of two prison guards. He was acquitted in his first trial, in November 1998, but was rearrested two years later and found guilty at a subsequent trial, in May 2002. Four months later, crime reporter Michel Auger was gunned down on a Montreal street by an aggrieved biker, but survived. Canadian authorities have responded to these outrages with a police crackdown and tough new laws directed at "criminal organizations." During the 1990s, the Bandidos and the Hells Angels also slugged it out in Scandinavia. Nordic bikers used rocket launchers and automatic weapons to battle each other in a conflict that caused a dozen deaths. Though the biker war in Quebec has sputtered out for now, it has erupted anew in other parts of Canada. In April 2006, the bodies of eight people were discovered in a farmer's field in southern Ontario. The dead included "full-patch" members of the Bandidos. Police arrested half a dozen suspects in what is one of the worst mass killings in Canadian history.

Sources: Canadian Broadcasting Corporation, "Biker Gangs in Canada," April 21, 2009. http://www.cbc.ca/canada/story/2009/04/01/f-biker-gangs.html; Yves Lavigne, *Hells Angels at War*, 1999; William Marsden and Julian Sher, *Angels of Death: Inside the Bikers' Global Crime Empire*, 2006; National Gang Intelligence Center, U.S. Department of Justice, Outlaw Motorcycle Gangs. http://www.usdoj.gov/ndic/pubs32/32146/appd.htm.

---

killed and a dozen injured. Largely comprised of Hispanic members, the Mongols seized control of Southern California from the HAMC in the 1980s.

Other major outlaw motorcycle gangs include the Pagan's Motorcycle Club, which has 200 to 250 members in 41 chapters in 11 states. Founded in Maryland in 1959, "the Pagan's have been tied to traditional organized crime groups in Philadelphia, Pittsburgh and New York and have engaged in criminal activities such as arson, assault, bombing, extortion and murder," states the U.S. Department of Justice.

OMGs often use smaller, local clubs to augment their ranks in times of war. These local clubs are typically referred to as "support," "puppet," or "duck" gangs. Members do the bidding of larger parent gangs, usually in the hope of joining them.

Outlaw bikers are unique among other organized crime groups in that they go out of their way to flaunt their allegiance to what police consider criminal bands. Successful underworld bosses such as Johnny Torrio and Meyer Lansky preferred to operate in the shadows; they were mysterious grey figures who wouldn't stand out in a crowd. Bikers, by contrast, are somewhat hard to miss in public. Most OMG members proudly wear "patches" on the back of their jackets depicting their club's logo and often what part of the country the club is based in. If nothing else, such self-identification makes it easier for authorities to identify OMG members when they commit crimes.

See Also: Barger, Ralph "Sonny"; Hells Angels

Further Reading

Bandidos Motorcycle Club. http://www.bandidosmc.dk.

Canadian Broadcasting Corporation, "Biker Gangs in Canada," April 21, 2009. http://www.cbc.ca/canada/story/2009/04/01/f-biker-gangs.html.

C.I. Dourghty Jr., "More on Hollister's Bad Time: 2000 "Gypsycycles" Chug Out of Town and the Natives Sigh "Never Again,'" *San Francisco Chronicle*, July 6, 1947.

Hells Angels Motorcycle Club. http://www.hells-angels.com.

Yves Lavigne, *Hells Angels at War*, 1999.

William Marsden and Julian Sher, *Angels of Death: Inside the Bikers' Global Crime Empire,* 2006.

National Gang Intelligence Center, U.S. Department of Justice, Outlaw Motorcycle Gangs. http://www.usdoj.gov/ndic/pubs32/32146/appd.htm.

Outlaws Motorcycle Club. http://www.outlawsmc.com.

Glenn Puit and Dave Berns, "Laughlin Shootout: Signs Told of Melee in the Making," *Las Vegas Review-Journal,* April 30, 2002.

P

PISTONE, JOSEPH (1939–)

Known as "Donnie Brasco," undercover FBI agent Joseph Pistone managed to infiltrate the Mafia, with spectacular results. His in-depth investigation resulted in major changes in the way the Mafia handles membership. In addition to putting away dozens of "wiseguys," Pistone provided a fascinating "mole's eye view" of the daily workings of a typical Mafia "crew."

Italian by heritage, Pistone was born in 1939 and raised first in Pennsylvania, then in Paterson, New Jersey. His father worked in a silk mill and ran some bars. Pistone played high school sports and went to college on a basketball scholarship. He dropped out at age 20 to get married, and spent a year doing construction and other kinds of physical labor. Pistone harbored a yearning to become an FBI agent. He spent a few years with Naval Intelligence, assisting with military investigations, then joined the Bureau. He was sworn in as a special agent on July 7, 1969, and underwent intensive training. After graduation, he was assigned to an FBI office in Florida.

By 1974, Pistone was working in New York City on a squad that investigated truck hijackings. The FBI was eager to crack a ring of thieves who specialized in stealing 18-wheel trucks and heavy equipment such as bulldozers and luxury cars along the east coast. It was decided to send an agent to infiltrate the gang and gather evidence. Thanks to the year he spent in construction, Pistone knew how to drive 18-wheelers and bulldozers. The FBI decided he would be the perfect man for the mission.

At the time, FBI undercover work was still something of a novelty. Long-time FBI director J. Edgar Hoover had frowned on such missions. "J. Edgar Hoover didn't want his FBI agents to work undercover because it could be a dirty job that could end up tainting the agents," Pistone later wrote. FBI undercover operations didn't begin in earnest until Hoover's death in 1972. Hoover's reluctance to authorize undercover missions meant that Pistone and the FBI had to improvise many aspects of his

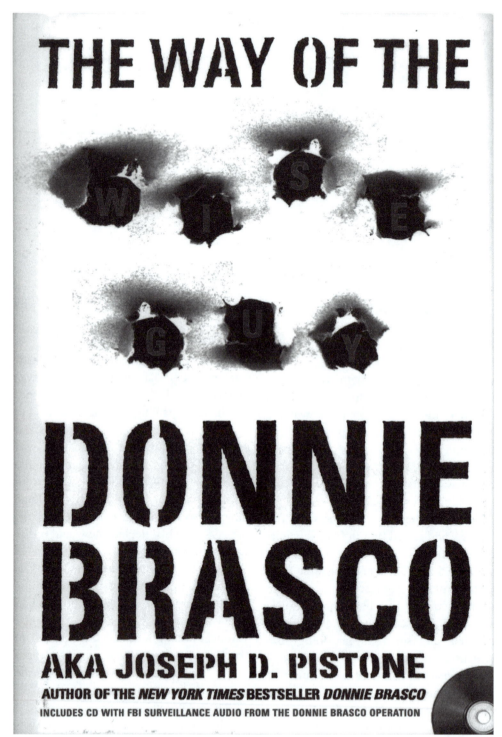

The cover of The Way of the Wiseguy, *by Joseph Pistone, published in 2004. [AP Photo/Running Press]*

operation. There were no set rules on how to go about infiltrating underworld organizations. With the help of his fellow agents, Pistone settled on the cover name "Donnie Brasco" and assumed a fake identity, complete with phony ID. As Donnie Brasco, Pistone easily penetrated the theft ring and joined their ranks. He was extremely successful at winning the trust of his fellow thieves. Thanks to Pistone's efforts, 30 members of the ring were arrested by the FBI and the Florida Highway Patrol in February 1976.

When the mission ended, Pistone went back to the truck and hijack squad in New York City. At the time, the city was plagued with a rash of truck hijackings, sometimes as many as five to six a day. Police intelligence suggested the Mafia might be involved in some of the hijackings. If the Mafia wasn't actually stealing the vehicles, it was believed they might be "fencing" (i.e., purchasing and selling) stolen goods from the trucks. Based on Pistone's success with the vehicle theft ring, his New York supervisor came up with a plan. The FBI would initiate a long-term undercover operation aimed at infiltrating "the upper echelon fences who handled these stolen loads," as Pistone put it later in testimony before the U.S. Senate.

Once again, Pistone was chosen for the mission. He had undercover experience, a Sicilian background, and spoke fluent Italian. He was also cool under pressure and had no reservations about tackling the Mafia. Pistone had grown up around mobsters in New Jersey and wasn't in awe of them or frightened by them as other young agents sometimes were. Nor did he bear any particular grudges against the mob. Penetrating the Mafia would simply be another job, albeit one in an extremely hazardous work environment. With the help of his FBI colleagues, Pistone spent months prepping for his new role. It was decided he would keep his previous pseudonym, Donnie Brasco. Much time was spent inventing a fake background for Brasco. Pistone had to be able to pass as a criminal, while avoiding situations that might force him to commit acts of violence. After much deliberation, it was decided that Donnie Brasco would be a jewel thief and a burglar who usually worked alone, avoided violence, and varied his time between New York City, Miami, and California. Brasco would also be a bachelor and an orphan, in the hopes this would take care of nosy questions about his family. The FBI gave the operation a six-month time span.

In September 1976, Pistone went undercover as Donnie Brasco. He couldn't tell friends, co-workers outside his immediate FBI circle, or relatives about his mission. For them, it was as if Pistone had fallen off the map. His own wife and three daughters only knew the barest details about his mission. The FBI set up some "hello phones"—numbers Mafia members could call for character references. The people answering the phones were either FBI agents or informants who had been prompted to say good things about Brasco if anyone called. Pistone opened a checking account, leased an appropriate gangster car (a 1976 yellow Cadillac Coupe de Ville with Florida tags), and got a one-bedroom apartment in Manhattan.

The FBI had a list of bars, nightclubs, and restaurants patronized by gangsters and "fences." Pistone started to frequent these places, alone. Pistone would have dinner or a drink by himself, and then leave without saying much. He didn't initiate conversation or ask nosy questions. The point was simply to get his face known in underworld circles. Among other locales, Pistone frequented a Manhattan restaurant called Carmello's that was owned by members of the Genovese Mafia family. He spent much time there and at other locales. In fact, for the first two months of the undercover operation, Pistone did little but hang out in known mob joints. He noticed that many of the gangsters at Carmello's liked to play Backgammon for money. Pistone sensed an opening. One day, he challenged the winner of a Backgammon match to a new game. For the first time, Pistone introduced himself (as "Don") and got to chat with some of the patrons. The bartender in Carmello's seemed friendly and appeared to know quite a few Mafia types. Pistone started drinking at the bar and chatting with the barkeep. After building the man's trust, Pistone asked him confidentially if he was interested in some jewelry. Pistone displayed some diamond rings and wristwatches, which he implied were stolen. He asked the bartender to hold onto the stash and see if he could sell it. Pistone and the bartender would split the proceeds. The bartender was unable to sell the cache, but this move did give Pistone criminal credibility with patrons of the restaurant.

Pistone continued to ingratiate himself with underworld figures. In early 1977, he was introduced to some members of the Colombo Mafia family. One of these members, "Jilly," ran a "crew" (i.e., a squad) of Mafiosi in Brooklyn. The crew used the back of a store in Bensonhurst as their headquarters and hangout. Pistone started spending time there, observing various low-echelon Mafiosi in action. He discovered, to his surprise,

the tedium of being a full-time gangster. Typically, Mafia members would arrive at Jilly's store around 10:30 or 11:00 in the morning. Members would sit around and chat while discussing scams and "scores" past, present, and future. One member would suggest a burglary or a hijacking, and the rest of the crew would mull the proposal over in fine detail. Everyone played cards (only gin rummy) and smoked cigarettes or cigars, which annoyed Pistone, a non-smoker. For lunch, someone would be sent out to buy fast-food for everyone, typically Chinese or hero sandwiches. Around 4:30–5:00 p.m., the men would go home for supper with their families or to meet their girlfriends. After eating, they hit the streets to pull off various robberies and hustles. If they weren't committing crimes, Jilly's crew would hang out in a night club until early the next morning. "It was easy to get lulled by this daily routine with these guys. Most of the time it was boring," Pistone later confessed.

FBI protocol meant Pistone couldn't take part in any burglaries, hijackings, or violent crimes with Jilly's crew. He made himself useful, however, by helping unload trucks that pulled up to the store with hijacked goods. These goods included everything from frozen food to liquor, clothes, TVs, and VCRs. Sometimes, Pistone brought in some "swag" (stolen jewels or other items, taken from FBI storage) to impress his peers. He had some close calls during this period. At one point, he was challenged about his identity. Pistone pretended to be extremely annoyed, and with great reluctance gave up the name and number of a contact who could vouch for him. The contact of course was one of the "hello phone" operators recruited by the FBI. Pistone sat around the store for hours, playing gin and trying to stay calm, as one of Jilly's crew touched base with the contact. Evidently, the contact performed as ordered and gave a resounding reference for "Donnie Brasco."

In March 1977, Pistone met Anthony Mirra, a "made" member of the Mafia. Through Mirra, Pistone was introduced to Benjamin "Lefty Guns" Ruggiero. Both Mirra and Ruggiero were "soldiers" in the Bonanno crime family. In his early 50s, Lefty was a lean, chatty hit man, with several murders to his credit. Ruggiero ran a social club in Little Italy that served as a headquarters and meeting place for Bonanno family members and associates. Pistone began to alternate between Jilly's store and Ruggiero's club. He was careful never to appear pushy or overeager. He never volunteered information about himself unless he was directly asked. When Ruggiero inquired, Pistone said he was a jewel thief and burglar, as per his cover story.

Pistone began to follow a routine. At around 10:00 a.m., he would go to Ruggiero's club, drink coffee, and read the papers. He did his best to listen in on conversations without seeming obvious about it. In the afternoon, Pistone would go to Brooklyn and hang out at Jilly's store for a few hours. In the evening, he would connect with Anthony Mirra, who struck him as extremely unstable and deadly. In later testimony before the U.S. Senate, Pistone revealed how frustrating the early part of this undercover operation was. Mafia members and associates were inevitably introduced to him by first name or a nickname. It was taboo to ask someone for their last name. Doing so would instantly peg you as an undercover cop or an informer. "No one asked about what other members were doing or even who they were. There were people

I worked with closely for six years who never told me their last names, only their nicknames," Pistone later explained.

Among other hustles, Ruggiero handled bookmaking operations for Nicky Marangello, underboss of the Bonanno family. In this capacity, Ruggiero was bringing in $20,000 to $25,000 every weekend. His overhead was extremely low; according to Pistone, Ruggiero ran his gambling operations from a single phone in the back of his Little Italy social club. Pistone was quick to realize the Mafia earned the lion's share of its profits from gambling, particularly sports betting and "numbers" (basically, illegal lotteries). Ironically, Pistone discovered that many Mafiosi also loved to gamble. Ruggiero himself was "degenerate" gambler in underworld lingo, who was constantly hustling to pay off his debts. Ruggiero started taking Pistone with him as he drove around town picking up money from bettors. Eventually, Ruggiero grew so comfortable with Pistone that he had him report to Marangello and provide updates on the bookmaking business.

Ruggiero took on the role of a mentor and began to "school" Pistone in the ways of the mob. This was a huge break, because usually "made" Mafia members don't offer insider information to nonmembers. Ruggiero offered detailed instructions on what Pistone would later describe as "the way of the wiseguy." Among other pointers, Pistone was told to dress sharply, keep his face clean-shaven, and, most importantly, show regal deference to made men. He was never, ever supposed to argue with a wiseguy, even if the wiseguy was in the wrong. As a mob "associate," Pistone was expected to keep in constant contact with Ruggiero, who had the right to boss him as he saw fit. If Pistone needed to leave town or wanted to pull a hustle, it had to be cleared with Ruggiero first.

Working with Ruggiero could be a challenge. In one incident, while driving along Third Avenue in New York, Ruggiero became enraged after a taxi cut him off twice. After the second occasion, the two cars stopped at a light. Ruggiero stepped out of his vehicle, grabbed a tire iron from the trunk and proceeded to smash the cabbie's window. Pistone couldn't intervene, for fear of blowing his cover. Ruggiero also had some personal habits that annoyed Pistone. He hated air conditioning and chain smoked cigarettes. Ruggiero wouldn't let Pistone turn on the air conditioning, even when they were driving. The combination of heat and tobacco smoke drove Pistone to the edge. Although he made thousands of dollars a week, Ruggiero was always broke and constantly borrowed money from Pistone to pay for his gambling habit.

Like most Mafiosi Pistone encountered, Ruggiero still lived in the same neighborhood near Little Italy where he had grown up. He was divorced, with four grown children. His son Tommy was a junkie, a condition he constantly fretted over. Ruggiero at one point married his girlfriend. He asked Pistone to be his best man. He also invited the FBI agent to come with him on a hit.

In many ways, Ruggiero was the perfect Mafiosi, always "on the job" so to speak, Pistone recalled. Mafia members "spend every waking hour thinking about how they were going to make money. They did not think or talk much about their wives, girlfriends, families, hobbies. The mob was their job as well as their whole life . . . what they did for a living was on their minds far more than

it is with ordinary 'straight' citizens," Pistone told the U.S. Senate.

At one point during his Mafia education, Pistone innocently asked his mentor what the advantages were of being a "made man." "Lefty looks at me like I'm the world's biggest moron. He gets excited and jumps out of his chair and starts yelling and waving his arms. 'What are you, fucking crazy?' he says. 'Are you fucking nuts? When you're a wiseguy, you can steal, you can cheat, you can lie, you can kill people—and it's all legitimate,'" wrote Pistone. Ruggiero wasn't trying to be witty: "The wiseguy does not see himself as a criminal or even a bad person; he sees himself as a businessman, a shrewd hustler, one step ahead of ordinary suckers," Pistone later wrote.

Pistone was surprised by the degree of dishonesty inherent in the Mafia. Members lied constantly, to victims, business partners, and fellow members. In the Mafia, all money flows upwards: any profit made by soldiers or associates has to be shared with the Mafiosi above them. There was no set rate for this share out; higher ranking Mafia leaders could take as much as they wanted from their underlings. Such a system encouraged dishonesty. "The way it works is every time you pull a score, a percentage of it has to go to the individual above you . . . so what the wiseguys do is they will pull a score and if the score is, say, $200,000, they will say the score was $150,000, because they know that if they are still on the bottom, the guy on top is going to get more of the proceeds," Pistone explained in Senate testimony. Ironically, "holding out" in this fashion could be grounds for execution, if mob bosses found out. Living under the constant threat of death for breaking some unwritten rule or siding with the wrong leader was all part of the Mafia mindset. Greed and fear were the prime motivators for most of the mobsters Pistone encountered.

By mid-summer 1977, Pistone had become deeply immersed in the underworld. Among other gangsters, he had a fleeting encounter with Bonanno family boss Carmine Galante. Along with Ruggiero and a clutch of other Mafiosi, Pistone helped guard a restaurant where Galante, fresh from jail, was having a meeting. Ruggiero made it clear that actually stepping into the restaurant and trying to chat up Galante would be an unspeakable breech of mob etiquette. Bosses such as Galante only talked with other bosses or high-ranking mobsters. It was the duty of Mafia soldiers and associates to loyally guard such great men and treat them with extreme deference, Ruggiero explained.

Every few days, Pistone phoned his FBI contact agent to give him a rundown of his activities. Once or twice a month, he met the agent in person to receive money for living expenses. Pistone only got to see his family every two or three weeks, if that. The undercover operation was starting to take on a new dimension. Though Pistone hadn't gotten particularly close to any mobster "fences," the FBI was delighted how deep he was getting with the Bonanno family, and to a lesser extent with the Colombo clan. The Bureau decided to extend, and alter, Piston's mission. His new assignment was to gather evidence against the New York Mafia. Pistone had to maintain a delicate balancing act. On one hand, he had to glean as much information as he could about Mafia activities. This meant paying close attention to conversations without being obvious. To put himself above suspicion, Pistone never asked anyone to repeat themselves, even if they had just blurted out a tantalizing piece of criminal gossip, and feigned disinterest in mob-talk, occasionally walking away in the middle of conversations or changing the topic being discussed. While hanging around mobsters, Pistone spent hours drinking coffee and reading newspapers cover to cover. This allowed him to surreptitiously listen in on Mafia chatter around him without appearing interested.

Occasionally, Pistone took part in underworld operations, albeit in a peripheral role. One time he pretended to sell some guns that one of Jilly's men had picked up in a robbery. Pistone handed the weapons over to the FBI, as well as the cash he made on the sale. He tried to avoid committing acts of violence, but occasionally this couldn't be helped. One time at a Miami nightclub, a comedian kept directing barbs against a table where Pistone sat with some wiseguys. At the prompting of one of his gangster acquaintances, Pistone warned the comedian to stop making Mafia cracks. He didn't. After his show was over, the gangsters followed the comedian to his dressing room. There, Pistone beat the man with his fists, to the delight of his colleagues.

In July 1979, Bonanno boss Galante was murdered, triggering a bitter innerfamily struggle for succession. Ruggiero was allied with rising Bonanno star Dominick "Sonny Black" Napolitano, who, in turn, was allied with Philip "Rusty" Rastelli. Rastelli had been the Bonanno boss, but stepped down to let Galante rule after he was released from prison in the late 1970s. Rastelli still aspired to the top position, however, and was one of the prime movers in the plot to kill Galante. After Galante was killed,

Rastelli took control of the Bonanno family once again. Napolitano was made a captain and became Ruggiero's immediate commander.

By doing nothing, Pistone found himself on the winning side in an underworld power struggle. Because he was an associate of Ruggiero, it was assumed he would be loyal to Napolitano and Rastelli. Napolitano was a swarthy man with jet-black dyed hair that gave him his nickname. Pistone worked his charm on the new mob boss and soon was on friendly terms with him. Napolitano liked to challenge Pistone to arm wrestling contests. The FBI agent always won, until one time Napolitano spat in his face during a match. Pistone was so startled Napolitano easily pinned his hand. Pistone continued to accompany Ruggiero on various operations. He journeyed to Milwaukee, where he met local Mafia boss Frank Balistrieri. In Florida, Pistone was introduced to Santo Trafficante, a big time Mafia leader.

Because the two spent a considerable amount of time in Miami on mob business, Pistone came up with the idea of entertaining Ruggiero and other gangsters on a boat. As it so happened, the FBI at the time was utilizing a white yacht for their ABSCAM investigation into political corruption. The FBI used the boat to impress targets of the ABSCAM probe. Pistone made inquiries and was given permission to use the yacht. He cooked up a cover story about being acquaintances with a boat owner, then took Ruggiero and a dozen mobsters and spouses on a cruise. As successful as the outing was, it nearly ruined Pistone's mission. After the ABSCAM scandal broke in early 1980, Ruggiero happened to be flipping through a copy of *TIME* magazine. There, in a story on ABSCAM, was a photograph of the very yacht Pistone had taken the mobsters out on. Ruggiero demanded an explanation. Pistone offered a quick alibi about being scammed, but his mentor remained suspicious.

By 1981, Pistone was close to becoming a "made" Mafiosi. Sonny Black Napolitano was willing to recommend "Donnie Brasco" for official entry into the ranks of the Mafia. His induction could take place as early as that December. No FBI agent had ever been "made" before. It would be a tremendous coup for law enforcement. There was only one catch: in order to be "made," Napolitano wanted Pistone to murder a mobster named Anthony "Bruno" Indelicato, a member of the Mafia faction opposed to Rastelli's rule. As part of the struggle, Indelicato's father, a mobster named Alphonse "Sonny Red" Indelicato, had been murdered, along with Philip "Philly Lucky" Giaccone and Dominick "Big Trin" Trinchera, in early May. The three men were summoned to a meeting and then killed on Rastelli's command. Bruno Indelicato was supposed to have been at the same meeting, but ducked out of it. Now Napolitano wanted to tie up loose ends and have the man "whacked." And Pistone seemed to be the perfect candidate to carry the hit out.

Pistone and his FBI handlers debated the issue. Pistone was eager to stay undercover and try to become "made" without murdering anyone. The Bureau thought it was too risky. "Donnie Brasco" would be put under tremendous pressure to kill Bruno Indelicato in order to advance up the Mafia hierarchy. To Pistone's disappointment, the six-year undercover operation was terminated on July 26, 1981.

Shortly after Pistone's undercover role ended, FBI agents approached

Napolitano and informed him who "Donnie Brasco" really was. Napolitano told his crew. There was disbelief. It was suspected that the FBI was merely playing mind games. For a few days, Napolitano and his men sat on this information, as they desperately tried to track Pistone down. In this, they failed. Pistone had completely withdrawn from the underworld and was busy giving information to the FBI and being reunited with his family. Feeling he had no choice, Napolitano broke the news about "Donnie Brasco" to his superiors. Seventeen days after Pistone's mission ended, Napolitano was ordered to attend a mob meeting in New Jersey. He headed off to the meeting, and no one saw him again. A few months later, Anthony Mirra was shot dead in the parking garage of an apartment in Manhattan. His assailants didn't bother taking the thousands of dollars in currency he had on him. This was a deliberate message, that robbery wasn't the motive for the murder. Ruggiero was also targeted for murder by the mob, but FBI agents tracked him down and arrested him before he could be murdered. Pistone and his family, meanwhile, were put under 24-hour FBI protection. In August 1982, a body was recovered from a creek on Staten Island. The body bore bullet wounds and the hands were cut off. This was a Mafia indication that the victim had violated mob secrecy. Through dental records, the body was determined to be Sonny Black Napolitano. "I was sorry it was Sonny. I was glad it wasn't me," wrote Pistone.

Pistone spent much of the 1980s testifying against his former colleagues in federal court. He ended up testifying at 10 trials and many more grand juries. His testimony led to 200 indictments and 100 convictions of members of the Mafia, including Ruggiero. Pistone didn't feel much guilt in "betraying" his comrades. "I felt close to Sonny Black. I felt a kind of kinship with him. But I didn't feel any guilt of betrayal because I'd always maintained in my own mind and heart the separation of our worlds," he wrote. "I knew that both Lefty and Sonny loved me in their own ways. [But] either would have killed me in a minute," he added. Indeed, following Napolitano's murder, the FBI heard through the underworld grapevine that a $500,000 "open contract" had been put on Pistone's life. Usually, the Mafia avoids murdering policemen and federal agents for fear of massive retaliation. They apparently were willing to make an exception for Pistone.

Pistone left the FBI in 1986. One year later, his book, *Donnie Brasco: My Undercover Life in the Mafia*, was released. This was turned into a successful movie in 1997, starring Johnny Depp as Pistone and Al Pacino as Ruggiero. Pistone lent his expertise to other police forces and helped Scotland Yard in the UK with an investigation into Asian Triad crime gangs. As part of the investigation, Pistone pretended to be a Mafiosi from New York.

It is believed that the contract against Pistone was eventually lifted. Nonetheless, Pistone continued to travel incognito under a fake name. He was also licensed to carry a gun. Pistone avoided going to Atlantic City, New Jersey, or any other place where the Mafia were known to congregate. In his 1988 Senate testimony, Pistone discussed steps that the Mafia had taken to prevent any future infiltration from FBI or police agents:

I understand that the New York families have instituted new rules to thwart further undercover penetrations. They have reinstituted the requirement that before someone is made a soldier, he will have to "make his bones," that is, he will have to kill someone. In addition, they are now requiring two "wiseguys" to vouch with their own lives for the new member, rather than as before, when only one did so.

He added, "I hope that just as the myth of [Mafia] invincibility has fallen, my infiltration and the recent criminal trials have also put to rest the romantic illusion that the Mafia is an 'honorable society' . . . there is no honor among these thieves. They deal in drugs, death and deception."

As for any residual personal feelings he might have had about his six-year mission, Pistone offering the following rationalization:

I knew that no matter what I did, I was not going to reform anybody, they were going to lie, steal, cheat, murder and kill, whether Joe Pistone [or] Donnie Brasco was there or not. So my main goal was to gather information for later prosecutions. I was not a reformist or a social worker nor a reformer and that is the mindset I had, and I also maintained that if they found out who I was, they would kill me just as soon as they have killed their best friends.

See Also: Mafia

Further Reading

Joseph Pistone, *Donnie Brasco: My Undercover Life in the Mafia*, 1987.

———, *The Way of the Wiseguy*, 2004.

Joseph Pistone, testimony before the U.S. Senate Permanent Subcommittee on Investigations of the Committee of Governmental Affairs, 1988. http://www.americanmafia.com/pistone_testimony.html.

Selwyn Raab, *Five Families: The Rise, Decline and Resurgence of America's Most Powerful Mafia Empires*, 2005.

PROHIBITION

Prohibition was the U.S. government's failed attempt to legislate sobriety. It lasted from 1920 to 1933 and was intended to stamp out alcohol by force of law. Instead, Prohibition led to the rise of powerful underworld bosses who grew rich peddling illicit spirits.

Prohibition came about following decades of lobbying by church groups, feminists, progressives, business owners, and bigots. These forces were responding to the United States' alcohol-saturated culture. Contrary to popular belief, the early Puritan settlers were not opposed to alcohol, just to drunkenness. When the Puritans sailed to Massachusetts, their cargo included 14 tons of water, 42 tons of beer, and 10,000 gallons of wine.

Heavy drinking was extremely common during the early years of the republic. Communal activities such as harvesting crops, building barns, and laying down roads were occasions for heavy imbibing. In parts of the United States, alcohol was used in lieu of currency, as a means of barter. Pioneers traded liquor with Indians (to devastating effect) and relied on alcohol as a means to endure a tough life in a largely unsettled, rural country. From the seventeenth century to the nineteenth century, alcohol was very common in U.S. society, and very cheap. Consumption of intoxicating spirits among adult

Beer barrels are destroyed by prohibition agents in an unknown location in 1920. [AP Photo]

white males was estimated at a staggering 10 to 12 gallons per year from 1750–1810.

Dr. Benjamin Rush, who served as surgeon general to the Continental Army during the U.S. Revolution, was one of the first to sound the alarm on liquor. In the 1780s, Dr. Rush came out against abuse of alcohol, on health and scientific grounds. He created a famous chart depicting the alleged impact of various spirits: punch could lead to "idleness, sickness and debt," brandy and water caused "fighting, inflamed eyes, red nose and rags," and drinking gin, brandy, and rum morning, day, and night inevitably lead to "murder, madness, despair and gallows." Dr. Rush also blamed alcohol for causing everything from diabetes and epilepsy to gout, jaundice, and "fetid breath."

Around the same time as Dr. Rush's fulminations, church bodies began to come out strongly against alcohol. The Methodists, Presbyterians, and Baptists all took positions favoring abstinence and sobriety. Lobby groups opposed to alcohol began to make their appearance in the nineteenth century. For example, in 1826 the American Temperance Society was founded. Five years later, the U.S. Army put an end to its tradition of giving soldiers regular alcohol rations. By 1835, the Temperance Society could claim 8,000 local chapters across the country. Some U.S. states began to clamp down on liquor. During the middle part of the

19th century, state governments in Maine, Oregon, Minnesota, Rhode Island, Massachusetts, Delaware, Nebraska Territory, Pennsylvania, New York, and New Hampshire passed legislation outlawing alcohol. Many of these laws were eventually repealed, vetoed by governors, or declared unconstitutional in court.

The Prohibition movement was temporarily sidetracked by the U.S. Civil War. After the war ended, the battle against the bottle resumed. New groups emerged: the Prohibition Party was founded in 1869, and the Woman's Christian Temperance Union (WCTU) was launched in 1874. These groups opposed alcohol for health and religious reasons. The WCTU introduced a degree of feminist politics into the temperance mix. Women from the WCTU and other organizations believed women and children suffered the brunt of alcoholism. They argued that alcohol made husbands recklessly spend their money and neglect and abuse their families. At the time, saloons were male-only preserves. The WCTU and likeminded groups sent women to picket and pray in front of bars and drug stores where liquor was sold to shame men into abandoning drink.

One WCTU member, who called herself Carrie Nation, took a more direct approach. The six-foot, fiery tempered activist began to burst into bars in the late Victorian era and smash them up with hammers, rocks, and a hatchet. She hurled billiard balls at expensive barroom mirrors, hacked away at bar counters, and slashed kegs containing intoxicating spirits. Male patrons were usually too stunned to respond. Ms. Nation launched her violent crusade in Kansas (which was technically a temperance state, although the law wasn't enforced with any urgency) then

expanded her reach to other locales. In the process, she became a national celebrity and a symbol of women's determination to crush Demon Rum (as alcohol was called).

A new group, called the Anti-Saloon League (ASL), was founded in 1893. Unlike the WCTU, the League was a secular organization that didn't have a religious agenda. Through astute lobbying and promotion, the ASL became a hugely powerful force for Prohibition. The ASL strongly supported "local option" laws, under which counties could vote to go "dry" even if the state itself was still "wet." The ASL wasn't aligned with any particular political party. They would support any candidate for any party, as long as they were against liquor.

The forces for Prohibition began to grow in strength. One reason was simply the fact there was a lot of drinking going on: by one estimate there was a saloon for every 300 people in the United States by the end of the 1800s. Saloons became more than just places where men gathered to drink. They were also the center of much political activity and served as quasi-employment exchanges, locations where men could find information about jobs. During the 1884 presidential election year, it was estimated that New York City hosted over 1,000 primaries and conventions. Nearly two-thirds of these were held in saloons.

The anti-alcohol movement was surprisingly broad. Religious leaders supported Prohibition because they felt alcohol led to sin and damnation. Feminists believed alcohol hurt women and children, progressives and union leaders felt it kept working people in a state of stupefied oppression, while capitalists fretted about the dangers of hungover workers on the production line. In addition to these pet causes, many social problems of the day, from violent crime to juvenile delinquency, poverty, spouse and child abuse, slum housing, prostitution, mental illness, and public disorder, were blamed on alcohol. "Liquor is responsible for 19% of the divorces, 25% of the poverty, 25% of the insanity, 37% of the pauperism, 45% of child desertion and 50% of the crime in this country," stated a pamphlet from the ASL, quoted in a report on Prohibition prepared for the National Commission on Marihuana [sic] and Drug Abuse, in the early 1970s. The League also claimed that alcohol caused 60,000 girls each year to fall into "lives of immorality."

There were some divisions within the temperance movement. Whereas radicals sought a total ban on all forms of alcohol, moderates felt a little bit of beer or wine was all right, as long as it wasn't consumed to excess. All sides, however, agreed that government action was needed to stop the wanton liquor trade. In addition to encouraging the government to pass laws against alcohol, temperance groups were strongly in favor of public education on the dangers of liquor. The WCTU encouraged children to sign abstinence pledges and sing ditties about the perils of intoxicating beverages. In a foreshadowing of drug education to come, teachers began to introduce anti-alcohol material in their curricula. By 1902, almost every state in the Union had some form of mandatory temperance education in their public schools.

At the turn of the twentieth century, a new element was added to the temperance ferment. In the 1890s and early 1900s, millions of new immigrants poured into America. Many were German, Italian, or Jewish, and viewed as "foreign" by more established Americans. It was also noted that many of these new immigrants were decidedly "wet." Germans, for example, were perceived as industrious, hardworking, and hard drinking, with a fondness for beer. Most immigrants came from countries where alcohol use was completely accepted and a normal part of life. The fact many new immigrants were Catholic caused further alarms among America's Protestant majority.

World War I compounded the situation. The United States entered the war in April 1917. As it happened, many U.S. brewers and saloonkeepers were of German descent. This added fuel to the Prohibitionist argument. Temperance groups did their best to associate alcohol with the hated "Huns." They considered it unpatriotic to drink, pointing to "wasted" labor and crops that went into making intoxicating beverages. The implication was the labor and crops could be put to better use, such as serving the war effort. Politicians, sensing a winning issue, began to clamor for a crackdown on alcohol.

Prohibitionists continued to hurl wild invectives against alcohol. "From the Great Lakes to the gulf, a militant majority of American people are crucifying that beastly, bloated bastard of Beelzebub, the liquor traffic . . . yet a few months more and we will bury the putrid corpse of John Barleycorn," stated Reverend Sam Small at the Worldwide Prohibition Congress in Columbus, Ohio, in November 1918, as quoted in *Prohibition: Thirteen Years That Changed America*. John Barleycorn was slang at the time for alcohol. At the same event, former secretary of state and failed presidential candidate William Jennings Bryan described alcohol as "man's greatest enemy."

On December 18, 1917, the House of Representatives took up the 18th Amendment to the U.S. Constitution. The amendment would ban the manufacture, transport and sale of "intoxicating liquors"—i.e., any beverage with an alcohol content of 0.5 or higher. Congress approved the amendment then passed it to the states for ratification. Three-quarters of the states would have to ratify the amendment for it to become law. Meanwhile, Congress was also debating a piece of legislation called the Volstead Act. Named for Andrew Volstead, a Minnesota Republican Congressman who facilitated passage of the bill, the Volstead Act spelled out the details covered by the 18th Amendment. Under the Volstead Act, it would become a crime to manufacture, sell, barter, transport, import, export, deliver, furnish, or possess intoxicating liquors. Exceptions were made for spiritual, industrial, and medicinal use. First-time offenders faced fines of $1,000 and 30 days in jail. Fines and jail time rose with subsequent offences. Interestingly, the law didn't touch on the use of alcohol within the privacy of one's home. Introduced May 27, 1919, the Volstead Act passed by a 255–166 vote. The Act went back and forth between House and Senate for some fine tuning. President Woodrow Wilson vetoed the final product, saying it was unconstitutional and unethical. The Congress easily overrode his veto. By January 16, 1919, some 36 states had ratified the 18th Amendment, making it part of the Constitution. Prohibition came into effect one year later, on midnight, January 16, 1920. "Dry" forces were overjoyed. Popular preacher Billy Sunday, addressing a rally in Norfolk, Virginia, famously observed, "The reign of tears is over. The slums will soon only be a memory. We will turn our prisons into factories and our jails into storehouses and corncribs. Men will walk upright now; women will smile and children will laugh. Hell will forever be rent."

The Prohibitionists believed that by passing a law, they would change everyone's behavior. Congress set up a Prohibition Unit (later called the Prohibition Bureau) to enforce the 18th Amendment, but set aside a mere $3 million for enforcement. The Prohibition Unit only had 1,500 officers, for the entire United States. Agents were poorly paid ($2,300 a year, a low salary even for that era) which also encouraged them to take bribes. These agents had their hands full: in 1921, authorities seized over 95,000 illicit distilleries, stills, and fermentation facilities. This rose to 170,000 in 1925, then to over 280,000 in 1930. Some 35,000 people were arrested in connection with these seizures in 1921, rising to 62,000 in 1925, and 75,000 in 1928.

As the Prohibition Unit soon realized, Americans didn't stop drinking just because of a law. Once Prohibition came into effect, some 15,000 physicians and nearly 60,000 retail druggists in Chicago alone applied to get licenses to sell medicinal alcohol. This flood of applicants was evidence of the desire to circumnavigate the law by any means necessary. Illegal bars called speakeasies opened up in major cities almost immediately. By the early 1920s, there were 5,000 speakeasies in New York City alone. By 1927, there would be over 30,000. What is remarkable is that this was double the number of bars, restaurants, and saloons that sold liquor legally *before* Prohibition.

Criminals were quick to realize the staggering profits that could be had by providing illicit liquor to thirsty citizens. Alcohol was smuggled into the United States from Canada, where it was still legal to manufacture; the Bahamas, where many distillers set up shop; and Europe. Authorities made 134 seizures of smuggler's boats in 1923 and 236 the following year. "Bootlegging," or trafficking alcohol, became extremely common. It's unclear where the term came from, although some sources suggest it referred to criminals who smuggled supplies of illicit spirits in their boots.

George Remus became one of the first fabulously wealthy bootleggers. Originally a pharmacist, optometrist, and lawyer living in Chicago, Remus moved his family to Cincinnati, Ohio, when Prohibition was enacted. The Cincinnati area (with a heavily German, pro-drinking population) was home to many shuttered distilleries and saloons. Remus began buying up distilleries that had been closed down. He started them up again and legally sold liquor to drug companies, under the guise that it was for "medicinal purposes." In fact, the drug companies were reselling liquor to gangsters who in turn supplied speakeasies, a fact Remus was certainly aware of. At his peak, Remus had 3,000 people on his staff. To ingratiate himself with proper Cincinnati society, Remus threw astonishingly lavish parties, at which diamonds and even new cars were given away to guests. Remus's time in the sun didn't last long, however. On May 1922, he was convicted in court after authorities raided a farm where he'd stocked liquor. It is believed Remus served as the inspiration for the social-climbing nouveau riche title character of *The Great Gatsby* by F. Scott Fitzgerald.

Other mobsters eagerly jumped into the liquor trade. Johnny Torrio, Al Capone, Dion O'Banion, and the Genna brothers kept Chicago well-stocked with bootlegged spirits. Dutch Schultz, Charles "Lucky" Luciano, Meyer Lansky, Arnold Rothstein, Jack "Legs" Diamond, and other mobsters did the same for New York City. A group of ambitious young thugs in Detroit formed what became known as the Purple Gang. The Purples organized a fleet of ships, dubbed "The Little Jewish Navy" (after the fact many of the gang members were Jews), that smuggled alcohol from Canada, across the Great Lakes, and into America.

Ironically, even though Prohibition had been sold, in part, as a public health measure, people began dying and becoming sick in huge numbers from tainted liquor. On New Year's Day 1927, a single New York City hospital recorded over 40 deaths from poisoned alcohol. The death rate across the United States from poisoned alcohol shot up from 1,064 in 1920 to 4,154 in 1925. This doesn't include numbers of people made blind or sick from tainted liquor. There were no health warnings or quality controls on bootleg alcohol. Consumers took a chance every time they sampled illicit spirits. People who drank poisoned spirits couldn't complain to the Better Business Bureau if the brew made them sick. Nor could bootleggers be sued; after all, the product they provided was illegal, which meant buyer beware.

Cocktails—that is, drinks containing alcohol and a mix of other beverages and flavors—became hugely popular during Prohibition. This was largely to mask the taste of inferior liquor. Prohibition changed drinking habits in other ways. For the first time, women were allowed inside drinking establishments. Speakeasy owners weren't strict about entry requirements and age limits. Bootleggers discovered they could make more money shipping hard liquor than beer. Beer is bulky and more difficult to conceal. So bootleggers concentrated solely on the hard stuff. Beer drinking went out style.

Prohibition engendered corruption and cynicism. Led by Capone and Torrio, gangsters took over the small city of Cicero, Illinois, outside of Chicago. They used brutal methods to get politicians they supported into office in the unfortunate municipality. In the 1920s, Capone donated over a quarter of a million dollars to the election campaign of Republican Big Bill Thompson. Thompson was a swaggering, do-nothing mayor who turned a blind eye to organized crime in Chicago. Capone could afford such generosity: at his peak, authorities estimated he was earning $100 million a year, of which $60 million came from liquor sales.

Far from reducing crime, Prohibition spawned lawbreaking the likes of which America had never seen before. Gangs in Chicago battled it out with rapid-fire machine guns and hand grenades. A total of 800 gangsters were killed in Chicago during the years of Prohibition. On February 14, 1929, gunmen acting for Al Capone murdered seven men connected to the rival "Bugs" Moran Gang in a cold garage in Chicago. The so-called St. Valentine's Day Massacre made headlines around the country. Chicago wasn't alone in terms of lawlessness. By the early 1920s, New York City had basically given up trying to enforce federal Prohibition laws.

Bootlegging enabled gangsters to amass firepower, followers, and political support. It also gave them the clout to move into other rackets. After getting started in bootlegging, for example, Dutch Schultz took over the "numbers" racket in New York City. Politicians began coming out against Prohibition. Al Smith, governor of New York, ran for president in 1928 on an anti-Prohibition platform. He lost, but one year later, the fiery Fiorello La Guardia became mayor of New York. As a congressman, and now mayor, LaGuardia was extremely opposed to Prohibition. Lobby groups began forming to repeal the 18th Amendment. The Women's Organization for National Prohibition Reform disliked the spirit of lawlessness that Prohibition caused. Prohibition made it hip to defy the law by drinking liquor and rubbing shoulders with bootleggers. Saloons had been bad enough, argued the Organization, but at least they weren't run by gangsters serving up a product with virtually no quality controls. Other anti-Prohibition groups included the Association Against the Prohibition Amendment, the Crusaders, and the Moderation League.

In the fall of 1929, the New York Stock Exchange crashed, which led to an economic unraveling known as the Great Depression. The Depression further turned people away from Prohibition. "Why was the government spending money chasing down bootleggers when millions of people were out of work?" argued critics. It was felt that money spent enforcing Prohibition could be better used for welfare programs and unemployment relief. Critics also pointed out that governments were losing a big source of tax revenue by keeping liquor illegal. New President Herbert Hoover tried to appease both the "drys" and the "wets." He maintained the ban on alcoholic beverages, but appointed former Attorney General George Wickersham to head a commission to look into the law. The Wickersham Commission released its report in early 1931. The Commission came out in favor of retaining Prohibition, but made note of widespread opposition to the law and the corruption it caused. "Throughout the country people of wealth, businessmen and professional men and their families, and the higher paid workingmen and their families are drinking in large numbers in open flouting of the law," read the Wickersham Commission report. As the Commission pointed out, it was extremely difficult to enforce a law that so many people disagreed with.

In the presidential election of 1932, Democratic Party candidate Franklin Roosevelt promised to repeal Prohibition. Once elected, Roosevelt was good to his word. He convinced Congress to modify the Volstead Act to allow for 3.2 percent alcohol beer (up from 0.5 percent). Congress easily passed this measure into law, which legalized "real beer." A measure to repeal the 18th Amendment was introduced in the Senate on February 14, 1933. The Senate approved the measure 63–23, followed by the House of Representatives, which voted 289–121 in favor. The amendment was passed to the states for ratification. In late 1933, Utah became the 36th state to ratify the 21st Amendment, which gutted the 18th Amendment. On December 5, 1933, it became legal once again to purchase hard liquor under federal law.

Prohibition was intended to get Americans to stop drinking alcohol. On this score, it was a total failure. According to a study by the Washington, D.C.-based CATO Institute, a libertarian think-tank, alcohol use was going down already in the years before Prohibition. In 1910, the average American consumed a little over 1.6 gallons of pure

alcohol on an annual basis. This dropped to 1.4 gallons in 1915, then below one gallon in 1919. By 1921, consumption had bottomed out at 0.2 gallons person. It looked like Prohibition had succeeded. Unfortunately for temperance supporters, consumption soon began to rise, reaching nearly 1.2 gallons per person in 1923, then nearly 1.4 gallons by the end of 1929. In other words, people were drinking almost as much alcohol as they had before Prohibition.

In a similar fashion, the death rate from alcoholism at first dropped with the advent of Prohibition. In 1910, the death rate from alcoholism was 5.4 per 100,000. This figure jumped around quite a bit, climbing to 5.9 per 100,000 in 1913, then declining to 1.6 in 1919. In 1920, the first year of Prohibition, the death rate fell even further, to 1.0 per 100,000. After that, it began rising once again. By 1923, the death rate from alcoholism had reached 3.2 per 100,000. Four years later, it was 4.0 per 100,000. Violent crime also skyrocketed during Prohibition. In 1910, the murder rate in the United States was under 2 per 100,000 people. By the early 1930s, this had reached nearly 10 per 100,000 people. When Prohibition was repealed, the murder rate dropped sharply, to roughly 6 per 100,000 by the mid-1930s then 5 per 100,000 by the mid-1940s.

Enforcement of Prohibition was abysmal. The Prohibition Bureau was riddled with corruption and incompetence. At most, Prohibition agents were never able to stop more than five percent of illicit alcohol coming into the United States. Prohibition generated a general disrespect for law and order. Ordinary citizens began to think nothing of flouting the law by drinking at speakeasies or buying liquor from criminals. Citizens began to lose faith in policemen, judges, politicians, and other forces of authority who were perceived as being in the pay of mobsters.

One of the most drastic effects of Prohibition, however, was that it turned petty thugs into millionaires. If Prohibition hadn't happened, chances are that Al Capone, Johnny Torrio, Dutch Schultz, the Purple Gang, and their peers would have remained small-time players running local neighborhood scams. Instead, bootlegging made minor mobsters rich beyond their wildest dreams. Pre-Prohibition gangs, such as the Five Pointers or the Eastman mob, were not national in scope. Their power only extended to the edges of the cities in which they were based. Old-time gang leaders such as Monk Eastman and Paul Kelly did not operate international smuggling operations of the kind that Al Capone and Lucky Luciano oversaw.

Once Prohibition was repealed, most gangsters got out of the bootleg business. With alcohol available once again in legitimate stores, the public no longer needed to buy poorly made and potentially dangerous liquor at a huge markup. Prohibition-Era gangs found new sources of income, in prostitution, drugs, labor racketeering, numbers, and especially gambling. In the end, Prohibition's main achievement was to enrich a massive, organized underworld. Remnants of this underworld, in the form of the American Mafia and other groups, are still active today.

See Also: Capone, Al; Drug Trade; Mafia; Schultz, Dutch

Further Reading

Edward Behr, *Prohibition: Thirteen Years That Changed America*, 1996.

Jane Lang McGrew, "History of Alcohol Prohibition," report prepared for the National Commission on Marihuana (sic) and Drug Abuse, 1972.

National Commission on Law Observance and Enforcement, (Wickersham Commission), "Report on the Enforcement of the Prohibition Laws of the United States," 1931.

Paul Sann, *The Lawless Decade*, 1957

David Southwell, *The History of Organized Crime: The True Story and Secrets of Global Gangland*, 2006.

Mark Thornton, assistant professor of economics at Auburn University, "Alcohol Prohibition Was a Failure," CATO Institute Policy Analysis, July 17, 1991.

Woman's Christian Temperance Union. http://www.wctu.org.

PURPLE GANG

The Purple Gang was a loosely knit group of thugs, most of whom were Jewish, who briefly dominated the Detroit underworld in the 1920s. The gang traced its origins to Detroit's old Jewish neighborhood around Hastings Street. There, shortly after the turn of the twentieth century, a group of juvenile delinquents coalesced around a charismatic youth named Abe Bernstein and his brothers, Ray, Joe, and Isadore ("Izzy"). The Bernstein-led gang was mostly made up of sons of first-generation immigrant Jews from Europe. Others had been born in the Old World and brought to America as infants or very young children.

At first, the embryonic Purple Gang was content to beat up drunks for money, steal from pushcarts, and generally cause mayhem in its community. According to one probably apocryphal tale, the gang acquired its name after a merchant compared its members to rotten meat, which sometimes takes on a purple hue. A more realistic suggestion is that the name was invented by journalists trying to fit a label on a fluid band of criminals.

The Purple Gang would have almost certainly remained a very small-scale organization were it not for Prohibition. Michigan was ahead of the national curve and went "dry" on May 1, 1918, over half a year before the Volstead Act came into effect across the country. Criminals of all types immediately raced to fill the void and provide Michigan residents with illegal alcohol, purchased in states where distilleries were still permitted. Once national prohibition was imposed in early 1920, Michigan criminals turned to Canada for their alcohol supplies. The province of Ontario, conveniently located directly across the Detroit River from the city of Detroit, had its own prohibition law. That law, however, did not ban the manufacture of alcohol for export—provided it went to a country where liquor was legal. American gangsters would simply cross the border, buy enormous amounts of alcohol, and claim it was destined for Cuba (where it was still legal to drink spirits). This one-way trade hugely benefited Canada, and Canadian officials didn't ask many questions.

In general, the Purple Gang didn't bother buying spirits in Canada or brewing liquor themselves. The gang specialized in hijacking trucks carrying alcohol that other gangs had purchased. The Purple Gang soon achieved a gruesome reputation for extreme brutality. Whereas most hijackers were only interested in the cargo and let drivers and guards off with a warning or a bribe, the Purples murdered everyone they encoun-

tered while heisting supplies. Drivers could expect no mercy if pulled off the road by the Purple Gang. This violence turned off some potential recruits. Jewish mobster Moe Davitz, for example, was originally a member of the Purple Gang, only to quit. A farsighted man, Davitz figured the Purples were too violent and irrational to last very long. Davitz moved to Ohio and set himself up as a power in Cleveland.

Back in Detroit, the Purples branched out into extortion, drugs, and murder for hire. Once again, the gang showed its entrepreneurial flair. The gang members didn't sell drugs themselves, but offered "protection" to dealers who did. Drug dealers were forced to kickback some of their profits to the Purples or face brutal retaliation. The Purple Gang also became involved in labor racketeering, a criminal art form later perfected by gangsters such as Dutch Schulz. The scam went as follows: mobsters would establish a "trade association" or "union" for a particular line of laborers, in the Purple Gang's case, Detroit based clothes cleaners and dryers, who occupied a vital niche in the days before home washing machines. Businesses would then be forced to pay exorbitant fees to join the trade association, membership in which conferred virtually no privileges beyond basic survival.

Like other Prohibition-Era gangs, the Purples used their newfound wealth to buy off city officials, policemen, and journalists. They weren't able to bribe everyone, however, and soon attracted the attention of the law. In the late 1920s, Detroit police charged 13 members of the Purple Gang with conspiracy to extort money from dryers and cleaners. Authorities claimed the Purples enforced their trade association with explosions, threats, fires, stink bombings, kidnappings, and beatings. When their trial came up, however, the gang members beat the charges.

Even as they rose in power and stature, the Purple Gang was never a formal organization with a permanent roster of members. The core gang numbered around a dozen men (mostly acquaintances of the Bernstein brothers). At its peak, the Purples could count about 20 thugs on their side, plus various associates. At one point, a small number of Purples broke away to form, along with some associates of Al Capone, something called the "Little Jewish Navy." The navy consisted of about 12 fast boats that plied the Detroit River, bringing alcohol from Canada to the United States.

Capone eyed the vast amounts of liquor flowing across the border with a covetous gaze. In the late 1920s, he met with the Purples and other gangs in Detroit. Capone explained that he wanted to set up operations in the Motor City. The Purples let Big Al know, in no uncertain terms, that they strongly opposed such a move. Capone could have crushed the Purples, but that would have meant a long, drawn out war with heavy casualties and lost income for both sides. Far simpler just to buy the Purple Gang off, which is what Capone ended up doing. He made the Purples his business agents in Detroit and bought liquor from them. The Purple Gang soon perfected their modus operandi: they would purchase (or steal) high quality Canadian Club whisky, slap their own labels on the bottles (for a made-up brand called "Old Log Cabin") then sell it to Capone.

The links to Capone didn't end there. Purple Gang members Phil and Harry Keywell took part in the St. Valentine's Day Massacre in Chicago, which saw Capone wipe out a rival gang led by George "Bugs" Moran. It's not clear if the Keywells were part of the death squad that murdered Moran's men in a cold, Chicago garage on February 14, 1929, or were just observers. In the post-Valentine fallout, police determined that the Keywell brothers had rented a room directly across the street from the crime scene. Their involvement beyond being simple lookouts is unknown.

The Capone relationship could rub the wrong way too. With Capone's encouragement, three Chicago hoods, identified by the *Detroit News* as Izzy Sutker, "Nigger" Joe Lebkowitz, and Hymie Paul, went to Detroit and became members of the Purple Gang. The trio were given a territory to sell liquor in, but started double-crossing their erstwhile allies. Needless to say, the Purple Gang was outraged. Ray Bernstein contacted a long-time Purple associate named Sonny Levine, who was on friendly terms with the Chicago threesome. Bernstein told Levine that all would be forgiven if the trio would only meet to sort things out. Levine arranged for Sutker, Lebkowitz, and Paul to meet Ray Bernstein at the Collingwood Manor apartments in Detroit. Ray showed up at the September 16, 1931, rendezvous with three Purple thugs in tow: Irving Milberg, Harry Fleisher, and Harry Keywell. On Bernstein's signal, the three Purples produced weapons and shot the three Chicago hoods to pieces. Levine, who was also in attendance, was not harmed. Ray Bernstein evidently valued his friendship and gave strict orders not to shoot Levine.

The Purple Gang soon had reason to regret this order. Police arrived and took the rather shocked Levine into custody. He was pressured into giving an eyewitness account of the slaughter. Within days of the Collingwood Manor Massacre, as the press called it, police arrested Ray Bernstein, Irving Milberg, and Harry Keywell. Fleisher disappeared and could not be found. Under extremely heavy police guard, Levine nervously testified in a fall 1931 trial. Bernstein, Milberg, and Keywell were convicted in early 1932 and given life sentences at Marquette prison in Michigan. These convictions heralded the Purple's decline as a major power. By this point, members were fighting each other, and the gang was self-destructing. Two key members, Abe Axler and Eddie Fletcher, were murdered by their peers in late 1933. Described as "machine gun terrorists of the Purple Gang," the *Detroit Times* speculated that the two were murdered to prevent them from seizing control of the floundering outfit.

By the late-1930s, the press and police had written off the Purple Gang as a spent force. A *Detroit News* story dated November 28, 1937, officially announced the gang's death throes. "Bullets write the gang's long overdue obituary," read the subheadline to a story on murdered gangster Harry Millman (described by the *Times* as the "Last of the Purples"). An FBI report from Detroit, Michigan, dated June 17, 1939, echoed these sentiments. "At present there are no known gangs or mobs of hoodlums operating as such in Detroit," stated the report. It continued:

Detroit four or five years ago was the headquarters for the notorious Purple Gang that operated for a while and controlled a great number of illicit and semi-illicit activities in this area. During its operations, the Purple Gang controlled such things as the malt industry, liquor labels, breweries, whisky smuggling, dope, etc. . . . This gang was dissolved through the activities of the Detroit Police department and its remnants, if not in the penitentiary, have become engaged in activities such as handbooks, big money gambling, the numbers racket and like operations.

Although their gang had fallen apart, the Bernstein brothers continued to make a living from underworld activity. The FBI report stated that Abe, Joe, and Izzie had moved into the racetrack wire service gambling business. Ray wasn't able to take part in this family enterprise, because he was still in jail. In this manner, the Bernstein's retained a toe-hold in organized crime, even as the Purple Gang became a historical curiosity.

Further Reading

"Axler and Fletcher Slain On Gang Ride and Bodies are Left in Car," *Detroit Times*, November 27, 1933.

Rich Cohen, *Tough Jews: Fathers, Sons and Gangster Dreams*, 1998.

Federal Bureau of Investigation, Purple Gang report. http://foia.fbi.gov/foiaindex/purp gang.htm.

"Millman, Last of Purples, Was Just a 'Tough Punk' To Police, *Detroit News*, November 28, 1937.

John William Tuohy, "The Purple Gang: An Interview with Paul Kavieff." http://www .americanmafia.com/Feature_Articles _50.html.

R

RELES, ABRAHAM "KID TWIST" (1907–1941)

Abraham "Kid Twist" Reles was a crass Jewish gangster who rose to a pinnacle of murderous underworld success, only to become a high-level turncoat. A key member of the elite band of killers known as Murder Incorporated, Reles provided authorities with inside information on scores of killings.

Born in 1907, Reles's parents were Austrian Jews who fled persecution in Europe. Raised on the mean streets of New York City, Reles took to crime early. As a teenager in the late 1920s, he worked for the Shapiro brothers (Meyer, Irving, and William), a brutal clan who controlled vice in the Brownsville neighborhood of Brooklyn. Reles performed a variety of tasks for the Shapiro's, such as beating up people, collecting loans, and other forms of mayhem. He usually worked in tandem with a partner named Martin "Buggsy" Goldstein. Short, fat, tough, and sly, Reles was a top-notch thug. He inspired fear and loathing,

Abe Reles, right, shown here with fellow Murder, Inc., member Al Tannenbaun, before testifying in a murder trial in 1940. [AP Photo]

despite his pudgy frame. "About the best you could say for Reles was that he was an animal in human guise," wrote assistant district attorney Burton Turkus in the book, *Murder, Inc.*

Not surprisingly, Reles drew the attention of police and was sentenced to a term in the Elmira Reformatory for various misdeeds. Released in the spring of 1930, Reles harbored a deep grudge against the Shapiro brothers, who had cut him loose after his arrest. Hanging out in a pool hall run by Buggsy Goldstein, Reles made the acquaintance of George Defeo. George's older brother, William Defeo, was an associate of Meyer Lansky and Ben Siegel, two well-established thugs who outranked the Shapiro's in the criminal hierarchy. Reles convinced Lansky and Siegel to supply him with slot machines (which were then new and illegal in many locales). Slot machines were provided, and Reles and Goldstein went into business, leasing them out to local bars and restaurants. This was done in defiance of the Shapiro's, who viewed Brownsville as their exclusive territory. Reles began to muscle in on other Shapiro rackets, including loan sharking and bookmaking (taking illegal bets).

War was declared between the Shapiro brothers and Reles and Goldstein. At first, the battle went poorly for Reles's side. Reles, Goldstein, and Defeo were shot at when they tried to vandalize vehicles parked near Shapiro headquarters. Reles was wounded in the altercation. After the ambush, Meyer Shapiro abducted Reles's teenage girlfriend at gun-point and brutally raped and beat her. Reles spent a few weeks recovering from his wounds and seething over the horrible offence committed against his girlfriend. The latter assault merely strengthened his resolve to get even. Once he had sufficiently recovered from his injuries, Reles contacted a former childhood acquaintance named Harry Strauss (later to pick up the nickname "Pittsburgh Phil") and two budding thugs, Harry "Happy" Maione and Frank "the Dasher" Abbandando. Other allies included Walter Sage and Gangy Cohen. Reles convinced the gang that they had to kill the Shapiros and take over their crime empire. Irving Shapiro was shot dead by Reles and Goldstein in the spring of 1931. Meyer Shapiro was killed next. Willie Shapiro was eventually killed a few years later, personally garroted by Reles. Once the Shapiro brothers had been neutralized, Reles' crew became the dominant crime faction in Brownsville.

Reles and Goldstein used a candy store as their headquarters. This same store served as the command center for what became known as Murder, Inc. Murder, Inc. was the enforcement arm of the national crime syndicate, established in the early 1930s to regulate vice. The syndicate recruited Reles, Goldstein, and many of their allies to serve as hired killers. They took to this work with glee, murdering hundreds of people in the course of a decade. Eventually, Reles became the street boss of Murder, Inc. In army terms, he would be the sergeant who led the troops on the ground. His commander in chief was crime boss Louis "Lepke" Buchalter. The sadistic Albert Anastasia served as Buchalter's adjutant, passing orders down the line.

In addition to being violent, Reles was cunning, as evidenced by his feud with a fellow hoodlum named "Jake the Painter." Reles and Jake had vowed to kill each other on sight. One evening in September 1932, Reles bumped into Jake on the street. Reles was unarmed, whereas Jake had a pistol. Thinking fast, Reles told Jake that killing him would be a mistake. If Reles was killed, Jake would surely be tracked down and slaughtered by Murder, Inc. Far better to join forces and go into business together. Jake was unsure, but agreed to discuss the matter further at a bar. Several rounds of hard liquor ensued. By the time they left the bar, Jake was light-headed and happy. Feelings of goodwill prevailed between the two former ene-mies. At this point, Reles told Jake he was foolish to keep a pistol on him. Police could charge him with carrying a concealed weapon. Why risk a criminal record? It was far smarter to get rid of the gun. Reles promised to ditch the weapon for his newfound friend. This sounded like a good idea to Jake, who handed the pistol over. Reles smiled, took the gun, and shot Jake the Painter dead with his own weapon.

Reles had other ways of dispatching enemies. He acquired his nickname, "Kid Twist," for his dexterity in stran-gling people. The name was also taken in honor of a turn-of-the-century gangster who had been called Kid Twist. Throughout the 1930s, "Kid Twist" was constantly in trouble with the law. In 1934, he was imprisoned after assaulting a black garage attendant for not working hard enough. By one estimate, Reles was arrested roughly every 80 days between 1930 and 1940. On January 15, 1940, Reles was picked up by police for vagrancy. At this conjuncture, Reles's criminal record featured 42 arrests. On January 24, 1940, a low-level miscreant named Harry Rudolph contacted assis-tant district attorney Turkus, offering him inside information in exchange for leniency. Rudolph stated that a hoodlum friend of his, Alex "Red" Alpert had been killed by three Murder, Inc. mem-bers: Reles, Buggsy Goldstein, and Dukey Maffetore.

On March 21, 1940, while in jail, Reles took a visit from his attorney. It is unclear what was discussed, but immedi-ately after this visit, Reles penned a note to his wife, Rose, asking her to speak with the Brooklyn district attorney, William O'Dwyer. Reles was ready to confess all he knew. It is believed Reles turned traitor because he feared his com-panions in Murder, Inc. had, for some reason, targeted him for death. He also worried that Murder, Inc. members might talk first, and thus get a deal that spared their lives while he went to the electric chair.

When talking to police, Reles didn't hide anything. He admitted committing at least 11 homicides (some sources put the total at 30). Reles offered details on these killings and roughly 200 other murders of which he had some knowl-edge. Thanks to his testimony, several Murder, Inc. members, including Harry Strauss, Louis Capone (no relation to Al), Buggsy Goldstein, Happy Maione, Dasher Abbandando, and Lepke Buchal-ter were put to death. Other Murder, Inc. members were given stiff prison terms. Assassin Charlie "the Bug" Workman changed his plea from not guilty to guilty after Reles told police about his role in the murder of crime boss Dutch Schultz. Workman figured a life sentence was better than a death sentence.

Reles himself died on November 12, 1941. Guarded by anywhere from six to 18 policemen at a Coney Island hotel (accounts vary), Reles somehow fell or was pushed out a six-story window. None of his police escorts claimed to have seen him go out the window, despite strict orders not to leave Reles alone at any time. It has been suggested that gangster boss Frank Costello bribed police, to the tune of $50,000–100,000, to toss Reles out the window. Underworld gossip sug-gested Costello didn't want Reles testify-ing against Anastasia and Siegel.

For all the insight he provided to police, Reles remained a deeply unsettling figure. The book *Murder, Inc.,* details a chilling exchange between Turkus and Reles. The exchange began when Turkus asked Reles if he ever felt a pang of conscience while killing. Reles responded with a question, asking the lawyer how he felt the first time he tried a case in court. Turkus said he was nervous. Kid Twist pressed on and asked Turkus how he felt when he tried his second case. Turkus said he was still nervous, but less so, and after that, he didn't feel bad at all trying cases. "You answered your own question," Reles rasped. "It's the same with murder. I got used to it."

See Also: Jewish Gangsters; Murder, Inc.

Further Reading

Rich Cohen, *Tough Jews: Fathers, Sons and Gangster Dreams*, 1998.

Thomas Reppetto, *American Mafia: A History of Its Rise to Power*, 2004.

Burton Turkus and Sid Feder, *Murder, Inc.: The Story of the Syndicate*, 1951.

ROTHSTEIN, ARNOLD (1882–1928)

Arnold Rothstein was famous for being the power behind the throne, a money man who was more financier than mob boss. He helped set up trans-Atlantic alcohol shipping routes during Prohibition and mentored a slew of up-and-coming gangsters. He was widely credited with "fixing" the 1919 World Series, when in fact he might have just provided seed money for the scam. A grey presence, Rothstein was smart enough to realize that being invisible was essential for longevity in the underworld. To this end, Rothstein let other people commit crimes from which he

Arnold Rothstein, c. 1923.

benefited financially. His personal style was all-charm and low-key good will; he was never known to swagger or act out in public, as less sophisticated gangsters were apt to do.

Unlike most mobsters, Rothstein came from a comfortable background. His father owned a dry goods store and a plant that processed cotton. Born in 1882, Rothstein spent his childhood in a townhouse on the Upper East Side of New York City. As a young teenager, Rothstein was drawn to the seedy underbelly of Manhattan. He started gambling in dives, rubbing shoulders with criminals and gang bosses. This caused a rift with his father, who frowned on gambling, even when his son won. Rothstein senior believed money was something you earned through hard work, not from skill with dice or cards. Despite his father's misgivings, Rothstein remained an avid gambler with a head for math. These were skills that would take him far from his father's respectable retail world.

In 1911, Rothstein demonstrated he had nerve as well as a vocation for making wagers. The downtown pool-room toughs and gamblers were getting annoyed at the presence of this well-spoken, upper-class Jewish kid in their midst. They decided to show him up by recruiting a star pool player to put him in his place. The hustler challenged Rothstein to a game, which the boy accepted. The air thick with cigarette and cigar smoke from dozens of curious onlookers, Rothstein and the pool shark had their match. The pool shark won, but Rothstein wouldn't quit. He challenged his opponent to another game. Rothstein began winning, as the two players engaged in game after game. The session became a marathon, lasting from Thursday evening until Saturday morning. Rothstein refused to give up, and finally pool hall management had to step in and end the game, as both players were exhausted. The pool hall patrons were impressed. Rothstein had shown his nerve and proven he didn't fold under pressure.

Well-spoken and clean-cut in appearance, Rothstein graduated from being a hobby gambler to a full-time professional. He would gamble on anything, and freely lent money to others so they could gamble, too. As he moved up in the world of gambling, Rothstein began paying off officials at Tammany Hall (the local, corrupt Democratic Party machine that ran New York City). He became the first Jew to have any clout with Tammany. He counted corrupt political bosses such as "Big Tim" Sullivan (who ran the Lower East Side) and, later, flamboyant New York mayor Jimmy Walker as friends.

With Sullivan's protection, Rothstein opened a casino on Broadway in midtown Manhattan. It was soon attracting rich New Yorkers and bringing in $10,000 a week. Rothstein put on the charm when the high society crowd frequented his casino. He usually wore a tuxedo, or else was nattily attired in silk suits, wing-tip shoes, and expensive hats. He carried a huge "bankroll" (a rolled up wad of cash) and was happy to make loans to fellow gamblers. The media called him "the Brain." Though Rothstein didn't deny being a gambler, he never revealed the extent of his criminal connections either. Some gullible newspaper readers might be forgiven for thinking Rothstein was just exceptionally lucky at poker.

When not at his casino, Rothstein presided from a table at Lindy's, a very chic Broadway eatery. From his table, he handled bookmaking and gambling operations. Rothstein also had an office on West 57th Street, but it dealt only with his legitimate investments such as real estate, race horses, and Broadway shows. Gangsters were not allowed inside.

For all his political connections, Rothstein did have a few close calls with the law. For example, on January 19, 1919, he was involved in a strange incident involving two policemen. Detectives John Walsh and John McLaughlin tried to enter an apartment at 301 West 57th Street, where they "suspected gambling was in progress," as the *New York Times* put it. The detectives were refused admission at the door, so they decided to force their way inside. Someone fired a pistol to ward off the intruders and the police fled. Six months later, a grand jury indicted Rothstein—who had been inside the apartment during the abortive raid—for assault in the first and second degrees.

He refused to tell police who was with him, much less who fired the shots at the detectives. Rothstein said he didn't know the two were police officers; he mistook them for hold-up men, so any gunplay was merely self-defense. It's unclear if authorities believed this or if Rothstein simply paid someone to make the case disappear. On July 24, 1919, the two indictments against Rothstein were dropped due to lack of evidence.

It was roughly around the same time that a confusing conspiracy began to take shape that immortalized Rothstein, even if his role in the affair is still open to question. The conspiracy centered on the powerhouse Chicago White Sox baseball team, which was the odds-on favorite to win the 1919 World Series. The poorly paid White Sox, however, succumbed to the blandishments of gamblers who offered them hard cash to blow games. The White Sox lost the Series, but players didn't have much opportunity to enjoy their bribes.

To quell rumors of a "fix," a grand jury was convened in Cook County, Illinois, in September, 1920, to examine rigged baseball games in general and the 1919 World Series in particular. Rothstein's name came up on more than one occasion. It was whispered that he contributed to a $100,000 bribe given to the White Sox players in on the scam. Rothstein himself received a subpoena and appeared before the grand jury on October 27, 1920. He evidently made a good impression; after he spoke, the State's Attorney's Office announced that Rothstein's testimony exonerated him "from complicity in the throwing of games in the 1919 World Series" according to the *New York Times*.

In the end, criminal indictments were handed down to eight White Sox players and the men who'd bribed them. Rothstein was not among the indicted. The trial began in June 1921. On July 23, 1921, Rothstein huffily issued a statement to the press from his home on West 84th Street. Although he admitted that former White Sox pitcher William Burns had approached him with a view to joining the scam, Rothstein insisted he didn't join the man's scheme. Rothstein's statement read:

> When Burns, with whom I had no previous acquaintance, sought me out in this city and advanced to me his proposition to enter into a scheme to fix the World Series, not only did I most emphatically refuse to have anything to do with him or his proposition, but I told him that I regarded his proposition as an insult and him as a blackguard, with whom I wanted no dealing whatsoever and warned him not to come near or speak to me on any pretext whatsoever.

In the end, the eight baseball players were acquitted in criminal court, but ended up being banned for life from professional ball. Rothstein, even though he wasn't indicted, much less convicted of anything, was forever known afterwards as the man who "fixed" the 1919 World Series.

Rothstein's fame was such that he entered pop culture consciousness. His persona formed the basis of the character Meyer Wolfsheim in F. Scott Fitzgerald's 1925 masterpiece, *The Great Gatsby*. Described as the gambler who fixed World Series, Wolfsheim is a shadowy bootlegger who provided the nouveau riche Jay Gatsby (whose character was allegedly based on real-life master bootlegger George Remus) with

---

THE BLACK SOX: DID GANGSTERS "FIX" THE 1919 WORLD SERIES?

In 1919, the Chicago White Sox were a powerhouse professional baseball team destined for the World Series. They were also very poorly paid. Shortly before the World Series, first baseman Chick Gandil approached a small-time gambler named Joseph Sullivan with a proposal. For $100,000, Gandil said he could ensure that the heavily favored White Sox lost. Sullivan agreed, and Gandil went about recruiting teammates to join in the scam. Sullivan didn't have $100,000 and needed co-investors. He recruited three gamblers: former boxer Abe Attell, former White Sox pitcher "Sleepy Bill" William Burns, and New York Giant first baseman Hall Chase. Underworld financier Arnold Rothstein also invested in the scam. Some accounts say Rothstein simply provided a share of the $100,000 bribe. Other crime historians believe Rothstein sent hoodlums to intimidate White Sox players to ensure their cooperation. The White Sox ended up losing the World Series to the Cincinnati Reds.

In September 1920, a grand jury in Cook County, Illinois, convened to examine allegations of rigged professional baseball games. The grand jury soon turned its attention to the 1919 World Series. Players, writers, gamblers, owners, and managers were called to testify. Rothstein appeared before the grand jury on October 27, 1920. Of course, he denied everything. In the end, eight White Sox players, plus Hal Chase, Abe Attell, Joe Sullivan, Bill Burns, and a handful of others, were indicted. Rothstein was not indicted, which was an indication of either his pull or his peripheral role in the scam. The trial began in June 1921. In the end, all eight players were acquitted, but were banned for life from professional baseball. Rothstein managed to escape any punishment, but was known forever afterwards as the "man who fixed the World Series."

Sources: Chicago Historical Society, The History Files, "Inside Story of Plot to Buy World Series." http://www.chicagohs.org/history/blacksox.html; Paul Sann, *The Lawless Decade*, 1957

---

his income. Rothstein was also depicted as the character Nathan Detroit in the short stories by Damon Runyon that would later become the musical *Guys and Dolls*.

The acclaim generated by the World Series scandal enhanced Rothstein's already inflated public image. If indeed all he did was provide seed money for the fix, then it certainly reflected his modus operandi. Rothstein was primarily a gang financier who put money up for other people's schemes. He didn't directly have a hand in rackets himself.

The way Rothstein responded to Prohibition exemplified his hands-off approach. After Prohibition was enacted in early 1920, Rothstein was approached by an associate named Irving Wexler (aka "Waxey Gordon"). Gordon wanted a loan of $175,000 to set up an alcohol smuggling ring. Gordon planned to buy liquor legally in Canada, then transport cases of it via speedboat across the Great Lakes to Chicago and other U.S. port cities.

Rothstein liked the plan, but suggested a few tweaks. He suggested that Gordon buy entire shiploads of alcohol in Europe and transport it across the Atlantic. Gordon agreed and soon was bringing in liquor by tramp steamer from Europe. The tramp steamer would halt just outside U.S. territorial waters, then the cargo would be unloaded on a collection of speed boats. These boats would drop the liquor off at secluded beaches, where it would be picked up and delivered to speakeasies, nightclubs, and bars that Rothstein had invested in.

Rothstein made sure that police and politicians were well paid to look the other way. To his chagrin, he discovered his greatest enemy was not the law, but his fellow gangsters. Rather than smuggle spirits themselves, some gangs simply hijacked liquor trucks belonging to other mobs. The victims of these robberies weren't exactly in a position to report the loss to police.

A command decision was made. Rothstein decided to hire "muscle" to protect his trans-Atlantic shipments. In this way, many up-and-coming gangsters got to ride shotgun on his liquor trucks and protect his bootlegging racket. Their ranks included Dutch Schultz, Ben Siegel, Meyer Lansky, Frank Costello, Lucky Luciano, Waxey Gordon, Louis "Lepke" Buchalter, and Gurrah Shapiro. Most of these mobsters were Jewish, though not all. In addition to financing criminal schemes, Rothstein was something of an underworld talent scout. He spotted budding criminals who looked like they had potential and offered them work and an underworld mentorship.

Rothstein also had some deep insights into the nature of organized crime. He was one of the first mobsters to realize that the best way for the underworld to operate was by stealth, by working in the shadows. Earlier gangsters in New York City, like Monk Eastman, had been rash,

violent showmen who drew attention to everything they did and behaved like thugs in public. They made little attempt to hide their felonious activities and almost made it a point of pride to get arrested. By contrast, Rothstein was smooth. His underworld financing was all done on the sly, with a handshake and a nod. There were no signed contracts, no photos in the newspaper, and no paperwork. All deals were kept in his head. Rothstein did not engage in bar brawls or gunfights on the street with police or rival gang members. He kept his hands clean, even in the dirtiest of deals. Rothstein's attorney, William Fallon once memorably described his client as "a man who dwells in doorways . . . a grey rat waiting for his cheese." Among other sources, this graphic quote appears in *Little Man: Meyer Lansky and the Gangster Life* by Robert Lacey.

Ever the far-seeing entrepreneur, Rothstein was one of the first mobsters to get involved in drug trafficking in a large way. He set up trafficking operations in the mid-1920s as an adjunct to bootlegging. Rothstein sent emissaries to Europe and Asia to purchase opium and other drugs, which would be smuggled into the United States.

If there was one weakness that Rothstein sustained all his life, it was gambling. He was obsessed with wagering. In the last year of his life, there was an indication that Rothstein was experiencing mental or physical problems. His betting became more manic and out of control. He started losing all the time. He went from charming to anxiety-ridden.

From September 8 to 10, 1928, Rothstein took part in a major, high-stakes, marathon poker game hosted by bookmaker and gambler George McManus. Rothstein ended up losing by a wide margin. He owed over $320,000 to a handful of well-heeled players. Rothstein mumbled something about IOUs and stormed out. Instead of paying up, Rothstein began loudly complaining that the game was fixed. He refused to pay his debts. It was an astonishing position to take. The city's best known gambler was welshing on his debts.

Weeks went by and Rothstein still had not paid off what he owed. By this point, McManus was being pressured by his poker friends to get Rothstein to settle up. To deal with the stress, McManus started drinking. On November 4, 1928, McManus angrily called Rothstein at Liddy's. He requested that the Brain come and see him right away at the Park Central Hotel. Rothstein grudgingly left his table at Liddy's and departed for the hotel. The Brain arrived on schedule and was shot in the stomach, by assailants unknown. The great gambler staggered downstairs, holding his wound. Witnesses found him wobbling around the employee entrance, conscious but gravely injured. A policeman arrived on the scene and summoned an ambulance. Rothstein was taken to New York Polyclinic Hospital, where it was determined he had suffered heavy internal bleeding. Rothstein lapsed into a coma.

Rothstein managed to regain consciousness. He chatted with his brothers and wife, Carolyn, and steadfastly refused to tell police who shot him. To the persistent questions from police, Rothstein kept saying he would take care of matters himself. He never got the chance. Rothstein fell back into a coma and died at 10:20 a.m. on November 6, 1928. Ironically, had he lived he almost certainly would have been able to pay off his gambling debts. Rothstein had bet heavily on the U.S. presidential election, wagering that Republican Herbert Hoover would defeat Democratic candidate Al Smith, from New York. Hoover won and Rothstein posthumously earned over $500,000. McManus was charged with shooting Rothstein, but was acquitted. The exact identity of Rothstein's shooter has never been definitively established.

Rothstein did not leave behind an empire. His legacy was in the form of an example of how to run an efficient underworld business: gangsters could do deals at arm's length, letting others take all the risks while keeping a low-profile, offering a smiling face to the public, enjoying the proceeds of crime. Interestingly, the multiple millions that Rothstein had earned through crime couldn't be found after his death. His wife, Carolyn, lived quite well on various legitimate investments Rothstein had made, but she did not enjoy his great fortune, which no one could locate.

See Also: Drug Trade; Jewish Gangsters; Prohibition; Schultz, Dutch

Further Reading

Chicago Historical Society, The History Files, "Inside Story of Plot to Buy World Series." http://www.chicagohs.org/history/blacksox.html.

Rich Cohen, *Tough Jews: Fathers, Sons and Gangster Dreams*, 1998.

Robert Lacey, *Little Man: Meyer Lansky and the Gangster Life*, 1991.

"Rothstein Cleared in Baseball Fixing," *New York Times*, October 27, 1920.

"Rothstein Quotes Burns in Defence," *New York Times*, July 24, 1921.

Paul Sann, *The Lawless Decade*, 1957.

S

SAIETTA, IGNAZIO "LUPO THE WOLF" (1877–1947)

Ignazio Saietta, aka "Lupo the Wolf," was one of the first well-known Italian American gangsters. Like many of his contemporaries, Lupo's reputation was highly exaggerated by both the media and by frightened Italian immigrants (who proved some of his earliest victims). A thug at heart, Lupo wasn't much of an organizer and couldn't put together the kind of vast, multi-level underworld organization that later criminals such as Al Capone established.

Born in 1877, Lupo fled Sicily in 1899, allegedly after killing a man. Lupo settled in New York City, where he connected with his brother-in-law, Giuseppe Morello, a leading Sicilian American crime boss. Almost immediately upon arrival, Lupo began preying on his fellow Italian immigrants. Lupo specialized in the primitive "Black Hand" scam. This racket was simple: an anonymous note would arrive at the home of an Italian immigrant threatening all manner of torture and violence unless a large fee was paid. The extortionist sending the letter would typically "sign" it by dipping his hand in black ink and pressing his palm against the paper. This would leave the impression of a black hand, which is how the scam got its name. The Black Hand racket was prevalent in any city with a large Italian population. Many new Italian immigrants were poorly educated, deeply superstitious, and had an inbred mistrust of police (who tended to be very corrupt in their homeland). Italians were unlikely to report Black Hand intimidation to authorities.

Lupo had initially acquired his nickname in Sicily. As he rose to prominence in America, the press anglicized his handle to "Lupo the Wolf," which, when translated literally, means "Wolf the Wolf." It suited his sinister, blood-thirsty image. A snappy dresser and something of a dandy, Lupo liked to ride around New York's Little Italy in a horse-drawn carriage. A cold-blooded thug at heart, Lupo was a feared presence on the street.

He still answered to his brother-in-law, Morello, however, who was on his way to becoming the top Sicilian mobster in New York.

Lupo and the men who worked for him ran a "Murder Stable" in Italian Harlem. This was a former horse stable where anyone who crossed Lupo was tortured and murdered. Some sources estimate Lupo killed 60 people during his career, mostly rival gangsters and people who balked at paying Black Hand tribute. When he wasn't victimizing his countrymen, Lupo was employed as a wholesale grocer.

In April 1903, Lupo and Morello were arrested as part of a wide sweep of Italian gangsters following an infamous "barrel murder." The mutilated corpse of a man named Benditto Madonia had been found stuffed in a barrel. It was known that Madonia was trying to collect money owed him by Morello when he disappeared. Police ended up focusing their investigation on one member of the Lupo/Morello gang. This sole suspect was put on trial, but no one would testify against him, so he was set free. Though they weren't put on trial themselves, it was strongly suspected that Lupo and Morello were involved in Madonia's murder.

A few brave souls fought back against Lupo the Wolf. A *New York Times* article from November 23, 1909, examined a court case in which Lupo (identified as "Ignazio Lupo") was "charged with extorting $4,000 from Salvatore Manzella . . . under threats of death." Manzella failed to appear in court and Lupo was discharged, only to be immediately hit with a federal warrant for other crimes. Those other crimes included counterfeiting. Lupo and Morello set up a counterfeiting operation in which they supplied criminal contacts in other cities with fake

greenbacks. Lupo, Morello, and a handful of others were arrested in 1910 by the Secret Service (the branch of U.S. Treasury department responsible for protecting politicians and the nation's currency). Lupo was found guilty and on February 19, 1910, was sentenced to 30 years in federal prison in Atlanta. Morello got 25 years.

The trial garnered huge coverage, much of it wildly inaccurate. For example, a *New York Times* article from April 3, 1910, described the Lupo/Morello gang as "the most dangerous band of foreign criminals ever known in this country." Other stories credited Morello with being the head of the American Mafia and Lupo "the reputed treasurer of the Mafia society." For good measure, *the Times* also called Lupo "proud and haughty." Lupo served 10 years and was paroled in mid-1920. Upon release, he visited Italy, then went into the wholesale fruit and baked goods business with his son. By this point, the Black Hand scam had pretty much run its course. The Italian community had become more sophisticated and less likely to fall for Black Hand threats. With the advent of Prohibition, gangsters found a much more lucrative source of income than simple extortion.

On top of his grocery business, Lupo ran a few low-key rackets, such as illegal lotteries, after getting out of prison. This proved to be a mistake. In 1936, New York governor Herbert Lehman asked President Franklin Roosevelt to have Lupo rearrested for racketeering. This was done, and Lupo was once again put behind bars in Atlanta's federal penitentiary. When he was released for a second time, he was a powerless figure who soon died in obscurity.

See Also: Black Hand; Mafia

Further Reading

Herbert Asbury, *The Gangs of New York*, 1927.

"Black Hand Manacled at Last," *New York Times*, April 3, 1910.

"Hold Lupo as Counterfeiter," *New York Times*, November 23, 1909.

"'Lupo the Wolf,' Notorious Criminal, Freed by Washington from Ellis Island," *New York Times*, June 13, 1922.

Thomas Reppetto, *American Mafia: A History of Its Rise to Power*, 2004.

SCHULTZ, DUTCH (1902–1935)

Dutch Schultz's time at the top was brief and brutal: a reminder that sheer luck can be as important as character in determining the fortunes of mob bosses. To this end, Schultz was incredibly lucky. He twice managed to beat the same tax rap that brought down Al Capone, and he stumbled onto a source of immense wealth that his fellow gangsters disdained. In the end, Schultz pushed his luck as far as it would go and ended up the victim of one of gangland's strangest hits.

Schultz's real name was Arthur Flegenheimer. He was born to a pair of German Jewish parents on New York's Lower East Side on August 6, 1902. Flegenheimer's family moved to the South Bronx when he was still a very young boy. His mother, Emma, hoped her son would grow up to be a good Orthodox Jew. His father abandoned the family when Arthur was 14, embittering him for the rest of his life. Flegenheimer spent his formative years in the rough Bergen Street and Webster Avenue section of the Bronx. Like many

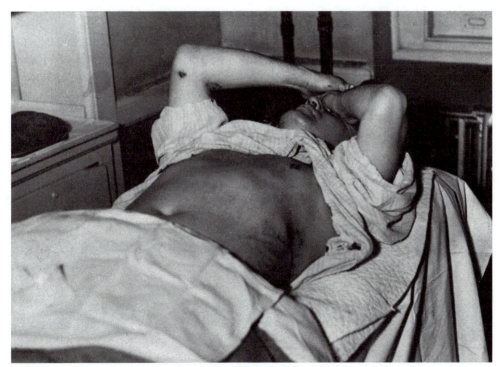

Dutch Schultz lays in a hospital cot, his arm and chest wounds exposed, in Newark, New Jersey, on October 23, 1935. Schultz died hours later from his gunshot wounds. [AP Photo]

juveniles in the same environment, he joined a street gang for protection and camaraderie. He also used his father's disappearance as an excuse to drop out of school. He began hanging around a clubhouse which was the haunt of a local gangster named Marcel Poffo. Poffo, who had a record for bank robbery and extortion, befriended little Arthur. To impress his mentor, Flegenheimer and his pals began robbing craps games that hadn't paid sufficient tribute to the neighborhood mob boss.

On December 12, 1919, Flegenheimer was arrested for burglarizing a Bronx apartment. He received his first and only prison sentence and found himself serving time in Blackwell's Island. The latter was a very tough penitentiary located on what is now Roosevelt Island in the middle of the East River. Flegenheimer proved to be a less than model prisoner and managed to get himself transferred to an even tougher facility called Westhampton Farms. Flegenheimer escaped from the Farms, only to be recaptured and have an additional two months added to his sentence.

At some point during the early 1920s, Flegenheimer was released from jail and returned to the Bronx. His Bergen Street buddies welcomed him back with open arms. In their eyes, going to jail was an important step on the road to manhood. The Bergen Street gang even had a new name for their pal: Dutch Schultz. The tag had originally belonged to an obscure but not forgotten street criminal from the area. Flegenheimer eagerly accepted the new moniker as he leapt back into a life of crime.

Schultz's timing couldn't have been better. Prohibition had just become national law in early 1920. There were fortunes to be made for youths brazen

enough to manufacture or distribute illegal alcohol. Fearless Schultz began driving a beer truck for rising Jewish gangster Arnold Rothstein. During this formative period, Schultz also worked sporadically as an enforcer. His paths occasionally crossed with another striving street kid, a Sicilian named Charles "Lucky" Luciano. Both Schultz and Luciano worked briefly as members of the Jack "Legs" Diamond gang. They also spent time guarding liquor trucks for underworld financier Arnold Rothstein.

By 1928, Schultz found himself employed as a bartender in a low-end speakeasy. In addition to serving drinks, he maintained order as a bouncer. The speakeasy was owned by a friend named Joey Noe. Schultz impressed Noe with his quick temper and proclivity for violence. Schultz and Noe decided to join forces. Noe became one of very few people, aside from family, allowed to address Schultz as "Arthur." The two men became close friends and allies. They began selling beer, which they purchased from an illegal brewery in Union City, New Jersey, throughout the Bronx. As farsighted entrepreneurs, Schultz and Noe put their profits back into their business. They purchased their own trucks and expanded their territory. Schultz typically rode "shotgun" in these vehicles, that is, he sat in the front passenger seat, gun in hand, to ward off would-be hijackers. Schultz had provided the same service during his brief tenure with Rothstein.

Schultz and Noe developed some persuasive sales techniques. Speakeasy owners who refused to buy their low-quality beer were threatened with brutal harm. Such was the fate of John and Joe Rock, two Irish brothers with whom Schultz and Noe wished to do business.

John Rock readily agreed to Schultz and Noe's sales pitch, but his more stubborn brother refused to be intimidated. Joe was kidnapped by thugs working for Schultz and Noe. The unfortunate Irishman was hung by his thumbs from a meat hook and tortured. A gauze bandage—liberally coated with the discharge from a gonorrheal sore—was slapped over his eyes. He was released after his family paid a $35,000 ransom, but soon went blind from gonorrheal infection.

Such tough guy exploits drew a crew of fledgling Jewish and Irish thugs to Schultz and Noe's side. Their gang soon came to include Abe "Bo" Weinberg and his brother George, and Vincent Coll and his brother Peter. Other gang members included Larry Carney, Thomas "Fatty" Walsh, Joey Rao, and Edward "Fats" McCarthy. The overconfident Schultz/Noe team started dealing beer across Manhattan's Upper West Side. They even moved their headquarters to this borough, setting up shop on East 149th Street. This meant they were encroaching on turf controlled by Schultz's former mentor, Legs Diamond.

Retribution was fast and merciless. On October 15, 1928, at 7:00 in the morning, Joey Noe stepped out of the Chateau Madrid nightclub on 54th Street and into an ambush. Gunmen working for Legs Diamond began firing at him. Noe had taken the precaution of wearing a bullet-proof vest, but the shots cut through his chest anyway, and tore up his spine. Noe managed to fire back, then collapsed on the sidewalk. Witnesses observed a blue Cadillac race away from the crime-scene. The car smashed into a parked vehicle and lost a door. Police located the door-less Cadillac one hour later. Inside was the body of Louis Weinberg, a gunman with the Legs Diamond crew. Weinberg (no relation to Bo or George) had been shot dead. Police figured some of Noe's bullets must have hit him during the brief skirmish in front of the Chateau Madrid. Noe survived the initial ambush, but ended up wasting away in hospital. By the time he expired, on November 21, 1928, Noe weighed less than 100 pounds. By all accounts, Schultz was genuinely grief stricken. From this moment on, he operated as a lone wolf, making all the major decisions himself.

Unlike most successful mobsters of the era, who decked themselves out in expensive, tailor-made wardrobes, Schultz resembled "an ill-dressed vagrant" in the words of the *New York Times* (as quoted in Paul Sann's book, *Kill the Dutchman!*). It was said the Dutchman never paid more than $2 for a shift or $35 for a suit. Nor did his physical attributes make up for his sartorial failures. A chorus girl once famously remarked that Schultz "looked like Bing Crosby with his face bashed in."

Seedy though he was, Schultz began to earn the grudging respect of his peers. In May 1929, he attended the Atlantic City conference, a major gathering of top-ranked mobsters from across America. It was a multicultural summit, with Sicilian and Italian gangsters rubbing shoulders with their Jewish counterparts. Among other things, the conference was called to discuss the end of Prohibition (which was beginning to look more and more likely as the decade progressed). The gangsters feared that the end of Prohibition meant the end of easy money from bootlegging. Were liquor to be legalized, they would have to find other avenues of work.

During the early 1930s, Schultz was peripherally involved in the great settling of accounts that became known as the Castellammarese War. The war was a battle between two old-time Sicilian mob leaders for the title of "capo di tutti capi" ("boss of the bosses"). The main antagonists were Giuseppe "Joe the Boss" Masseria and Salvatore Maranzano, both of whom hailed from Castellammare del Golfo, Sicily (which is how their underworld struggle gained its name). Schultz supported Masseria, but largely stayed out of the war. The struggle continued for over a year, with at least 50 known dead. Actual fatalities were probably higher. Members of the mob did not go to police when one of their own was murdered.

On January 24, 1931, Schultz got into a fight with Charles "Chink" Sherman at the Club Abbey, a popular Manhattan nightspot. Sherman was associated with a rival bootlegger named Waxey Gordon. The brawl allegedly had to do with a wisecrack made about a woman one of the men was dating. In the melee, Sherman was hit with a chair and stabbed several times. Schultz took a bullet in the shoulder. When police arrived, Sherman stayed true to the underworld code and refused to identify his assailant. In a similar fashion, the 80 customers at the nightclub all developed faulty memories when quizzed by police. Schultz managed to escape from the fracas with nothing more than a shoulder injury.

Shortly after the Club Abbey incident, Schultz's former street acquaintance, Lucky Luciano, brought the Castellammarese War to an abrupt end. Luciano theoretically worked for "Joe the Boss" Masseria. Luciano, however, cut a deal with Maranzano and set his boss up for the slaughter. On April 15, 1931, Masseria was murdered in a restaurant in the Coney Island section of Brooklyn. Maranzano quickly took charge following Masseria's death (and was subsequently killed himself, thanks again to Luciano). The Castellammarese War was over.

By this point, Schultz had taken up residence in a swanky ninth floor apartment on Fifth Avenue in Manhattan, near Central Park. Schultz registered the apartment under the alias "Russell Jones." An anonymous call to police revealed that "Mr. Jones" was none other than Dutch Schultz. Police began staking out Schultz's Fifth Avenue apartment. On June 18, 1931, Schultz and an associate named Danny Iamascia got into a violent confrontation with two undercover police detectives who were watching the apartment. Schultz mistook the men for a pair of assassins. Guns were drawn and Iamascia was shot; he was hit in the stomach and left wrist. Schultz and two other thugs took off running. One of the lawmen fired a warning shot that brought Schultz to a halt. Schultz dropped his own gun on the ground and tried to charm the detectives, offering them $50,000 each and a home in exclusive Westchester, New York, if they let him go. The police wouldn't bite. They commandeered a taxicab, tossed the moaning Iamascia on the floor then pushed Schultz inside. The detectives ordered the startled cabbie to stop at the nearest hospital, then the police station. Iamascia died of his injuries in the hospital. Schultz was bailed out of jail quickly and told to appear for a trial date. Policemen at the station were bemused to find nearly $19,000 in cash in Schultz's pockets when he was booked.

Around this time, a lawyer, named Richard "Dixie" Davis, entered Schultz's orbit. Davis was renowned for defending criminals involved in the numbers racket. The numbers racket was simply an illegal lottery. Customers would place a penny or two on a three digit number. The gangsters organizing the racket would then select a winning number from an objective source, such as stock reports or sports scores, so players could check for themselves whether or not they picked a winner. If your number "hit" then you won a few dollars. Most of the criminals Davis defended were African American. Davis put on a flamboyant show in court, shouting and waving his arms dramatically, which endeared him to his ill-educated clients. Likewise, most of the people who played the numbers were black. It was a cheap, hugely popular form of gambling in Depression-Era Harlem.

The city's established Jewish and Italian gangsters turned their noses up at numbers. They considered it beneath their dignity to get involved with what they dismissed as "nigger pennies." As a result, numbers was one of very few rackets in New York City run by African Americas. Though his peers were dismissive, Schultz sensed that huge profits were to be made at numbers. With the help of Dixie Davis, who had insider knowledge of the key players in the racket, Schultz began to take over the numbers industry. He violently persuaded African American "policy bankers" (that is, criminals who organized numbers games) to become "partners" with him. Schultz soon seized control of the New York numbers racket, reducing the black mobsters who had been running it to the status of very junior leaders. To his peers' astonishment, Schultz was soon making $12 to $14 million a year just from numbers.

For all the money he was making from African Americans, Schultz harbored less than brotherly feelings toward his new business partners. In financial statements detailing income and expenses, Schultz referred to his black workers as niggers. He also agreed to a plan to rig the numbers game to make it tougher to win. As suggested by professional gambler Otto "Abbadabba" Berman, the plan involved manipulating the odds at a horse-racing track where Schultz derived his winning numbers. The scheme was mind-bogglingly complex, but it worked. Berman soon increased the Dutchman's profit margin by a healthy share. Abbadabba was put on Schultz's payroll, to the tune of $10,000 a week. The numbers racket remained as lucrative as ever, even as the odds of getting a winning number grew steeper.

Schultz also benefited from another racket. One of his underlings, Julius Modgilewsky (aka "Jules Martin") seized control of two union locals that represented restaurant wait staff. Martin then founded a group called "The Metropolitan Restaurant & Cafeteria Owners Association." Martin would contact restaurant owners and threaten a strike among their unionized workers. Labor strife could be averted, however, if the restaurateur joined the Association, for a fee that ranged from $250 to $25,000. Restaurant owners who resisted suffered from strikes and stink bombs. These were explosives containing butyric acid that dowsed everything in their wake with a sordid stench that was almost impossible to get rid of. Facing such ruinous tactics, most restaurant owners submitted and joined the Association. The restaurant racket was soon bringing in another $2 million a year for Schultz.

In late January 1933, Schultz was indicted for income tax evasion.

According to the authorities, Schultz had neglected to file income tax returns for 1929, 1930, and 1931. The federal government said he owed them $92,000, based on earnings of nearly half-a-million dollars from bootlegging. Schultz faced the prospect of decades in jail. On the surface, going after gangsters for undeclared income seemed like a strange tactic, however, a Supreme Court decision from the late 1920s made clear that even illegal income had to be declared on income taxes. Failure to do so could result in huge fines or jail time—as Al Capone discovered in a spectacular Chicago trial in the early 1930s.

Instead of taking his chances at trial, Schultz became a fugitive. He "hid" in plain view, in various locales around New York City. While supposedly on the run from the law, Schultz found plenty of time to visit his girlfriend Frances, a former nightclub hat-check girl, and escort her about town.

In early 1934, there was more bad news for Schultz. The fiery Fiorello LaGuardia was elected mayor of New York on a reform ticket. LaGuardia promised to crack down hard on city mobsters. LaGuardia backed his words with action. In a well-covered media stunt, the mayor dumped a barge of illegal slot machines (seized from gangster controlled stores and bars) into the East River. Schultz faced another determined "gangbuster" in the form of prosecutor Thomas Dewey. A straight-laced graduate of Columbia University Law School, Dewey became a chief assistant to the United States attorney for the Southern District of New York. Dewey was determined to wage legal war against the underworld.

Schultz got a slight respite from the bad news in June 1934, when Frances had a baby girl. Her loving parents named her Anne Davis Flegenheimer (in honor of Dixie Davis). Schultz also began delving into Catholic rituals and beliefs. He had long been a non-practicing Jew before suddenly becoming interested in religion. Schultz's spiritual awakening might have had something to do with his increasing legal problems.

In late 1934, Schultz found himself labeled an "undercover" Public Enemy Number One by FBI director J. Edgar Hoover. Meanwhile, Schultz's lawyers tried to negotiate a settlement of his tax problems, but federal authorities rebuffed their attempts. On November 28, 1934, Schultz decided he'd had enough of the outlaw life. He surrendered to police in Albany, New York, on his income tax indictment. Schultz spent a few weeks in jail before being released on bail. Upon his release, the Dutchman (as the news media had taken to calling him) held a press conference. The press noted Schultz's lack of sartorial grace and seedy presence. The *New York Times* wrote that he "had a special talent for looking like a perfect example of the unsuccessful man." Schultz himself touched directly on his lack of fashion sensibility. "You take silk shirts now," Schultz told the reporters, "I think only queers wear silk shirts. I never bought one in my life. Only a sucker will pay $15 or $20 for a silk shirt."

Schultz also took the time to deny he was ever a "beer baron" and to express disgust at being labeled a Public Enemy Number One. Schultz's fashion commentary and the *Times'* put-down of his dressing habits are both cited in *Kill the Dutchman!*,

While plotting his trial defense, Schultz had an employee problem to deal with. He suspected Jules Martin—

mastermind of the restaurant rackets—had stolen some $70,000 from him. Martin was sent by train to visit Schultz at a hotel in Cohoes, New York, where he was staying. Under threat of violence, Martin confessed to stealing funds. Schultz personally shot him dead and had the body disposed of. All of this was a backdrop to Schultz's tax trial, which opened April 16, 1935, in Syracuse, New York. The prosecution had a tough time—two dozen witnesses disappeared rather than testify against Schultz. It didn't help that New York was a "wet" state that had been strongly against Prohibition. New Yorkers weren't as likely as, say, residents of "dry" Mississippi, to view bootlegging as a serious crime.

On April 29, 1935, the jury announced it couldn't come to a decision. The justice had to discharge the case and let Schultz go. Schultz was delighted to have beaten the same rap that had put Al Capone behind bars. "This tough world ain't no place for dunces," Schultz told reporters, as quoted in *Kill the Dutchman!*, "And you can tell those smart guys in New York that the Dutchman is no dunce and as far as he is concerned Alcatraz doesn't exist. I'll never see Alcatraz. Al Capone was a dunce for going to Alcatraz."

Schultz's triumph was short-lived. In June 1935, New York Governor Herbert Lehman appointed Thomas Dewey as a special prosecutor. Dewey promptly launched an investigation into Schultz's control of the numbers racket. In addition to this, Schultz was hit with a new series of tax evasion charges. Schultz was set to face trial in small-town Malone, New York. The Dutchman proved to be a wily opponent. He arrived in Malone a week before his trial began and threw money around. He bought meals and drinks for townspeople and ingratiated himself with the locals. Schultz presented the image of an off-beat businessman who was being taken to task over a regrettable tax mix-up. Small-town Malone residents sympathized with Schultz's plight. On August 1, 1935, the jury voted nine to three for acquittal. One day later, they voted not guilty. Schultz was a free man.

Just because he had beaten the rap a second time, however, didn't mean Schultz was completely off the hook. Mayor LaGuardia made it clear Schultz wasn't welcome to return to New York. There was also the Dewey investigation to worry about. Schultz retreated to Connecticut and took up residence at various hotels in Bridgeport. Accompanied by his loyal bodyguard, Bernard "Lulu" Rosenkrantz, Schultz found himself the toast of the local high society. He was invited to cocktail parties and other soirees with the upper crust, where he was treated like a naughty boy who had beaten the system.

While Schultz kept his spirits up, some of his underlings were looking to jump ship. Bo Weinberg, in particular, became concerned that Schultz's empire was falling apart. The Dutchman's legal problems were costing a fortune, and he wasn't able to keep a steady eye on business. Weinberg allegedly approached New Jersey mobster Abner "Longy" Zwillman for assistance. Zwillman arranged a meeting between Weinberg and Schultz's old street acquaintance, Lucky Luciano. Weinberg offered Luciano insider information that would allow him to take over Schultz's business concerns. In return, Weinberg wanted a share of the profits.

Luciano heard Weinberg out, then called a meeting at his Waldorf Towers headquarters in New York. Those in attendance included Zwillman, Joe Adonis, Frank Costello, Meyer Lansky, Louis "Lepke" Buchalter, Tommy Lucchese, and Vito Genovese. Luciano explained Weinberg's proposal to the assembled gangsters. The mobsters were excited by the idea of seizing and dividing up Schultz's empire. They mulled over how this could be achieved. Unaware of this scheming, Schultz asked for a meeting with Luciano. He rambled on about his newfound commitment to Catholic spirituality, which further convinced Luciano that Schultz was not paying sufficient attention to business.

For all his newfound spirituality, Schultz remained a dangerous thug. He found out about Weinberg's betrayal and was infuriated. Schultz's crew staked out Zwillman's mansion in New Jersey. On September 9, 1935, Weinberg was intercepted, either on his way to or from a meeting with Zwillman. Schultz's men forced him into a car and drove him off to see the Dutchman. According to rumor, Schultz killed the traitorous mobster with his bare hands. Another rumor suggested Weinberg had been tossed into the East River, still alive, with his feet encased in cement. A couple of weeks after Weinberg's disappearance, Schultz moved from Connecticut to Perth Amboy in New Jersey. There, he managed to get arrested on "suspicion of being a fugitive."

On October 1, 1935, Schultz was bailed out of jail. Afraid to enter Manhattan proper for fear of being arrested again, Schultz moved his headquarters to Newark, New Jersey. He took a suite at the Robert Treat hotel and settled on the local Palace Chop Shop restaurant as his base of operations. Rosenkrantz, joined by another bodyguard, Abe Landau, kept a close eye on everyone who wanted to see the boss. A few days after he was released from jail, a federal grand jury indicted Schultz on a variation of older charges. The government couldn't arrest him on the same felony tax evasion counts because to do so would constitute double jeopardy. So instead, the U.S. government hit Schultz with 11 different misdemeanor counts for failing to file income tax returns in 1929, 1930, and 1931.

By this point, Schultz had found a new target for his wrath. He became fixated on Tom Dewey. Dewey's heavily pregnant wife began to receive threatening phone calls. FBI chief J. Edgar Hoover sent Dewey a letter, citing underworld rumors that the prosecutor had been targeted for death. Schultz made it clear he wanted Dewey murdered. Killing a special prosecutor went against the gangster code, however. It had long been a mob tenet not to harm prosecutors, policemen, journalists, and politicians. This had less to do with morality than the fear of massive retaliation and exposure.

Luciano was approached by Albert Anastasia, a sadistic mobster known as "The Mad Hatter" or the "Lord High Executioner of Murder, Inc."—a collection of killers for hire. Anastasia informed Luciano that Schultz had ordered him to target the special prosecutor. Schultz wanted Anastasia to keep watch on Dewey's apartment, with an eye toward assassinating the prosecutor. Luciano held a meeting with gangster chiefs. A lengthy discussion ensued, in which it was decided that killing Dewey was technically possible (Anastasia had discovered the prosecutor spent a few minutes each morning checking phone messages in a local pharmacy before going to his office, which offered an ideal opportunity for a hit), but extremely inadvisable. Murdering Dewey would bring way too much heat down on the mob.

A slightly different take suggests Schultz himself attended Luciano's meeting to personally lobby for Dewey's murder. When his peers vetoed the idea, Schultz flew into a rage and announced he was going to take care of the special prosecutor himself. He stormed off, to the alarm of his fellow mobsters. The latter decided on the spot that Schultz had to be murdered in order to prevent a hit on Dewey. On the evening of October 23, 1935, two assassins burst into the Palace Chop House in Newark, New Jersey where Schultz had set up his temporary HQ. The gunmen rushed into the dining area—empty but for three Schultz associates (Abe Landau, Lulu Rosenkrantz, and Otto "Abbadabba" Berman)—and sprayed the room with fire. Schultz himself was shot in the bathroom. Despite being hit at point-blank range, no one died in the initial attack. Berman lingered for a few hours then expired, followed by Landau.

Schultz, lying delirious in a hospital bed in Newark, held out a little longer. Schultz had taken a bullet in the stomach and infection had set in. He was running an extremely high fever and babbling incoherently. Police thought this was a golden moment to capture some deathbed confessions. They installed stenographers by Schultz's side to take down his every word. The resulting verbal tapestry proved of no use at all to police, but made a fascinating document. Schultz rambled:

There are only 10 of us and there are 10 million fighting somewhere in front of you, so get your onions up and we will throw up the truce flag. . . . Communistic . . . strike . . . baloney. . . . Please, he eats like a little sausage baloney maker . . . please crack down on the Chinaman's friends and Hitler's commander . . . mother is the best bet and don't let Satan draw you too fast.

On the afternoon of October 24, 1935, Schultz uttered his last intelligible words, "French-Canadian bean soup!" then lapsed into a coma and died. Rosenkrantz died a few hours after his boss expired. Some three decades later, Schultz's deathbed ramblings would become the basis of a book by cult-writer William Burroughs. As bizarre as Schultz's last words were, they captured the fiercely individualistic spirit of a maverick gangster who followed no one's lead but his own.

See Also: Jewish Gangsters; Numbers Racket

Further Reading

Rich Cohen, *Tough Jews: Fathers, Sons and Gangster Dreams*, 1998.

Nate Hendley, *Dutch Schultz: The Brazen Beer Baron of New York*, 2005.

Paul Sann, *Kill the Dutchman!*, 1971.

Dutch Schultz deathbed transcript, *New York Times*, October 26, 1935.

Burton Turkus and Sid Feder, *Murder, Inc.: The Story of the Syndicate*, 1951.

SHAKUR, SANYIKA (1963–)

On June 15, 1975, Sanyika Shakur (birth name, Kody Scott) graduated from sixth grade in South Central Los Angeles. Whereas most kids might celebrate with soft drinks and a dance party, Shakur and

Sanyika Shakur, aka "Monster" Kody Scott, at Pelican Bay prison in June 1993. [AP Photo/Susan Ragan]

his comrades marked their graduation by committing several felonies. The youthful crew stole a car, then smoked pot and drank beer. At a certain point in the evening, Shakur was viciously beaten by his friends, but this but was no cause for alarm. He was simply being "jumped in"—a gang initiation. After the beating, Shakur's pals gathered up some weapons. Shakur was given a pump action shotgun. The crew drove into the neighborhood of a warring gang and let loose with a furious barrage. Shakur watched in delight as people dropped from his shots. "It was the proudest moment in my life," he later wrote. At the time, Shakur was 11 years old.

In many ways, Shakur's career arc was similar to that of his mentor, Stanley "Tookie" Williams, an early leader of the Crips gang that Shakur belonged to:

violent youth, incarceration, then enlightenment. They also shared a penchant for brutality, "I have pushed people violently out of this existence," Shakur matter-of-factly notes in his autobiography.

Born in 1963, Shakur was the product of an affair between his mother and Dick Bass, a professional football player with the Los Angeles Rams. If Shakur inherited any athletic skills, he didn't use them. Instead, he gravitated toward gang culture at a very early age. At 12, he was already hanging around with Tookie Williams, who was a full decade older. Shakur was impressed by Williams's muscular physique and macho attitude. Among other activities, the pair smoked PCP together. "I learned a lot of Crip etiquette from Tookie," Shakur later noted.

At age 13, in 1977, Shakur acquired the nickname "Monster" after inflicting a particularly severe beating on an unlucky victim. He had finished schooling by this point to concentrate on being a full-time gangbanger. To this end, Shakur was a proud member of the "Eight Tray Gangster Crips"; Eight-Tray means "83"—the street number in the gang's neighborhood.

Though he kept a loaded .44 Bulldog pistol on him at all times, Shakur insists that the gangbanging milieu was far less dangerous in the late 1970s than in later decades. Gangs such as the Bloods and Crips were smaller and relied on pistols and shotguns to settle their grievances, not automatic weapons, which were expensive and hard to come by. Also, crack cocaine had yet to arrive on the scene.

At age 15, Shakur was arrested for auto theft and assault and was sentenced to nine months in a youth detention camp. Upon release, he met a young lady named Tamu who became the love of his life. She was soon pregnant. Shakur wasn't much of a father; he was too busy gangbanging. In his autobiography, Shakur cites a mind-numbing litany of shootings, beatings, scouting missions in "enemy" territory, and acts of street bravado. Shakur also presents an almost sociological examination of street gang culture and the importance of maintaining loyalty to your "set." A set is a sub-section of a larger gang, similar to a platoon in the army. As Shakur explains, set members typically adhere to a complicated series of shifting alliances. Sometimes, the Eight Tray Crips allied themselves with a set from the supposedly hated Bloods against another Crip set. Gang bangers are expected to constantly reaffirm allegiance to their set by spray-painting elaborate graffiti, making complicated hand signs, and shouting slogans.

All of this gang activity nearly came to a shattering end on New Year's Eve 1980. That evening, Shakur was ambushed in a parking lot and shot several times at pointblank range by rival gangsters. The latter left Shakur for dead, but he somehow managed to survive.

Shakur recovered from the shooting and resumed gangbanging. While serving time in the early 1980s, he was exposed to black revolutionary writing. A religious figure who went by the name "Muhammad" introduced Shakur to Black Muslim teachings and the militant Black Panther Party.

Paroled on March 7, 1984, Shakur hooked up with Muhammad again, who continued to supply him with reading material, including the *Autobiography of Malcolm X* and rants from Black Panther leaders. Muhammad taught Shakur that his real enemy was the white power structure, not fellow gangbangers. Shakur was impressed, but remained a gangster at heart. On August 27, 1984, he shot up some rivals. One month later, he was found guilty of one count of mayhem and two counts of attempted murder and given a seven year term. He was shipped to county jail prison, then Chino state penitentiary.

Inside the county jail, Shakur found other mentors. Some prisoners had started a group called Consolidated Crip Organization (CCO), which aimed to unify various squabbling Crip sets. People in the CCO espoused a strong sense of black empowerment and pride, which Shakur embraced.

In the mid-1980s, Shakur served time at Soledad prison and San Quentin. During this period he decided to adopt a new name. He dropped the sobriquet "Monster" and began calling himself

"Sanyika"—a name derived from the east African language of Kiswahili. Shakur continued to read extensively in jail. Although partial to black history, he also devoured works by various left-wing leaders such as Fidel Castro and Mao Tse-Tung. He began to identify with the New Afrikan Independence Movement, which espoused a radical, pro-Afro-American line, and tried to live down his Crips heritage.

After being paroled in November 1988, Shakur returned to South Central L.A. He took a job as a file clerk, rising to assistant loan advisor. He refused to sell drugs with his peers. He reunited with Tamu and his family.

While ostensibly straight, some old habits die hard. In January 1991, Shakur was convicted of assault and grand theft auto after beating a crack dealer and taking his van. Shakur later wrote that the man deserved what he got because he "refused to stop selling his product on my corner." Shakur pled guilty and received seven years.

Shakur spent much of the early 1990s in lockdown. He read the dictionary for amusement and got married to Tamu. He also became a writer. His articulate but brutal autobiography, *Monster,* was a bestseller when released in 1993. In his book, Shakur expressed regret for his early gangster behavior. "Today, no school, library or institution, business, detention center or church is exempt from being touched in some way by the gang activity in South Central," he notes.

Despite his remorse, Shakur has found it difficult to stay on the straight and narrow. In February 2007, he made the Los Angeles police department's "Top 10 Most Wanted Gang Members" list after being suspected of beating a man and stealing his car. One month later, Shakur was arrested. At his May 2008 trial he pled no contest to charges of carjacking and robbery. He was given six years to serve in state prison.

See Also: Bloods; Crips; Williams, Stanley "Tookie"

Further Reading

Mandalit del Barco, "Gang Member Turned Author Arrested in L.A.," *National Public Radio*, February 6, 2009.

Leon Bing, *Do or Die*, 1991.

Patrick Mcgreevy, "Throwing the Book at 'Monster,'" *Los Angeles Times*, February 15, 2007.

Sanyika Shakur (aka Monster Kody Scott), *Monster: The Autobiography of an L.A. Gang Member*, 1993.

SIEGEL, BENJAMIN "BUGSY" (1906–1947)

Flashy, womanizing Benjamin "Bugsy" Siegel helped put Las Vegas on the map as an epicenter of legal gambling and tawdry excess. Siegel was dangerous, erratic, and extremely impulsive—traits that helped propel him into the elite ranks of the underworld, but later turned him into a liability.

The Siegel's most unique quality was his vision: whereas other gangsters were content to act like pirates, ravaging and pillaging businesses for quick profits with no thought to the future, Siegel was determined to lay the foundations of a long-lasting gambling empire. He envisioned a hotel/casino, in the middle of the Nevada desert that would offer games of chance and top-of-the-line entertainment in an atmosphere of affordable luxury. Siegel paid for this vision with his life, but can be credited

Benjamin "Bugsy" Siegel. [Library of Congress]

with turning Las Vegas—once a dreary desert town—into a gambling Mecca.

This underworld visionary was born February 28, 1906, in a poor neighborhood in Brooklyn. His parents were Russian Jews. Siegel joined a street gang as a boy (par for the course in the area he grew up in) and started stealing. Siegel teamed up with another juvenile delinquent named Moe Sedway. The two budding thugs settled on extortion as a prime way to make some fast cash: the pair would approach push cart operators and threaten to burn their merchandise if they didn't pay "protection" money on the spot.

At some point, Siegel struck up a friendship with a third Jewish boy, Meyer Lansky. Temperamentally, the two had little in common: Siegel was handsome, charming, and action-oriented, whereas Lansky was stolid, quiet, and more of a thinker than a thug. Nonetheless, each of the two budding gangsters saw something in the other man that he admired and respected. When Prohibition became law in 1920, Siegel and Lansky joined forces and entered the bootlegging business.

According to his FBI file, Siegel quickly rose to the top of the bootlegging business thanks to "his ruthlessness and ability to handle men." The same file notes that Siegel picked up the nickname "Bugs" because "he was regarded by his intimate acquaintances as insane along certain lines." At the time, "bugs" was slang for "crazy." Siegel earned this disparaging sobriquet for his tendency to explode in rage "at the slightest provocation," according to the FBI. Being filled with rage did have its advantages. Siegel channeled his anger into murder and became an accomplished hit-man for the fledgling Siegel/Lansky mob. "Siegel and Lansky shared the dictatorial powers of the gang but Siegel was responsible for the terroristic practices of their group," noted the FBI.

As a young adult, Siegel stood 5'9" and weighed around 160 pounds. He had dark brown hair and was quite good-looking. He could be charming when he wanted to be, but remained a thug at heart. For example, during the 1920s he was arrested for a variety of offences, including rape and carrying a concealed weapon. Siegel beat the rape rap and married his childhood sweetheart, Esther Krakower, on January 28, 1929. Marriage, however, didn't stop Siegel from pursuing women and keeping mistresses. He would remain sexually insatiable all of his life.

On April 15, 1931, Siegel took part in one of the most spectacular mob hits of the day: the murder of Giuseppe Joe "The Boss" Masseria in a Coney Island restaurant. Masseria was killed on the orders of Salvatore Maranzano, another crime leader with whom he was at war. Siegel was part of the four-man death squad that dispatched Masseria.

Siegel himself was the target of underworld violence. On November 9, 1932, a soldier from a rival gang lowered an explosive device down the chimney of a Manhattan house used by Siegel and Lansky as their headquarters. The bomb got stuck so its explosive force was largely contained. Nonetheless, Siegel suffered "rather severe head injuries," according to his FBI file. "Siegel still has the scars on his head caused by the flying bricks. One of these scars, about 1.5 inches long on the upper side (left) of his head is visible through his thinning hair."

In 1937, following the repeal of Prohibition, Siegel sold off his liquor interests and headed west to California. He invested mob money in hotels, restaurants, and real estate and helped organize a racing wire service that relayed sports information to bookies in the east, who used it for their gambling operations. Rumor suggests Siegel also spent time in Mexico setting up heroin smuggling rings. Siegel was supposed to answer to local Los Angeles mob boss Jack Dragna, but he mostly went his own way. He had a reputation for brutality that even gave crime bosses pause.

Siegel rented a mansion in the L.A. area and moved in his wife and two daughters. He continued to womanize and enjoy the southern California high life. He particularly liked hanging out with the Hollywood elite. He was introduced to the latter by a former childhood pal turned movie star named George Raft. Thanks to Raft, Siegel was soon rubbing shoulders with movie stars such as Clark Gable, Jean Harlow, Gary Cooper, and others. Around such an illustrious crowd, Siegel toned down his gangster act and turned on the charm. He began entertaining notions of acting in movies himself.

Even as he partied with movie stars, Siegel looked after the interests of the underworld. In the fall of 1939, Lansky requested that Siegel murder Harry "Big Greenie" Greenberg, a mobster turned police informant who had fled to California. The murder was carried out on November 22, 1939, by a team led by Siegel. Siegel was arrested for Greenberg's death and put on trial. Although Siegel was acquitted, the trial churned up a huge amount of publicity. Reporters delved into Siegel's past and drew out his old nick-name. The press began to refer to Siegel as "Bugs" or "Bugsy" in print. Siegel hated this nickname and would physically attack anyone who said it to his face.

During the Second World War, Siegel kept busy with a number of tasks. Among other activities, he ran a manufacturing plant, organized drug smuggling from Mexico, and poked around Nevada on behalf of his mob superiors. Desperate to raise tax revenues during the Depression, Nevada legalized casino gambling in 1931. Over a decade later, the legal gambling industry was still underdeveloped. There were a few casinos and gambling dens in Las Vegas, but it remained a sleepy backwater. The larger hotel/casinos were relatively upscale, but still exuded a hick cowboy air.

William Wilkerson wanted to break this mould. The founder of the *Hollywood Reporter* newspaper and a string of upscale nightclubs in L.A., Wilkerson planned to create a hotel/casino that would be different from anything in Vegas at the time. The hotel/casino he envisioned would feature the best amenities, including a restaurant, a pool, a café, tennis courts, and gaming rooms, and attract celebrities and high rollers. Guests would be entertained by top musicians and singers. There wouldn't be a hint of cowboy décor or ambience.

Wilkerson picked up some investment funds for this project from the underworld. In the mid-1940s, Lansky, Siegel, and 20 other partners, including Moe Sedway, founded The Nevada Project Corporation. The Corporation would be the vehicle by which the mob helped fund Wilkerson's hotel/casino project. Lansky asked Siegel to oversee the Corporation's investment in the Nevada sands.

While this was going on, Siegel was also heavily involved with a temperamental new mistress named Virginia Hill. A brunette, Alabama-born siren Hill was notorious for throwing showy parties in Los Angeles. Gorgeous and short-tempered, Hill was also a courier for the mob, moving huge amounts of money from the United States to secret accounts in Europe.

Siegel's FBI report rather prissily refers to Hill as a woman who "wears daring clothes, smokes and drinks excessively, uses foul language and considerable makeup, speeds money freely." The Bureau described her reputation as "bad, promiscuous." All of which seemed to appeal to Siegel, who was soon cavorting around town with the brunette vixen. Siegel and his wife, meanwhile, split up.

Back in Vegas, construction on Wilkerson's dream hotel/casino began in early 1946. Crews worked night and day at the massive site. Siegel became more closely involved in the project. Even though building supplies were hard to come by in post-war Nevada, Siegel managed to get his hands on black-market materials. Wilkerson was supposed to be Siegel's boss, but Bugsy was soon chafing under his leadership. Siegel started ordering changes without seeking Wilkerson's approval. Some of these changes deviated from the blue-prints for the hotel/casino, but Siegel didn't care.

The hotel/casino was now dubbed "The Flamingo," Siegel's pet name for Hill. As Siegel gained more control over the Flamingo, he began spending money with manic glee. He insisted on the finest materials, such as rare wood and expensive marble, and was constantly altering plans and changing his mind about aspects of construction. Ironically, Siegel was likely the victim of petty racketeers. It was rumored that shady contractors sold goods to Siegel at inflated prices, only to steal them from the worksite and then sell them back to the distracted gangster. Siegel was so wrapped up in his mistress and his dream casino that he was oblivious to such thievery.

Costs for the Flamingo soared, eventually nearing $6 million, a staggering amount of money in the late 1940s. Siegel shuttled back and forth between Los Angeles and Las Vegas, all the while dealing with increasingly nervous mob investors. The underworld was deeply unhappy with the cost overruns on the project and openly questioned whether the hotel/casino would be a success. Siegel's legendary charm didn't assuage them. "Benjamin 'Bugs' Siegel has just about run out of 'show money,'" noted an FBI memorandum from the era. Even as FBI director J. Edgar Hoover publicly denied the very existence of organized crime, his minions kept close tabs on several gangsters, including Siegel. A report from Siegel's FBI file read:

During the evening of August 22, 1946, Special Agent [blacked out] observed Benjamin "Bugs" Siegel and his mistress Virginia Hill at the House of Murphy, a well-known eating place, at Fourth and LaCienega, Beverly Hills, California. Siegel was observed to leave the House of Murphy Café at approximately 10 p.m. in a Pontiac automobile bearing the license plate no. 97 S 764. Siegel was loosely surveilled (sic) to 816 North Kenmore.

Throughout late 1946, Siegel and Wilkerson scrounged up cash from banks and mobsters alike to keep construction going. Under extreme pressure from his underworld partners, Siegel doubled the size of the workforce and paid extravagant overtime rates to encourage productivity. Siegel also foolishly moved up the opening date of the Flamingo from March 1, 1947 (the date Wilkerson preferred) to December 26, 1946.

Sure enough, the Flamingo opened the day after Christmas, even though the facility was not complete. A large crowd of local residents turned out (partly out of curiosity) but only a handful of celebrities, aside from the ubiquitous George Raft. Construction was still going on during the opening, and the dealers working the casino tables were raw and unsteady. The Flamingo lost money on its opening night, and continued losing money for

several days after. The place might have recouped costs by renting out expensive hotel rooms, except the hotel wasn't finished and there was nowhere for guests to stay. Far from being a cash-cow, the Flamingo was draining mob coffers. Siegel shut the place down in late January 1947, so workers could finally finish construction. Lansky and his underworld partners were not happy.

On March 1, 1947, the Flamingo was reopened. The hotel was finally done and the operation began making money. Still, the mob wasn't satisfied. Lansky and other crime bosses wanted Siegel to promptly pay them back the millions he had borrowed, plus interest. Siegel refused, telling the bosses he would pay on his terms and schedule. It was typical, impulsive Siegel, thumbing his nose at some of the most powerful gang bosses in the country.

By this point, Siegel's checks were bouncing. In the spring of 1947, two huge checks—one for $100,000, the other for $50,000—were returned to him. The checks had been made out by Siegel to Del. E. Webb Construction, the company that built the Flamingo. The $100,000 check had its payment stopped while the $50,000 check was returned for insufficient funds.

In June 1947, Hill and Siegel got into a violent quarrel. He allegedly beat her, leaving bruises that lasted for weeks. Hill overdosed on drugs after the argument, was taken to hospital, then set to Europe after her release. This incident didn't mark the end of Siegel and Hill's relationship. In fact, Siegel was sitting on a couch in Hill's Beverly Hills mansion, reading a paper, when he was killed. On June 20, 1947, a sniper with a .30 caliber military M1 carbine snuck into Hill's backyard and shot Siegel four times. The steel-jacketed bullets hit him with such force they knocked out one of his eyes, which police located about 15 feet from his body.

In an interview with a district attorney, published in the *Los Angeles Herald and Express* on June 27, 1947, Siegel's distraught ex-wife Esther described Bugsy as "a good husband, a good father to our two daughters and a splendid man. . . . I never heard a single soul who didn't love him. Even after the divorce we remained on the best of terms." It was never clear who ordered Siegel's murder. Lansky always denied involvement, although he was one of the investors closet to Siegel.

In some ways, Siegel had the last laugh. The Flamingo quickly got over its growing pains and proved to be a massive draw. Soon, the mob was pouring money into Las Vegas. By the early 1960s, the city was dotted with huge casino/hotels that offered legal gambling amidst luxurious accommodations, just like the Flamingo.

See Also: Jewish Gangsters; Lansky, Meyer

Further Reading

Federal Bureau of Investigation report on Bugsy Siegel
(http://foia.fbi.gov/foiaindex/siege.htm)

Robert Lacey, *Little Man: Meyer Lansky and the Gangster Life*, 1991.

"Murder in Beverly Hills," *TIME*, June 30, 1947.

"Mrs. Siegel Tells of Romance and Life With 'Bugsy'" *Los Angeles Herald and Express*, June 27, 1947.

V

VALACHI, JOSEPH (1904–1971)

There were underworld turncoats before Joseph Valachi—Abe "Kid Twist" Reles comes to mind. But never before had a full-member of the U.S. Mafia come forward and revealed so many secrets to authorities. Some critics questioned how much Joseph Valachi really knew, and suggested he merely mouthed information police already had on file for the benefit of the press. Even so, Valachi remains a fascinating figure: the man who depicted the inner workings of one of the most secretive crime societies in America.

Valachi was born September 22, 1904, in the then-thriving Italian community of East Harlem, New York City. Valachi's father was an alcoholic pushcart peddler and wife beater. A school truant, Valachi became a petty criminal when he was still a boy. From 1919 to 1923, he was the getaway driver for a burglary gang that committed hundreds of crimes. Throughout the 1920s, Valachi alternated between burglary

Joseph Valachi testifies to a U.S. Senate rackets subcommittee of the inner workings of the crime organization, 1963. [AP photo/stf]

sprees and stints in jail. His activities drew the attention of more established criminals in the city.

In the late 1920s , the vicious Castellammarese War erupted between Sicilian-American gang leaders Salvatore Maranzano and Joe "The Boss"

Masseria. Both gangsters were eager to bolster their ranks. This is how Valachi wound up getting formally inducted into Maranzano's gang.

In late 1930, Valachi was taken to a private house, where he found himself in a room with 40 other gangsters, sitting around a rectangular table. Valachi recognized rising mobsters such as Thomas Lucchese, Joe Bonanno, and Joe Profaci. Valachi was introduced to Maranzano, then asked to sit down. He did as he was told. On the table in front of him rested a .38 caliber pistol and a knife. Maranzano began the induction ritual. In a private memoir written decades later that became the basis of a book called *The Valachi Papers*, Valachi recalled the intensity of the moment: Speaking in Italian, Maranzano told Valachi that the weapons "represent that you live by the gun and the knife and you die by the gun and knife," wrote Valachi. Valachi was instructed to put his fingers together to form a cup. A piece of paper was placed in his hands, which was set alight. As it flickered, Valachi was required to say, "This is the way I will burn if I betray the secret of this Cosa Nostra" in Italian, recorded Valachi.

Cosa Nostra—Italian for "our thing"—was the name Maranzano's mobsters used to describe their organization. The term "Mafia" was frowned on. It was seen as a foreign expression that referred to organized crime in Sicily. Valachi was told to value Cosa Nostra over family, friends, religion, and country. He was also expected to live by the code of omerta—silence. If caught by authorities, he was supposed to reveal nothing nor help the police in any way. In addition, Valachi was instructed not to sleep with other members' wives, on pain of death, he recalled in his memoir.

After another ritual, Maranzano announced that Bonanno would serve as Valachi's "godfather"—someone who would watch out for him. Bonanno pricked Valachi's trigger finger, drawing blood, as Maranzano intoned, "This blood means that we are now one family," wrote Valachi.

According to Valachi, the whole ceremony took about 10 minutes. When all the rituals were over, food was brought in and the men feasted. In spite of the colorful pageantry, Valachi's initial duties with the Mafia were anything but glamorous. Among other chores, he served as a bodyguard and chauffeur for higher ranking mobsters. During his whole criminal career, Valachi never rose above the level of "soldier"—the lowest rank in the Mafia hierarchy. Nonetheless, by virtue of Mafia membership, Valachi did get to witness underworld events of historic proportions, if only as a bystander.

For example, in the summer of 1931, following the murder of Joe "The Boss" Masseria in a Coney Island restaurant, Maranzano held a mass meeting. In front of hundreds of gangsters, including Valachi, Maranzano outlined his vision of an orderly underworld. He divided New York City's Mafia into five "families" and proclaimed himself "capo di tutti capi"—boss of the bosses. Maranzano himself was murdered shortly after this meeting, but the structure he established endured.

Valachi was called to perform his first "hit" as a Mafia member in late November 1932. The target was a man named Michael Reggione (aka "Little Apples"), whom Valachi didn't know. Valachi carried out the hit and, over the next three decades, committed roughly

30 additional murders (he wasn't sure of the exact total). Valachi also engaged in a variety of other rackets, including loan sharking, numbers, gambling, and slot machines, among others. During World War II, he dealt in black market ration and gasoline stamps. After the war, he got into jukeboxes in a big way. He "earned a living" in mob parlance, but wasn't particularly affluent and certainly was no powerhouse in the Mafia leadership.

In addition to other scams, Valachi also dealt drugs, which went against Mafia principles. Officially, the Mafia was opposed to drug trafficking for fear of incurring stiff penalties. Unofficially, many Mafia members found the enormous profits in the illegal drug business too alluring to ignore. The Bureau of Narcotics (forerunner of the Drug Enforcement Administration) started keeping tabs on Valachi in the 1940s. Valachi's record with the Bureau of Narcotics stated that he "wholesales heroin to major Mafia traffickers on the Upper East Side of NYC." Valachi's record, and scores of others, was listed in the 2007 book, *Mafia*, which compiled criminal profiles drawn up by the Bureau of Narcotics.

In early 1956, Valachi was arrested on drug charges. Found guilty, he was given five years in jail. Valachi got out on bail pending an appeal, then his conviction was reversed. Following this close call, Valachi plunged back into the drug trade and was arrested again in November, 1959. This time, he jumped bail and hid out. Learning that his Mafia masters were displeased with him, Valachi decided to take his chances at trial. He turned himself in, and promptly drew a 15-year sentence, to be served at the federal penitentiary in Atlanta.

In August 1961, Valachi went through a new drug trial in New York, for which he received another 20 years, to be served concurrently with his first sentence. Upon returning to Atlanta, Valachi was unnerved to find himself ostracized by imprisoned Mafia boss Vito Genovese. Genovese, who had a lot of power over other incarcerated Mafiosi, suspected Valachi was going to turn informer. Valachi caught wind of this and began to fear for his life. Even though Valachi had loyally served the underworld for decades, he was certain he was going to be murdered.

On June 22, 1962, at 7:30 a.m., Valachi was approached by a fellow convict named John Saupp. Saupp meant no harm, but Valachi mistook him for a Mafia assassin. In rage and terror, Valachi grabbed an iron-pipe from a jail-yard construction site. Wielding the pipe like a club, he attacked Saupp and viciously beat him. The shocked convict didn't have a chance to fight back. Saupp lingered for a couple days in the hospital, but eventually succumbed to his injuries.

Following this assault, Valachi was transported to Westchester County Jail, north of New York City. It was there he began to tell authorities what he knew about organized crime. It's unclear why Valachi broke omerta. Valachi himself claimed he wanted to warn the public about the menace posed by Cosa Nostra. This seems rather unlikely, in light of Valachi's lengthy career as a criminal. A more likely explanation is that Valachi hoped that by talking he could avoid a death sentence for killing Saupp. Coming forward also gave Valachi a feeling of being important. After a lifetime spent toiling in the Mafia's lower ranks, Valachi was treated as a criminal superstar by the federal government.

In September and October 1963, Valachi testified before a U.S. Senate subcommittee chaired by Senator John McClellan that was investigating organized crime. Valachi was guarded by scores of federal marshals to prevent anyone from collecting the $100,000 "contract" the Mafia had put on his head.

Valachi described the Mafia's structure to the subcommittee: it was divided into "families" run by bosses assisted by underbosses and consiglieres (advisors). As a soldier, Valachi was one of several thugs that made up a Mafia "crew" or regime. This crew carried out the mob's dirty work, under the supervision of a "caporegime" or capo.

Valachi explained that the Mafia was ruled by a board of 9–12 top bosses, "The Commission." With Maranzano's ill-fated attempt at dictatorship in mind, there was no one single boss of the whole organization. According to *The Valachi Papers*, the Mafia boasted 5,000 members across the United States at the time of Valachi's defection.

Some of the information Valachi gave was erroneous. He repeated the myth of the "Night of the Sicilian Vespers" (a supposed nationwide purge of old-time Mafia members that followed Maranzano's murder) and was known to get names wrong. His testimony also gave the erroneous impression that the Mafia was as rigidly organized and hierarchical as the U.S. government or police departments. This was incorrect; the very strength of organized crime is its fluidity. Alliances are forged, only to be broken or abandoned, as old enemies become new allies and vice-versa. Although bosses have a huge amount of power within their own families, their ability to influence or control events outside their purviews (such as rackets run by a rival

family) is limited. The Mafia chain of command can sometimes be blurry as well, with some mob leaders taking a direct hand in street crimes (as in case of Salvatore Gravano or "Sammy the Bull"—a well ensconced mobster in the 1980s who enjoyed personally taking part in hits).

The biggest question around Valachi, however, was how a lowly soldier could know so much about upper level Mafia management. It has been suggested that federal authorities used Valachi as a "mouthpiece." According to this theory, Valachi simply echoed information about top Mafia leaders that the government wanted to put on record, but that he himself couldn't have possibly known about. As the book *American Mafia*, written by former Chicago commander of police detectives Thomas Reppetto notes, some mobsters were contemptuous of Valachi's recall. Mafia boss Joseph Bonanno famously compared Valachi's committee appearance to, "a New Guinea native who had converted to Catholicism, describing the inner workings of the Vatican," noted Reppetto.

Although the veracity of some of Valachi's observations was dubious, he did throw a light on day-to-day Mafia practices. Mafia members, he revealed, weren't paid a salary (though some members receive pay for phony "no-work" or "no-show" jobs with legitimate companies). Membership in the Mafia was considered remuneration enough, Valachi explained. "Made" Mafiosi, such as himself, were expected to generate their own income and give a cut of their proceeds to the mobster above them. Being a formal member of the Mafia meant having the support of the "Family" behind you. Whereas common criminals had to constantly worry about arrest, Mafia members could count on sympathetic policemen, judges, and politicians who were in the pay of their family.

Mafiosi were "connected" in other ways as well; they had access to rackets that were out of reach of ordinary criminals and could rely on an unlimited number of "associates" for support. Joining the Mafia was like becoming a franchise owner; though opportunities abounded, profits were by no means guaranteed. Valachi also revealed the use of the term "Cosa Nostra," which had previously been a well-kept secret.

In June 1964, the Department of Justice encouraged Valachi to write an autobiography of his life in crime. Valachi diligently spent the next 13 months scribbling away, eventually churning out 300,000 words. Excerpts from this massive work would eventually appear in for *The Valachi Papers*.

Despite the huge bounty on him, Valachi wasn't brought down by Mafia bullets. He died of a heart attack at federal prison in El Paso, Texas, in April 1971. As a legacy, he left behind the first definitive, insider's look at the Mafia. Valachi's confessions also helped squash any lingering doubts as to whether an American Mafia really existed or not. After Valachi's testimony, FBI director J. Edgar Hoover no longer denied the existence of an organized Mafia in the United States. The federal government in general became much more involved in fighting organized crime following Valachi's confessions. That said, it's suspected Valachi not only recited information that had been fed to him by his handlers, but greatly exaggerated the underworld's strength. "Nobody will listen. Nobody will believe. You know what I mean? This Cosa Nostra, it's like a second government. It's too big," Valachi is quoted as saying, in the book that bears his name.

See Also: Mafia; Reles, Abraham "Kid Twist"

Further Reading

Pierre de Champlain, *Mobsters: Gangsters and Men of Honour*, 2004.

"His Life and Crimes," *TIME*, January 17, 1969.

"Killers in Prison," *TIME*, October 4, 1963.

Peter Maas, *The Valachi Papers*, 1968.

Thomas Reppetto, *American Mafia: A History of Its Rise to Power*, 2004.

United States Treasury Department, Bureau of Narcotics, *Mafia*, 2007.

W

WEAPONS

Urban gangsters of the 19th century generally relied on low-tech weapons such as knives, hatchets, brass knuckles, blackjacks (small clubs with a weighted end and a grip), slungshots (a contraption made from rope and a weighted object that worked somewhat like a yo-yo, only with much more devastating impact) and brickbats. A brickbat was simply a chunk of brick or stone that was either thrown or launched from a sling-shot. Occasionally, Victorian-era thugs would also use revolvers, rifles, and shotguns.

The latter three weapons were extremely common among gangsters of the Old West. Early percussion cap revolvers required a complex loading process that involved putting gunpowder and lead balls into each of the pistol's six chambers. The chambers would then be fitted with mercury-filled percussion caps which would ignite the charge when struck by the pistol's hammer. Loading was so laborious that bandits would typically wear a brace of them into battle. Outlaws such as Jesse James

A Ruger Mini-14 .53-caliber semiautomatic rifle and other weapons seized or bought in an undercover operation targeting Los Angeles street gangs in 2007. [AP Photo/Reed Saxon]

carried up to half-a-dozen percussion cap revolvers in their belts so they wouldn't have to reload during an engagement.

Later revolvers, like the Colt Single Action Army pistol, used cartridges that packed gunpowder and a bullet in a single lethal package and were considerably easier to load. Nonetheless, all revolvers were limited in their range and accuracy. When the Dalton gang made their ill-fated raid on Coffeyville, Kansas, in 1892, they relied on Winchester repeating rifles, not revolvers.

The Sicilian Mafia introduced a new firearm into the mix in the form of the "lupara"—a double or single-barreled, sawed-off shotgun, sometimes with a retractable stock. These weapons were originally intended to be used by shepherds to ward off wolves (hence the name "lupara" from "lupus" for wolf), however, it was quickly determined that luparas were equally effective against people.

When New Orleans police chief David Hennessy was gunned down by unknown assailants on October 15, 1890, police found four luparas left at the scene of the crime. Although their range was limited, luparas were devastating at close-quarters and could easily be concealed and carried.

Chicago crime boss Al Capone nearly became a victim of the astonishing leap in firepower demonstrated by gangs during Prohibition. On September 20, 1926, as Capone sipped coffee in the Hawthorne Inn in Cicero, Illinois, a convoy of seven vehicles idled up to the restaurant. As each vehicle drew abreast of the Inn, a group of assassins poked their weapons through the car windows and let loose a blistering broadside. Every vehicle in the convoy took a turn shooting at the Hawthorne's facade. Inside the restaurant, the rounds smashed up bricks, masonry, mirrors, windows, and furniture, but didn't hit Capone. Police would later estimate that over 1,000 rounds had been fired in total.

Amazingly, none of the 60-odd patrons inside the restaurant, including Capone, were killed. A graphic description of this near-massacre is detailed in Laurence Bergreen's book, *Capone: The Man and the Era.*

The weapon of choice in this dramatic assault was the Thompson sub-machine gun, better known as the "Tommy Gun" or "Chicago Piano." The Thompson sub-machine gun represented something new in the underworld. Machine guns had been around since the late 19th century. They were big and bulky, however, and generally required a two-man crew, to shoot, load and carry. Weighing only 10 pounds, the Thompson was light enough for a single operator to use.

Though light, the Thompson was lethal: it had been designed shortly after World War One as a "trench broom"—a weapon that could spray devastation on ranks of soldiers packed in tight quarters. The Tommy Gun shot 800 bullets a minute from a drum or box- shaped magazine. A quick burst was enough to tear a man to shreds.

Although it had been made with military use in mind, Tommy Guns weren't popular with the army. For a start, the weapon wasn't very accurate and gobbled up vast amounts of ammunition. If the military wasn't interested in the weapon, gangsters were. They eagerly snatched up Tommy Guns, sometimes paying hundreds or even thousands of dollars for the weapons on the black market. Capone was quick to realize the potential of the Tommy Gun. His gang used two of them (among other weapons) when they executed seven men in a Chicago garage on Valentine's Day in 1929.

Some gangsters preferred the Browning Automatic Rifle (BAR) over the Tommy Gun. It had a much greater range (Thompson sub-machine guns weren't very accurate beyond 50 yards, whereas BARs could still hit targets at 600 yards) and a deadlier kick. On the other hand, BARs were large and bulky which limited their appeal.

The introduction of crack cocaine in the mid-1980s dramatically escalated the drug war and led to another leap in underworld firepower. Crack gangs funneled their profits into new weapons, particularly Uzi and Mac-10 machine pistols. Like Tommy Guns, these weapons had originally been designed for military use. Uzis and Mac-10s were smaller and more compact than Thompson sub-machine guns, and could spit a huge number of bullets in the general direction of a target. Machine pistols were extremely inaccurate, however, which meant a lot of stray rounds. The end-result was a rising death toll of innocent bystanders, shot during crack gang "drive-by" shootings and ambushes.

Drug gangs in the 1980s were also partial to high capacity automatic or semi-automatic pistols, particularly those made by the Austrian company Glock. Ironically, Glock pistols are also popular with military and police personnel.

Some gangbangers, looking to increase their lethality even further, invested in AK-47 assault rifles. Originally used by the Soviet army, these weapons are a direct descendant of the Browning Automatic Rifle of decades before. AK-47s are highly popular with both soldiers and terrorists alike and have a well-earned reputation for durability, reliability, and stopping power. Observers can only hope that the underworld arms race doesn't accelerate any further and that gangsters of the future don't start using grenade launchers,

tanks, and armored personal carriers to settle their grievances.

See also: Capone, Al

Further Reading

Bryan Burrough, *Public Enemies: America's Greatest Crime Wave and the Birth of the FBI, 1933–1934*, 2004.

Nate Hendley, *Al Capone: Chicago's King of Crime*, 2006.

Nate Hendley, *Bonnie and Clyde: A Biography*, 2007.

T. J. Stiles, *Jesse James: Last Rebel of the Civil War*, 2002.

WILLIAMS, STANLEY "TOOKIE" (1953–2005)

One of the most controversial criminals in American history, Stanley "Tookie" Williams was both a feared gang leader

Stanley "Tookie" Williams in prison, 1993. [AP Photo/J. Patrick Forden]

and an apostle of nonviolence. He helped found the Crips, one of the most dangerous street gangs in the United States, only to become a passionate critic of the gangster lifestyle. A celebrated writer, he was nominated for a Nobel Prize while on death row.

"I grew up in South Central Los Angeles, amidst poverty, street gangs, pimps, prostitutes, police tyranny, illegal drugs, criminality and other social injustices," Williams later wrote on "Tookie's Corner," a website dedicated to his musings. Soon, young Williams was skipping school, hanging around fellow tough kids, and sniffing glue. In the early 1970s, Williams became acquainted with a young black teenager named Raymond Lee Washington. In 1969, Washington founded a group called the Baby Avenue Cribs. Accounts differ as to the nature of this organization. Some researchers believe it was a criminal street gang. Other sources indicate the Cribs had a vague mission of protecting black neighborhoods from predatory gangsters.

In either case, the "Baby Avenue" tag was soon dropped and "Cribs" morphed into "Crips." In 1971, Williams joined the fledgling organization and quickly established himself as one of the gang's leaders. At the time, Williams was building a fearsome persona. He lifted weights obsessively, grew an Afro and handlebar moustache, and strutted about his neighborhood like a preening general.

Another former gang member-turned-author, Sanyika Shakur (aka "Monster Kody Scott"), offered a graphic description of Williams in the late 1970s, "Tookie was a Crip through and through—walk, talk and attitude. He had a Cadillac and never drove it, preferring to walk everywhere . . . his entire living room was filled with weights. No furniture whatsoever, just pig iron. Tookie was huge, beyond belief at the time: 22 inch arms, 58 inch chest and huge tree-trunk legs. And he was dark, Marcus Garvey dark, shiny, slick and strong. He had the physique, complexion and attitude that intimidated most American people." wrore Shakur, in his 1993 autobiography.

According to Shakur, Williams was also fond of the drug PCP, an animal tranquilizer that can put human users into a semi-psychotic daze in which they're immune to pain. In addition, he had no qualms about personally committing violent crimes. By contrast, leaders of traditional Mafia gangs typically let their subordinates handle any dirty work.

On the evening of February 27, 1979, Williams met an acquaintance identified only as "Darryl" in subsequent court documents. Williams introduced Darryl to another man, Alfred Coward, nicknamed "Blackie" because of his dark complexion. Darryl drove Williams in his brown station wagon to a house where a fourth man, James Garrett, lived. Coward followed behind in a 1969 Cadillac. Williams stayed over at Garrett's place from time to time and had personal items at his residence, including a 12-gauge slide action shotgun with a sawed off handle. The two vehicles remained parked outside while Williams retrieved his shotgun. Weapon in hand, Darryl and Williams drove off to another residence, followed again by Coward. The men smoked a PCP-laced cigarette then got back in their respective cars.

Williams, Coward, and Darryl went to yet another man's home, that of Tony Sims in Ponoma, California. Williams left his friends for a time. When he returned, he had a .22 caliber pistol on him, which he placed in the station wagon. Now armed with a pistol and shotgun, the men began discussing various ways to make some fast cash; they quickly settled on robbery.

Darryl and Williams climbed into the station wagon, while Coward and Sims took the Cadillac. Both cars headed out onto the freeway. They exited near Whittier Boulevard and drove to a Stop-N-Go market. Darryl, armed with the .22 pistol Williams had put in his car, and Sims made an abortive attempt to rob the Stop-N-Go; they entered the store but didn't actually steal anything or hold the clerk up. Infuriated, Williams insisted that the group find a new target.

With a renewed sense of mission, the group drove to a 7–11 at 10437 Whittier Boulevard. The clerk on duty was 26-year-old Albert Lewis Owens. His was sweeping up the store parking lot when Williams and Co. arrived in their two vehicles. Owens stopped sweeping and stepped into the 7–11, followed by the four men. Williams got behind Owens, took out his shotgun, and ordered the man into a storage room at the back of the store. Owens was told to lie down. According to court records, three shots were heard. Williams had blasted the hapless clerk twice at point-blank range and put another round through a security video monitor. The murder netted the four men $120 from the store cash register. Back in their cars, Williams allegedly joked about the homicide, explaining that he killed Owens to eliminate any witnesses, and because the clerk was white.

At 5 a.m. on March 11, 1979, Williams committed another violent felony. Brandishing his shotgun once again, Williams broke into the Brookhaven Motel at 10411 South Vermont Avenue in South Central Los Angeles. The motel was run by 76-year-old Yen-l Yang and his 63-year-old wife, Tsai-Shai Yang. The Yangs were recent immigrants from Taiwan. Assisting the two elderly Yangs was their son, Robert Yang. A daughter Yee-Chen Lin, who was visiting her family from Taiwan, also happened to be at the motel.

Once inside the Brookhaven, Williams smashed down a door leading to a private office. He encountered the Yang father, mother, and daughter, and shot them. After shooting the family, Williams raided the cash register—netting about $100—then left. Asleep in another room, Robert Yang was awakened by the sound of gun shots and screams. He raced into the motel office to discover his family lying grievously wounded and the cash register empty. Yang called 911 and two deputies were dispatched to the bloody scene. The deputies reported that Yee-Chen Lin was dead, and that Yen-l Yang and Tsia-Shai Yang were still alive, although horribly injured. Soon after, they, too, died from their wounds.

Deputies on the scene retrieved an expended 12-gauge shotgun shell. In the course of the investigation, police recovered Williams' shotgun. Ballistics matched the shell to the weapon. The serial number on the shotgun was traced back to a purchase record Williams had filled out, in which he used his driver's license for identification purposes. He was promptly taken into custody.

In early 1981, Williams went on trial for robbery and murdering Owens and the Yang family. Among other witnesses, Alfred Coward offered a detailed description of the events surrounding the murder of store clerk Owens. Tony Sims (who didn't speak in court because he wasn't granted immunity) also furnished additional information about Owens's murder.

On March 13, 1981, Williams was found guilty of committing four murders and robbery. The jury recommended the death penalty. Williams's main reaction was to sneer at the jurors, referring to them as "sons of bitches," according to court documents. One month after the verdict, the court sentenced Williams to die. While still proclaiming his innocence, Williams became an inmate at San Quentin State Prison. He wasn't exactly a model prisoner. A 2005 report written by the Los Angeles district attorney's office in response to a petition for clemency cited nearly a dozen violent prison altercations involving Williams. "Williams demonstrated violent behavior consistent with a hardened murderer," stated the report.

For example, in January 1982, Williams on two occasions tossed what the district attorney's office referred to as "chemical substances" at guards. On February 16, 1984, a guard had to fire a warning shot to get Williams to stop beating another prisoner. Four years later, Williams was stabbed in a prison fight. During this period, Williams still maintained the loyalty of some of his associates. In 1981, prior to being convicted, Williams married Bonnie Williams-Taylor, with whom he had a son, Travon Williams.

In 1988, Williams was confined to solitary confinement for his bad behavior. While in "the Hole" Williams began to ponder his violent existence. He started reading extensively and prayed to God. He began to view his violent youth and manhood as destructive and nihilistic, rather than heroic. Williams recognized that many young men like him were caught up in an unending cycle of violence and macho posturing, usually projected against other young black men. Conditions in the inner city would never change unless the gangsters who terrorized their own communities tried to follow a different road.

Williams decided to lead by example and denounce his gangster past. His timing was auspicious; throughout the 1980s, the Crips and other street gangs, such as the Bloods, rose to national prominence. The Crips, Bloods, and other gangs shot it out with automatic weapons on the street while trying to gain dominance in the burgeoning crack trade.

Williams's transformation was a slow process. On July 6, 1993, he took part in a brawl in the prison shower area. A warning shot was fired to break up the melee, and Williams found himself back in solitary confinement. During this spell in the Hole, Williams made a firm commitment to speak out against the perils of gangs and crime. He came up with the idea of writing children's books that would warn kids about the realities of street life and the gangster existence. In 1993, Williams was interviewed in prison by author Barbara Cottman Becnel, who was writing a book on the Crips and Bloods. Williams convinced Becnel to make a video-taped speech of him denouncing gang violence.

According to a 2005 Petition for Clemency, these video-taped remarks were played at an April 1993 "peace summit" featuring 400 male and female gangsters and gang associates in Los Angeles. "It is not an exaggeration when I say that the future of this country is literally tied to the success or failure of anti-violence and anti-gang programs,"

Williams told the assembled crowd. If media reports are to be believed, the young thugs in attendance at the summit greeted Williams' videotaped remarks with rapturous applause. It's unclear, however, if the message Williams was trying to convey took hold among his young listeners.

In 1994, Williams was released from solitary confinement. Using Becnel as his co-author, sounding board, and conduit to the outside world, Williams began writing a series of children's books. His prodigious output included tomes on gangs, drugs, violence, weapons, self-esteem, and community values. These books began appearing in 1996 as part of a series called "Tookie Speaks Out Against Gang Violence." Titles included, *Gangs and Drugs, Gangs and the Abuse of Power, Gangs and Wanting to Belong, Gangs and Self-Esteem,* and *Gangs and Violence.* The overall message in all the books was the same: gang life is a dead end.

On April 13, 1997, Williams made another monumental break with his past. He posted an apology on his Web site (run by Becnel) for having helped found the Crips:

> 25 years ago when I created the Crips youth gang with Raymond Lee Washington in South Central Los Angeles, I never imagined Crips membership would one day spread throughout California, would spread to much of the rest of the world . . . so today I apologize to you all . . . who must cope with dangerous street gangs. I no longer participate in the so-called gangster lifestyle and I deeply regret that I ever did," wrote Williams, on "Tookie's Corner."

Raymond Lee Washington, for his part, was shot dead in 1979.

Williams also took the time to pen a "Letter to Incarcerated Youth, Number One" in which he urged prisoners to educate themselves. "You or I can complain 24x7 about the problems of poverty, drugs, violence, racism and other injustices, but unless we choose to initiate a personal change, we will remain puppets of unjust conditions," stated Williams. Other letters blasted gang members for being mentally enslaved to a violent lifestyle that oppressed them as much as real slavery in America's past.

In 2000, Williams published an online "Protocol for Peace" on his Web site. The protocol was designed to serve as a template for warring gangs that wanted to strike up a truce. The Protocol urged parties to stop "any verbal, written or physical violence against one another," become educated, and stop abusing alcohol and drugs. The Protocol also talked—somewhat wistfully—about establishing mediators, peacekeepers, and neutral "buffer zones."

One year after the Protocol appeared, Williams was nominated for a Nobel Peace Prize, for his anti-gang work. In 2004, Williams published his memoir, *Blue Rage, Black Redemption.* His autobiography followed a familiar arc—childhood poverty, followed by several wild years as a young gangster, followed by enlightenment in prison. It was similar in theme to the much heralded *The Autobiography of Malcolm X*, the 1965 book in which the Black Muslim leader outlined a past as desultory and violent as Williams's.

Williams was successful in attracting many supporters to his side. These supporters didn't claim he was innocent (Williams's guilt was pretty much established beyond doubt), but focused instead on getting him off death row. The movement tried to convince California governor Arnold Schwarzenegger to grant clemency and spare Williams's life. To bolster this request, supporters cited Williams's anti-gang activity and apparent redemption. This was an unusual step; usually, clemency is granted on the basis of innocence, not post-conviction behavior.

The legal establishment was less than impressed by Williams's about-face. In their 2005 report, responding to the clemency petition, the LA district attorney's office claimed that Williams still held fast to certain gangster tenets. For a start, he refused to tell police what he knew about the Crips organization and Crip activity in jail. Williams defended his inaction, on the grounds that telling all would be akin to "snitching." The district attorney's office also pointed out that Williams never apologized to the families of the four people he murdered. In interviews with the media, Williams said he couldn't take responsibility for the murders because he was innocent—a position even his strongest supporters found difficult to swallow. Major organizations, such as the National Association for the Advancement of Colored People (NAACP), and celebrities, such as rapper Snoop Dogg, became involved in the pro-clemency battle. Dogg was seen sporting a "Save Tookie" T-shirt and wrote a song about Williams. Actor Jamie Foxx, meanwhile, portrayed Williams in a flattering TV movie about his life.

In late November 2005, Williams did an interview with the *New York Times*. He was appropriately contrite. "I have a despicable background," he stated. "I was a criminal. I was a co-founder of the Crips. I was a nihilist. . . . I functioned primarily on street wit. I managed to make it to the 12th grade. The teachers were insipid in their methodology. Cripping was all I knew. I lived it. I breathed it. I walked it and talked it," he continued. For all his openness, Williams continued to deny he had actually murdered anyone.

In December 2005, Governor Schwarzenegger held a hearing on clemency. The hearing was a closed-door affair. At the end of it, the governor turned down the petition for clemency. Williams would die as scheduled. In press statements, the governor made it clear that while it was nice that Williams found redemption, he was still a cold-blooded, unrepentant murderer. The governor even questioned the sincerity of Williams's change of heart, pointing out that a book he wrote contained the name of George Jackson, a notorious African American prison thug and activist, on the dedication list.

In one of his last interviews, conducted with radio station Pacifica Radio WBAI, Williams waxed philosophic about his impending execution:

> Well, I feel good and my redemption signs—I got up this morning, I cleansed myself, I prayed, I exercised and now I'm talking to you—or prior to talking to you, I was talking to my mother . . . and my lack of fear of this barbaric methodology of death, I rely upon my faith. It has nothing to do with machismo or manhood or with some pseudo former gang street code . . . yes, I have been a wretched person, but I have redeemed myself,"

Williams told interviewer Kat Aaron, in a radio interview broadcast December 12, 2005.

On December 13, 2005, as 1,000 people milled about holding a vigil,

Williams was executed by lethal injection in San Quentin. Six days later his lifeless body was laid out for viewing. Some 2,000 people filed past his corpse to pay their respects. His funeral packed the Bethel AME church with 1,500 mourners.

Redemption aside, Williams's main legacy—besides his powerful words—is the Crips street gang, now one of the largest of its kind in the United States. "The Crips are a collection of structured and unstructured gangs that have adopted a common gang culture," reads a U.S. Department of Justice backgrounder on gangs. "Crips membership is estimated to consist of between 30,000 to 35,000 individuals, most of whom are African American males from the Los Angeles metropolitan area." The same report notes that the Crips remain—in spite of Williams's best efforts—heavily involved in various felonious activities, including drug dealing, auto theft, burglaries, homicide, and assault.

See Also: Bloods; Crips; Shakur, Sanyika

Further Reading

Leon Bing, *Do or Die*, 1991.

CURTIS, MALLET-PREVOST, COLT AND MOSLE LLP, New York, New York, Petition for Executive Clemency on Behalf of Stanley Tookie Williams, November 8. 2005. http://www.cm-p.com/pdf/executiveclemency.pdf.

District Attorney County of Los Angeles, Los Angeles District Attorney's Response to Stanley Williams' Petition for Executive Clemency, November 16, 2005. http://da.co.la.ca.us/pdf/swilliams.pdf.

Institute for the Prevention of Youth Violence, "Tookie's Corner." http://www.tookie.com.

Sanyika Shakur (aka Monster Kody Scott), *Monster: The Autobiography of an L.A. Gang Member*, 1993.

U.S. Department of Justice, Street Gangs. http://www.usdoj.gov/criminal/gangunit/gangs/street.html.

Stanley Tookie Williams, "Excerpts From an Interview with Stanley Tookie Williams," *New York Times*, December 12, 2005.

Stanley Tookie Williams, interviewed by Kat Aaron, *Wake-Up Call*, Pacifica Radio station WBAI, December 12, 2005.

Glossary

Associate—someone who works with Mafia members but isn't actually in the Mafia

Bookmaking—taking bets (also "making book" or "book")

Capo—mid-level Mafia commander, in charge of a crew

Chicago Piano—1920s term for a Thompson sub-machinegun

Citizen—Mafia term for someone who isn't in the Mafia

Consigliere—an advisor to a Mafia boss

Contract—underworld term for marking someone for assassination, as in "taking out a contract" on someone

Crew—a group of individuals who work for a crime boss

Degenerate gambler—a gambling addict

Drive-by—a shooting in which members of a gang fire out the windows of a vehicle in motion

Forfeiture—term used to describe the seizure of underworld assets (money, property, automobiles, etc.) on the part of law enforcement agencies

Full patch—an official member of an outlaw motorcycle gang

Gat—gun

Hangaround—a potential member of an outlaw motorcycle gang who hasn't reached the prospect stage

Hit—an assassination

La Cosa Nostra—literally "our thing," another name for the U.S. Mafia

Loan shark—someone who provides loans at an exorbitant rate of interest

Made man—a formal member of the Mafia

Moustache Pete—an old-time Mafia boss

No show job—a job, typically in construction or unions, in which a Mafia member receives full pay for no work

Numbers—an illegal lottery

Omerta—Mafia term, meaning silence to authorities in the case of arrest

One percenter—term of pride for outlaw motorcycle gangs; stems from the American Motorcyclist Association's alleged claim that 99 percent of riders were law-abiding citizens

Open the books—practice of inducting a new member of the Mafia

Patch—stylized logo of an outlaw motorcycle gang along with the name of the city or region the chapter is based in, typically worn on the back of a denim or leather jacket

Patch over—process by which members of a smaller outlaw motorcycle gang join a larger, more established gang

Piece—gun

Prospect—a potential member of an outlaw motorcycle gang

Puppet gang—a smaller outlaw motorcycle gang that does the bidding of a larger, more established gang

RICO—Racketeer Influenced and Corrupt Organizations Act, a piece of legislation that makes it illegal to belong to an organization that engages in a pattern of "racketeering" (i.e., criminal activity)

Set—a sub-division of a larger street gang

Shylock—a loan shark

Sit down—Mafia term for a meeting

Skimming—the practice of diverting casino profits before they are taxed (also: skim)

Straightened out—the process of becoming a made man

Taken for a Ride—specifically, the act of kidnapping someone in a vehicle, driving to an isolated locale and murdering him; more generally, a slang term of murder

Vigorish—the rate of interest on a shylock loan (also called "vig")

Whacked—killed

Wiseguy—the term Mafia members use to describe themselves

Bibliography

PRINTED SOURCES

"Accused of Four Murders." *New York Times,* May 12, 1907.

"After the Dalton Gang." *New York Times*, August 1, 1892.

"After the Don: A Donnybrook?" *New York Times*, November 1, 1976.

"After 24 Years on Death Row, Clemency Is Killer's Final Appeal." *New York Times*, December 2, 2005.

"'Alarming Alliance' of Mafia and Street Gang is Broken Up." *New York Times*, December 19, 2007.

"Al Capone Died Here." *Chicago Tribune*, February 15, 2007.

"All Classes Mingle at Colosimo Funeral." *New York Times*, May 16, 1920.

"America's Crusade." *TIME*, September 15, 1986.

"An Archetypal Mob Trial: It's Just Like in the Movies." *TIME*, May 23, 2004.

"Another Train Robbery." *New York Times*, October 14, 1892.

"Anti-Cocaine Bill Passed." *New York Times*, March 29, 1907.

"Antigang 'Role Model' Is Up for a Nobel and Execution." *New York Times*, December 6, 2000.

"Armed, Sophisticated and Violent, Two Drug Gangs Blanket Nation." *New York Times*, November 25, 1988.

Asbury, Herbert. *The Gangs of New York*. New York: Thunder's Mouth Press, 1927.

"Axler and Fletcher Slain On Gang Ride and Bodies are Left in Car," *Detroit Times*, November 27, 1933.

"Bad, Bad Leroy Barnes." *TIME*, December 12, 1977.

"Badfellas." *New York Times*, January 18. 2004.

Barger, Ralph "Sonny" with Keith Zimmerman and Kent Zimmerman. *Hell's Angel: The Life and Times of Sonny Barger and the Hell's Angels Motorcycle Club*. New York: HarperCollins, 2000.

"Barrell Murder Mystery Deepens." *New York Times*, April 20, 1903.

Baum, Dan. *Smoke and Mirrors*. New York: Little, Brown & Company, 1996.

"Bawdy Business." *TIME*, May 25, 1936.

Behr, Edward. *Prohibition: Thirteen Years That Changed America*. New York: Arcade Publishing, 1996.

Bergreen, Laurence. *Capone: The Man and The Era*. New York: Simon & Schuster, Inc., 1994.

"Billy the Kid's Life and Death." *New York Times*, July 31, 1881.

"Billy the Kid's Slayer Thanked." *New York Times*, July 20, 1881.

Bing, Leon. *Do Or Die*. New York: HarperCollins Publishers, 1991.

"Black Hand Manacled At Last." *New York Times*, April 2, 1910.

"Black Hand Suspect Was Bled Himself." *New York Times*, November 13, 1909.

"Blood, Business, 'Honor.'" *TIME*, October 15, 1984.

"Blood in the Streets: Subculture of Violence." *TIME*, April 24, 1972.

"Blowing the Whistle on Gangsta Culture." *New York Times*, December 22, 2005.

Blumenthal, Ralph. *Last Days of the Sicilians*. New York: Simon & Schuster, Inc., 1988.

"Books of the Times; A Don Pays the Price of Carelessness." *New York Times*, May 23, 1991.

"Books of the Times; Illuminating Gang Life in Los Angeles: It's Raw." *New York Times*, July 23, 1993.

Bringing Down the Mob. New York: Henry Holt and Company, 2006.

"Bronx Boy." *TIME*, April 29, 1935.

"Bugging Big Paul." *TIME*, June 10, 1991.

"Bugging the FBI." *TIME*, March 20, 1978.

Bureau of Alcohol, Tobacco, Firearms and Explosives, *Most Wanted, Randy Michael Yager*, February 13, 2009, http://www.atf.gov/wanted/pages/15yager.htm.

Burns, Walter Noble. *The Saga Of Billy the Kid*. New York: Konecky & Konecky, 1953.

Burrough, Bryan. *Public Enemies*. New York: Penguin Books, 2004.

"Capone Coup." *TIME*, May 27, 1929.

"Capone's Week." *TIME*, May 19, 1930.

CBC-TV Web site, "Biker Gangs in Canada." April 5, 2007, http://www.cbc.ca/canada/story/2009/04/01/f-biker-gangs.html.

Centers for Disease Control and Prevention, *Quick Stats: General Information on Alcohol Use and Health*. http://www.cdc.gov/alcohol/quickstats/general_info.htm.

De Champlain, Pierre. *Mobsters: Gangsters and Men of Honour*. Toronto: Harper-Collins Publishers, 2004.

Chicago Historical Society, "Black Sox," http://www.chicagohs.org/history/blacksox .html.

"A Chronicle of Bloodletting." *TIME*, July 12, 1971.

"City Boy." *TIME*, July 25, 1949.

"City Prisons Filled With Drug Victims." *New York Times*, June 11, 1915.

"Clemency For a Crip?" *New York Times*, December 2, 2005.

"Cocaine Evil Among Negroes." *New York Times*, November 3, 1902.

"Cocaine Forbidden in the U.S. Mails." *New York Times*, July 17, 1908.

"The Cocaine Habit." *New York Times*, June 20, 1909.

"Cocaine Habit Horrors." *New York Times*, April 30, 1905.

"Cocaine in Hay Fever." *New York Times*, July 31, 1885.

"The Cocaine Remedy." *New York Times*, August 29, 1885.

"The 'Cocaine' Trademark." *New York Times*, February 25, 1860.

"Cocaine User Shoots Seven." *New York Times*, December 6, 1907.

"Cocaine's Destructive Work." *New York Times*, January 25, 1887.

"Cocaine's Terrible Effect." *New York Times*, November 30, 1885.

Cohen, Rich. *Tough Jews*. New York: Random House, 1998.

"The Conglomerate of Crime." *TIME*, August 22, 1969.

Corbitt, Michael, and Sam Giancana, *Double Deal*. HarperCollins Publishers, 2003.

"Crime and Its Results." *New York Times*, January 6, 1880.

"Crime's 'Mr. Untouchable' Emerges From the Shadows." *New York Times*, March 4, 2007.

"Criminal Justice: Well-Organized Crime." *New York Times*, March 21, 2004.

"Criminal Mastermind." *TIME*, December 7, 1998.

"The Curious and the Police Abound at a Wake for Gotti." *New York Times*, June 14, 2002.

Curtis, Mallet-Prevost, Colt & Mosle LLP, *Petition for Executive Clemency on Behalf of Stanley Tookie Williams,* New York, New York, November 5/2005.

Davis, John H. *Mafia Dynasty: The Rise and Fall of the Gambino Crime Family*. New York: HarperCollins Publishers, 1993.

"The Dead Rabbits At Work Again." *New York Times*, February 12, 1863.

"Death After Battle With Paul Kelly's Gang." *New York Times*, November 27, 1905.

"Decline and Fall of an Empire." *New York Times*, January 17, 1999.

District Attorney County of Los Angeles, *Los Angeles County District Attorney's Response to Stanley Williams' Petition for Executive Clemency*, November 16, 2005.

"Dixie, Doxie & Dewey." *TIME*, February 14, 1938.

"The Don is Done." *New York Times*, January 31, 1999.

"Dr. Farley Becomes Insane." *New York Times*, February 6, 1886.

"Drug Habit Curable, Says Dr. Lambert." *New York Times*, October 7, 1909.

"An East Side Vendetta." *New York Times*, September 17, 1903.

"80s Plot to Hit Giuliani? Mob Experts Doubt It." *New York Times*, October 26, 2007.

"Ellison Convicted of Manslaughter." *New York Times*, June 9, 1911.

"Enforcer Paints Picture of Gotti as a Powerful Don." *New York Times*, February 23, 2006.

Excerpts From an Interview with Stanley Tookie Williams, *New York Times*, December 12, 2005.

"Ex-Mobster of 'Goodfellas' Fame Wanted in California." Yahoo.com news, May 17, 2009.

"Extend Drug Law to Guard the Poor." *New York Times*, November 18, 1910.

Federal Bureau of Investigation, http://www.fbi.gov/.

"Federal Jury Convicts Boscarino." *New York Times*, December 11, 1910.

James O. Finckenauer, *La Cosa Nosta in the United States*, National Institute of Justice, http://www.ncjrs.gov/pdffiles1/nij/218555.pdf.

"Finds Drug Evil Pervades the City." *New York Times*, December 5, 1916.

"For a Third Time, a Jury Fails to Convict Gotti." *New York Times*, September 28, 2006.

"A Fortnight Under the Pure Food Law." *New York Times*, January 13, 1907."

"Founder of East Coast Bloods Is Given 50 Years." *New York Times*, April 15, 2003.

"Gambino Group Seen As Country's Biggest." *New York Times*, March 31, 1984.

"A Game of Casino." *TIME*, January 20, 1958.

"Gangsters Again Engaged in a Murderous War." *New York Times*, June 9, 1912.

"Gannon Finds No Vice in his Own Precinct." *New York Times*, August 30, 1901.

Giancana, Sam, and Chuck Giancana. *Double Cross*. New York: Warner Books, 1992.

"Glum Gorilla." *TIME*, December 19, 1927.

"The Godfathers." *New York Times*, May 5, 1996.

"Goodbye Fellas." *New York Times*, February 27, 2007.

"Good Word for Eastman." *New York Times*, June 21, 1909.

"Gotti Accused of Role in Castellano Slaying." *New York Times*, December 13, 1990.

"Gotti's Angry Words Taped in Prison." *New York Times*, December 15, 2004.

"Governor Schwarzenegger Denies Clemency for Gang Co-Founder." *New York Times*, December 12, 2005.

Gray, Mike. *Drug Crazy*. New York: Random House, 1998.

Greenberg, David. "Civil Rights: Let 'em Wiretap!" *History Network News*, George Mason University, October 22, 2001, http://hnn.us/articles/366.html.

"Hampton Negro Conference." *New York Times*, July 16, 1903.

"Hard Days for the Mafia." *TIME*, March 4, 1985.

"Have No Words of Blame." *New York Times*, October 8, 1892.

"Held Up An Express Train." *New York Times*, July 16, 1892.

Hells Angels Official Web site, http://www.hells-angels.com/.

Hendley, Nate. *Al Capone: Chicago's King of Crime*. Canmore, Alberta: Altitude Publishing, 2006.

Hendley, Nate. *Crystal Meth*. Canmore, Alberta: Altitude Publishing, 2006.

Hendley, Nate. *Dutch Schultz: The Brazen Beer Baron of New York*. Canmore, Alberta: Altitude Publishing, 2005.

Henry Hill's official Web site, http://henryhill90290.tripod.com/.

Hill, Gregg, and Gina Hill. *On the Run: A Mafia Childhood*. New York: Time Warner Book Group, 2004.

"His Life and Crimes." *TIME*, January 17, 1969.

"Hitting the Mafia." *TIME*, June 24, 2001.

"Hold Lupo as Counterfeiter." *New York Times*, November 23, 1909.

"Hold Nine as Pupils of Lupo the Wolf." *New York Times*, December 2, 1910.

"Hoyne Says 1920 World Series Was About to be Fixed." *New York Times*, October 2, 1920.

"Indict Arnold Rothstein." *New York Times*, June 7, 1919.

"Informers Under Fire." *TIME*, April 17. 1972.

"An Inspiration from Death Row." *San Francisco Chronicle*, December 11, 2000.

"Interpret Harrison Law." *New York Times*, June 6, 1916.

"Jailing of Crime Figure Called Telling Blow to Mafia in Philadelphia." *New York Times*, January 18 1987.

"Jesse James's Death." *New York Times*, April 6, 1882.

"Jesse James Shot Down." *New York Times*, April 4, 1882.

"John Gotti Dies in Prison at 61; Mafia Boss Relished the Spotlight." *New York Times*, June 11, 2002.

Johnson, Mayme, and Karen Quinones. *Harlem Godfather: The Rap on My Husband, Ellsworth "Bumpy" Johnson*, Oshun Publishing Company Inc., 2008.

"Jury Hears Gotti Discuss Organization on Tapes." *New York Times*, February 18, 1992.

Katz, Helena. *Gang Wars: Blood and Guts on the Streets of Early New York*. Canmore, Alberta: Altitude Publishing, 2005.

Kill the Dutchman! New Rochelle, NY: Arlington House, 1971.

"Killers in Prison." *TIME*, October 4, 1963.

"The Killing of Jesse James." *New York Times*, November 5, 1879.

"Killing That Made the Wolf an Exile." *New York Times*, February 17, 1910.

Klaus von Lampe, "Organized Crime Research," http://www.organized-crime.de/.

Kobler, John. *Capone: The Life and World of Al Capone*. Cambridge, MA: Perseus Books Group, 1971.

Lacey, Robert. *Little Man: Meyer Lansky and the Gangster Life*. Boston: Little, Brown and Company, 1991.

Lamothe, Lee, and Adrian Humphreys. *The Sixth Family*. Mississauga, ON: John Wiley & Sons Canada, 2006.

Langton, Jerry. *Iced*. Toronto: Key Porter Books, 2007.

"'Last Don' Reported to be First One to Betray Mob." *New York Times*, January 28. 2005.

"Last of the Dalton Gang." *New York Times*, October 6, 1892.

Lehr, Dick, and Gerard O'Neill. *Black Mass*. New York: HarperCollins Publishers, 2000.

"Licit and Illicit Drugs." *Consumer Reports*, 1972, http://www.druglibrary.org/schaffer/Library/studies/cu/cumenu.htm.

"Lords of Dopetown." *New York*, October 25, 2007.

Los Angeles County District Attorney's Office, "Monster Author Pleads No Contest, Sentenced to Six Years Prison," news release, May 5, 2008.

"Losers and Outsiders." *The Nation*, May 17, 1965.

"Low Profile." *TIME*, November 4, 1991.

Lunde, Paul. *Organized Crime*. New York: DK Publishing, 2004.

"Lupo Gang Off to Prison." *New York Times*, February 21, 1910.

"'Lupo the Wolf' Notorious Criminal, Freed by Washington From Ellis Island." *New York Times*, June 12, 1922.

Maas, Peter. *The Valachi Papers*. New York: HarperCollins Publishers, 1968.

"The Mafia: Back to the Bad Old Days?" *TIME*, July 12, 1971.

"The Mafia Big, Bad and Booming." *TIME*, May 16, 1977.

Mannion, James. *The Everything Mafia Book*. Avon, MA: Adams Media Corporation, 2003.

Marsden, William, and Julian Sher. *Angels of Death*. London: Hodder Headline, 2006.

"Masked Men Rob a Train." *New York Times*, September 9, 1881.

McGrew, Jane Lang. *A History of Alcohol Prohibition,* prepared for the National Commission on Marihuana and Drug Abuse, 1972, http://www.druglibrary.org/schaffer/Library/studies/nc/nc2a.htm.

"Meyer Lansky is Dead at 81; Financial Wizard of Organized Crime." *New York Times*, January 16, 1983.

"Milestones." *TIME*, December 19, 2005.

"Millman, Last of Purples, Was Just a 'Tough Punk' To Police, *Detroit News*, November 28, 1937.

"The Minnesota Banditti." *New York Times*, October 14, 1876.

"Missouri Railroad Robbers." *New York Times*, August 13, 1876.

"Mob Metaphysician." *New York Times*, May 25, 1997.

"'Mob Yuppies' Said to Reshape Organized Crime." *New York Times*, April 23, 1988.

"Mobster Recalls Schemes in Days as a Gotti Soldier." *New York Times*, March 1, 2006.

"'Monk' Eastman Caught After Pistol Battle." *New York Times*, February 3, 1904.

"Monk Eastman Free on Prison Parole." *New York Times*, June 20, 1909.

"Monk Eastman Gang All Scattered Now." *New York Times*, June 21, 1909.

"'Monk' Eastman, Gangster, Murdered; Found in Union Square, Shot Five Times; His Partner in Bootlegging Suspected." *New York Times*, December 27, 1920.

"Monk Eastman Sentenced." *New York Times*, July 2, 1915.

"More 'Dead Rabbits' In the Field." *New York Times*, December 9, 1857.

"More On Hollister's Bad Time." *San Francisco Chronicle*, July 6, 1947.

"Morphia Disease." *New York Times*, April 30, 1876.

"Morphine Victims Sentenced." *New York Times*, November 3, 1900.

"Murder in Gang Haunt; Then Paul Kelly Fled." *New York Times*, November 23, 1905.

Mustain, Gene, and Jerry Capeci. *Mob Star: The Story of John Gotti*. New York: Bantam Doubleday Dell Publishing Group, 1988.

"Must Purify East Side." *New York Times*, August 9, 1903.

Nash, Jay Robert. *Look For the Woman*. London: HARRAP Limited 1981.

National Alliance of Gang Investigators Associations, http://www.nagia.org/.

National Cancer Institute, *Actual Causes of Death in the United States*, http://cancercontrol.cancer.gov/od/causes.html.

National Drug Intelligence Center, U.S. Department of Justice, http://www.usdoj.gov/ndic/.

National Institute on Drug Abuse, *NIDA InfoFacts: Understanding Drug Abuse and Addiction*, http://www.nida.nih.gov/Infofacts/understand.html.

"Nations Uniting to Stamp Out Use of Opium and Many Other Drugs." *New York Times*, July 25, 1909.

"Negro Cocaine Evil." *New York Times*, March 20, 1905.

"Negro Cocaine 'Fiends' Are a New Southern Menace." *New York Times*, February 8, 1914.

"Negro Kills 3 In Saloon." *New York Times*, August 1, 1909.

"New Mafia Killer: A Silenced .22." *New York Times*, April 18. 1977.

"The New Poison Squad." *New York Times*, November 1, 1907.

"New York Day by Day; Seeing Castellano's Killers." *New York Times*, December 30 1985.

Newton, Michael. *The FBI Encyclopedia*. Jefferson, NC: McFarland & Company, Inc., Publishers, 2003.

"Non-Returnable Lansky." *TIME*, September 25, 1972.

"A Notorious Outlaw Murdered." *New York Times*, November 4, 1879.

Office of National Drug Control Policy, http://www.whitehousedrugpolicy.gov/.

The Officer Down Memorial Page, Inc., http://www.odmp.org/.

"An Old Accomplice's Comment." *New York Times*, April 5, 1882.

"One Big Shot." *TIME*, November 3, 1930.

"150 Years In All for the Lupo Gang." *New York Times*, February 20, 1910.

"Opium Conference Today." *New York Times*, December 1, 1911.

"Organized Crime An Offer they Can't Refuse." *TIME*, November 25, 1991.

"An Outlaw Band Surrounded." *New York Times*, October 12, 1891.

Outlaws Motorcycle Club official Web site, http://www.outlawsmc.com."Patent Medicine Bill to Curb Drug Users." *New York Times*, March 15, 1908.

Paul Kavieff, interview by John William Tuohy, AmericanMafia.com, July 10, 2000. http://www.americanmafia.com/feature_articles_50.html

"Paul Kelly Examined." *New York Times*, December 3, 1905.

"Paul Kelly Found In Cousin's House." *New York Times*, December 2, 1905.

"Paul Kelly's Men Cheered." *New York Times*, April 6, 1905.

PBS Frontline Web site, "The Opium Kings," May 20, 1997, http://www.pbs.org/wgbh/pages/frontline/shows/heroin/.

Pistone, Joseph, with Richard Woodley. *Donnie Brasco: My Undercover Life in the Mafia*. London: Hodder, 1987.

"Police Unearth Cocaine Dives." *New York Times*, September 14, 1908.

"Poorer Drug Users in Pitiful Plight." *New York Times*, April 15, 1915.

"Private Anguish Emerges in Gotti's Conversations." *New York Times*, September 11, 2006.

"Prosecutors Shift Attack Against Mafia." *New York Times*, January 24, 1993.

Raab, Selwyn. *Five Families*. New York: St Martin's Press, 2005.

"Race Riot at Little Ferry." *New York Times*, July 31, 1912.

"A Remedy for Many Ills." *New York Times*, September 2, 1885.

"Reporter's Notebook: What Mobsters Chat About: Glory Days and Bad Teeth." *New York Times*, June 10, 2001.

Reppetto, Thomas. *American Mafia*. New York: Henry Holt and Company, 2004.

"Reputed Street Gang Leader Gets 37-Year Prison Sentence." *New York Times*, July 21, 2006.

"Rich Italian Gone; Once Mafia Leader." *New York Times*, December 5, 1908.

"Riot in the Sixth Ward." *New York Times*, February 14, 1859.

Robbins, David. *Heavy Traffic*. New York: Penguin Group, 2005.

"Rothstein Called in Chicago Inquiry." *New York Times*, October 16, 1920.

"Rothstein Cleared in Baseball Fixing." *New York Times*, October 27, 1920.

Russo, Gus. *The Outfit*. New York: Bloomsbury, 2001.

Saan, Paul. *The Lawless Decade*. New York: Crown Publishers, 1957.

Sabbag, Robert. *Snow Blind*. New York: Avon Books, 1976.

"Says Ellison Fired." *New York Times*, June 7, 1911.

Shakur, Sanyika. *Monster: The Autobiography of an LA Gang Member*. New York: Penguin Group, 1993.

"Shot By Shot, an Ex-Aide to Gotti Describes the Killing of Castellano." *New York Times*, March 4, 1992.

Sifakis, Carl. *The Mafia Encyclopedia*. New York: Checkmart Books, 2005.

"Skillful Detective Work." *New York Times*, March 19, 1882.

"Slaughter on 46th Street." *TIME*, December 30, 1985.

"Slaves to the Cocaine Habit." *New York Times*, May 26, 1886.

Smith, Denis Mack. *Mussolini*. New York: Random House, 1982.

Smith, Jo Durden. *Mafia: The Complete History of a Criminal World*. London, UK: Arcturus Publishing Limited, 2003.

Sonny Barger's official Web site, http://www.sonnybarger.com/.

Southwell, David. *The History of Organized Crime*. London: Carlton Publishing Group, 2006.

"Special Report: Organized Crime." *TIME* , September 3, 1990.

Stanley "Tookie" Williams, interview by Kat Aaron, *Wake Up Call,* Pacifica Radio Station WBAI, December 12, 2005, http://www.democracynow.org/2005/12/13/stanley_tookie_williams_i_want_the.

Stiles, T.J. *Jesse James: Last Rebel of the Civil War*. New York: Random House, 2002.

"Tales From Mr. Untouchable, and a Stroll Among the Statues." *New York Times*, January 28. 2007.

"Tammany's Rothstein." *TIME*, December 16, 1929.

"Telling Tales." *TIME*, January 30, 1984.

"10 Dead, 20 Hurt in a Race Riot." *New York Times*, September 29, 1913.

"Their Thing." *TIME*, August 16, 1963.

"Thinks Paul Kelly's a Nest of Floaters." *New York Times*, November 24, 1905.

Thompson, Hunter. *Hell's Angels*. New York: Ballantine Books, 1966.

Thornton, Mark. *Alcohol Prohibition Was a Failure*, CATO Institute Policy Analysis, July 17, 1991, http://www.cato.org/pub_display.php?pub_id=1017&full=1

"Throwing the Book at 'Monster.'" *Los Angeles Times*, February 15, 2007.

"A Thug in a Great Looking Suit" John Gotti biography, http://www.cnn.com/.

T.J. Stiles' official Web site, http://www.tjstiles.net/index.htm.

Tookie's Corner, http://tookie.com/.

"Tookie's Mistaken Identity." *LA Weekly*, December 15, 2005.

"To Surpass Jesse James." *New York Times*, October 7, 1892.

"A Train Robber's Story." *New York Times*, April 1, 1882.

"Trial on Rackets Delayed in Boston." *New York Times*, July 11, 1985.

Turkus, Burton, and Sid Feder. *Murder, Inc.: The Story of the Syndicate*. Cambridge, MA: Perseus Books Group, 1979.

"Uncle Sam Is the Worst Drug Fiend in the World." *New York Times*, March 12, 1911.

United Nations Office on Drugs and Crime, *2008 World Drug Report*, http://www.unodc.org/documents/wdr/WDR_2008/WDR_2008_eng_web.pdf

United States Treasury Department, Bureau of Narcotics. *Mafia: The Government's Secret File on Organized Crime.*. New York: HarperCollins Publishers, 2007.

"U.S. Attorney Seeks Release of Informer." *New York Times*, February 22, 1992.

U.S. Congress. Senate. Permanent Subcommittee on Investigations on the Committee of Government Affairs, *Testimony of Angelo Lonardo*, 1988.

U.S. Congress. Senate. Permanent Subcommittee on Investigations on the Committee of Government Affairs, *Testimony of Joseph Pistone*, 1988.

U.S. Congress. Senate Special Committee to Investigate Organized Crime in Interstate Commerce, *Kefauver Committee final report*, August 31, 1951.

U.S. Department of Justice, http://www.usdoj.gov/.

U.S. Drug Enforcement Administration, U.S. Department of Justice, http://www.usdoj.gov/dea.

"Victims of Cocaine." *New York Times*, May 25, 1886.

"Vincent Gigante, Mafia Leader Who Feigned Insanity, Dies at 77." *New York Times*, December 19, 2005.

"Volk Asks Congress for 'Dry' Inquiry." *New York Times*, January 6, 1921.

Wallace, Stone. *Dustbowl Desperadoes*. Edmonton: Folk Lore Publishing, 2003.

The Way of the Wiseguy. Philadelphia: Running Press, 2004.

Wellman, Paul. *A Dynasty of Western Outlaws*. Garden City, NY: Doubleday, 1961.

"Western Outlaws Arrested." *New York Times*, December 29, 1880.

"What Elmer Did." *TIME*, December 6, 1948.

"What the Mexicans Might Learn from the Italians." *New York Times*, June 1, 2008.

"Where Primaries Are Not Run by 'Bosses.'" *New York Times*, September 22, 1901.

"Who Wouldn't Be Worried?" *TIME* , October 19, 1931.

"Will the Real Mob Please Stand Up." *New York Times*, March 5, 2006.

"Witness Describes Scene at Murder of Castellano." *New York Times*, February 27, 1992.

"Word For Word/New York Gangs; The Dapper Don and Company Were a Bunch of Copycats." *New York Times*, May 3, 1998.

World Encyclopedia of Organized Crime. New York: Da Capo Press, 1993.

"Yale Avenged." *TIME*, September 17, 1928.

"Youth Gangs From West Coast Become Entrenched in New York." *New York Times*, August 28. 1997.

Index

About the Author

Nate Hendley is a Toronto-based writer who is the author of *Bonnie and Clyde: A Biography* (published by Greenwood) and several other non-fiction books. He graduated with an Honors BA in Cultural Studies from Trent University in Peterborough, Ontario. His website is located at www.natehendley.com.